Police Sergeant, Lieutenant, and Captain Promotion Exams

2nd Edition

Francis M. Connolly
George J. Mullins

ARCO
THOMSON LEARNING

Australia • Canada • Mexico • Singapore • Spain • United Kingdom • United States

An ARCO Book

ARCO is a registered trademark of Thomson Learning, Inc., and is used herein under license by Peterson's.

About Peterson's
Founded in 1966, Peterson's, a division of Thomson Learning, is the nation's largest and most respected provider of lifelong learning online resources, software, reference guides, and books. The Education Supersite℠ at petersons.com—the Web's most heavily traveled education resource—has searchable databases and interactive tools for contacting U.S.-accredited institutions and programs. CollegeQuest® (CollegeQuest.com) offers a complete solution for every step of the college decision-making process. GradAdvantage™ (GradAdvantage.org), developed with Educational Testing Service, is the only electronic admissions service capable of sending official graduate test score reports with a candidate's online application. Peterson's serves more than 55 million education consumers annually.

Thomson Learning is among the world's leading providers of lifelong learning, serving the needs of individuals, learning institutions, and corporations with products and services for both traditional classrooms and for online learning. For more information about the products and services offered by Thomson Learning, please visit www.thomsonlearning.com. Headquartered in Stamford, Connecticut, with offices worldwide, Thomson Learning is part of The Thomson Corporation (www.thomson.com), a leading einformation and solutions company in the business, professional, and education marketplaces. The Corporation's common shares are listed on the Toronto and London stock exchanges.

For more information, contact Peterson's, 2000 Lenox Drive, Lawrenceville, NJ 08648; 800-338-3282; or find us on the World Wide Web at: www.petersons.com/about

An American BookWorks Corporation Project

ISBN 0-7689-0706-3

Printed in the United States of America

10 9 8 7 6 5 4 3 2 1   03 02 01

CONTENTS

PART FOUR: MODEL EXAMINATIONS

PART FIVE: CIVIL SERVICE CAREER INFORMATION RESOURCES

APPENDIX: HOW TO INCREASE YOUR SKILLS IN MATHEMATICS

WHAT THIS BOOK WILL DO FOR YOU

Arco Publishing has followed testing trends and methods ever since the firm was founded in 1937. We *specialize* in books that prepare people for tests. Based on this experience, we have prepared the best possible book to help *you* score high.

To write this book we carefully analyzed every detail surrounding the forthcoming examinations. Since there is such variation in exams, we cannot predict exactly what your exam will be like. *However*, after studying many announcements and many exams, we have written this book to prepare you for the most probable question types. The instructional chapters will prepare you for questions that you are likely to face. The model exams, while they are not actual exams, will give you excellent practice and preparation for your police sergeant, lieutenant, or captain promotion exam. Other features of this book include details about:

- the job itself

- official and unofficial announcements concerning the examination

- all the previous examinations, although many not available to the public

- related examinations

- technical literature that explains and forecasts the examination

CAN YOU PREPARE YOURSELF FOR YOUR TEST?

You want to pass this test. That's why you bought this book. Used correctly, your "self-tutor" will show you what to expect and will give you a speedy brush-up on the subjects tested in your exam. Some of these are subjects not taught in schools at all. Even if your study time is very limited, you should:

- become familiar with the type of examination you will have

- improve your general examination-taking skill

- improve your skill in analyzing and answering questions involving reasoning, judgment, comparison, and evaluation

- improve your speed and skill in reading and understanding what you read — an important part of your ability to learn and an important part of most tests

This book will help you in the following ways:

Present every type of question you will get on the actual test. This will make you at ease with the test format.

Find your weaknesses. Once you know what subjects you're weak in, you can get right to work and concentrate on those areas. This kind of selective study yields maximum test results.

Give you confidence *now.* It will build your self-confidence while you are preparing for the test. As you proceed, it will prevent the kind of test anxiety that causes low test scores.

Stress the multiple-choice type of question because that's the kind you'll have on your test. You must not be satisfied with merely knowing the correct answer for each question. You must find out why the other choices are incorrect. This will help you remember a lot you thought you had forgotten.

After testing yourself, you may find that you are weak in a particular area. You should concentrate on improving your skills by using the specific practice sections in this book that apply to you.

HOW DO I USE THIS BOOK?

If you already know what type of career you wish to pursue, this book will help you prepare for any of the major exams. If you don't know what type of job you'd like to apply for, this book will also help you. Not only will you be able to prepare for your exam, but you will also find information here about various types of careers, and perhaps it will narrow down your choices. This book offers you an overview of the world of civil service, a brief introduction to federal, state, and city employers and their hiring requirements, and in-depth descriptions of a number of widely used examinations.

PART ONE

There are five parts to this book. Part One covers the major employment sectors: federal, state, municipal (city), and private industry careers. There's more than enough for everyone here. Each sector has its own requirements and tests. However, as you will see, there are certain types of questions that will appear on most of these exams, regardless of the type of test you will take.

Also in this section is important information on test-taking techniques. This will give you guidelines to help you prepare for the actual test. Feeling anxious before you take a test is a normal reaction. We provide you with tips on feeling relaxed and comfortable with your exam so you can get a great test score.

PART TWO

Part Two is an overview of the various types of careers available. If you haven't already been in the field, you will be surprised by the number of different job opportunities there are as well as the varied jobs within an area. For example, did you know that there are almost 2,000 different job titles just within the United States Postal Service? This is just *one* federal agency.

If you are beginning your career or job shopping at this time, you should read this section carefully. It will help introduce you to the different jobs and the many opportunities that await you. We hope you will be inspired and excited and will be motivated to apply for, study for, and land one of those jobs. If this section helps you narrow your area of interest, you can then concentrate on the exams that will help you prepare for the job you want. If you are still wide open, give equal attention to each exam.

PART THREE

That leads us into Part Three of this book. In this section, we detail test-types and requirements. We've also given you a review section so that you can practice on a variety of different question types. We suggest you go through this chapter to get an idea of where your strengths lie and what weaknesses you'll have to deal with on the actual test.

We've also provided you with a variety of different types of tests that you will encounter in almost any job you apply for in the civil service, since there are certain basics that need to be covered. For example, in most tests, you will be asked to understand vocabulary and the use of grammar. Some tests will test your memory abilities and your ability for recall. Can you alphabetize easily and quickly? That's an area also covered on many of these tests.

PART FOUR

In Part Four, there are either real examinations, (official sample examinations) or others are model examinations closely patterned on the actual exams. Timing, level of difficulty, question styles, and scoring methods all conform closely to the examinations for which they are meant to prepare. And a special feature of this book is that all the correct answers are explained.

When you do take the sample exams, try to set aside the full measure of time to take the exam at one sitting. Time yourself accurately (a stopwatch or a kitchen timer will work well) and stop working when the time is up. If you have not completed all of the questions when the time expires, stop anyway. Check your answers against the provided correct answers and score your paper. Then continue with the remaining questions to get in all the practice you can. Carefully study all the answer explanations, even those for questions that you answered correctly. By reading all of the explanations, you can gain greater insight into methods of answering questions and the reasoning behind the correct choices.

One very important suggestion: We strongly believe that regardless of the test that you think you're planning to take—or the career path you want to follow—try to take *all* of the exams in this book. It may seem like a lot of extra work, but you never know where you may end up. You may think you're interested in a job with the local city government, and end up instead in a private company. Or the exam you were hoping to take is not being given for another year, but some other test is being given next month. It is always better to be prepared.

PART FIVE

Finally, Part Five contains civil service career information resources. Here you will find out how to go about looking for available jobs, as well as important addresses, phone numbers, and Internet websites that will help you pursue your career in civil service.

The most important thing is to *use* this book. By going through all of the sections and reading them, reviewing question types, and taking the practice exams, you will be using what you learned here to the best of your ability to succeed in your intended career path.

PART ONE

So You Want to Work for The Government

overnment service is one of the nation's largest sources of employment. About one in every six employed persons in the United States is in some form of civilian government service. Of those government employees, five out of six workers are employed by state or local governments, and the remainder work for the federal government.

As you can see, government employees represent a significant portion of the nation's work force. They work in large cities, small towns, and remote and isolated places such as lighthouses and forest ranger stations, and a small number of federal employees work overseas. In this chapter, we will outline the various types of careers that are available in the federal, state, and local governments.

WHERE THE JOBS ARE: FEDERAL CIVILIAN EMPLOYMENT

The federal government is the nation's largest employer. It employs almost 3 million civilian workers in the United States and an additional 130,000 civilian workers—half of them U.S. citizens—in U.S. territories and foreign countries. The headquarters of most government departments and agencies are in the Washington, D.C., area, but only one out of eight federal employees works there.

Federal employees work in occupations that represent nearly every kind of job in private employment as well as some unique to the federal government such as regulatory inspectors, foreign service officers, and Internal Revenue agents. Most federal employees work for the executive branch of the government.

The executive branch includes the Office of the President, the cabinet departments, and about 100 independent agencies, commissions, and boards. This branch is responsible for activities such as administering federal laws, handling international relations, conserving natural resources, treating and rehabilitating disabled veterans, delivering the mail, conducting scientific research, maintaining the flow of supplies to the armed forces, and administering other programs to promote the health and welfare of the people of the United States.

The Department of Defense, which includes the Departments of the Army, Navy, and Air Force, is the largest department. It employs about one million civilian workers. The Departments of Agriculture, Health and Human Services, and the Treasury are also big employers. The two largest independent agencies are the U.S. Postal Service and the Veterans Administration.

There is also federal civilian employment available in the legislative branch, which includes Congress, the Government Printing Office, the General Accounting Office, and the Library of Congress. The judicial branch, the smallest employer, hires people for work within the court system.

WHITE-COLLAR OCCUPATIONS

Because of its wide range of responsibilities, the federal government employs white-collar workers in a great many occupational fields. About one of four of these are administrative and clerical workers.

General clerical workers are employed in all federal departments and agencies. These include office machine operators, secretaries, stenographers, clerk-typists, mail- and file-clerks, telephone operators, and workers in computer and related occupations. In addition, there are the half million postal clerks and mail carriers.

Many government workers are employed in engineering and related fields. The engineers represent virtually every branch and specialty of engineering. There are large numbers of technicians in areas such as engineering, electronics, surveying, and drafting. Nearly two-thirds of all engineers are in the Department of Defense.

Of the more than 120,000 workers employed in accounting and budgeting work, 35,000 are professional accountants or Internal Revenue officers. Among technician and administrative occupations are accounting technicians, tax accounting technicians, and budget administrators. There are also large numbers of clerks in specialized accounting work. Accounting workers are employed throughout the government, particularly in the Departments of Defense and the Treasury and in the General Accounting Office.

Many federal employees work in hospitals or in medical, dental, and public health activities. Three out of five are either professional nurses or nursing assistants. Other professional occupations in this field include physicians, dieticians, technologists, and physical therapists. Technician and aide jobs include medical technicians, medical laboratory aides, and dental assistants. Employees in this field work primarily for the Veterans Administration; others work for the Departments of Defense and Health and Human Services.

Other government workers are engaged in administrative work related to private business and industry. They arrange and monitor contracts with the private sector and purchase goods and services needed by the federal government. Administrative occupations include contract and procurement specialists, production control specialists, and Internal Revenue officers. Two out of three of these workers are employed by the Departments of Defense and Treasury.

Another large group works in jobs concerned with the purchase, cataloging, storage, and distribution of supplies for the federal government. This field includes many managerial and administrative positions such as supply management officers, purchasing officers, and inventory management specialists, as well as large numbers of specialized clerical positions. Most of these jobs are in the Department of Defense.

Throughout the federal government, many people are employed in the field of law. They fill professional positions, such as attorneys or law clerks, and administrative positions, such as passport and visa examiners or tax law specialists. There also are many clerical positions that involve examining claims.

The social sciences also employ many government employees. Economists are employed throughout the government; psychologists and social workers work primarily for the Veterans Administration; and foreign affairs and international relations specialists, for the Department of State. One third of the workers in this field are social insurance administrators employed largely in the Department of Health and Human Services.

About 50,000 biological and agricultural science workers are employed by the federal government, mostly in the Departments of Agriculture and Interior. Many of these work in forestry and soil conservation activities. Others administer farm assistance programs. The largest number are employed as biologists, forest and range fire controllers, soil conservationists, and forestry technicians.

The federal government employs another 50,000 people in investigative and inspection work. Large numbers of these are engaged in criminal investigation and health regulatory inspections, mostly in the Departments of Treasury, Justice, and Agriculture.

Physical sciences is another area of government employment. Three out of four workers in the physical sciences are employed by the Departments of Defense, Interior, and Commerce. Professional workers include chemists, physicists, meteorologists, cartographers, and geologists. Aides and technicians include physical science technicians, meteorological technicians, and cartography technicians.

And in the mathematics field are professional mathematicians and statisticians and mathematics technicians and statistical clerks. They are employed primarily by the Departments of Defense, Agriculture, Commerce, and Health and Human Services.

Entrance requirements for white-collar jobs vary widely. A college degree in a specified field or equivalent work experience is usually required for professional occupations such as physicists and engineers.

Entrants into administrative and managerial occupations usually are not required to have knowledge of a specialized field, but must instead indicate a potential for future development by having a degree from a 4-year college or responsible job experience. They usually begin as trainees and learn their duties on the job. Typical jobs in this group are budget analysts, claims examiners, purchasing specialists, administrative assistants, and personnel specialists.

Technician, clerical, and aide-assistant jobs have entry-level positions for people with a high school education or the equivalent. For many of these positions, no previous experience or training is required. The entry level position is usually that of trainee. Persons who have junior college or technical school training or those who have specialized skills may enter these occupations at higher levels. Typical jobs are engineering technicians, supply clerks, clerk-typists, and nursing assistants.

BLUE-COLLAR OCCUPATIONS

Blue-collar occupations—craft, operative, laborer, and some service jobs—provide full-time employment for more than half a million federal workers. The Department of Defense employs about three fourths of these workers in establishments such as naval shipyards, arsenals, the Air or Army depots, as well as on construction, harbor, flood control, irrigation, or reclamation projects. Others work for the Veterans Administration, U.S. Postal Service, General Services Administration, Department of the Interior, and Tennessee Valley Authority.

The largest single blue-collar group consists of manual laborers. Large numbers also are employed in machine tool and metal work, motor vehicle operation, warehousing, and food preparation and serving. The federal government employs a wide variety of individuals in maintenance and repair work, such as electrical and electronic equipment installation and repair, and in vehicle and industrial equipment maintenance and repair. All these fields require a range of skill levels and include a variety of occupations comparable to the private sector.

Although the federal government employs blue-collar workers in many different fields, about half are concentrated in a small number of occupations. The largest group, the skilled mechanics, works as air-conditioning, aircraft, automobile, truck, electronics, sheet-metal, and general maintenance mechanics. Another large number of craft workers is employed as painters, pipefitters, carpenters, electricians, and machinists. A similar number serves as warehouse workers, truck drivers, and general laborers. An additional group of workers is employed as janitors and food service workers.

ENTRANCE REQUIREMENTS

Persons with previous training in a skilled trade may apply for a position with the federal government at the journey level. Those with no previous training may apply for appointment to one of several apprenticeship programs. Apprenticeship programs generally last four years; trainees receive both classroom and on-the-job training. After completing this training, a person is eligible for a position at the journey level. There are also a number of positions which require little or no prior training or experience, including janitors, maintenance workers, messengers, and many others.

THE MERIT SYSTEM

More than nine out of ten jobs in the federal government are under a merit system. The Civil Service Act, administered by the U.S. Office of Personnel Management, covers six out of ten federal titles. This act was passed by Congress to ensure that federal employees are hired on the basis of individual merit and fitness. It provides for competitive examinations and the selection of new employees from among the most qualified applicants.

Some federal jobs are exempt from civil service requirements either by law or by action of the Office of Personnel Management. However, most of these positions are covered by separate merit systems of other agencies such as the Foreign Service of the Department of State, the Federal Bureau of Investigation, the Nuclear Regulatory Commission, and the Tennessee Valley Authority.

EARNINGS, ADVANCEMENT, AND WORKING CONDITIONS

Most federal civilian employees are paid according to one of three major pay systems: the **General Pay Schedule,** the **Wage System**, or the **Postal Service Schedule.**

GENERAL PAY SCHEDULE

More than half of all federal workers are paid under the General Schedule (GS), a pay scale for workers in professional, administrative, technical, and clerical jobs, and for workers such as guards and messengers. General Schedule jobs are classified by the U.S. Office of Personnel Management in one of fifteen grades, according to the difficulty of duties and responsibilities and the knowledge, experience, and skills required of the workers. GS pay rates are set by Congress and apply to government workers nationwide. They are reviewed annually to see whether they are comparable with salaries in private industry. They are generally subject to upwards adjustment for very high-cost-of-living regions. In low-cost areas, the GS pay scale may exceed that of most private-sector workers.

Most employees receive within-grade pay increases at one-, two-, or three-year intervals if their work is acceptable. Within-grade increases may also be given in recognition of high-quality service. Some managers and supervisors receive increases based on their job performance rather than on time in grade.

High school graduates who have no related work experience usually start in GS-2 jobs, but some who have special skills begin at grade GS-3. Graduates of 2-year colleges and technical schools often can begin at the GS-4 level. Most people with bachelor's degrees appointed to professional and administrative jobs such as statisticians, economists, writers and editors, budget analysts, accountants, and physicists, can enter at grades GS-5 or GS-7, depending on experience and academic record. Those who have a master's degree or Ph.D. or the equivalent education or experience may enter at the GS-9 or GS-11 level. Advancement to higher grades generally depends upon ability, work performance, and openings in jobs at higher grade levels.

FEDERAL WAGE SYSTEM

About one quarter of federal civilian workers are paid according to the Federal Wage System. Under this system, craft, service, and manual workers are paid hourly rates established on the basis of "prevailing" rates paid by private employers for similar work in the same locations. As a result, the federal government wage rate for an occupation varies by locality. This commitment to meeting the local wage scale allows the federal wage earner to bring home a weekly paycheck comparable to that which he or she would earn in the private sector and to enjoy the benefits and security of a government job at the same time. The federal wage earner has the best of all possible worlds in this regard.

Federal government employees work a standard 40-hour week. Employees who are required to work overtime may receive premium rates for the additional time or compensatory time off at a later date. Most employees work eight hours a day, five days a week, Monday through Friday, but in some cases, the nature of the work requires a different workweek. Annual earnings for most full-time federal workers are not affected by seasonal factors.

Federal employees earn 13 days of annual (vacation) leave each year during their first three years of service; 20 days each year until the end of 15 years; after 15 years, 26 days each year. Workers who are members of military reserve organizations also are granted up to 15 days of paid military leave a year for training purposes. A federal worker who is laid off, though federal layoffs are uncommon, is entitled to unemployment compensation similar to that provided for employees in private industry.

Other benefits available to most federal employees include: a contributory retirement system, optional participation in low-cost group life and health insurance programs which are partly supported by the government (as the employer), and training programs to develop maximum job proficiency and help workers achieve their highest potential. These training programs may be conducted in government facilities or in private educational facilities at government expense.

GENERAL SCHEDULE
(Range of Salaries)

Effective as of January 1, 2001

GS Rating	Low	High
1	$14,244	$17,819
2	16,015	20,156
3	17,474	22,712
4	19,616	25,502
5	21,957	28,535
6	24,463	31,798
7	27,185	35,339
8	30,107	39,143
9	33,254	43,226
10	36,621	47,610
11	40,236	52,305
12	48,223	62,686
13	57,345	74,553
14	67,765	88,096
15	79,710	103,623

WHERE THE JOBS ARE: STATE AND LOCAL GOVERNMENTS

State and local governments provide a very large and expanding source of job opportunities in a wide variety of occupational fields. About fifteen million people work for state and local government agencies; nearly three fourths of these work in units of local government such as counties, municipalities, towns, and school districts. The job distribution varies greatly from that in federal government service. Defense, international relations and commerce, immigration, and mail delivery are virtually non-existent in state and local governments. On the other hand, there is great emphasis on education, health, social services, transportation, construction, and sanitation.

EDUCATIONAL SERVICES

About one half of all jobs in state and local government are in educational services. Educational employees work in public schools, colleges, and various extension services. About half of all education workers are instructional personnel. School systems, colleges, and universities also employ administrative personnel, librarians, guidance counselors, nurses, dieticians, clerks, and maintenance workers.

HEALTH SERVICES

The next largest field of state and local government employment is health services. Those employed in health and hospital work include physicians, nurses, medical laboratory technicians, dieticians, kitchen and laundry workers, and hospital attendants. Social services make up another aspect of health and welfare. Unfortunately, the need for welfare and human services has been increasing greatly. As the need grows, the opportunities for social workers and their affiliated administrative and support staff also grows.

GOVERNMENT CONTROL/FINANCIAL ACTIVITIES

Another million workers work in the areas of general governmental control and financial activities. These include chief executives and their staffs, legislative representatives, and persons employed in the administration of justice, tax enforcement and other financial work, and general administration. These functions require the services of individuals such as lawyers, judges and other court officers, city managers, property assessors, budget analysts, stenographers, and clerks.

STREETS AND HIGHWAYS

The movement of people is of great concern to both state and local governments. Street and highway construction and maintenance are of major importance. Highway workers include civil engineers, surveyors, operators of construction machinery and equipment, truck drivers, concrete finishers, carpenters, construction laborers, and, where appropriate, snow removers. Toll collectors are relatively few in number, but they too are state or county employees or employees of independent authorities of the states or counties. Mass transportation within municipalities and between the cities and their outlying suburbs is also the province of local government. Maintaining vehicles, roadbeds and signaling systems, and staffing the vehicles themselves, requires a large and varied work force.

POLICE AND FIRE PROTECTION SERVICES

Police and fire protection is another large field of employment. Along with uniformed officers, these services include extensive administrative, clerical, maintenance, and custodial personnel.

MISCELLANEOUS STATE AND LOCAL OCCUPATIONS

Other state and local government employees work in a wide variety of activities, including local utilities (water in most areas, electricity in some); natural resources; parks and recreation; sanitation; corrections; local libraries; sewage disposal; and housing and urban renewal. These activities require workers in diverse occupations such as economists, electrical engineers, electricians, pipefitters, clerks, foresters, and bus drivers.

CLERICAL, ADMINISTRATIVE, MAINTENANCE, AND CUSTODIAL WORKERS

A large percentage of employment in most government agencies is made up of clerical, administrative, maintenance, and custodial workers. Among the workers involved in these activities are word processors, secretaries, data processors, computer specialists, office managers, fiscal and budget administrators, bookkeepers, accountants, carpenters, painters, plumbers, guards, and janitors. The list is endless.

Most positions in state and local governments are filled by residents of the state or locality. Many localities have residency requirements. Exceptions are generally made for persons with skills that are in special demand.

EARNINGS

Job conditions and earnings of state and local government employees vary widely, depending upon occupation and locality. Salary differences from state to state and even within some states tend to reflect differences in the general wage level and cost of living in the various localities.

As with the federal government, a majority of state and local government positions are filled through some type of formal civil service test; that is, personnel are hired and promoted on the basis of merit. State and local government workers have the same protections as federal government workers: they cannot be refused employment because of their race; they cannot be denied promotion because someone else made a greater political contribution; and they cannot be fired because the boss's son needs a job. Jobs tend to be classified according to job description and pegged to a salary schedule that is based upon the job classifications. Periodic performance reviews also are standard expectations. Nearly every group of employees has some sort of union or organization, but the functions and powers of these units vary greatly.

Since states and local entities are independent, the benefits packages they offer their employees can be quite different. Most state and local government employees are covered by retirement systems or by the federal social security program. Most have some sort of health coverage. They usually work a standard week of 40 hours or less with overtime pay or compensatory time benefits for additional hours of work.

PREPARING YOURSELF FOR THE CIVIL SERVICE EXAMINATION

Most federal, state, and municipal units have recruitment procedures for filling civil service positions. They have developed a number, of methods to make job opportunities known. Places where such information may be obtained include:

1. The offices of the State Employment Services. There are almost two thousand throughout the country. These offices are administered by the state in which they are located, with the financial assistance of the federal government. You will find the address of the one nearest you in your telephone book.

2. Your state Civil Service Commission. Address your inquiry to the capital city of your state.

3. Your city Civil Service Commission. It is sometimes called by another name, such as the Department of Personnel, but you will be able to identify it in your telephone directory under the listing of city departments.

4. Your municipal building and your local library.

5. Complete listings are carried by such newspapers as *The Chief-Leader* (published in New York City), as well as by other city and state-wide publications devoted to civil service employees. Many local newspapers run a section on regional civil service news.

6. State and local agencies looking for competent employees will contact schools, professional societies, veterans organizations, unions, and trade associations.

7. School boards and boards of education, which employ the greatest proportion of all state and local personnel, should be asked directly for information about job openings.

You will find more in-depth information at the end of this book.

THE FORMAT OF THE JOB ANNOUNCEMENT

When a position is open and a civil service examination is to be given for it, a job announcement is drawn up. This generally contains everything an applicant has to know about the job.

The announcement begins with the job title and salary. A typical announcement then describes the work, the location of the position, the education and experience requirements, the kind of examination to be given, and the system of rating. It may also have something to say about veteran preference and the age limit. It tells which application form is to be filled out, where to get the form, and where and when to file it.

Study the job announcement carefully. It will answer many of your questions and help you decide whether you like the position and are qualified for it. We have included sample job announcements in a later chapter.

There is no point in applying for a position and taking the examination if you do not want to work where the job is. The job may be in your community or hundreds of miles away at the other end of the state. If you are not willing to work where the job is, study other announcements that will give you an opportunity to work in a place of your choice. A civil service job close to your home has an additional advantage since local residents usually receive preference in appointments.

The words **Optional Fields**—sometimes just the word **Options**—may appear on the front page of the announcement. You then have a choice to apply for that particular position in which you are especially interested. This is because the duties of various positions are quite different even though they bear the same broad title. A public relations clerk, for example, does different work from a payroll clerk, although they are considered broadly in the same general area.

Not every announcement has options. But whether or not it has them, the precise duties are described in detail, usually under the heading, **Description of Work.** Make sure that these duties come within the range of your experience and ability.

Most job requirements give a **deadline for filing** an application. Others bear the words, **No Closing Date** at the top of the first page; this means that applications will be accepted until the needs of the agency are met. In some cases a public notice is issued when a certain number of applications has been received. No application mailed past the deadline date will be considered.

Every announcement has a detailed section on **education and experience requirements** for the particular job and for the optional fields. Make sure that in both education and experience you meet the minimum qualifications. If you do not meet the given standards for one job, there may be others open where you stand a better chance of making the grade.

If the job announcement does not mention **veteran preference,** it would be wise to inquire if there is such a provision in your state or municipality. There may be none or it may be limited to disabled veterans. In some jurisdictions, surviving spouses of disabled veterans are given preference. All such information can be obtained through the agency that issues the job announcement.

Applicants may be denied examinations and eligible candidates may be denied appointments for any of the following reasons:

- intentional false statements

- deception or fraud in examination or appointment

- use of intoxicating beverages to the extent that ability to perform the duties of the position is impaired

- criminal, infamous, dishonest, immoral, or notoriously disgraceful conduct

The announcement describes the **kind of test** given for the particular position. Please pay special attention to this section. It tells what areas are to be covered in the written test and lists the specific subjects on which questions will be asked. Sometimes sample questions are given.

Usually the announcement states whether the examination is to be **assembled** or **unassembled.** In an assembled examination applicants assemble in the same place at the same time to take a written or performance test. The unassembled examination is one where an applicant does not take a test; instead, he or she is rated on his or her education and experience and whatever records of past achievement the applicant is asked to provide.

In the competitive examination all applicants for a position compete with each other; the better the mark, the better the chance of being appointed. Also, competitive examinations are given to determine desirability for promotion among employees.

Civil service written tests are rated on a scale of 100, with 70 usually as the passing mark.

FILLING OUT THE APPLICATION FORM

Having studied the job announcement and having decided that you want the position and are qualified for it, your next step is to get an application form. The job announcement tells you where to send for it.

On the whole, civil service application forms differ little from state to state and locality to locality. The questions that have been worked out after years of experimentation are simple and direct, designed to elicit a maximal amount of information about you.

Many prospective civil service employees have failed to get a job because of slipshod, erroneous, incomplete, misleading, or untruthful answers. Give the application serious attention, for it is the first important step toward getting the job you want.

Here, along with some helpful comments, are the questions usually asked on the average application form, although not necessarily in this order.

- **Name of examination or kind of position applied for.** This information appears in large type on the first page of the job announcement.

- **Optional job** (if mentioned in the announcement). If you wish to apply for an option, simply copy the title from the announcement. If you are not interested in an option, write *None*.

- **Primary place of employment applied for.** The location of the position was probably contained in the announcement. You must consider whether you want to work there. The announcement may list more than one location where the job is open. If you would accept employment in any of the places, list them all; otherwise list the specific place or places where you would be willing to work.

- **Name and address.** Give in full, including your middle name if you have one, and your maiden name as well if you are a married woman.

- **Home and office phones.** If none, write *None*.

- **Legal or voting residence.** The state in which you vote is the one you list here.

- **Height without shoes, weight, sex.** Answer accurately.

- **Date of birth.** Give the exact day, month, and year.

- **Lowest grade or pay you will accept.** Although the salary is clearly stated in the job announcement, there may be a quicker opening in the same occupation but carrying less responsibility and thus a lower basic entrance salary. You will not be considered for a job paying less than the amount you give in answer to this question.

- **Will you accept temporary employment if offered you for (a) one month or less, (b) one to four months, (c) four to twelve months?** Temporary positions come up frequently and it is important to know whether you are available.

- **Will you accept less than full-time employment?** Part-time work comes up now and then. Consider whether you want to accept such a position while waiting for a full-time appointment.

- **Were you in active military service in the Armed Forces of the United States?** Veterans' preference, if given, is usually limited to active service during the following periods: 12/7/41–12/31/46; 6/27/50–1/31/55; 6/1/63–5/7/75; 6/1/83–12/1/87; 10/23/83–11/21/83; 12/20/89–1/3/90; 8/2/90 to end of Persian Gulf hostilities.

■ **Do you claim disabled veterans credit?** If you do, you have to show proof of a war-incurred disability compensable by at least 10 percent. This is done through certification by the Veterans Administration.

■ **Special qualifications and skills.** Even though not directly related to the position for which you are applying, information about licenses and certificates obtained for teacher, pilot, registered nurse, and so on, is requested. List your experience in the use of machines and equipment and whatever other skills you have acquired. Also list published writings, public speaking experience, membership in professional societies, and honors and fellowships received.

■ **Education.** List your entire educational history, including all diplomas, degrees, and special courses taken in any accredited or armed forces school. Also give your credits toward a college or a graduate degree.

■ **References.** The names of people who can give information about you, with their occupations and business and home address, are often requested.

■ **Your health.** Questions are asked concerning your medical record. You are expected to have the physical and psychological capacity to perform the job for which you are applying. Standards vary, of course, depending on the requirements of the position. A physical handicap usually will not bar an applicant from a job he can perform adequately unless the safety of the public is involved.

■ **Work history.** Considerable space is allotted on the form for the applicant to tell about all his past employment. Examiners check all such answers closely. Do not embellish or falsify your record. If you were ever fired, say so. It is better for you to state this openly than for the examiners to find out the truth from your former employer.

On the following pages are samples of a New York City Application for Examination and a state application from Louisiana.

WHY PEOPLE CHOOSE GOVERNMENT SERVICE

There are many similarities between work in the private sector and work for the government. Within each occupation, the similarities of the daily duties far outweigh the differences in employers. Regardless of the nature of the employer—government, private business, nonprofit organization—typists type; doctors heal, teachers teach; electricians install wiring.

As was mentioned at the beginning of this chapter, one in six of employed persons in the United States is in government service. The five in six persons who are employed by nongovernmental employers all hope for just compensation for their work, for promotions when merited, and for fair and equal treatment with reference to their co-workers. They all hope that they will not be discriminated against for any non-job-related reasons, that they will not be fired capriciously, and that their opinions and suggestions will be taken seriously. In the great majority of cases, these expectations will be met.

But, in the private sector, there are no guarantees of employment practices. In government service these guarantees are a matter of policy and law. Each governmental jurisdiction has its own body of rules and procedures. In other words, not all government service is alike. The Federal Civil Service does serve as a model for all other governmental units.

NEW YORK CITY APPLICATION FOR EXAMINATION

DEPARTMENT OF CITYWIDE ADMINISTRATIVE SERVICES
DIVISION OF CITYWIDE PERSONNEL SERVICES
1 Centre Street, 14th floor
New York, NY 10007

APPLICATION FOR EXAMINATION

(Directions for completing this application are on the *back* of this form. Additional information is on the Special Circumstances Sheet)

Download this form on-line: nyc.gov/html/dcas

FOLLOW DIRECTIONS ON BACK
Fill in all requested information clearly, accurately, and completely.

The City will only process applications with complete, correct, legible information which are accompanied by correct payment or waiver documentation.

All unprocessed applications will be returned to the applicant.

1. EXAM #:

Check One:
☐ Open Competitive
☐ Promotion

2. EXAM TITLE:

3. SOCIAL SECURITY NUMBER:

4. LAST NAME:

5. FIRST NAME:

6. MIDDLE INITIAL:

7. MAILING ADDRESS:

8. APT. #:

9. CITY OR TOWN:

10. STATE:

11. ZIP CODE:

12. PHONE:

13. OTHER NAMES USED IN CITY SERVICE:

14. RACE/ETHNICITY (Check One):
☐ White
☐ American Indian/ Alaskan Native
☐ Black
☐ Asian/Pacific Islander
☐ Hispanic

15. SEX (Check One):
☐ Male
☐ Female

Questions 14 & 15:
Discrimination on the basis of sex, sexual orientation, race, creed, color, age, disability status, veteran status or religious observance is prohibited by law. The City of New York is an equal opportunity employer. The identifying information requested on this form is to be used to determine the representation of protected groups among applicants. This information is voluntary and will not be made available to individuals making hiring decisions.

16. ARE YOU EMPLOYED BY THE HEALTH AND HOSPITALS CORPORATION? (Check One)   ☐ YES   ☐ NO

17. CHECK ALL BOXES THAT APPLY TO YOU: (Directions for this section are found on the "Special Circumstances" Sheet)
☐ I AM A SABBATH OBSERVER AND WILL REQUEST AN ALTERNATE TEST DATE (Verification required. See Item A on Special Circumstances Sheet).
☐ I HAVE A DISABILITY AND WILL REQUEST SPECIAL ACCOMMODATIONS (Verification required. See item B on Special Circumstances Sheet).
☐ I CLAIM VETERANS' CREDIT (For qualifications see item C on Special Circumstances Sheet).
☐ I CLAIM DISABLED VETERANS' CREDIT (For qualifications see item C on Special Circumstances Sheet)

18. Your Signature: _____   **Date:** _____

STATE OF LOUISIANA APPLICATION—page 1

SF10
(Page 1)
REV. 1/97

**STATE PRE-EMPLOYMENT
APPLICATION**

STATE OF LOUISIANA
DEPARTMENT OF CIVIL SERVICE
P.O. Box 94111, Capitol Station
Baton Rouge, Louisiana 70804-9111

FOR OFFICE USE

Special _____
Promo _____
Action(s) _____

Session _____

Data Entry Completed _____

1. TEST LOCATION-Check only one.

AN EQUAL OPPORTUNITY EMPLOYER

| Baton Rouge (3) (Weekday) ☐ | New Orleans (6) (Weekday) ☐ | Lafayette (4) (Sat. only) ☐ | Shreveport (7) (Sat. only) ☐ |
| | New Orleans (12) (Saturday) ☐ | Lake Charles (5) (Sat. only) ☐ | West Monroe (8) (Sat. only) ☐ |

2. Enter Name and Complete Address below.

3. Parish of Residence

4. Are you 18 or older? ☐ Yes ☐ No

5. Other names ever used on SF-10

NAME - First   Middle   Last

Mailing Address

City   State   Zip Code

6. Social Security Number (For identification purpose)

Work Telephone No.

Home Telephone No.

L A S T → P R I N T F I R S T N A M E → M I D D L E

JS No.

V.P.

S.R.

7. REGISTER TITLE(S) APPLIED FOR	**FOR OFFICE USE**					**ADDITIONAL TITLES**	**FOR OFFICE USE**				
	SER	CD	REJ	GRD	TR		SER	CD	REJ	GRD	TR

ALL TITLES LISTED ABOVE MUST HAVE THE SAME SERIES NO.

8. JOB LOCATION AVAILABILITY - IMPORTANT: Read Item 9 on the Instruction Page before completing this item. Mark at least one (1), but no more than twenty (20) parishes.

01 Acadia	09 Caddo	17 E. Baton Rouge	25 Jackson	33 Madison	41 Red River	49 St. Landry	57 Vermillion
02 Allen	10 Calcasieu	18 E. Carroll	26 Jefferson	34 Morehouse	42 Richland	50 St. Martin	58 Vernon
03 Ascension	11 Caldwell	19 E. Feliciana	27 Jeff Davis	35 Natchitoches	43 Sabine	51 St. Mary	59 Washington
04	12 Cameron	20 Evangeline	28 Lafayette	36 Orleans	44 St. Bernard	52 St. Tammany	60 Webster
05 Avoyelles	13 Catahoula	21 Franklin	29 Lafourche	37 Ouachita	45 St. Charles	53 Tangipahoa	61 W. Baton Rouge
06 Beauregard	14 Claiborne	22 Grant	30 LaSalle	38 Plaquemines	46 St. Helena	54 Tensas	62 W. Carroll
07 Bienville	15 Concordia	23 Iberia	31 Lincoln	39 Pte. Coupee	47 St. James	55 Terrebonne	63 W. Feliciana
08 Bossier	16 DeSoto	24 Iberville	32 Livingston	40 Rapides	48 St. John	56 Union	64 Winn

9. ☐ Permanent ☐ Temporary—Type of employment you will accept

NOTE: Most Temporary Appointments are 3 - 12 months

10. ☐ YES ☐ NO   Do you possess a valid driver's license?

11. ☐ YES ☐ NO   Do you possess a valid commercial driver's license?

12. ☐ YES ☐ NO   Are you currently holding or running for an elective public office?

13. ☐ YES ☐ NO   Have you ever been on probation or sentenced to jail/prison as a result of a felony conviction or guilty plea?

14. ☐ YES ☐ NO   Have you ever been fired from a job or resigned to avoid dismissal?

NOTE: If answers to Items 13 and/or 14 are "YES", you MUST complete Item 24 on Page 2 of this application

15. ☐ YES ☐ NO   Are you claiming Veteran's Preference points on this application? (If "YES", see Item 20 on Page 2.)

The following information is collected to complete Equal Opportunity Reports required by law. You ARE NOT LEGALLY OBLIGATED to provide this information.

16. RACIAL/ETHNIC GROUP   **16A.** DATE OF BIRTH   **17.** SEX ☐ Male ☐ Female

_____   _____

I HAVE READ THE FOLLOWING STATEMENTS CAREFULLY BEFORE SIGNING THIS APPLICATION:

18. Date   Social Security No. (for verification)

19. Signature of Applicant

AUTHORITY TO RELEASE INFORMATION: I consent to the release of information concerning my capacity and/or all aspects of prior job performance by employers, educational institutions, law enforcement agencies, and other individuals and agencies to duly accredited investigators, personnel technicians, and other authorized employees of the state government for the purpose of determining my eligibility and suitability for employment.

I certify that all statements made on this application and any attached papers are true and complete to the best of my knowledge. I understand that information on this application may be subject to investigation and verification and that any misrepresentation or material omission may cause my application to be rejected, my name to be removed from the eligible register and/or subject me to dismissal from state service.

STATE OF LOUISIANA APPLICATION—page 2

20.	ACTIVE MILITARY SERVICE/VETERAN'S PREFERENCE

See Item 10 on the Instruction Page to determine your eligibility for Veteran's Preference. If you are a first-time applicant or if you are claiming Veteran's Preference for the first time, required PROOF MUST BE ATTACHED to this application to have preference points added to your score.

List the dates (month and year) and branch for all ACTIVE DUTY military service. Was this service performed on an active, full-time basis with full pay and allowances? (Check YES or NO for each period of service.)

FROM	TO	BRANCH OF SERVICE	YES	NO

List all GRADES held and dates of each grade. Begin with the highest grade. IMPORTANT: Use E-, O-, or WO-grade.

FROM	TO	GRADE HELD	FROM	TO	GRADE HELD

21.	TRAINING AND EDUCATION		☐ YES	Date received _____

Have you received a high school diploma or equivalency certificate? ☐ NO Highest grade completed _____

A. LIST BUSINESS OR TECHNICAL COLLEGES ATTENDED	NAME/LOCATION OF SCHOOL	Dates Attended (Month & Year) FROM — TO	Did You Graduate? YES — NO	TITLE OF PROGRAM	CLOCK HOURS PER WEEK

List any accounting practice sets completed:

B. LIST COLLEGES OR UNIVERSITIES ATTENDED (Include graduate or professional schools)	NAME OF COLLEGE OR UNIVERSITY/ CITY AND STATE	Dates Attended (Month & Year) FROM — TO	Total Credit Hours Earned Semester — Quarter	Type of Degree Earned	Major Field of Study	Date Degree Received (Month & Yr.)

C. MAJOR SUBJECTS	CHIEF UNDERGRADUATE SUBJECTS (Show Major on Line 1.)	Total Credit Hours Earned Semester — Quarter	CHIEF GRADUATE SUBJECTS (Show Major on Line 1.)	Total Credit Hours Earned Semester or Qtr.
1				
2				
3				

22.	LICENSES AND CERTIFICATION		23. TYPING SPEED

List any job-related licenses or certificates that you have (CPA, lawyer, registered nurse, etc.)

TYPE OF LICENSE OR CERTIFICATE (Specify Which One)	DATE ORIGINALLY LICENSED/ CERTIFIED	EXPIRATION DATE	NAME AND ADDRESS OF LICENSING OR CERTIFYING AGENCY	
				WPM
1				DICTATION SPEED
2				**WPM**

24. Explain a "YES" answer to Items 13 and/or 14 here. A "YES" ANSWER WILL NOT NECESSARILY BAR YOU FROM STATE EMPLOYMENT. WE WILL CONSIDER THE DATE, FACTS, AND CIRCUMSTANCES OF EACH INDIVIDUAL CASE. For Item 13, give the law enforcement authority (city police, sherrif, FBI, etc.), the offense, date of offense, place, and disposition of case.

_____

_____

Name _____

STATE OF LOUISIANA APPLICATION—page 3

Name _____

25.   WORK EXPERIENCE — <u>IMPORTANT</u>: Read Item 11 of Instruction Page carefully before completing these items. List all jobs and activities including military service, part-time employment, self-employment, and volunteer work. BEGIN with your FIRST job in Block A; END with your MOST RECENT or PRESENT job.

A

EMPLOYER/COMPANY NAME	KIND OF BUSINESS

STREET ADDRESS	YOUR OFFICIAL JOB TITLE

CITY AND STATE	BEGINNING SALARY	ENDING SALARY

DATES OF EMPLOYMENT (MO/DA/YR)	AVERAGE HOURS WORKED PER WEEK	REASON FOR LEAVING	NO. OF EMPLOYEES YOU DIRECTLY SUPERVISED
FROM	TO		

NAME/TITLE OF YOUR SUPERVISOR)	LIST JOB TITLES OF EMPLOYEES YOU DIRECTLY SUPERVISED
NAME/TITLE OF PERSON WHO CAN VERIFY THIS EMPLOYMENT (IF OTHER THAN SUPERVISOR)	

DUTIES: List the major duties involved with job and give an approximate percentage of time spent on each duty.

% OF TIME	MAJOR DUTIES
100%	

B

EMPLOYER/COMPANY NAME	KIND OF BUSINESS

STREET ADDRESS	YOUR OFFICIAL JOB TITLE

CITY AND STATE	BEGINNING SALARY	ENDING SALARY

DATES OF EMPLOYMENT (MO/DA/YR)	AVERAGE HOURS WORKED PER WEEK	REASON FOR LEAVING	NO. OF EMPLOYEES YOU DIRECTLY SUPERVISED
FROM	TO		

NAME/TITLE OF YOUR SUPERVISOR)	LIST JOB TITLES OF EMPLOYEES YOU DIRECTLY SUPERVISED
NAME/TITLE OF PERSON WHO CAN VERIFY THIS EMPLOYMENT (IF OTHER THAN SUPERVISOR)	

DUTIES: List the major duties involved with job and give an approximate percentage of time spent on each duty.

% OF TIME	MAJOR DUTIES

STATE OF LOUISIANA APPLICATION—page 4

100%

USE REVERSE SIDE OF THIS PAGE IF ADDITIONAL SPACE REQUIRED FOR WORK EXPERIENCE

Name _____

25. WORK EXPERIENCE (Continued)

C

EMPLOYER/COMPANY NAME	KIND OF BUSINESS
STREET ADDRESS	YOUR OFFICIAL JOB TITLE
CITY AND STATE	BEGINNING SALARY / ENDING SALARY
DATES OF EMPLOYMENT (MO/DA/YR) / AVERAGE HOURS WORKED PER WEEK	REASON FOR LEAVING / NO. OF EMPLOYEES YOU DIRECTLY SUPERVISED
FROM / TO	
NAME/TITLE OF YOUR SUPERVISOR	LIST JOB TITLES OF EMPLOYEES YOU DIRECTLY SUPERVISED
NAME/TITLE OF PERSON WHO CAN VERIFY THIS EMPLOYMENT (IF OTHER THAN SUPERVISOR)	

DUTIES: List the major duties involved with job and give an approximate percentage of time spent on each duty.

% OF TIME	MAJOR DUTIES

100%

D

EMPLOYER/COMPANY NAME	KIND OF BUSINESS
STREET ADDRESS	YOUR OFFICIAL JOB TITLE
CITY AND STATE	BEGINNING SALARY / ENDING SALARY
DATES OF EMPLOYMENT (MO/DA/YR) / AVERAGE HOURS WORKED PER WEEK	REASON FOR LEAVING / NO. OF EMPLOYEES YOU DIRECTLY SUPERVISED
FROM / TO	
NAME/TITLE OF YOUR SUPERVISOR)	LIST JOB TITLES OF EMPLOYEES YOU DIRECTLY SUPERVISED
NAME/TITLE OF PERSON WHO CAN VERIFY THIS EMPLOYMENT (IF OTHER THAN SUPERVISOR)	

DUTIES: List the major duties involved with job and give an approximate percentage of time spent on each duty.

% OF TIME	MAJOR DUTIES

TEST-TAKING TECHNIQUES

Many factors enter into a test score. The most important factor should be ability to answer the questions, which in turn indicates the ability to learn and perform the duties of the job. Assuming that you have this ability, knowing what to expect on the exam and familiarity with techniques of effective test taking should give you the confidence you need to do your best on the exam.

There is no quick substitute for long-term study and development of your skills and abilities to prepare you for doing well on tests. However, there are some steps you can take to help you do the very best that you are prepared to do. Some of these steps are done before the test, and some are followed when you are taking the test. Knowing these steps is often called being "test-wise." Following these steps may help you feel more confident as you take the actual test.

"Test-wiseness" is a general term which simply means being familiar with some good procedures to follow when getting ready for and taking a test. The procedures fall into four major areas: (1) being prepared, (2) avoiding careless errors, (3) managing your time, and (4) guessing.

BE PREPARED

Don't make the test harder than it has to be by not preparing yourself. You are taking a very important step in preparation by reading this book and taking the sample tests which are included. This will help you to become familiar with the tests and the kinds of questions you will have to answer.

As you use this book, read the sample questions and directions for taking the test carefully. Then, when you take the sample tests, time yourself as you will be timed in the real test.

As you are working on the sample questions, don't look at the correct answers before you try to answer them on your own. This can fool you into thinking you understand a question when you really don't. Try it on your own first,.then compare your answer with the one given. Remember, in a sample test, you are your own grader; you don't gain anything by pretending to understand something you really don't.

On the examination day assigned to you, allow the test itself to be the main attraction of the day. Do not squeeze it in between other activities. Be sure to bring admission card, identification, and pencils, as instructed. Prepare these the night before so that you are not flustered by a last-minute search. Arrive rested, relaxed, and on time. In fact, plan to arrive a little bit early. Leave plenty of time for traffic tie-ups or other complications that might upset you and interfere with your test performance.

In the test room, the examiner will hand out forms for you to fill out. He or she will give you the instructions that you must follow in taking the examination. The examiner will tell you how to fill in the grids on the forms. Time limits and timing signals will be explained. If you do not understand any of the examiner's instructions, ASK QUESTIONS. It would be ridiculous to score less than your best because of poor communication.

At the examination, you must follow instructions exactly. Fill in the grids on the forms carefully and accurately. Misgridding may lead to loss of veteran's credits to which you may be entitled or misaddressing of your test results. Do not begin until you are told to begin. Stop as soon as the examiner tells you to stop. Do not turn pages until you are told to do so. Do not go back to parts you have already completed. Any infraction of the rules is considered cheating. If you cheat, your test paper will not be scored, and you will not be eligible for appointment.

The answer sheet for most multiple-choice exams is machine scored. You cannot give any explanations to the machine, so you must fill out the answer sheet clearly and correctly.

HOW TO MARK YOUR ANSWER SHEET

1. Blacken your answer space firmly and completely. ● is the only correct way to mark the answer sheet. ◗, ✖, ⊘, and ⊘ are all unacceptable. The machine might not read them at all.

2. Mark only one answer for each question. If you mark more than one answer, you will be considered wrong, even if one of the answers is correct.

3. If you change your mind, you must erase your mark. Attempting to cross out an incorrect answer like this ✖ will not work. You must erase any incorrect answer completely. An incomplete erasure might be read as a second answer.

4. All of your answering should be in the form of blackened spaces. The machine cannot read English. Do not write any notes in the margins.

5. MOST IMPORTANT: Answer each question in the right place. Question 1 must be answered in space 1; question 52 in space 52. If you should skip an answer space and mark a series of answers in the wrong places, you must erase all those answers and do the questions over, marking your answers in the proper places. You cannot afford to use the limited time in this way. Therefore, as you answer each question, look at its number and check that you are marking your answer in the space with the same number.

6. For the typing tests, type steadily and carefully. Just don't rush, since that's when the errors occur. Keep in mind that each error subtracts 1 wpm from your final score.

AVOID CARELESS ERRORS

Don't reduce your score by making careless mistakes. Always read the instructions for each test section carefully, even when you think you already know what the directions are. It's why we stress throughout this book that it's important to fully understand the directions for these different question-types before you go into the actual exam. It will not only reduce errors, but it will save you time—time you will need for the questions.

What if you don't understand the directions? You will have risked getting the answers wrong for a whole test section. As an example, vocabulary questions can sometimes test synonyms (words which have similar meanings), and sometimes test antonyms (words with opposite meanings). You can easily see how a mistake in understanding in this case could make a whole set of answers incorrect.

If you have time, reread any complicated instructions after you do the first few questions to check that you really do understand them. Of course, whenever you are allowed to, ask the examiner to clarify anything you don't understand.

Other careless mistakes affect only the response to particular questions. This often happens with arithmetic questions, but can happen with other questions as well. This type of error, called a "response error," usually stems from a momentary lapse of concentration.

Example

The question reads: "The capital of Massachusetts is …." The answer is (D) Boston, and you mark (B) because "B" is the first letter of the word "Boston."

Example

The question reads: "8 - 5 = …." The answer is (A) 3, but you mark (C) thinking "third letter."

A common error in reading comprehension questions is bringing your own information into the subject. For example, you may encounter a passage that discusses a subject you know something about. While this can make the passage easier to read, it can also tempt you to rely on your own knowledge about the subject. You must rely on information within the passage for your answers—in fact, sometimes the "wrong answer" for the questions are based on true information about the subject not given in the passage. Since the test-makers are testing your reading ability, rather than your general knowledge of the subject, an answer based on information not contained in the passage is considered incorrect.

MANAGE YOUR TIME

Before you begin, take a moment to plan your progress through the test. Although you are usually not expected to finish all of the questions given on a test, you should at least get an idea of how much time you should spend on each question in order to answer them all. For example, if there are 60 questions to answer and you have 30 minutes, you will have about one-half minute to spend on each question.

Keep track of the time on your watch or the room clock, but do not fixate on the time remaining. Your task is to answer questions. Do not spend too much time on any one question. If you find yourself stuck, do not take the puzzler as a personal challenge. Either guess and mark the question in the question booklet or skip the question entirely, marking the question as a skip and taking care to skip the answer space on the answer sheet. If there is time at the end of the exam or exam part, you can return and give marked questions another try.

MULTIPLE-CHOICE QUESTIONS

Almost all of the tests given on civil service exams are multiple-choice format. This means that you normally have four or five answer choices. But it's not something that should be overwhelming. There is a basic technique to answering these types of questions. Once you've understood this technique, it will make your test-taking far less stressful.

First, there should only be one correct answer. Since these tests have been given time and again, and the test-developers have a sense of which questions work and which questions don't work, it will be rare that your choices will be ambiguous. They may be complex, and somewhat confusing, but there will still be only one right answer.

The first step is to look at the question, without looking at the answer choices. Now select the correct answer. That may sound somewhat simplistic, but it's usually the case that your first choice is the correct one. If you go back and change it, redo it again and again, it's more likely that you'll end up with the wrong answer. Thus, follow your instinct. Once you have come up with the answer, look at the answer choices. If your answer is one of the choices, you're probably correct. It's not 100 percent infallible, but it's a strong possibility that you've selected the right answer.

With math questions you should first solve the problem. If your answer is among the choices, you're probably correct. Don't ignore things like the proper function signs (adding, subtracting, multiplying, and dividing), negative and positive numbers, and so on.

But suppose you don't know the correct answer. You then use the "process of elimination." It's a time-honored technique for test-takers. There is always one correct answer. There is usually one answer choice that is totally incorrect—a "distracter." If you look at that choice and it seems highly unlikely, then eliminate it. Depending on the number of choices (four or five), you've just cut down the number of choices to make. Now weigh the other choices. They may seem incorrect or they may be correct. If they seem incorrect, eliminate them. You've now increased your odds at getting the correct answer.

In the end, you may be left with only two choices. At that point, it's just a matter of guessing. But with only two choices left, you now have a 50 percent chance of getting it right. With four choices, you only have a 25 percent chance, and with five choices, only a 20 percent chance at guessing correctly. That's why the process of elimination is important.

SHOULD YOU GUESS?

You may be wondering whether or not it is wise to guess when you are not sure of an answer (even if you've reduced the odds to 50 percent) or whether it is better to skip the question when you are not certain. The wisdom of guessing depends on the scoring method for the particular examination part. If the scoring is "rights only," that is, one point for each correct answer and no subtraction for wrong answers, then by all means you should guess. Read the question and all of the answer choices carefully. Eliminate those answer choices that you are certain are wrong. Then guess from among the remaining choices. You cannot gain a point if you leave the answer space blank; you may gain a point with an educated guess or even with a lucky guess. In fact, it is foolish to leave any spaces blank on a test that counts "rights only." If it appears that you are about to run out of time before completing such an exam, mark all the remaining blanks with the same letter. According to the law of averages, you should get some portion of those questions right.

If the scoring method is *rights minus wrongs*, such as the address checking test found on Postal Clerk Exam 470, DO NOT GUESS. A wrong answer counts heavily against you. On this type of test, do not rush to fill answer spaces randomly at the end. Work as quickly as possible while concentrating on accuracy. Keep working carefully until time is called. Then stop and leave the remaining answer spaces blank.

In guessing the answers to multiple-choice questions, take a second to eliminate those answers that are obviously wrong, then quickly consider and guess from the remaining choices. The fewer choices from which you guess, the better the odds of guessing correctly. Once you have decided to make a guess, be it an educated guess or a wild stab, do it right away and move on; don't keep thinking about it and wasting time. You should always mark the test questions at which you guess so that you can return later.

For those questions that are scored by subtracting a fraction of a point for each wrong answer, the decision as to whether or not to guess is really up to you.

A correct answer gives you one point; a skipped space gives you nothing at all, but costs you nothing except the chance of getting the answer right; a wrong answer costs you 1/4 point. If you are really uncomfortable with guessing, you may skip a question, BUT you must then remember to skip its answer space as well. The risk of losing your place if you skip questions is so great that we advise you to guess even if you are not sure of the answer. Our suggestion is that you answer every question in order, even if you have to guess. It is better to lose a few 1/4 points for wrong guesses than to lose valuable seconds figuring where you started marking answers in the wrong place, erasing, and re-marking answers. On the other hand, do not mark random answers at the end. Work steadily until time is up.

One of the questions you should ask in the testing room is what scoring method will be used on your particular exam. You can then guide your guessing procedure accordingly.

SCORING

If your exam is a short-answer exam such as those often used by companies in the private sector, your answers will be graded by a personnel officer trained in grading test questions. If you blackened spaces on the separate answer sheet accompanying a multiple-choice exam, your answer sheet will be machine scanned or will be hand scored using a punched card stencil. Then a raw score will be calculated using the scoring formula that applies to that test or test portion—rights only, rights minus wrongs, or rights minus a fraction of wrongs. Raw scores on test parts are then added together for a total raw score.

A raw score is not a final score. The raw score is not the score that finds its way onto an eligibility list. The civil service testing authority, Postal Service, or other testing body converts raw scores to a scaled score according to an unpublicized formula of its own. The scaling formula allows for slight differences in difficulty of questions from one form of the exam to another and allows for equating the scores of all candidates. Regardless of the number of questions and possible different weights of different parts of the exam, most civil service clerical test scores are reported on a scale of 1 to 10. The entire process of conversion from raw to scaled score is confidential information. The score you receive is not your number right, is not your raw score, and, despite being on a scale of 1 to 100, is not a percentage. It is a scaled score. If you are entitled to veterans' service points, these are added to your passing scaled score to boost your rank on the eligibility list. Veterans' points are added only to passing scores. A failing score cannot be brought to passing level by adding veterans' points. The score earned plus veterans' service points, if any, is the score that finds its place on the rank order eligibility list. Highest scores go to the top of the list.

Test-Taking Tips

1. Get to the test center early. Make sure you give yourself plenty of extra time to get there, park your car, if necessary, and even grab a cup of coffee before the test.

2. Listen to the test monitors and follow their instructions carefully.

3. Read every word of the instructions. Read every word of every question.

4. Mark your answers by completely darkening the answer space of your choice. Do not use the test paper to work out your answers.

5. Mark only ONE answer for each question, even if you think that more than one answer is correct. You must choose only one. If you mark more than one answer, the scoring machine will consider you wrong.

6. If you change your mind, erase completely. Leave no doubt as to which answer you mean.

7. If your exam permits you to use scratch paper or the margins of the test booklet for figuring, don't forget to mark the answer on the answer sheet. Only the answer sheet is scored.

8. Check often to be sure that the question number matches the answer space, that you have not skipped a space by mistake.

9. Guess according to the guessing suggestions we have made.

10. Stay alert. Be careful not to mark a wrong answer just because you were not concentrating.

11. Do not panic. If you cannot finish any part before time is up, do not worry. If you are accurate, you can do well even without finishing. It is even possible to earn a scaled score of 100 without entirely finishing an exam part if you are very accurate. At any rate, do not let your performance on any one part affect your performance on any other part.

12. Check and recheck, time permitting. If you finish any part before time is up, use the remaining time to check that each question is answered in the right space and that there is only one answer for each question. Return to the difficult questions and rethink them.

PART TWO

What Kind of Work Will You Be Doing?

TO GET PROMOTED

This book targets police promotion and has been carefully designed to assist the motivated officer to achieve a higher rank within his or her agency by competing successfully in promotion examinations.

In recent years, the courts have become key players in police promotion examinations because of their involvement in job-related and nondiscriminatory testing procedures. Court involvement should not be used to justify less than a full effort by those who seek advancement. In situations where the courts have insisted that promotion lists reflect the racial, ethnic, or gender composition of those who competed, a pragmatic approach by the candidate is mandatory. Students who prepare properly will be in the top percentile of their particular group.

A student was heard to exclaim, "You've got to be lucky to get promoted." Our response to that statement and its inherent implication is, "Yes, and the harder you study the luckier you get." It should be noted that in many jurisdictions the written examination and/or an assessment center or oral board is only a portion of the qualifications deemed necessary for promotion. In some agencies, evaluations by supervisors and peers are an integral component in the qualifying process. In some departments, the chief or top administrator is permitted to promote a candidate with a lower written mark than that attained by another. Many argue that such a procedure is arbitrary at best and capricious at worst, but such a system does have some merit.

A chief is ultimately responsible for "getting the job done" and it is universally accepted that a supervisor or manager at whatever level gets the job done *through people*. It follows then, that the chief should have a certain amount of input into the selection of those who are going to direct police operations at the level of execution. Would it not be appropriate for a chief to consider the reputation of a candidate in his decision-making process? Reputations in police work, as in other professions, are usually earned. Examine the following list of reputations that could accompany candidates being considered for promotion. Assume that you must select some candidates and reject others.

- "If you can find her."

- "He likes the ladies."

- "She knows the job."

- "Tough, but fair."

- "Helluva guy when sober."

- "He knows how to get the job done."

- "An empty suit."

- "A take-charge guy."

- "Loyal and dependable."

- "If it needs to be done, then give it to her."

It would be difficult to argue that these kinds of reputations should not be considered in the promotion process. As previously mentioned, peer group and supervisory evaluations play an important role in a valid promotion procedure. Additionally, seniority and academic achievement are promotional considerations that are easily and objectively measured.

THE PROMOTION

The first promotion, usually to the rank of sergeant, is the big one. This promotion is the most demanding. The new boss is now in the position of being responsible for the work of other people. He or she must now plan, direct, and evaluate the work of others. The transition from "one of the boys" to one of the bosses is a most difficult adjustment. As a supervisor, he or she becomes a vital link in the vertical communications process and must gain the loyalty of subordinates while maintaining loyalty to the department and its mission.

As one advances to higher ranks within the agency, the concept of being a supervisor does not change. The lieutenants and captains are still responsible for getting certain jobs done through people and, because there is an inverse relationship between the rank attained and the number of people directly supervised, the ability to delegate properly becomes critical. The interpretation of crime statistics, the proper allocation of available manpower, the response to community pressures, and budget considerations are ongoing challenges to police management. The prestige and economic rewards of a promotion are the obvious and measurable advantages of higher rank, but even more important is the self-satisfaction and sense of accomplishment that is experienced by the true professional.

ADMINISTRATION AND SUPERVISION

Supervising personnel, commanding units, and dealing with personnel problems are the concerns of executives in every organization. Consequently, examiners throughout the nation are inclined to reflect those concerns in questions designed to test candidates for supervisory and administrative positions. Students should realize that supervisors and administrators respond to similar demands. Most experts agree that the major duties of supervisory personnel differ only in degree from those of highly placed administrators.

Our coverage of supervision, administration, and personnel considerations will consist of a series of concepts followed by questions based on those concepts. And each question will have an explained answer.

We will begin this series with a discussion of important organizational considerations.

ORGANIZATIONAL STRUCTURES

Line Organization—An arrangement where the channels of authority and responsibility extend in a direct line from the chief executive officer to those involved at the level of execution. This approach is seldom utilized in its pure form.

Functional Organization—A situation where the organization is divided among special units. A functional organizational structure divides responsibility and authority among separate units. For example, the police department may have a personnel unit, a traffic unit, a juvenile unit, a patrol unit, and a detective unit. This approach is seldom utilized in its pure form.

Line and Staff Organization—This type of organization combines special units with a line organization approach. In this kind of structure, the line commanders receive advice and help from special units, but do not receive commands or orders. This approach is widely utilized.

THE PRINCIPLES OF ORGANIZATION

Division of Work—The principle that tasks that are similar should be combined into one function. They should not be fragmented and, where possible, should be under the direct control of one person. *Note*: A worker should be assigned a limited number of tasks to increase the quality of work.

Unity of Command—Each employee should be directly supervised by only one supervisor. This principle also holds that only one person should be in complete command of any given situation.

Span of Control—This refers to the number of persons that one supervisor can effectively supervise. The many factors that help determine the number of people who may be effectively supervised include the ability of the supervisor, the readiness of the employees, the complexity of the tasks, and other demands on the supervisor's available time. *Note*: As one attains a higher rank the span of control becomes smaller. Consequently, there is an inverse relationship between one's place in the organization and the span of his or her control.

Delegation—A primary objective of a supervisor is "to get the job done through people." Supervisors may delegate orally or in writing and should not be reluctant to delegate. Delegation is not blind trust; a person with authority must be held accountable for this authority. Both authority and responsibility must be delegated in equal amounts.

Note: A supervisor may delegate tasks and assignments, but the ultimate responsibility for completion of the task rests with the supervisor. Responsibility can't be delegated.

Personnel Development—It is a supervisory duty to develop and train subordinates. And it is noted that those who do delegate contribute to the development of their subordinates.

Specialization—A by-product of the division of work by function. Most police administrators agree that the patrol force is the backbone of the department and that as the number of specialized units increases this backbone is weakened. There is a kind of Catch-22 principle involved with the formation of specialized units. If, for example, patrol officers who receive outstanding evaluations are rewarded by assignment to specialized units (such as detective or youth divisions), the patrol division suffers because it loses talented personnel. Additionally, specialization may complicate direction, coordination, and control.

Chain of Command—Ordinarily, police officers should proceed through a sergeant and a lieutenant before arriving at the captain's office. In the usual scheme of things, communications should go upward and downward through established channels in the hierarchy. If a supervisor is bypassed by a directive going downward and has no official knowledge of it, he or she is unable to contribute to the accomplishment of such a directive and cannot be held responsible for its enforcement. *Note*: Do not confuse unity of command with chain of command.

ADMINISTERING THE ORGANIZATION

Whether we say "administering" the organization or "managing" the organization we are talking about the same thing. The words "management" and "administration" are used interchangeably in most texts. We suggest that you use Luther Gulick's acronym POSDCORB to help remember the administrative (or management) duties of a chief executive officer. POSDCORB stands for the following:

- *Planning*—Working out in a broad outline what needs to be done and the methods for doing it.

- *Organizing*—Establishing a formal structure or arrangement based on what is to be done and by whom. This includes both long- and short-term planning.

- *Staffing*—The personnel function that includes recruitment and training.

- *Directing*—Giving orders, delegating, instructing, following up, and being a leader.

■ *Coordinating*—Making sure that units and personnel within units are working together (not at odds) in an effort to accomplish agency objectives.

■ *Reporting*—Keeping subordinates informed by utilizing oral and written reports, research, and inspections.

■ *Budgeting*—The usual fiscal planning that aims at operating the agency in an economical and efficient manner.

Note: Many maintain that the major duties of supervisory personnel differ only in degree from those of the chief executive officer. Ongoing evaluation of an organization is an important part of the management team.

DISCIPLINE AND TRAINING

A well-disciplined organization is highly trained. It can even be argued that discipline is a form of training that has as its objectives the changing of attitudes, improvement of skills, and imparting of knowledge.

Discipline may be viewed as positive or negative. Positive discipline is that form of attitudinal conditioning that has as its objective the correction of inadequacies without punishment. Negative discipline consists of punishment and is usually applicable when positive methods of training have been tried, but have failed to achieve the desired conformity to acceptable standards of performance. The principal responsibility for maintaining an appropriate level of discipline in the unit should rest with the immediate line supervisor.

Insofar as punishment is concerned, supervisors and managers should realize that morale is more adversely affected by punishment that is perceived to be unfair than by punishment that is severe. And if punishment is to be looked upon as fair, then there are certain fundamental requisites.

Punishment should be

1. provided with advance warning.

2. certain.

3. swift.

4. fair and impartial.

5. consistent.

6. a deterrent for others.

Discipline, morale, and esprit de corps are interdependent. When one falls, the others usually follow.

In theory, job-related problems result from management's failure to provide the needed training. And one of the principal duties of the supervisor is the training of subordinates.

The need for police training never ends. The more complex the society it serves, the more complex the police department's training must be.

The following series of questions has been specifically designed to help students more fully appreciate some of the concepts involved in discipline and training.

EVALUATIONS AND RATINGS

Many supervisors find evaluations and ratings to be among the most distasteful of the tasks assigned to them. Although it is argued that many employees find their evaluation and rating interviews to be somewhat stressful, the good workers view them as an opportunity to earn recognition. Nonetheless, employees must be evaluated and supervisors must do the job. The objectives of the evaluation and rating process are as follows:

- Assist substandard employees to improve their job performance

- Provide management with an inventory of employee capabilities

- Assist in the advancement and placement of personnel

- Provide for a degree of recognition that employees desire

- Improve job performance and thereby deliver better service

- Provide criteria for validating the selection process

- Defend against charges of discrimination

Although the objectives of a good evaluation and rating procedure are laudatory, the actual process of one individual auditing another's performance is inherently subjective. Many of the traits that supervisors are required to rate cannot be measured by precise tests. Consequently, the undesirable factor of subjectivity creeps into the evaluation process. Subjectivity may be minimized by supervisors who systematically record observations made in the course of performing their supervisory duties.

Selecting the rating method that is most appropriate for the particular group involved and that will provide the most reliable results is one of the major problems associated with evaluations and ratings. Some of these methods are listed as follows:

Ranking Employees—From highest to lowest level in the unit, or on the basis of most valuable to least valuable.

Selected Employee Standard—The rater compares the employee being rated with others who have been identified as having the greatest, average, or least value.

Ideal Employee Standard—The rater determines (in his or her own mind) the qualities of an ideal employee and then compares the work product of those being evaluated with the "ideal."

Numerical Standards—The person being evaluated is given a numerical grade for each trait being measured.

Forced Choice Standard—The rater must select from a group of statements (for each trait) the one that most accurately describes the person being rated.

It should be obvious that in the preceding rating methods the problem of subjectivity has the potential of being reflected in the overall evaluation. However, it follows that good supervisors are good raters, and the good supervisor is usually more objective because he or she relies heavily on recorded data gathered throughout the rating period. In addition to the failure to properly train supervisors on how to rate and evaluate employees (a management failure), there are some common rating errors with which we should be familiar. These include the following:

Leniency—The most common rating error. This is usually the course of least resistance for the weak boss who wants to minimize the discomfort of the always necessary, face-to-face, post-evaluation interview with the person rated.

Personal Bias—An error that allows the rater's personal feelings about an employee to impact on the rating.

Error of Related Traits—This occurs when the rater assumes that because a person possesses one particular strength or weakness, that he automatically possesses another. (If the employee is overweight, he is probably lazy.) This is also known as logical error or association error.

Central Tendency—A tendency to group those being rated in the center of the scale rather than at either (good or bad) extreme. This tendency is often reinforced by a policy that requires extreme ratings to be supported by independent documentation. In this kind of error, the outstanding (extreme) employee suffers.

Halo Effect—This occurs when a rater evaluates on the basis of a general impression: good or bad.

Error of Subjectivity—This error occurs when the rater is overly impressed by one or two characteristics that have special appeal to him.

Error of Overweighting—This error occurs when the supervisor is influenced by a single occurrence (good or bad) that takes place at or near the end of the rating period. Sometimes referred to as the error of recency.

It is noted that some organizations have abandoned ratings as such in favor of Management By Objectives (MBO) that typically involves goal setting by supervisors and subordinates working together. In this approach, the subordinate is judged by standards that he or she helped to determine in terms of setting goals, participation, and appraisal.

Every performance evaluation or rating must be followed by a discussion between the supervisor and the employee concerned. This interview provides an excellent opportunity for the supervisor to provide recognition for good performance. It is an ideal time to discuss means for improving the work performance of the marginal employee. The supervisor should appropriately schedule follow-up interviews to discuss improved effort and performance. If properly utilized, the post-rating interview can be the most productive element in the rating process.

Reasons why rating systems fail include the following:

- Indifference of supervisors to the need for accuracy in ratings

- Employee pressures

- Failure to train raters in an effort to reduce the more common rating errors

- Rating abuses—ratings should be utilized only as they were intended

- Slipshod procedures and shortcuts

Note: The first-line supervisor is usually a sergeant in the police service and is the key figure in any rating system. The job involves the productivity of the officers that are under his or her command. The first-line supervisor plays a prime part in setting the standards of performance for subordinates. Although it is true that rating systems are inherently subjective, good supervisors can keep subjectivity to a minimum.

ASSESSMENT CENTERS

Some agencies utilize a sophisticated method of identifying managerial personnel who have the ability for administrative and executive advancement. The method, referred to as an "assessment center," is a procedure whereby selected personnel interact with each other and individually with role players in job-related exercises. The behavior and reactions of the employees in varying degrees of stress and problem-solving exercises are evaluated by trained personnel. In many of the exercises, the subjects are not aware of the parameters being measured. For example, the ability to work with others, the ability to lead, innovativeness, and the ability to work within a time constraint. Assessment centers may last from one to several days and have proven most successful in identifying personnel that possess the desired assets.

CONFERENCES

A conference is a problem-solving device and usually involves an exchange of ideas, attitudes, and knowledge among persons with a common problem. In order to succeed, a conference must be well planned and effectively directed by a conference leader. It is generally accepted that the participants should be of somewhat equal rank if drawn from the same organization.

The leader must have a well-thought-out plan and must adhere to it if the conference is to be successful. The wise leader will consider the nature and depth of the problem, the availability of people with the necessary expertise, and a host of other things such as the following:

- Arranging for timely notification to participants

■ Actual agenda

■ Preparation of an opening statement to identify the problem

■ Preparation of pertinent and thought-provoking questions

Although the conference leader need not be an expert in the matter to be discussed, he or she should know enough about the problem to properly introduce it and to stimulate meaningful discussion in an effort to arrive at a solution.

Once the conference leader has introduced the problem, he or she should promote participation by all of the conferees. This may be accomplished by maintaining a permissive attitude and a position of strict neutrality throughout the discussions. The good conference leader will frequently summarize contributions, but will not evaluate them. (Evaluation would obviously be inconsistent with neutrality.) The conference leader should not hesitate to use questions in order to stimulate thinking.

Questions should not be framed in a manner that would allow a simple "yes" or "no" answer. *Overhead questions* are general in nature, directed at the entire group, and answerable by any member. A *directed question* is asked of a specific person and is often used to obtain a point of view from a knowledgeable member or to force a reticent member to more actively participate. *Relay questions* are a means by which the leader, rather than answering a question directed at him or her, relays the question to another member of the conference.

The skillful leader must keep in mind that participants bring divergent personalities to the conference setting. Dealing with these personalities, while at the same time keeping the conference on course, often presents a serious challenge to the leader. Some of the more common personalities and recommended ways for dealing with them are as follows:

■ *Overtalkative Member*—It is important to use him or her as a summarizer or scribe.

■ *Hostile Member*—It is important to remain neutral. In many situations, the group will police him or her.

■ *Quiet Retiring Member*—This member should be encouraged and his or her comments never ignored.

■ *Obstructionist (Against Everything)*—The leader may ignore his or her contributions or give someone else credit for them.

■ *Dogmatic Member*—Control this individual by asking a technical question that he or she will not be able to answer.

In addition, the able conference leader must remain neutral in handling delicate or controversial problems and must control disturbances without embarrassing those involved. While directing the conference, the leader must never lose sight of his or her primary function is to seek solutions to the problem at hand. The leader is not involved in a brainstorming exercise. The purpose of the conference is to arrive at well-thought-out solutions and not spontaneous responses that are immediately recorded and examined at a later time (as in the "brainstorming" approach to problem solving).

Although conferences have a place in organizational life, they do have limitations, pitfalls, and a failure rate. Some of the more common limitations are as follows:

■ Conferences are time-consuming.

■ The conference procedure often takes key personnel from their regularly assigned duties.

■ Skillful conference leaders are not always available.

When a conference fails it is usually the fault of the conference leader. Reasons for failure include, but are not limited to, the following:

- Poor techniques by the leader

- Failure to summarize contributions

- The leader assumes the role of "expert"

- Improper or careless selection of participants

- Too much formality

- Prior solution of the problem with the conferees' knowledge

- An inclination to evaluate contributions

Before concluding our brief discussion on conferences it is appropriate that we mention the "vertical staff meeting." Although we indicated that most conferences should be composed of people of somewhat equal rank drawn from the same organization, the vertical staff meeting contains a representative of each rank from the very top of the level of execution. A vertical staff meeting allows the chief to obtain input from each rank represented. This kind of meeting provides an effective means for identifying rather than solving problems. It also allows for training of the leadership at each level of the organization. Some writers use the terms "conference" and "vertical staff meeting" interchangeably, even though these terms have different functions in organizational life.

THE IMPORTANCE OF PATROL

The patrol force is often referred to as the backbone of the police department and is the largest unit. In large departments, most officers serve in the patrol bureau, and in smaller departments the patrol force is the entire department.

The patrol force is the eyes and ears of the police administrator. Solutions to police problems depend heavily on the information gathered and reported by the men and women involved at the level of execution.

The more effective the patrol force, the less the need for specialized units. Specialized units are necessary only to the extent that the patrol force fails to prevent crime and apprehend criminals.

The elimination of the actual opportunity, or elimination of the belief of opportunity for successful misconduct, is the basic purpose of patrol. A thief's desire to steal is not diminished by the presence of a police officer, but the opportunity for successful theft is reduced.

Patrol is the form of police service that directly attempts to eliminate the opportunity for misconduct. Nevertheless, when misconduct occurs the patrol force is immediately available to: 1) investigate offenses, 2) arrest offenders, 3) collect evidence, and 4) recover stolen property.

The police officer is the ultimate in the decentralization of municipal service. An officer may perform various inspectional services for other municipal agencies while on routine patrol, but if these services seriously interfere with his or her duties, they should be performed by the primary department.

Depletion of the patrol force to staff specialized units should be avoided. The patrol bureau is so important that it should be kept as strong as possible by the assignment of all tasks that it may perform substantially as well as specialists and that do not interfere with patrol duties. There is no formula to determine the exact optimum proportional strength of the patrol and special divisions.

Most of the perils of specialization are found at the levels of execution. For example, the performance by specialists of tasks that should be handled by police officers in the course of their regular duty. However, specialization for planning and inspection is nearly always essential to ensure suitable attention to the accomplishment of each of the primary police tasks.

Patrol by specialized divisions has limited value because officers so engaged are not alert to conditions demanding attention outside the field of their special interest. Routine patrol by detectives is particularly wasteful and should not be permitted.

PATROL ACTIVITIES

Most authorities divide the activities of a police officer into two broad categories. These are called-for services and preventive patrol.

Called-for services refer to activity generated by crime complaints, requests for services, and other police work that cannot be categorized as preventive patrol activity, administrative activity, or time out of service. There are two kinds of called-for services. They are the investigation of crimes and the handling of noncriminal incidents and miscellaneous complaints. Among called-for services are both incidents reported by police officers and complaints of crime and requests for service received from citizens.

Preventive patrol encompasses all patrol activities not included in called-for services. Preventive patrol is directed primarily at diminishing less tangible hazards that are not readily identified. A major result of preventive patrol is to create a sense of omnipresence.

IMPORTANT PATROL ISSUES

There are a number of issues with regard to patrol that are the subjects of frequent controversy. There are many aspects of staffing and scheduling and each has its advocates and its critics. We will discuss the pros and cons of each of these issues in turn.

Frequent Change of Beat—The only real argument in favor of frequent changes of beat is that it inhibits corruption. The police officer who is moved frequently does not have the opportunity to develop a payoff or protection racket. In fact, however, there is very little of this sort of corruption and the many drawbacks of frequent change of beat far outweigh the advantage of preventing petty corruption.

The highest quality of patrol service results from permanent assignment of an officer to a beat. The officer who patrols the same location becomes well acquainted with persons, hazards, and facilities on the beat. The officers who patrol a certain beat on a regular basis can readily assume responsibility for conditions that exist or are allowed to develop, and they are well positioned to spot and rectify incipient problems. A real drawback connected with frequent changes of beat is that the rotation of personnel disrupts the investigation and disposition of cases, neglect, and delay result.

Rotation of Shifts—The premise of shift rotation is that less desirable assignments should be evenly distributed among the personnel. With rotation, everyone gets to spend some working hours in the daylight. Without scrutiny, rotation of shifts seems to be a good idea and it does have its proponents.

However, the most efficient patrol service is attained by the permanent assignment of an officer to a platoon. Officers who regularly work together develop efficient methods and fierce loyalties, which makes for good police work. Those who have worked both rotational shifts and fixed shifts have found that the set schedules makes for less tension in one's home life. The body tends to adapt to a regular waking-sleeping regimen and stable daily rhythms and routines are conducive to better physical and mental health. Fixed shifts easily accommodate officers' personal lives. Students, for instance, can arrange their lives according to regular working hours, whatever they may be.

If fixed shifts are a regular policy, then transfer from one shift to another can be used as a promotional device. Conversely, transfer to less desirable platoons can be used as a disciplinary measure.

Fixed shifts also allow for the assignment of personnel to the duty that is most appropriate to their stage of development. For example, it may be reasonable to assign recruits to late tours because of the less frequent citizen contact at those hours. Some argue that the recruit should be assigned for training and experience to the first platoon where less frequent contact with more critical citizens offsets the disadvantages of inexperience.

The very active evening shift (4 P.M. to midnight) should be manned by well-trained, experienced officers with proven efficiency and effectiveness.

Finally, the day tour should be offered to the older officer who has become less active physically, but who has a wealth of experience. The day shift may be a reward for long, efficient service. In the day shift, the older officer's knowledge of police service and an acquaintanceship with the general public will prove most useful and he or she will be subject to less physical strain. The philosophy here is, "Well done, thou good and faithful servant!"

Permanent Supervisors—This patrol issue is among the least controversial. The only drawback to the assignment of permanent supervisors is the possibility of favoritism and the development of cliques. A good supervisor does not play favorites; there should be no accommodation for supervisors who are not good supervisors. The permanent supervisor can become acquainted with the strengths and weaknesses of the officers under his or her control and develop and utilize them most effectively. The permanent supervisor who knows the officers well can develop squad spirit and is more effective at evaluation time. The permanent supervisor can more logically be held responsible for the activities of the officers.

Canine Corps—The use of dogs is very controversial, mainly because of the possibility of using them inappropriately. Dogs should not be used where there is strong community hostility against them; to do so would be counterproductive. The use of dogs for riot control raises "considerable doubt." It may increase violence and can further damage community relations. In such situations, the emotional issue outweighs the utility of the dogs. By the same reasoning, dogs should not be used at rallies or sit-ins of any kind, including civil rights, student antiwar, or labor dispute gatherings.

On the other hand, the use of dogs in high crime areas for routine patrol and for hazardous searches is being accepted throughout the country. Dogs can be used to control street gangs and street robberies. Dogs are fine adjuncts in antiburglar patrols in commercial areas and streets, in narrow alleys and yards, and are effective in searches of vast unoccupied buildings, warehouses, and stores. Most recently, dogs have proven themselves to be very effective in sniffing out the presence of drugs and bombs.

Community Control of Police—The final area of controversy is community control of police. Community control sounds democratic, but the public should not control the police. The concept of community control ignores the mobility of police between and among communities within the larger municipality. In effect, the police are already under the substantial local control of the mayor and the local legislative body. The community can advise and make suggestions, but responsible control must remain within the department.

COMMUNITY-ORIENTED POLICING

Ideally, this style of policing is designed to promote the quality of living throughout the community. Its principle is to assign two or three officers to specified communities. These officers serve as a liaison to governmental agencies to rectify and improve the overall quality of the communities. These officers have complete autonomy in decision-making and other aspects of their duties. There are variations of this style of policing ranging from focusing attention on one or two neighborhoods to developing a philosophy for the whole department to follow. Generally speaking, the most successful community-oriented police agency is one in which there is total integration of the department.

Most police officers do not see this as "real" police work, since little time is focused on the idea of "crime fighting." Here we find that there is an overall misconception of the true focus of the patrol function, which should be public order or peacekeeping. Ideally, community-oriented policing provides a stronger component toward crime fighting by eliminating the social ills that often trigger deviant behavior. Hence, crime fighting is indirectly achieved by improving the overall quality of life in the community.

COMPLAINTS AGAINST POLICE PERSONNEL

Police personnel are carefully selected and are highly trained. Even so, they are human beings and will occasionally commit infractions of various sorts. Some infractions may be observed by a supervisor and others are reported as complaints from the public.

Minor infractions observed by the supervisor can be addressed informally. In every instance of an observed breach of discipline, the supervisor should call the matter to the attention of the employee promptly and, when possible, in private. The supervisor must discuss the incident with the offending employee, and, if indicated, give a warning. A record of the circumstances of the incident and of the action taken must be made in every instance where a breach of discipline requires punitive action by a supervisor; then follow-up must be maintained to assure correction of the offending behavior or practice. The recording of an incident in the employee's file without calling the act to the offending employee's attention and hearing his or her side is absolutely indefensible. Your goal is to correct behavior, not to make a case against the employee.

More serious complaints require formal procedures. The techniques of investigating personnel complaints are similar to those used in other investigations. Prompt investigation is essential to determine the exact allegation and its validity. It may be useful to set up a fact-finding inquiry. Every allegation must be answered, investigated, and concluded.

The following are some basic rules regarding the investigation of complaints against police personnel:

- Oral complaints should be reduced to writing as soon as possible after they are received.

- Anonymous complaints cannot be ignored, but they must be treated with caution and discretion because of the impact they may have upon the morale of the employees involved.

- Persons making complaints while intoxicated should be interviewed at the time, then re-interviewed when sober.

- Complaints received from second parties on behalf of an alleged victim of police action must be investigated; they cannot be rejected merely because they are not made directly by the person claiming to be aggrieved.

- Statements should be taken from people who were in a position to observe what supposedly happened, but who say that they heard or saw nothing.

- Personnel records of the accused employee should be carefully examined for evidence of similar complaints in the past.

Thorough investigation of a complaint must lead to decisive conclusions. No complaint may be left unresolved. Basically, at the end of an investigation a complaint may be classified as the following:

- *Sustained*—The facts obtained support the complaint.

- *Exonerated*—The evidence indicates that the act complained of actually occurred but was legal, proper, and necessary.

- *Unfounded*—The act complained of did not occur.

- *Not Sustained*—There is insufficient evidence or there are material conflicts in the evidence. Thus, the case must be resolved in favor of the accused employee.

- *Misconduct Not Based on the Complaint*—From the point of view of the employee, an unfortunate byproduct of the investigation is uncovering misconduct that is not part of the original complaint.

The investigative report should contain a statement of the complaint, a summary of the investigation backed up with details of the investigation, conclusions and recommendations concerning the disposition of the case, and statement of corrective action taken if charges were sustained. Follow-up is the duty of the supervisor.

INTERVIEWING AND HANDLING EMPLOYEE GRIEVANCES

INTERVIEWING

An interview is an interchange of views and ideas between two or more persons. The primary purpose of the interview is to obtain or impart information or to influence attitudes or behavior. Interviewing or consulting with others is a prime activity of every supervisory officer at every level; it consumes a great deal of time. An interview is decidedly not an interrogation. The interview differs from the interrogation in its most basic purpose. The purpose of an interrogation is to obtain information, not to give out information. In fact, the interrogator will seldom place himself or herself in a position of giving any information at all. Suspects are always subject to interrogation.

Personnel are interviewed, not interrogated. The personnel interview serves the following purposes: to obtain information; to communicate or give information; to motivate employees; to help solve group and personal problems through the consultation process; and to appraise the past, present, or future situation of the employee.

Personnel interviews are not all alike. There are a number of different kinds of personnel interviews that include the following:

- Informal interviews that occur in the course of day-to-day personal contacts between supervisors and subordinates.

- Progress interviews that are scheduled to inform an employee of his or her progress.

- Grievance interviews that are generally initiated by the employee.

- Disciplinary interviews that serve to change attitude, to improve skills, and to impart knowledge.

- Separation interviews to be held at the time of separation of the employee, regardless of the reason for the separation.

- Problem-solving interviews are often referred to as consultation interviews or "chaplain's interviews." These are aimed at helping the subordinate solve personal problems.

Not all personnel interviews need to be recorded. When a record is desirable or needed, the results should be recorded immediately upon conclusion of the interview. The record should be made promptly to prevent omissions, inaccuracies, and faulty information from filtering into the record.

Some interviews fail. The reasons for failure include breakdown in communication, ignorance, faulty recollection, and the tendency of the person being interviewed to say what he or she thinks is expected. Subjective reporting of the results is also an aspect of the failed interview. The interviewer must be alert and flexible enough to adapt the principles and techniques of interviewing to the problem at hand.

GRIEVANCES

Grievances may be real or imagined; they may be expressed or internalized. Whether verbalized or not, grievances have the effect of stifling initiative and of causing a drop in morale and performance. Expressed grievances can be identified and dealt with. If the problem cannot be cured, it can be discussed and alleviated. Morale improves when employees recognize that the supervisor is working to correct a situation. Nonverbalized grievances may be more serious to the supervisor and the organization than expressed grievances. They are harder to identify, yet may severely hamper the functioning of the unit. Once the supervisor senses symptoms that strong feelings of discontent or dissatisfaction are growing among subordinates, he or she should try to determine the root cause.

There are a number of causes of employee dissatisfaction, one of which is the working environment. Problems such as unsatisfactory operational equipment and the cleanliness of facilities are often the kinds of problems that the supervisor cannot directly correct. The supervisor can, however, bring these matters to the attention of higher management and can let the employees know that higher management has been alerted.

Inept supervisory practices also give rise to unhappiness. Some inept supervisory practices include failure to give earned recognition, use of intemperate language, favoritism, dual standards of conduct, excessive supervision, and the promotion or toleration of cliques. The supervisor must examine his or her own behavior for these signs of ineptitude. Misunderstandings of policies, rules, and procedures can lead to unnecessary discontent. It is the job of the manager to constantly work at improving communication skills.

Management failures may give rise to justified negative reactions of workers. Toleration by supervisors of wasted time, unjustified use of equipment, supervisory negligence in protecting the interests of the organization, and violations of employee "due process" rights all fall under the categorization of management failures. By adhering to basic tenets of leadership the supervisor can prevent much employee dissatisfaction.

TACTICS

Many departments rely on "in-house" procedures in an effort to respond to certain kinds of situations that require unique reactions due to the variations of people, places, and things with which they are confronted.

PART THREE

Preparing Yourself for the Civil Service Examination

TECHNIQUES FOR ANSWERING CIVIL SERVICE QUESTIONS

There is no substitute for knowledge when it comes to answering a civil service question (or any question). But it is unreasonable to expect that you will know, with certainty, the answer to every question appearing on your examination. The proper application of test-taking technique can help you over some tough hurdles when you are not sure of the answer.

You must understand that the examiner, in asking the usual multiple-choice question, must present you with three correct statements and one incorrect statement, or three incorrect statements and one correct statement. In either event, the examiner must present you with one statement that he or she considers to be the correct answer. Furthermore, the person asking the question must use words and/or phrases in the suggested answers. The words used by the examiner are the key to a successful approach.

MULTIPLE-CHOICE QUESTIONS

A multiple-choice question consists of two parts: a stem, which asks a question or states a problem, and several alternatives, which are possible answers to the question or problem posed. Go through each of the following steps in arriving at the answer to a multiple-choice question:

1. Read the stem quickly.

2. Reread the stem at a slower pace. What is the examiner trying to tell you? What is the examiner asking of you?

3. Underline or circle key words in the stem. Circle the words that tell you what the examiner wants as a correct choice. The following list is a sampling of the kinds of words civil service examiners use to tell you what they want as the answer to the question. Some of them are tricky; for example, "least inaccurate" means the same as "most accurate."

least accurate	most advisable
most valuable	most correct
least inaccurate	least proper
highest	is not
approximately	bad
least correct	greatest value
false	most invalid
is	poorest
wrong	least inadvisable
most accurate	true
least valid	greatest error
best	right
lowest	good

4. Read the alternatives (choices) quickly.

5. Mentally eliminate any obviously incorrect alternatives.

6. Reread the remaining alternatives at a slower pace.

7. Underline or circle the key words in each alternative that are under consideration. In particular, look for the following key words:

Universal Words (Deadly)	**Safe or Hedging Words (Best)**
all	probably
every	partial
total	should
anything	commonly
entire	potentially
completely	usually
nobody	may
everywhere	average
each	almost
forever	some
any	may be
eliminate	seldom
lone	frequently
alone	generally
nothing	could
never	often
only	nearly
always	few
none	might
wholly	normally
whole	sometimes
sole	essentially
Note: The above words are usually contained in *incorrect* statements.	occasionally
	more or less
Strong Words (Dangerous)	*Note*: These words are usually contained in *correct* statements.
main	
major	
ignore	
chief	
eliminate	
rarely	
paramount	
regardless	
postpone	
avoid	
shall	
must	
primarily	
will	
too ____	
inevitable	
impossible	
absolutely	

8. Cross out the small letter preceding obviously wrong alternatives.

9. Choose your answer from the remaining alternatives.

10. Cross out the small letter preceding alternatives that you think are incorrect.

11. In the margin, print a large letter that represents the alternative you have selected for the answer. This practice, once it becomes a habit, should materially reduce errors in transcribing your answer to the answer sheet.

It may be hard for you to believe, but these key words can be your clue to the correct answers when you do not really know the material. In an effort to convince you that our technique works, let's answer a few questions without even seeing the questions.

Directions: Examine the following suggested answers. Select the *correct* answer without being able to read the question.

(A) The actions of a single officer at a scene of a police incident may reflect on the quality of service performed by the entire department.

(B) A police officer may be thought of as the cynosure of the public's eye.

(C) As the backbone of the service, under no circumstances should the patrol force be weakened by the creation of specialized units.

(D) A police officer can be termed as the ultimate in decentralization of a city's service.

SOLUTION:

1. In choice (A), the word "may" appears. (A *safe* word.)
2. In choice (B), the word "may" appears. (A *safe* word.)
3. In choice (C), the phrase "under no circumstances" appears. (A *deadly* or *universal* phrase that means "never.")
4. In choice (D), the word "can" appears. (A *safe* word.)
5. Choices (A), (B), and (D) contain *safe* words, while choice (C) contains a *deadly* word or phrase.
6. The correct answer is (C).

And now for the question: "Relative to the image and function of a patrol force, select the incorrect statement." (And you could have answered it even if you did not know the meaning of the word cynosure.)

Let's try another—just the answers:

(A) Gives direct orders only in extreme emergency situations

(B) Assigns work and instructs his subordinates on the basis of individual differences

(C) Eliminates favoritism by maintaining an impersonal relationship with his subordinates

(D) Explains clearly to his subordinates the reason for each order that he issues to them

(E) Allows subordinates full discretion in the performance of their duties

SOLUTION:

(A) "only"— *deadly*

(B)

(C) "eliminates"— *deadly*

(D) "each"— *deadly*

(E) "full discretion"— *deadly*

The correct answer is (B).

The question was: "Leadership is best exemplified by a supervising officer who:"

Experience with past police promotion examinations demonstrates that often you must make a choice between two alternatives. The following techniques will be valuable to you in the future:

OPPOSITE-CHOICE METHOD

In questions where two of the alternatives are diametrically opposite to each other and they both relate to the stem, one usually is the correct answer. Disregard the other choices.

BROADEST-CHOICE METHOD

If two alternatives seem correct (i.e., they relate to the stem) and the broader in scope of the two encompasses the idea contained in the more restricted, alternative—take the broader one as your answer.

MANDATORY-CHOICE METHOD (TRUE OR FALSE)

If the four alternatives offered begin with words such as "true," "false," "desirable," or "undesirable" followed by a supporting statement, answer the question in this manner:

1.   Do not read the supporting statements.

2.   Make up your mind as to whether the idea in the stem is true or false, desirable or undesirable, etc.

3.   Cross out the small letters preceding the alternatives that disagree with your determination. Do not read the supporting statements in the discarded alternatives.

4.   Read the supporting statements in the remaining alternatives. Look for and underline key words, ect.

5.   Cross out the small letter preceding the alternative that you are discarding.

6.   Print your answer in the margin.

GROUPED-ALTERNATIVES METHOD

In some questions, three of the four alternatives will be found to fit into a general category. Normally, the remaining alternative is the correct answer.

ELIMINATION METHOD

Many times you will find questions in which you are able to eliminate all but one of the alternatives. However, you are unhappy with the remaining alternative. Nothing in the world is perfect; why should examination questions be the exception? Take the remaining alternative as your answer and hope for the best. Above all, do not fight the question or look for hidden meanings.

GENERAL CONSIDERATIONS

■   A correct choice may be extremely simple (to you). Do not shy away from the obvious.

■   A correct choice may be only partly complete, but it is never partly wrong.

■   Sometimes quotation marks are placed around an incorrect statement. Do not rely on the quotation marks. Each statement must stand on its own merits.

■   Choices that restate the stem in different words usually are not the choices that the examiner is looking for except in reading comprehension questions.

■ Incorrect statements may sound good, or be *gobbledygook*. If you do not clearly understand the meaning of a choice, beware, it may not have a meaning.

■ If you are asked for a specific number and you must guess, avoid the highest and lowest choices.

For example, what is the maximum age of a sergeant?

    (A) 61
    (B) 62
    (C) 63
    (D) 64

If you must guess, choose choice (B) or (C).

Never choose choices that do any of the following:

a.   Allege stupidity or ineptness on the part of any group.

b.   Allege unworthy or criminal characteristics in police officers.

c.   Suggest that public opinion should be the sole determinant of an action to be taken. The public is often wrong. An action should stand on its own merits.

TECHNIQUES FOR ANSWERING SPECIFIC TYPES OF QUESTIONS

READING INTERPRETATION

1. Read the entire passage and all question stems quickly. (Do not read alternatives.)

2. Reread passage—this time more slowly. Mark off with brackets different ideas or thoughts in the passage. Underline key words. By now you should have the flavor of the passage along with the main idea or ideas.

3. Read the first question and the alternatives given:

   a. Identify the thought involved. Normally, only one thought is involved in each question.
   b. Go to the bracketed section in the passage that relates to the thought.
   c. Reread the bracketed material.
   d. Reread the alternatives offered.
   e. Eliminate the obviously wrong alternatives. Remember the tips on universal words, etc.
   f. Select your choice of the remaining alternatives.
   g. Go back to the bracketed material and make sure your answer agrees with it.

4. Read and answer the second question in the same manner.

5. Complete the rest of the questions in the same manner.

JUDGMENT QUESTIONS

These questions attempt to measure your ability to solve problems through the exercise of common sense. This type of question is losing popularity with the examiners since judgment questions can be easily attacked, or if made protest-proof, they are ridiculously easy and therefore of no value to the examiners. But you may still find judgment questions on your exam. Other than utilizing the regular techniques for answering multiple-choice questions, there is no specific method for answering the judgment type of question other than the use of common sense.

PARAGRAPH REARRANGEMENT

These questions require you to read several sentences and then arrange them in a logical sequence to form a comprehensive paragraph. They are designed to test your logical thinking processes. Let's look at a simple four-sentence paragraph, isolate the sentences, and present them as a paragraph rearrangement question. In effect, we will assume the role of an examiner.

Then we will suggest a practical approach in answering this kind of question.

TYPICAL QUESTION

Arrange the following sentences in proper paragraph order:

1. Therefore, it is incumbent upon arresting officers to take necessary precautions when dealing with young law violators.

2. Delinquent acts, particularly by those under 16 years old, are a cause of concern to everyone involved in the criminal justice system.

3. On many occasions they have inflicted serious physical injuries to arresting officers.

4. Some young delinquents are capable of causing serious harm to those with whom they come in contact.

    (A)   2—3—4—1
    (B)   3—4—2—1
    (C)   2—4—3—1
    (D)   2—3—1—4

THE TECHNIQUE

1. Before reading the sentences, look at the suggested answers. Looking at the suggested answers listed above. It is obvious that either sentence 2 or 3 must be the opening sentence. It is obvious that sentence 2 and not 3 is the better opener.

Note: If sentence 2 was obviously not acceptable as an opening sentence, and sentence 3 was acceptable, only choice (B) could be the answer.

2. Look for an obvious sequence that exists between two sentences. For example, would the proper sequence for sentences 3 and 4 be 3—4 or 4—3— In sentence 4 there is a reference to "some young delinquents," and in sentence 3 there is a reference to "they." Obviously, the word "they" refers back to "some young delinquents." The conclusion is obvious; the proper sequence is 4—3.

3. Look for a sentence that is probably a closing-sentence. Words such as "however," "but," and "therefore" are likely to begin a sentence that concludes a paragraph. Three of the suggested answers above indicate that sentence 1 is the concluding sentence.

Therefore, we conclude that the opening sentence is sentence 2, the appropriate sequence is 4—3, and the concluding sentence is 1. The correct answer is (C): 2—4—3—1.

PARAGRAPH

Delinquent acts, particularly when committed by individuals less than 16 years of age, are a cause of concern to everyone involved in the criminal justice system. Some young delinquents are capable of causing serious harm to those with whom they came in contact. On many occasions they have inflicted serious physical injuries to arresting officers: Therefore, it is incumbent upon arresting officers to take necessary precautions when dealing with young law violators.

SENTENCE COHERENCE

This kind of question gives the candidate several ideas and requires the candidate to select a sentence which embodies all of the ideas and which is also grammatically correct. It is meant to be a predictive measure of the candidate's report writing skills.

1. Read all the ideas quickly.

2. Reread all the ideas at a slower pace.

3. Count the number of ideas given.

4. Read the proposed answer choices quickly.

5. Eliminate any (usually two) answer choices that do not state all of the ideas.

6. Reread the remaining answer choices at a slower pace.

7. Eliminate the choice with a grammatical error.

8. Select the remaining answer choice.

9. Check the answer choice again to be certain that it contains all of the ideas and does not have any obvious errors in grammar.

SOME TIPS ABOUT ORAL EXAMINATIONS

Oral examinations used by civil service examiners fall info the following four broad categories: The Interactive Oral, The Oral Assessment Board, The Job Knowledge Interview, and The Speech to a Group.

1. *The Interactive Oral* takes the form of a role-playing situation. The candidate for promotion "assumes" the rank being sought, receives a set of instructions and directives from the "commanding officer," and is required to transmit them to a "subordinate." The other role players will not make the task easy for you. You may be required to train or coach a subordinate, monitor his or her performance, and resolve conflicts (job-related or personal). Your objective is to be certain that all of your commanding officer's orders are given and understood. The scoring system can be very involved and sophisticated. The examiners will be checking that you get feedback, cover the required points, and arrange for a follow-up of the subordinate's performance.

2. *The Oral Assessment Board* is a three- to five-person panel. You may be required to justify your tenure in your current position and to justify your rights to the promotion you seek. Although technical expertise will not play a large part before the oral assessment board, you may find it useful to fall back on technical knowledge to get you out of a tight spot.

The panel will be looking for and evaluating the following:

■ Command presence

■ Communication skills

■ Attitudes

■ Ability to think and react under stress

■ Experience

■ Job knowledge

In this situation, you must be careful not to become emotionally involved. Although you usually cannot answer "yes" or "no," try to limit your responses to the questions posed by the panel members. If you cannot answer a question, do not be afraid to admit it. Do not ramble just to have something to say. And remember, there is no one right answer to these questions.

3. *The Job Knowledge Interview* is nothing more than an unwritten technical essay. In the job knowledge interview, the candidate appears before a panel and is asked to handle various problems such as the following:

■ Serious public disorder

■ Intoxicated police officer

■ Firearms discharge

■ Another job-related problem

In recent police captain's and chief's examinations on which this question style has appeared, scoring was based entirely upon accurate responses to the problems presented. A perfect score could be achieved by simply reciting all required steps as they appear in rules and regulations, law, etc. Sometimes a mathematics or graph problem dealing with the assignment of personnel is included. If so, the candidate is given time to study the chart and then must respond orally to the problem presented.

4.   *The Speech to a Group* is just what it sounds like. The candidate is given a topic and sufficient time to outline and prepare the presentation. If you must give a speech to a group, keep in mind the following important points:

■ What is the purpose of the address?

■ Who is the audience? Is it friendly or hostile? Will the press be present? Will the audience be "stacked" with hecklers?

■ How long must you speak?

■ Will there be a question and answer session?

■ Did you stick to the announced script?

Your subject matter and your presentation must be well organized. A good rule to adhere to is the following:

1.   Tell them what you are going to tell them.

2.   Tell them.

3.   Tell them what you told them.

Your oral examination may also include a written report. This sounds like a contradiction in terms, but it may happen. The oral examiners may assign you to write a report based on information that they supply. If you are required to prepare a written report, we suggest that you prepare a rough draft by way of an outline, then write a legible copy. The process of writing a spontaneous police report is similar to the process of writing any other report. If you do not know the code word NEOTWY for gathering facts and preparing a report, then you should learn it today.

WHEN   N

WHERE   E

WHO   O

WHAT   T

HOW   W

WHY   Y

The last letter of each word makes up the code word. If you stick to NEOTWY, it is almost impossible not to prepare a complete and accurate report.

READING INTERPRETATION

There is a growing trend toward the use of reading interpretation in civil service promotion examinations. Currently, they are the eliminators that frequently make the difference between success and failure.

The two basic elements in reading interpretation are speed and comprehension. Contradictory as it may sound, the more slowly a person reads, the less he absorbs. The more rapidly he reads, the more he understands and retains. This is probably because heavier concentration is required for rapid reading, and concentration enables a reader to grasp important ideas contained in the reading material. Remember that speed and comprehension work together.

One of the techniques that will help you is scanning, which enables you to pull out facts or main ideas. You do this by moving your eyes rapidly across the lines of type. Do not permit your eyes to stop for individual words. Continue reading the paragraph without backtracking in order to maintain the continuity of the ideas of the author. However, if you think you have missed the point of the paragraph, reread it two or three times, but always read quickly. In the end, you will be amazed haw much you do understand.

You cannot "cram" for reading interpretation questions. The only way you can develop this skill is by practice and more practice. The key to the answer will always be found in the paragraph.

In some recent promotion examinations, the examiners began using a new style of reading interpretation question. They gave the competitors a record of facts upon which a report was to be prepared. The questions that followed the record of facts were very closely drawn and difficult to handle. An example would be as follows:

Fact: "Mr. Jones told me that a person who sounded like a young boy telephoned his store and said that a bomb would go off in one hour."

Based on the above, the most clear and accurate presentation would be:

(A) "Mr. Jones, said that a young boy telephoned his store and said that a bomb would go off in one hour." Not the correct answer. The person *sounded* like a young boy.

(B) "A person who sounded like a young boy telephoned Mr. Jones' store and said that a bomb would go off in one hour." Not the correct answer. Mr. Jones *said* this occurred. Maybe it did, but maybe it did not.

(C) "One hour before a bomb was scheduled to go off, a person who sounded like a young boy telephoned his store Mr. Jones said." Not the correct answer. Obviously wrong; note the misplaced modifier. Does *his store* refer to the person who sounded like a young boy, or to Mr. Jones?

(D) "According to Mr. Jones, a person who sounded like a young boy telephoned his store and said that a bomb would go off in one hour." Not the correct answer. The second comma results in a lack of clarity. If you remove the second comma, then this would be correct.

Directions: Consider the following two sentences and determine if they relay the same information:

1. "One half hour before the bomb exploded, Mr. Jones said he felt ill."

2. "One half hour before the bomb exploded, Mr. Jones said, he felt ill." Does the comma placement change the meaning of the sentence? Yes, it does!

These are the kinds of problems the examiners concentrate on in the fact report questions.

SAMPLE:

You took the following notes while you were conducting an undercover surveillance. You will be required to prepare a report based on the notes:

1. Frank left school at about 1 P.M.

2. Frank met Roger at the local health club.

3. Roger threatened Frank with a lawsuit.

4. Frank left the health club hurriedly.

5. Frank went to George's house.

Directions: Select the one choice that is the most clear and accurate presentation of the information contained in the notes. Grammar and style are important only if they affect clarity and accuracy.

(A) Frank met Roger in the local health club, and he left the health club hurriedly after Roger threatened him with a lawsuit.
(B) Frank met Roger in the local health club, and he left the health club hurriedly after he threatened him.
(C) Frank met Roger in the local health club, he threatened him with a lawsuit, and then he left the health club hurriedly.
(D) Roger threatened Frank with a lawsuit when he met him in the local health club; then he left the health club hurriedly.

The correct answer is (A).
  In choice (B), who threatened whom? Who left the club?
  In choice (C), who threatened whom?
  In choice (D), who left in a hurry?

PRACTICE QUESTIONS

Directions: Base your answers to questions 1 through 7 on the following instructions and information.

Assume that you and Police Officer Tracy have conducted a robbery investigation. You are going to be required to write a report based on your notes. Following your notes there are seven questions. Each of these questions concerns how best to express one or more of the facts presented in the notes. You may refer to the notes at any time.

NOTES:

1. At 7 A.M., P.O. Tracy received a call from Frank Marx. Marx said he is a janitor at the Roth Bar. Marx reported that a robbery had taken place at the bar. P.O. Tracy and I went to the bar to investigate.

2. Found Mr. Roth in his storeroom sitting on a barrel looking dazed. His legs were bruised and bleeding slightly. Wallet lying open next to him on the barrel. The storeroom in great disorder.

Marx relayed the following information:

3. He had come to work at 5 A.M. Worked in bar cleaning the floor and came to storeroom a little before 7 A.M. for supplies.

4. He found Mr. Roth bound and gagged. Feet tied together with a telephone cord. Hands tied together at his ankles with another telephone cord, with telephone still attached.

Mr. Roth told us:

5. Bar door had opened shortly before 2 A.M. Saw three young men enter bar. Recognized one of them as Danny Maloney. He said he had worked for him at one time as a bartender.

6. One of the other two men asked to use the phone. He let them do so. They pushed him and bound and gagged him. Said they needed money. Proceeded to ransack bar. About $70 missing from the register. Two trophies that had been on a rack near the front door also missing. Did not know if anything else taken.

7. P.O. Tracy and I looked around outside with Marx. We found the two trophies. Marx noticed then that the 1982 delivery truck was missing. Said it was usually parked outside the bar and usually had the keys in it. Said Maloney would have known this.

8. Mr. Roth did not want to be taken to a hospital. Said he would, get Marx to drive him to his doctor later in the morning.

Directions: In questions 1 through 7, select the one choice that most clearly and accurately presents the information given in the notes. Circle the letter of your choice.

---

1. (A) At 7 A.M., P.O. Tracy took a call reporting a robbery at the Roth Bar by Frank Marx, who said he is a janitor at the bar.

   (B) Frank Marx, who said he is a janitor at the Roth-Bar, called at 7 A.M. to report a robbery. P.O. Tracy took the call.

   (C) At 7 A.M., P.O. Tracy took a call from Frank Marx, who identified himself as a janitor at the Roth Bar and reported that a robbery had taken place at the bar.

   (D) At 7 A.M., Frank Marx, who said he is a janitor, called to report that a robbery had taken place at the Roth Bar. P.O. Tracy took the call.

2. (A) We found Mr. Roth in the storeroom, which was in great disorder. He looked dazed, and his legs were bruised and bleeding slightly. His open wallet was next to him.

   (B) We found Mr. Roth, sitting on a barrel dazed and bleeding slightly. His legs were bruised, and his open wallet was next to him on the barrel. The storeroom was in great disorder.

   (C) We found Mr. Roth sitting on a barrel in the storeroom, in great disorder. His wallet was next to him on the barrel. He looked dazed, and his legs were bruised and bleeding slightly.

   (D) We found Mr. Roth sitting on a barrel in the storeroom, which was in great disorder. He looked dazed and his legs were bruised and bleeding slightly. His wallet was next to him on the barrel.

3. (A) Marx informed us that he had found Mr. Roth, bound and gagged, when he came to the storeroom for supplies shortly before 7 A.M. after working in the bar cleaning the floor.

   (B) Marx informed us that Mr. Roth had been found bound and gagged shortly before 7 A.M. He said that he had come to the storeroom for supplies at that time after working in the bar cleaning the floor.

   (C) Marx informed us he had found Mr. Roth bound and gagged after working in the bar cleaning the floor. He found him when he came to the storeroom for supplies shortly before 7 A.M.

   (D) After he had worked in the bar clearing the floor Marx told us that he had found Mr. Roth bound and gagged in the storeroom, when he came for supplies shortly before 7 A.M.

4. (A) Marx said that a telephone cord and a telephone cord with the phone still attached, had been used to tie Mr. Roth's hands and feet.

   (B) Marx said that Mr. Roth's hands and feet were bound together behind his back and at his ankles with a telephone cord and a telephone cord, which still had the phone attached.

   (C) Marx said that Mr. Roth's feet were tied together with a telephone cord and his hands bound together at his ankles with a telephone cord. The phone was still attached to this cord.

   (D) Marx said that the robbers had tied Mr. Roth's hands together with a telephone cord. His feet had been tied together at his ankles with a telephone cord which still had the phone attached.

5. (A) Mr. Roth said that when the bar door opened shortly before 2 A.M. he saw three young men enter the bar. He said that he had recognized one of them Danny Maloney, who had worked for him at one time as a bartender.

   (B) Mr. Roth said that three young men had entered the bar shortly before 2 A.M. He recognized Danny Maloney, who had worked for him at one time as a bartender.

   (C) Mr. Roth said that when the bar door opened shortly before 2 A.M. There were three people who entered the bar; two other young men and Danny Maloney, who had worked for him at one time.

   (D) Mr. Roth said that when the bar door opened shortly before 2 A.M. he saw three young men enter the bar. He said he recognized one of them, Danny Maloney, who worked for him as a bartender.

6. (A) Mr. Roth said the missing items from the bar included about $70 from the register, and two trophies from a rack near the front door.

   (B) Mr. Roth said about $70 was missing from the register and two trophies were missing from a rack near the front door.

(C)   Mr. Roth said the men had found about $70 in the register and two trophies on a rack near the front door.

(D)   Mr. Roth, said about $70 in the register and also two trophies that had been on a rack near the front door were missing.

7.   (A)   When Marx, P.O. Tracy, and I looked around outside we found the two trophies, and Marx noticed that the 1982 delivery truck was missing. Marx told us it was usually parked outside the bar and the keys were usually left in it. He said Maloney would have known this.

(B)   When P.O. Tracy and I looked around outside with Marx, we found the two trophies and he noticed that the 1982 delivery truck was missing. He told us Maloney would have known that the truck was usually parked outside the bar and that the keys were usually left in it.

(C)   When P.O. Tracy and I looked around outside, we found the two trophies with Marx. He also noticed that the 1982 delivery truck was missing. Marx told us that it was usually parked outside the bar and usually had the keys left in it, and that Maloney would have known this.

(D)   When Marx, P.O. Tracy and I looked around outside, we found the two trophies. Marx said the missing 1982 delivery truck was usually parked outside the bar and usually had the keys left in it, and Maloney would have known this.

The following report, submitted by an officer at the scene, concerns a street demonstration.

On August 16th, a group of women, each holding a young child by the hand, were involved in a street demonstration in front of the ABC factory. They began by blocking a train and preventing it from leaving the factory. The factory owners are very concerned that the hot weather may damage or spoil the contents of the train.

The C.O. of the police detail on the scene calls for additional assistance of five female police officers, a nurse, a bus, and a police photographer equipped with a motion picture camera. The C.O. is aware of the fact that several press members are present at the scene, some of whom have camera equipment.

When the call for additional assistance arrives, the C.O. directs the women to disperse. He justifies this order on the grounds that the hot weather and intense sun is not right for the children. The women ignore the order to disperse and the C.O. orders them to be removed.

Another group of demonstrators who had been standing to the side of the train demonstrate their dissatisfaction with the police action by charging the police. Several police are injured during this melee.

Eventually order is restored. That evening, the press coverage presented a neutral and fairly accurate account of the incident.

Directions: Questions 8 through 10 are to be answered on the basis of the above report. Clarity and accuracy are important considerations in your answer. Grammar, punctuation, and sentence structure are only important if poor grammar, improper punctuation, or poor sentence structure affect clarity and accuracy. In each of the following questions, choose as your answer the choice that most clearly and accurately reflects the contents of the report.

---

8.   (A)   A group of women, some of whom were holding young children were involved in a street demonstration in front of the ABC factory.

(B)   A group of women who were holding a young child by the hand, were involved in a street demonstration in front of the ABC factory.

(C)   A group of women, each holding a small child by the hand, was involved in a street demonstration in front of the ABC factory.

(D)   A group of women, each holding a young child by the hand, was involved in a street demonstration in front of the ABC factory.

9. (A) The C.O. of the police detail, aware of the fact that the press was present called for additional assistance.

    (B) When the C.O. of the police detail called for additional assistance of the five female police officers, some of the press members were in possession of camera equipment.

    (C) Several press members with camera equipment were on the scene when the C.O. of the police detail called for additional assistance.

    (D) The C.O. of the police detail was aware of the fact that some members of the press present at the scene had camera equipment.

10. (A) Because the demonstrators were dissatisfied with the police activity at the scene, several police officers were injured during a struggle that followed a charge against the police.

    (B) Several demonstrators in charging the police caused some police officers to suffer injuries.

    (C) The press coverage of the incident that occurred that evening presented an accurate and fairly neutral account.

    (D) A neutral and fairly accurate account of the incident appeared in the press that evening.

Directions: Questions 11 through 15 will be based on the information given below.

Assume that you and your partner, Police Officer Roger, have investigated the report of a terrorist threat to derail a passenger train on the Amtrak line passing through your command. Assume further that you will have to prepare a report based on the notes below.

NOTES:

1. Station Master, Breckenridge Hockenfelder, received a threat by telephone.

2. I searched the train station and tracks with Roger and Hockenfelder; found no bomb.

3. Hockenfelder said the caller sounded like a Russian immigrant.

4. He reported that the caller said, "A bomb will go off in a half hour on the tracks just outside the station platform and then hung up.

5. Hockenfelder said that a man entered the station about a half hour before the call; he studied several booklets of train schedules.

6. He said that he asked the man where he wanted to go and the man replied, "I want free passage to New York City."

7. Mr. Hockenfelder said that he replied, "There are no free passages. If you want a ticket you must pay. If you won't pay, please leave the station."

8. A bystander heard the commotion, saw the man leave, and recognized him as a chauffeur for a foreign ambassador who lives at 767 Brook Street.

9. We went to the address and spoke with a man who said his name was Fyodor Szathmary, and that he was a chauffeur for the Hungarian Embassy.

10. Mr. Szathmary said he had been home all day and had not been at the train station.

Directions: In each of the following questions, select the choice that most clearly and accurately restates the relevant information from the notes. Grammar and style are important only if they affect clarity and accuracy.

11. (A) Roger, Hockenfelder, and I searched the train station and tracks, but there was no bomb.

    (B) By searching the station and tracks, Roger, Hockenfelder, and I found there was no bomb.

    (C) Roger, Hockenfelder, and I searched the station and the tracks and found no bomb.

    (D) After a search of the station and tracks, Roger, Hockenfelder, and I found no bomb.

12. (A) Hockenfelder reported that the caller, a Russian immigrant, said, "A bomb will go off in 1/2 hour on the tracks just outside the station platform."

    (B) According to Hockenfelder, the caller sounded like a Russian immigrant and said, "A bomb will go off in 1/2 hour on the tracks just outside the station platform."

    (C) Hockenfelder reported that a Russian immigrant caller had said, "A bomb will go off in 1/2 hour on the tracks just outside the station platform."

    (D) A person who sounded like a Russian immigrant called and said, "A bomb will go off in 1/2 hour on the tracks just outside the station platform."

13. (A) According to Hockenfelder, he asked the man to leave the station after telling him that if the man would not pay he would have to leave.

    (B) According to Hockenfelder, the man did not have the money to buy a ticket so he asked him to leave the station.

    (C) Hockenfelder said that the man refused to buy a ticket when he told him he would have to leave the station.

    (D) Hockenfelder said that the man was asked to leave the station because he could not buy a ticket.

14. (A) One-half hour before the call, Hockenfelder said, a man entered the station; he said that the man studied several booklets of train schedules.

    (B) One-half hour before the call, Hockenfelder said that a man entered the station and studied several booklets of train schedules.

    (C) One-half hour before police arrived, Hockenfelder said, he received a telephone threat about a bomb.

    (D) Hockenfelder stated that one-half hour before he received a telephone bomb threat, a Russian immigrant was at the station studying train schedules.

15. (A) The chauffeur for the Hungarian Embassy said he had been home all day.

    (B) The chauffeur who lived at 767 Brook Street worked for the Hungarian Embassy and was at home all day.

    (C) Mr. Szathmary, who said he was a chauffeur for the Hungarian Embassy was at home all day and had not been at the train station.

    (D) A man who identified himself as Fyodor Szathmary and a chauffeur for the Hungarian Embassy said that he had been home all day and had not been at the station.

ANSWER KEY

1.	C	6.	B	11.	C
2.	D	7.	A	12.	B
3.	A	8.	D	13.	A
4.	C	9.	D	14.	A
5.	A	10.	D	15.	D

SENTENCE COHERENCE

The examiners may include as many as ten sentence coherence questions. They involve several statements of fact presented in a very simple way. These statements of fact are followed by four or five choices that attempt to incorporate all of the facts into one logical, properly constructed, and grammatically correct sentence. These questions can hurt you if you are not careful. You must have a basic understanding of sentence structure and grammar in order to handle them properly.

I. 1. Mr. Smith was sweeping the sidewalk in front of his house.
    2. He was sweeping it because it was dirty.
    3. He swept the refuse into the street.
    4. P.O. Jones gave him a ticket.

Which one of the following best presents the information given above?

(A) Because his sidewalk was dirty, Mr. Smith received a ticket from P.O. Jones when he swept the refuse into the street.
(B) P.O. Jones gave Mr. Smith a ticket because his sidewalk was dirty and he swept the refuse into the street.
(C) P.O. Jones gave Mr. Smith a ticket for sweeping refuse into the street because his sidewalk was dirty.
(D) Mr. Smith, who was sweeping refuse from his dirty sidewalk into the street, was given a ticket by P.O. Jones.

II. 1. An arrest was made by P.O. Nunno.
    2. Evidence was seized after a search following the arrest.
    3. The judge ruled that the evidence must be suppressed.
    4. His reason was that probable cause for the arrest did not exist.

The choice that *most* clearly and accurately describes the above statements is which of the following:

(A) Because the judge ruled that the evidence must be suppressed, the arrest made by P.O. Nunno was found to be without probable cause.
(B) Probable cause is necessary before evidence seized during an arrest will withstand a constitutional attack.
(C) Because the arrest made by P.O. Nunno was not based on probable cause, the evidence seized during a search after the arrest was suppressed.
(D) Because P.O. Nunno made a search that was not supported by probable cause, the judge ruled that the evidence must be suppressed.

III.
1. Roger was clearing his driveway after a heavy snowstorm.
2. He was clearing it in order to get to work on time.
3. He suffered a heart attack and died before he finished the job.

Which one of the following best presents the information given above?

(A) Because he was in a hurry to get to work, Roger suffered a fatal heart attack while clearing his driveway after a heavy snowstorm.

(B) Because of a heavy snowstorm, Roger suffered a fatal heart attack in order to get to work after it.

(C) Roger, while clearing his driveway in order to get to work after a heavy snowstorm, suffered a fatal heart attack before finishing the job.

(D) Because he was shoveling his driveway after a heavy snowstorm, Roger suffered a fatal heart attack before he finished and could not get to work.

IV.
1. An auxiliary police officer named Tondelayo was patrolling her post.
2. She surprised a woman trying to break into a liquor store.
3. The woman tried to hit Tondelayo with a pinch bar.

Which of the following best presents the information given above?

(A) While Auxiliary P.O. Tondelayo was patrolling her post, she surprised a woman trying to break into a closed liquor store. The woman tried to hit her with a pinch bar.

(B) While she was patrolling her post, Auxiliary P.O. Tondelayo surprised a woman trying to break into a closed liquor store and she tried to hit her with a pinch bar.

(C) The woman trying to break into a closed liquor store was surprised by Auxiliary P.O. Tondelayo who was patrolling her post and tried to hit her with a pinch bar.

(D) The woman tried to hit Auxiliary P.O. Tondelayo, who was patrolling her area, and surprised her while she was trying to break into a closed liquor store.

V.
1. The assigned detective returned from investigating the crime.
2. When he returned he gave some details to his supervisor.
3. The supervisor included these details in a written report.

Which of the following best presents the information given above?

(A) When he returned from investigating the crime, the detective gave some details to his supervisor, and he included this information in a written report..

(B) Upon returning from investigating the crime, the supervisor included the details the detective gave him in a written report.

(C) Upon his return from investigating the crime, the detective gave some details to his supervisor and then included them in a written report.

(D) When he returned from investigating the crime the detective gave some details to his supervisor, who then included the details in a written report.

VI.
1. In order to properly prepare a budget, facts are needed.
2. These facts must be current and accurate.
3. Without such facts, no budget can be prepared.

Which of the following best presents the above information?

(A) Without facts that are up-to-date and accurate, a budget cannot be prepared.

(B) Because facts are needed to prepare a budget, they must be current and accurate.

(C) Without facts, which are needed to properly prepare a budget, no budget can be prepared.

(D) Facts are the *sine qua non* of budget preparation.

ANSWER KEY

I.	D	IV.	A
II.	C	V.	D
III.	C	VI.	A

PARAGRAPH REARRANGEMENT TECHNIQUE

On some recent police promotion examinations, competitors have been required to successfully answer from five to ten questions on paragraph rearrangement. These can cause a serious problem for the poor reader. We have researched the problem, and have come up with a pragmatic approach that should materially assist all competitors to score higher on this type of question.

The paragraphs that you will see on police examinations will contain four or five sentences that may or may not be jumbled. Your responsibility will be to arrange them in the proper order.

Most paragraphs will contain one central thought or topic. For the most part, this main thought will be expressed in the opening sentence. However, there is no rule that requires this kind of construction. The topic sentence may do one of two things: It may announce the subject to be discussed, which lets you know immediately what the paragraph is about. Or it may state the writer's attitude toward a subject; what he or she thinks about it.

From this point (the topic sentence), the remaining sentences should appear in a clear and logical order. This does not present a difficult problem when a paragraph describes how to do something. The order in this case is usually chronological. However, when the objective of the paragraph is to give information or to persuade someone, the logical order becomes more difficult to perceive.

HINTS

- All sentences pertaining to the same idea should usually be kept together.

- Ideas that are necessary for a full understanding of the paragraph should appear early in the paragraph.

- Connecting language should be looked for so that you can determine which sentence or sentences logically flow from another.

- Final sentences may summarize or conclude. They may be introduced by language such as "Consequently," "In conclusion," and "Therefore."

- If one sentence uses a noun as the subject, and another sentences uses a pronoun for the same subject, the noun subject will usually precede the pronoun. For example, "John drove the car. He drove it fast."

- Transitional expressions may be used to move smoothly from one idea to another. Some of these expressions are as follows:

  he—his—they—this—that—these—those—them—it.

These words refer to a person or an idea just mentioned. Therefore, you will have to link these sentences with a prior sentence in the paragraph. They will not ordinarily be contained in the opening sentence.

■ There are certain words or expressions that connect ideas in the paragraph. Some of them are as follows:

accordingly	in fact
again	in short
also	likewise
although	moreover
as a result	nevertheless
at last	next
at the same time	on the contrary
besides	on the other hand
consequently	otherwise
equally important	second
finally	similarly
first	since
for example	then
furthermore	therefore
hence	thus
however	too (also)
in addition	whereas
in conclusion	

When these expressions are used they will indicate that one sentence is connected to a sentence that precedes it. They usually will not be used in the opening sentence.

Now try to rearrange the following sentences into coherent paragraphs. Note the key words in the first example and make a conscious effort to tie the thoughts together logically. A practical technique is to look at the answers first and consider only the given openers as possibilities.

I. 1. A wave has height from trough to crest.
     2. It has length; the distance from its crest to that of the following wave.
     3. Before constructing an imaginary life history of a typical wave, we need to become familiar with some of its physical characteristics.
     4. The period of the wave refers to the time required for succeeding crests to pass a fixed point.
     (A) 1—2—3—4
     (B) 3—2—1—4
     (C) 3—1—2—4
     (D) 3—4—1—2

SOLUTION

The idea of the paragraph is to describe some physical characteristic of a wave. This thought is contained in sentence 3. We choose this, then, as our first sentence and thus eliminate choice (A) from consideration.

Sentences 1 and 2 give us true physical characteristics, height and length. But which comes first? In sentence 1 the noun "wave" is used, while in 2 the pronoun it is used. Therefore, sentence 1 must precede 2. The only choices that start with 3 and have 1 preceding 2 are choices (C) and (D). When we look back at the paragraph, we see that sentence 4 does not truly give us a physical characteristic of a wave, but gives us a time period. The answer is choice (C): 3—1—2—4.

II.
1. If your favorite uncle is a police officer, maybe you will make a good police officer too, but not necessarily.
2. Sometimes young people make the mistake of picking a job just because a much-admired relative or friend likes that job.
3. It is risky to choose an occupation just because you admire or are fond of someone who has chosen it.
4. You may admire Joe Namath, F. Lee Bailey, or a good homicide detective. But this does not mean that you can count an being successful or happy as a professional ball player, criminal lawyer, or famous detective.

(A) 1—2—3—4—5
(B) 3—5—1—2—4
(C) 2—1—3—4—5
(D) 2—4—5—1—3

SOLUTION

As you look at this paragraph, it becomes apparent that the opening sentence is not easy to choose. Obviously it is a choice between sentence 2 or 3. In cases such as this, choose the sentence that seems to be broader—in this case, sentence 2. We can now disregard choices (A) and (B), but not with absolute certainty. When you have a difficult time choosing the first sentence, try to locate the concluding sentence. Logic tells us that 5 should be last. We need go no further. The only choice with sentence 5 last and either 2 or 3 first is (C). That is the correct answer: 2—1—3—4—5.

III.
1. The objective of the program was to relieve the tensions caused by hard studying and to meet the need of many students to learn to use their bodies effectively in trained ways.
2. Each location played one sport for a week, by turns, for four weeks.
3. In the afternoons during the school year, all students of P.T.S. were required to participate in an athletic program.
4. The sports were tennis, baseball, track, and soccer.
5. Each location had one week of coaching by competent coaches.

(A) 1—2—3—4—5
(B) 3—1—2—4—5
(C) 3—2—1—4—5
(D) 3—1—4—2—5

SOLUTION

In this grouping there is no problem choosing sentence 3 as your first sentence. Unfortunately, we can only eliminate choice (A). Using common sense, sentence 3 must be followed by 1; 3 talks of an athletic program and 1 gives us the program's objectives.

The choice is narrowed to either (B) or (D). Again, using common sense, sentence 2 should precede 4. The answer then is choice (B): 3—1—2—4—5.

IV.
1. They are words from special fields with which he has no contact.
2. Although the largest English dictionaries contain over a million words, the average adult is said to have a use and recognition vocabulary of only between thirty and sixty thousand words.
3. This means that nine out of ten words recognized by the present-day official language are as strange to him as they would be if they were part of a foreign tongue.
4. Fortunately, he hardly ever misses them.
5. A highly literate adult is not likely to go much beyond one-hundred thousand.

(A) 2—3—1—5—4
(B) 2—1—5—3—4
(C) 2—5—3—1—4
(D) 2—5—4—3—1

SOLUTION

You should not have a problem selecting sentence 2 as the opening sentence. Sentence 2 speaks of the number of words in the average adult's vocabulary. Logically following this, as a comparison, should be the sentence that tells us how many words are in the above average (highly literate) adult's vocabulary —5. Thus, the sequence starts with 2—5. We can now eliminate choices (A) and (B). Choosing the next sentence is difficult, but logical. Since the dictionary is said to contain over a million words, and the highly literate adult understands one hundred thousand of these, there must be nine out of ten words that are unfamiliar even to the highly literate. Therefore, sentence 3 is next, and the sequence is 2—5—3 so far. We can stop there and pick our answer as choice (C).

But let us go further. Sentence 1 must follow 3, since it tells us what words the highly literate adult does not understand. Sentence 4 is a tongue-in-cheek concluding sentence. The correct answer is (C): 2—5—3—1—4.

V. 1. For one thing, despite the objections of the administration and most business leaders, we must move to a shorter workweek or, work year, combined, if desired, with multiple-shift operations.

2. If the national goal is to minimize technological displacement and unemployment without resorting to horse-and-buggy production methods, then a variety of possible policies would achieve optimum employment.

3. For another, young people should be required to stay in school longer.

4. This would keep more people employed and would prevent expensive equipment from standing idle.

5. This requirement, combined with an earlier retirement age, would cut persons off from both ends of the labor force thereby reducing the number of job seekers.

(A) 2—1—4—3—5

(B) 2—1—4—5—3

(C) 3—1—5—2—4

(D) 2—1—3—5—4

SOLUTION

Now we separate the guessers from the analysts. This is a tough one. There is no problem choosing 2 as the opening sentence. The connecting words and transitional words, as well as the choices force us to pick sentence 2 as the opener. Sentence 2 speaks of a variety of policies. Common sense and the choices given tell us that sentence 1 must follow 2.

Here the real test starts. Is it 2—1—3 or 2—1—4? You cannot really decide until you look at 5. What requirement does 5 relate to? Logic tells us that it must relate to 3, since keeping youngsters in school longer plus an earlier retirement age would cut persons off from both ends of the labor farce. The transitional word "this," used in 4, must relate to sentence 1. The answer is choice (A): 2—1—4—3—5.

Directions: Rearrange the following sentences in proper paragraph order.

I. 1. Obstacles to the coordination or consolidation of the police services of different jurisdictions are similar to the barriers faced in restructuring and relocating other functions of local government.

2. They tend to be among the most formidable for the police, principally because police service is generally among the most local of governmental services, and because even the smallest local governmental jurisdictions like to believe that they can provide at least minimal police service.

3. Often political and social pressures linked to the desire for local self-government, rather than legal restrictions, offer the most significant barriers to the coordination and consolidation of police service.

4. But it is important for all jurisdictions to be aware of any legal obstacles to coordination or consolidation that may exist.

(A) 4—2—3—1
(B) 1—3—4—2
(C) 1—2—3—4
(D) 1—4—3—2

II. 1. All of the councils have been active on an informal basis in promoting interjurisdictional agreements.

2. A council of governments, with a committee on law enforcement, can be an effective vehicle in metropolitan areas for promoting consolidation or cooperation in law enforcement activities.

3. It is a simple step to include law enforcement as part of a council's total program.

4. Four of the councils are now engaged in negotiating cooperative agreements among member units and three also mediate disputes.

(A) 3—2—1—4
(B) 2—4—1—3
(C) 1—2—4—3
(D) 4—3—1—2

III. 1. However, in their attempts to uncover basic feelings regarding these factors, the researchers found that direct questions designed to find out how the subjects felt about specific aspects of their jobs resulted in superficial, lifeless answers.

2. These studies were primarily concerned with the determinants of morale and productivity.

3. Management first became aware of the value of interviewing in industrial relations during the 1930s as a consequence of studies conducted at the Hawthorne plant of the Western Electric Company.

4. Also, instead of giving straightforward responses, some of the people interviewed tended to talk about what interested them most at the moment.

(A) 2—1—4—3
(B) 3—2—1—4
(C) 1—2—3—4
(D) 3—2—4—1

IV. 1. Provisions should be made for use of the system by federal and regional law enforcement agencies, but parallel or duplicatory systems should be avoided unless for specific backup purposes.

2. It is intended to complement, not to replace local and state systems.

3. The national system should be a coordinating mechanism that will further the exchange of information of mutual concern among smaller, independent, but coordinated, systems.

4. The concept of the National Crime Information Center (NCIC) is clear.

(A) 4—2—3—1
(B) 2—4—1—3
(C) 2—3—1—4
(D) 4—1—3—2

V.
1. If we had no sense of urgency about our work, we would probably feel no need to use all of our ability and energy to do it.
2. But pressure may become so intense that people are no longer able to cope with it.
3. Most of us need a certain amount of tension to motivate us to do our best work.
4. When this happens, they may make as much effort as before and find themselves accomplishing half as much.
5. Anxiety intrudes on their efforts to work and thought is disrupted.
   - (A) 3—1—2—5—4
   - (B) 3—2—1—5—4
   - (C) 3—2—4—5—1
   - (D) 3—2—5—0—1

VI.
1. It is scarcely different from enterprises selling shoes or grass seed.
2. Murder, robbery, rape, arson, and drug dealing are fairly commonplace in New York City.
3. Like any other business, it obeys the law of supply and demand, and most newspapers have discovered that a description of a crime attracts more customers than does a description of a French cabinet crisis.
4. Despite all its pretenses of representing the public, the average newspaper is simply a business enterprise that sells news.
5. The newspaper editor, as a result, can choose that brand of crime he or she thinks customers will most want to buy.
   - (A) 3—4—2—1—5
   - (B) 4—1—2—3—5
   - (C) 4—1—3—2—5
   - (D) 4—3—1—2—5

VII.
1. People in the television industry have long defended violence in television programming by saying that programs containing violence are intended only for adults.
2. And it seems that such programs, far from serving as safety valves, stimulate aggressive children and they seek overt means of acting out their aggressions.
3. But recent research has cast doubt on these arguments.
4. They have further maintained that if a child should happen to see a program containing violence, the violence would serve as a safety valve, offering a harmless outlet for his aggressions.
5. Several studies have reported that even children in the early elementary school years see more adults' programs than children's programs.
   - (A) 1—3—5—4—2
   - (B) 1—4—3—2—5
   - (C) 1—4—3—5—2
   - (D) 4—3—1—2—5

VIII.
1. People do not understand how difficult it is to be a police officer.
2. This statement is often expressed and deeply felt by many police officers.
3. Yet, for many reasons, such mutual understanding has been hard to achieve.
4. Presumably, better police-public cooperation and accommodation would result if police were better able to communicate with citizens.
   - (A) 1—2—3—4
   - (B) 1—4—3—2
   - (C) 1—2—4—3
   - (D) 4—1—2—3

IX. 1. A positive public image can help a department recruit and hold good personnel, maintain high morale, and gain public cooperation.

2. One of the most important positions within a department for achieving these positive results is the uniformed patrol officer.

3. His contacts with law-abiding citizens within the community may be the only contacts those citizens have with a member of the criminal justice system.

4. It is necessary, therefore, for him to make a conscious effort to positively influence all those persons with whom he comes in contact during his routine daily activities.

(A) 1—2—3—4
(B) 2—3—4—1
(C) 1—4—3—2
(D) 4—1—2—3

X. 1. Such experiments are based on the recognition that typically the only meeting between the private citizen and the police is under circumstances of crises or confrontation where the police officer appears in only one segment of his or her role, and the citizen is likely to be out of character.

2. Hopefully, the benefits of such exposure will be bilateral.

3. Frequently, these efforts take the form of observational experience, whereby citizens are invited to observe the officers firsthand as they carry out their duties.

4. Increasing efforts have been made in recent years to overcome the often strained relationship between police officers and citizens.

5. Whether expressed or not, the intent of experiments involving citizen observation of police work is to display the police officer to the public in a more total perspective.

(A) 1—5—3—4—2
(B) 5—3—4—2—1
(C) 4—5—3—1—2
(D) 4—3—1—5—2

ANSWER KEY

I.	B	VI.	C
II.	B	VII.	C
III.	B	VIII.	C
IV.	A	IX.	A
V.	A	X.	D

QUESTIONS ON ADMINISTRATION AND SUPERVISION

> **Directions:** Read each question and choose the best answer. Circle the letter of your choice.

1. "It is desirable and advantageous to leave a maximum measure of planning responsibility to operating agencies or units rather than to remove the responsibility to a central planning staff agency." Adoption of the former policy, or decentralized planning, would lead to

    (A) less effective planning; operating personnel do not have the time to make long-term plans.

    (B) more effective planning; operating units are usually better equipped technically than any staff agency and consequently are in a better position to set up valid plans.

    (C) less effective planning; a central planning agency has a more objective point of view than any operating agency can achieve.

    (D) more effective planning; plans are conceived in terms of the existing situation and their execution is carried out with the will to succeed.

2. The planning process in administrative work is of great importance in developing procedures and methods of operation. The statement that represents the *best* principle to follow in providing for the planning process is that

    (A) the department's planning unit should do the planning for all divisions of the department.

    (B) the operating personnel who are to execute the plan should participate with the planning unit in the preparation of plans.

    (C) the larger operating divisions should have sole responsibility for preparation of plans affecting them, with the planning unit providing plans for the small divisions.

    (D) the operating divisions, large or small, should be responsible for the preparation of plans, with the planning unit's approval required.

3. "As an organization grows larger, the amount of personal contact between the top administrative officials and the rank and file diminishes. Consequently, management comes to rely more heavily upon written reports and records for securing information and exercising control." The *most* valid implication of this quotation is that, as an organization grows larger

   (A) evaluation of the work of rank and file employees becomes more objective because of greater reliance upon written reports and records.
   (B) relations between first-line supervisors and their subordinates grow more impersonal.
   (C) top administrative officials depend upon less direct methods for controlling the work of their subordinates.
   (D) it becomes more difficult for top administrative officials to maintain high morale among rank and file employees.

4. Budgeting is most properly a phase of

   (A) directing.
   (B) organizing.
   (C) planning.
   (D) coordinating.

5. Of the following, the most fundamental reason for the use of budgets in governmental administration is that budgets

   (A) minimize seasonal variation in workloads and expenditures of public agencies.
   (B) facilitate decentralization of functions performed by public agencies.
   (C) provide advance control on the expenditure of funds.
   (D) establish valid bases for comparing present governmental activities with corresponding activities in previous periods.

6. "Specialization in the performance of administrative planning duties is not an example of an undesirable specialization of duty being made at the expense of the patrol force." This statement should be considered as generally

   (A) false; specialization of any kind inevitably results in some depletion of the patrol force.
   (B) true; specialization is desirable to the extent that it efficiently performs part of the actual patrol duty.
   (C) false; this type of duty can be efficiently performed by the individual patrol supervisor.
   (D) true; these duties cannot be performed by subordinates in the course of their regular patrol duty.

7. "The extent of specialization is important because, while some specialization is essential to effective operation, overspecialization may have the opposite effect." Of the following, the statement that is the best support for this quotation is that

   (A) excessive specialization tends to create uncontrolled independent units.
   (B) effective operation is essential regardless of the degree of specialization.
   (C) interdependence of operating units exists regardless of the establishment of new units.
   (D) subdivision of department activities should proceed only where clearly necessary.

8. "The tasks of coordination, supervision, and control are likely to become more complicated as the specialization of a police department increases." This statement is generally

   (A) false; better performance of these tasks is likely to result because of the concentrated attention given to particular problems.

   (B) false; the proportion of a total force that is specialized is too small to have any effect on these tasks.

   (C) true; the increased number of interrelationships that results from specialization are sources of potential conflict and friction.

   (D) true; the individual specialist resents direction from superior officers who are not themselves specialists.

9. It has been said that the structure of the organization can have an influence on the morale of its members. With reference to a large municipal agency, this statement is

   (A) false; morale depends more on the individual job experience and the personal satisfactions derived from job performance than on the organizational structure.

   (B) true; members of the agency are most likely to be uncertain and frustrated where the organizational relationships are unsound, confused, or blurred.

   (C) false; morale is more a matter of interpersonal relationships in an agency than a consequence of the organizational structure, regardless of whether or not such a structure is sound.

   (D) true; members of the agency will be unaware of their status if the organizational structure is poorly devised.

10. Assume that a nationwide survey reveals that a particular police administrative practice is widely used and that it is quite different from that of your department. The one of the following that is the most reasonable implication of results of this survey is that

    (A) the more widely accepted practice should be instituted in your department on a trial basis immediately.

    (B) your department's practice should be evaluated in an effort to determine if it can be improved.

    (C) your department's practice should be revised to conform to the more widely accepted practice.

    (D) police problems of your department are unique and it is unlikely that any administrative changes ought to be made.

11. Arranging the personnel of a police unit with a common purpose in a manner to enable the performance by specified persons of related work grouped for the purpose of assignment, and the establishing of areas of responsibility with clearly delineated channels of communication and authority is called

    (A) planning.
    (B) staffing.
    (C) organizing.
    (D) budgeting.

12. An advantage of decentralization in a police department is that it

    (A) facilitates the adoption of uniform policies.

    (B) eliminates the need for any centralized direction in the activity that is decentralized.

    (C) reduces the risk of duplication and overlapping.

    (D) tends to develop administrative and supervisory ability on the part of a greater number of individuals.

13. "An organization such as a police agency is not generally confronted by such unique problems as to make impossible the application of certain administrative principles that have found applicable in other organizations." The most valid deduction to make from this statement is that

    (A) practices of other organizations reveal that police problems are not generally susceptible to solution by standardized management techniques.
    (B) questions of size are relevant in evaluating the applicability of common administrative principles.
    (C) some management guides can serve both police and nonpolice administrators equally well.
    (D) superficial familiarity with police organization often leads to the application of invalid administrative techniques.

14. The attitude of an employee toward the organization employing him is largely an outgrowth of an attitude toward

    (A) his immediate supervisor.
    (B) his co-workers.
    (C) the personnel office.
    (D) the administrators of the organization.

15. The primary responsibility of every supervising officer is to

    (A) create among his or her subordinates a negative attitude towards the departmental objectives.
    (B) make certain that all subordinates are treated equally as to the assignment of tasks.
    (C) see that the required work is performed properly.
    (D) establish a relationship of mutual confidence between himself or herself and the subordinates.

16. Of the following, the most important reason for periodic staff conferences is to

    (A) brief the staff on the plans and prospects of the organization.
    (B) hear the grievances and problems of the subordinate members of the staff.
    (C) obtain suggestions from subordinate members of the staff.
    (D) obtain uniformity in interpretation of policies and procedures

17. For a supervisor to give equally close supervision to all officers would be

    (A) desirable; all officers can benefit from the supervisor's guidance.
    (B) undesirable; the degree of supervision needed varies with the capabilities of each officer.
    (C) undesirable; the demands on the supervisor's time would be too great.
    (D) desirable; all subordinates would be assured of fair and equal treatment.

18. "You can pass the buck up, but you can't pass it down." Of the following, the most accurate statement on the basis of the above quotation is that

    (A) a superior is responsible for the actions of his or her subordinates regardless of the issuance of orders or instructions.
    (B) a supervisor who receives positive orders from a superior is more likely to accept responsibility for their execution than is the superior.
    (C) discretionary actions by subordinates relieves the superior of responsibility for this aspect of their actions.
    (D) the superior officer is more likely to accept responsibility than is a subordinate officer.

19. An essential element of administrative control over the operations for which a superior is responsible is that the superior

   (A) should perform an important task herself instead of assigning a competent subordinate to perform the task.
   (B) should personally check every ordered action taken by her subordinates to insure that all actions have been properly performed.
   (C) who has issued an order to a subordinate should ascertain that it has been carried out properly.
   (D) who has assigned an important task to a subordinate should inform her that he, the subordinate, will be held fully accountable for its proper execution.

20. "Regardless of the sincerity of purpose and the soundness of personnel policies and relationships formulated by top police management, either with or without consultation with representatives of the rank-and-file officers, such policies cannot succeed in helping to create a contented and efficient body of rank-and-file officers unless the supervisory officers at all levels are made aware of the contents of these policies and consciously apply the philosophy underlying them in their daily work." This statement is generally true, chiefly because

   (A) the superior officers on all levels in the chain of command should personally interpret both the letter and the spirit of these policies to the rank-and-file officers.
   (B) the rank-and-file officers will tend to accept grudgingly any personnel policies created without consulting them and will tend to regard with suspicion the real motives behind the seeming kindliness of the administrative and supervisory echelons who created the policies.
   (C) the real personnel policies, as far as the individual officers are concerned, are those interpersonal relationships that are manifested in their daily contacts with their immediate superiors.
   (D) personnel policies should not be implemented until all the officers who will be affected by them are made fully aware of the contents of the policies.

21. Of the following, the *least* valid reason for a policy of delegating authority from supervisors to subordinates is to

   (A) relieve supervisors of responsibility for execution of specific operations.
   (B) give subordinates training and experience for higher responsibility.
   (C) assure performance of essential tasks in the absence of the supervisors.
   (D) improve the morale of subordinates by giving them challenging assignments.

22. "The supervisor who is responsible to several superiors is in an advantageous position since she has the benefit of intimate contacts with more people in higher positions." This statement is generally

   (A) false, because a supervisor should not normally be directly responsible to more than one superior at the same time.
   (B) true, since the supervisor is in a position to learn more about the overall operation of the agency.
   (C) false, because there is a tendency in such a case for the supervisor to lose touch with her own subordinates.
   (D) true, since she can sometimes receive more favorable treatment for her subordinates by judicious use of such contacts.

23. The effective "span of control" in the administration of services varies *least* with the

   (A) accessibility and efficiency of a central records system.
   (B) level of responsibility.
   (C) necessary degree of supervision and direction.
   (D) personalities of the supervisor and subordinates.

24. The one of the following which, if increased, would most likely result in an increased span of control on the part of a supervisory officer is

   (A) an intervening period of time required for orders to reach subordinates not actually present.
   (B) his ability to supervise subordinates effectively.
   (C) the complexity of the jobs to be performed by subordinates.
   (D) the effort which must be devoted to extra-departmental conferences and programs.

25. "Some of the most persistent and acute problems of administration, especially in a large or decentralized organization such as a large urban police department, stem from deficiencies in horizontal communication." Of the following methods, the one that will tend to diminish this problem the most is the

   (A) provision for more face-to-face contacts on policy between subordinate and superior officers.
   (B) greater use of conferences to exchange information between officers of the same rank.
   (C) greater emphasis on the use of clear concise language in the issue of commands or orders.
   (D) provision for a more orderly downward flow of information which increases knowledge of the organization and its work.

26. Provision for effective communication between superior and subordinate levels of command will have a number of valuable results. Of the following, the one that is *least* likely to be a result of an effective communication system is the

   (A) development of policy decisions at all levels.
   (B) dovetailing, rather than overlapping, of separate police activities.
   (C) execution of directives in the manner intended.
   (D) identification of failures or sore spots in the department.

27. It has been suggested that all subordinate officers be kept currently informed about general departmental actions, changes in other departmental work units, and new developments of general interest in their department. For an agency to put this suggestion into effect is generally

   (A) inadvisable; subordinate officers should perform the duties specifically assigned to them and not get involved in matters that do not concern them directly.
   (B) advisable; subordinate officers may often need to know such information in order to coordinate their work properly with that of other officers or work units.
   (C) inadvisable; changes in other units have little effect on the work performed by officers not assigned to these units.
   (D) advisable; broad knowledge of the activities in an agency tends to improve management skills.

28. Coordination of the functions of the various component organizational units of a large organization would be *least* facilitated by

   (A) staff supervision and inspection.
   (B) grouping related activities under one control.
   (C) utilizing auxiliary units as control devices.
   (D) enlarging the span of control of upper levels of command.

29. Assume that your supervisor has asked you to present to her comprehensive, periodic reports on the progress that your unit is making in meeting its work goals. For you to give your supervisor oral rather than written reports is

    (A) desirable; it will be easier for her to transmit your oral reports to her superiors.
    (B) undesirable; the oral reports will provide no permanent record to which she may refer.
    (C) undesirable; there will be less opportunity for you to discuss the oral reports with her than the written ones.
    (D) desirable; the oral reports will require little time and effort to prepare.

30. The principal advantage of making an oral report is that it

    (A) affords an immediate opportunity for two-way communication between the subordinate and the superior.
    (B) is an easy method for the superior to use in transmitting information to others of equal rank.
    (C) saves the time of all concerned.
    (D) permits more precise pinpointing of praise or blame by means of follow-up questions by the superior.

ANSWERS TO ADMINISTRATION AND SUPERVISION QUESTIONS

1. **The correct answer is (D).** Planning should permeate the entire organization. The people who are to implement a plan should take part in its preparation. Choice (B) indicates that operating units are "better equipped technically than any staff agency . . ." Absolute statements such as this are seldom the correct answer choice.

2. **The correct answer is (B).** The concept is the same as in the preceding question. Planners and operating personnel should work together to the fullest extent.

3. **The correct answer is (C).** Top administrative officials are usually not in a position that allows for face-to-face feedback and must rely more and more on written reports for needed information.

4. **The correct answer is (C).** A budget may be defined as a financial plan.

5. **The correct answer is (C).** Budget execution is the administrative task of controlling the expenditure of appropriations so as to carry out the plans as provided in the budget.

6. **The correct answer is (D).** Specialization in administrative planning is essential to the accomplishment of the primary police tasks.

7. **The correct answer is (A).** Specialized units sometimes tend to operate independently and even at cross-purposes from other units in the department. For example, homicide squads are usually not too interested in burglary or traffic control, yet certain cooperation may be advantageous at times.

8. **The correct answer is (C).** As previously stated, specialized units have a tendency to work independently and a tendency to de-emphasize common objectives.

9. **The correct answer is (B).** If the organizational structure allows for work that includes duplication of effort, over-specialization, and unrealistic spans of control, then uncertainty and confusion will result.

10. **The correct answer is (B).** This question merely requires that you not act until you get the facts, but that you should be open to change if deemed worthwhile. It's possible that your agency is following a course that is already appropriate.

11. **The correct answer is (C).** This is an acceptable definition of organizing.

12. **The correct answer is (D).** Decentralization results in decision making being pushed down from the headquarter complex to smaller units such as areas, districts, and precincts. When the decisions are made at the lower echelons, administrative and supervisory ability are usually strengthened—even if some mistakes are made initially.

13. **The correct answer is (C).** The question asks, "What is the most valid deduction to make from this statement?" This is actually a reading interpretation question.

14. **The correct answer is (A).** The immediate supervisor is the one from whom orders are taken and the one to whom an employee usually reports.

15. **The correct answer is (C).** The objective is to get the job done through people.

16. **The correct answer is (D).** Staff conferences promote the flow of information from higher to lower levels within the organization and one result is uniformity in the interpretation of policies and procedures.

17. **The correct answer is (B).** Employees bring different strengths and weaknesses to the job situation. Employees are not equal and should not be treated equally. They should be treated fairly and according to their needs.

18. **The correct answer is (A).** This is another reading interpretation question. It does make the point that supervisors cannot give away or delegate responsibility.

19. **The correct answer is (C).** If a supervisor is not in the habit of ascertaining whether his or her orders have been carried out properly, such supervisor will lose control of the operation.

20. **The correct answer is (C).** This question is similar in concept to question 14. (The rank-and-file experience personnel policies as applied by immediate supervisors.)

21. **The correct answer is (A).** Responsibility is not delegated. The supervisor may (and should) delegate jobs and tasks, but the ultimate responsibility for getting the job done is hers.

22. **The correct answer is (A).** The quotation is obviously false. It describes a violation of the concept of unity of command, which requires that people in the organization receive orders from only one person. Unity means "oneness."

23. **The correct answer is (A).** Suggested answer choices (B), (C), and (D) would all impact an effective span of control:

    (B) The higher one is in the organization, the narrower the span of control.

    (C) The more direction and supervision needed, the narrower the span of control.

    (D) If personalities clash and prevent harmonious relationships, the effective span of control is reduced.

    Note: The availability of the central records system would not impact on the span of control.

24. **The correct answer is (B).** Obviously, if the supervisor's ability to supervise effectively is increased, then it follows that he will be able to increase the number of people he can effectively supervise.

25. **The correct answer is (B).** Careful reading would have helped on this one.

    Choice (A) pertains to vertical communication.

    Choice (B) pertains to horizontal communication, or "officers of the same rank."

    Choice (C) pertains to orders—downward or vertical communication.

    The (D) choice refers to downward (vertical) communication.

26. **The correct answer is (A).** Policy decisions are not made at all levels. They are made at the top, are broad, and usually not reduced to writing.

27. **The correct answer is (B).** It would be difficult for one unit to coordinate with the activities of another if it were unaware of changes in the other unit. A unit that is operating in the dark, or in a vacuum, would be hard-pressed to dovetail its work output with that of other units.

28. **The correct answer is (D).** Coordination of effort may be more readily realized if the span of control is reduced at the upper levels of command. Remember, there is an inverse relationship between rank and the span of control—the higher the rank, the smaller the span.

29. **The correct answer is (B).** The question states that the supervisor wants "comprehensive" (large in scope) reports. Periodic reports that are large in scope should be in writing.

30. **The correct answer is (A).** A primary advantage of oral interaction is the ability to engage in immediate face-to-face, or two-way communication.

QUESTIONS ON DISCIPLINE AND TRAINING

> **Directions:** Read each question and choose the best answer. Circle the letter of your choice.

31. It has been suggested that a supervisor should continuously strive to develop all subordinates to the limit of their ability and skills. This suggestion is generally

    (A) advisable; although basically alike, individuals possess widely different backgrounds and each officer must be given training in the specific duties of the immediate job.

    (B) inadvisable; individuals differ from each other, and urging an unambitious employee to greater effort against his or her will may cause the employee to become a reluctant and less satisfactory worker.

    (C) advisable; only by full utilization of each officer's talents can maximum service be obtained.

    (D) inadvisable; assisting officers to develop themselves may result in their dissatisfaction when insufficient opportunities for promotion are available.

32. The main objective of a precinct training program is to

    (A) prepare members for higher responsibilities.
    (B) develop skills needed on the job.
    (C) keep members abreast of the latest professional developments.
    (D) stimulate members to pursue further studies.

33. In a police training program, the group (or conference) method of instruction, in addition to being an acceptable method of imparting knowledge and improving skills, is of value chiefly because of the

    (A) stimulation afforded the individual members as the result of joint efforts toward a common goal.

    (B) adaptability of such instruction to the needs of each individual in a group.

    (C) enhancement of department morale resulting from the spirit of cooperation and good fellowship engendered by the use of this method.

    (D) minimization of competition, which is a generally undesirable ingredient in the learning process.

34. "The ultimate responsibility for police training lies with the top echelon of command, and the patrol sergeant should not properly be held accountable for any part of this supervisory function." This statement is

    (A) true; the patrol sergeant should devote the major portion of his time to the performance of patrol.
    (B) false; the patrol sergeant is in a key position to assist in training.
    (C) true; the duty of a patrol sergeant to correct the improper patrol performance of subordinates cannot be classified as training.
    (D) false; the patrol sergeant's primary responsibility is the training of subordinates.

35. "Most areas of police work requiring original police training also require periodic retraining." This statement is generally considered to be

    (A) correct, chiefly because people do not have a firm grasp of material when presented.
    (B) correct, chiefly because police personnel must be kept abreast of changes in law enforcement.
    (C) incorrect, chiefly because training time is too valuable to be wasted on experienced personnel.
    (D) incorrect, chiefly because police officers are retrained to learn what they already know.

36. You have been directed to provide certain members of the internal affairs unit with specialized training. Which of the following would be the *least* desirable approach for you to pursue?

    (A) You would utilize a coaching approach to a small group of employees.
    (B) An approach by you that would insist on employee participation.
    (C) The utilization of an instructor who would teach individuals in instructional interview approach.
    (D) A lecture approach whereby selected experts would address the group.

37. "Differences in initial ability are relevant in any discussion of learning. Everyone knows that there are slow learners and rapid learners." For an officer with training responsibility it would be *correct* to state that, in general,

    (A) although slow learners take longer, they retain what they learn longer.
    (B) fast learners maintain their advantage and retain material longer.
    (C) slow learners and fast learners are approximately equal in their ability to retain what has been learned.
    (D) there is no relationship between the speed of learning and how long it is retained.

38. While giving job instructions on a new riot-control device, a lieutenant is asked by a subordinate why the device was not utilized in a manner different from the way the lieutenant indicated was proper. The method suggested by the subordinate included several procedures that were unsafe and could result in serious injury to those using the device. The lieutenant answered by stating that the method he was demonstrating was correct, that the suggested method was unsafe, and that there was no point in discussing improper methods. The lieutenant's approach to the question was

    (A) proper, mainly because the members will not have the chance to pick up bad habits.
    (B) improper, mainly because the lieutenant did not consider the possibility of modifying the suggestion to make it safer.
    (C) proper, mainly because the speed of learning is most rapid when only one method is followed.
    (D) improper, mainly because hazards of incorrect methods can be avoided if they are known.

39. Studies of the learning process indicate that the speed of absorption of new skills is not constant. Plateaus, or periods in which little or no progress is made, are regularly encountered. The most important implication of these findings for the officer conducting a training program is that

    (A) training sessions should be spaced to avoid the plateau period.
    (B) trainees should be encouraged during the plateau period.
    (C) before the training program starts, trainees should be warned to expect the plateau period.
    (D) training efforts should be concentrated on the plateau period.

40. When training a subordinate in the performance of her duties, it is desirable for a lieutenant to explain the theory or reasons for certain procedures mainly because

    (A) the subordinate cannot perform specific duties properly if she does not know the theory behind them.
    (B) a basic understanding of her duties enables a subordinate to more readily apply what she has learned to new situations.
    (C) explaining the reasons for performing a task serves as the lieutenant's justification for ordering the subordinate to do it.
    (D) a basic understanding of duties assures that every subordinate will learn the one best way of performing each task, thus enabling her to work harmoniously with other employees.

41. Supervisory training is designed to develop skills in human relationships while work-skill training attempts to alter the relationship between a person and a machine or material of some sort. The following statement that most accurately describes an important difference between these two types of training is that

    (A) resistance to work-skill training is likely to be greater than resistance to supervisory training.
    (B) skills acquired from supervisory training should be less flexible than skills acquired from work-skill training.
    (C) skills acquired from supervisory training are usually less directly and routinely applied than skills acquired from work-skill training.
    (D) trainees are more apt to feel more secure in attempting to utilize skills acquired through supervisory training than those acquired from work-skill training.

42. Sergeant A, just before instructing an officer in the correct method of searching a premises for contraband, explained to the officer why it was important to follow the correct procedure. The sergeant's action was

    (A) good; a procedure is less likely to be forgotten if its purpose is understood.
    (B) poor; the importance of searching for contraband is obvious and the explanation is a waste of time.
    (C) good; repetition is an effective aid in learning an operation.
    (D) poor; such an explanation will distract the officer from the main points in the instruction.

43. One of the best indications of interest in the job on the part of subordinates is that they ask questions. Such questions are of value chiefly because they

    (A) provide an excellent guide to the reassignment of subordinates.
    (B) serve to enhance the status of the supervisor when he or she answers them.
    (C) indicate the efficiency of the personnel involved.
    (D) can be utilized as part of the training process.

44. Police Officer William Chaney asks Sergeant Collins the following question, "Sarge, don't you think we spend too much time processing truants?" The sergeant responds by asking Officer Chaney how he thinks truants should be processed. This response by the sergeant is

    (A) inappropriate because the officer will not ask questions in the future.
    (B) appropriate because it is a way of motivating the officers to form a solution to a perceived problem.
    (C) inappropriate because Police Officer Chaney will resent the sergeant's lack of interest.
    (D) appropriate because the sergeant should have replied directly to the question.

45. A lieutenant from the police academy is explaining a soon-to-be instituted method for the processing of domestic violence situations to a group of police officers. During the presentation the lieutenant realizes that the group is neither impressed by, nor interested in, the new procedure. The lieutenant should

    (A) ask questions based on job-related situations that would stimulate thoughtful responses.
    (B) order the group to take notes so that they would have access to the procedure when needed.
    (C) present the new procedure carefully and methodically and refrain from asking questions.
    (D) reschedule the training for a time when the group receptiveness is likely to be more positive.

46. In general, specific training of a police officer in a particular duty should be continued to the point at which the

    (A) police officer has no further questions about how to perform the duty.
    (B) police officer states that he or she knows how to perform the duty and is ready to do the job.
    (C) instructor is reasonably certain that the police officer understands how to perform the duty.
    (D) police officer has given a perfect demonstration of performance of duty.

47. In order to teach effectively a newly appointed employee who must learn to do a kind of work that is unfamiliar, the supervisor should realize that during this *first* stage in the learning process the subordinate is generally experiencing

    (A) acute consciousness of self.
    (B) acute consciousness of subject matter with little interest in persons or personalities.
    (C) inertness or passive acceptance of the assigned role.
    (D) understanding of problems without understanding the means of solving them.

48. Of the following kinds of work, the one that a manual process is most usually preferred over a mechanized process is one in which the transactions are very

    (A) numerous.
    (B) similar.
    (C) dissimilar.
    (D) predictable.

49. The most accurate of the following principles of education and learning for a supervisor to keep in mind when planning a training program for the assistant supervisors under her supervision is that

    (A) assistant supervisors, like all other individuals, vary in the rate at which they learn new material and in the degree to which they can retain what they learn.

(B) experienced assistant supervisors who have the same basic college education and agency experience will be able to learn new material at approximately the same rate of speed.

(C) the speed with which assistant supervisors can learn new material after the age of 40 is half as rapid as at ages 20 to 30.

(D) with regard to any specific task, it is easier and takes less time to break an experienced assistant supervisor of old, unsatisfactory work habits than it is to teach him or her new, acceptable ones.

50. The officer who has had much experience in the training of new employees knows that the most accurate of the following statements is that

(A) generally, the stronger the incentive an employee has the faster he will learn to perform the duties of the position.

(B) the average employee can accurately perform an operation after he has observed a skilled employee perform the operation.

(C) the chief difficulty in teaching an older employee a new method of performing an operation is usually that his mind functions more slowly than that of a younger person.

(D) it is easier for an employee to change his accustomed way of performing an operation than to adopt a new way.

51. A supervisor will be able to train employees better if he or she is familiar with basic principles of learning. Which one of the following statements about the learning process is most *correct*?

(A) An employee who learns one job quickly will learn any other job quickly.

(B) Emphasizing correct things done by the employee usually gives her an incentive to improve.

(C) Great importance placed on an employee's mistakes is the best way to help her to get rid of them.

(D) It is very hard to teach new methods to middle-aged or older employees.

52. Most authorities in police supervision agree that punishment for similar breaches of conduct should be uniform. Uniformity may involve giving consideration to the conditions under which the infraction occurred and to whether the infraction was intentional, careless, or out of lack of knowledge of the rule. Which one of the following choices best reflects the extent to which "conditions" and "intentions" should be taken into account in maintaining uniformity of penalties?

(A) Both conditions and intentions should be factors in uniformity.

(B) Neither conditions nor intentions should be a factor in uniformity.

(C) Conditions should be a factor in uniformity, but intentions should be disregarded.

(D) Intentions should be a factor in uniformity, but conditions should be disregarded.

53. A proposal has been made that a table of standard penalties be established for infractions of the rules whereby there would be a set penalty for each kind of infraction and this penalty would be applied automatically. To institute such a system would be

(A) undesirable; it would be almost impossible to work out a fair and equitable table of penalties.

(B) desirable; it would assure that no police officer would be subjected to a more drastic penalty than any other.

(C) undesirable; it would prevent the exercise of judgment in fitting the penalty to the individual and the background of the situation.

(D) desirable; it would create an understanding among police officers as to what they might expect, thereby causing them to be less likely to question the application of a proper penalty.

54. As a recently appointed sergeant, you have decided that disciplinary action is to be taken against a police officer under your supervision. In this situation, it is most important for you to realize that

    (A) disciplinary action, once decided upon, should be taken quickly.
    (B) disciplinary action should be postponed for reconsideration at a later date when you have acquired more supervisory experience.
    (C) the mildest form of discipline should be tried first.
    (D) you should request your commanding officer to decide whether or not any disciplinary action should be taken.

55. It is a generally accepted principle of supervision that disciplinary action should be taken quickly when it needs to be taken. Which of the following statements best supports the taking of prompt disciplinary action?

    (A) The accuracy of official disciplinary records will thereby be insured.
    (B) The offender is more likely to feel that the disciplinary action will be severe.
    (C) The supervisor is more likely to remember the details surrounding the offender's breach of discipline.
    (D) There is an avoidance of the prolonged aggravation caused by later disposition of the case.

56. When dealing with newly assigned subordinates, a supervisor has been following the practice of bringing promptly to their attention their first violation of the rules and regulations. This practice is generally

    (A) advisable, chiefly because the subordinates must be taught as promptly as possible just who is in charge.
    (B) inadvisable, chiefly because the subordinate is relatively new at this point and should be treated with greater leniency.
    (C) advisable, chiefly because at this point mild disciplinary measures may be very effective.
    (D) inadvisable, chiefly because the subordinate may come to feel that the superior is setting too high a standard of expected performance.

57. "It has come to be realized that, from the standpoint of control, the certainty of punishment for a breach of duty is more important than the severity of punishment." According to this statement, it follows that

    (A) disciplinary action for errors or violations should be administered without exception.
    (B) dismissal is an admission of failure to supervise a police officer effectively.
    (C) it is less important to impress an offender with his guilt than with the inevitability of punishment.
    (D) more emphasis should be placed on the punishment aspect as the offense increases in seriousness.

58. A certain authority on police supervision makes both of the following statements on the same page of a textbook: "Punishment must be meted out swiftly after detection and proof of the infraction," and "An immediate supervisor, discovering misconduct on the part of a subordinate, should allow his emotions to cool before taking punitive action against him." Which one of the following inferences in regard to this apparent inconsistency is most logically based on the above selection?

    (A) Quality of discipline is always more important than speed.
    (B) Even an expert may be inconsistent when it comes to taking punitive action.
    (C) There is no real inconsistency between the two statements, since the second quotation merely balances the speed and effectiveness.
    (D) Most employees would rather be penalized immediately, even though in the heat of anger, rather than wait for the penalty until emotions have cooled.

59. In order to build a spirit of cooperation among the staff, a supervisor must call attention to correct as well as incorrect behavior in a manner that subordinates will feel is consistent and reasonable. Of the following, the best rule for the supervisor is

   (A) call attention to incorrect behavior only if it is insignificant, but give praise for any form of correct behavior.
   (B) in discussing deficiencies, treat them as problems to be overcome rather than personal criticisms.
   (C) never single out one subordinate for praise in front of the entire staff.
   (D) all instances of criticism should be preceded by instances of commendation of equal significance.

60. For a superior who is supervising patrol to make a notation in a memorandum book whenever he or she strongly reprimands a subordinate verbally is

   (A) inadvisable, chiefly because an undue amount of supervisory time will be devoted to recording such information.
   (B) advisable, chiefly because the superior is developing a fund of information that will be useful in the future handling of the subordinate.
   (C) inadvisable, chiefly because the subordinate may resent such a procedure.
   (D) advisable, chiefly because all subordinates will make greater efforts to improve their job performance since they will not be sure of the nature of the notations.

61. During a disciplinary interview with a subordinate, a sergeant believes that she is unable to maintain an objective attitude because of anger and resentment toward the police officer. Under these circumstances, it would be most appropriate for the sergeant to

   (A) let the officer know exactly how she feels and that it will not be easy to "forgive and forget."
   (B) tell the officer she is passing the case on to the precinct commander who will be unbiased in meting out the deserved punishment.
   (C) postpone the interview until a later date before it develops into a subjective discussion.
   (D) try to keep her feelings under control by discussing the behavior that necessitated the interview.

62. When your supervisor complains to you concerning a serious error on the part of one of your subordinates, the most proper response should be to

   (A) assure him or her that you will check on it to prevent a similar mistake in the future.
   (B) accept the complaint and report the subordinate for disciplinary action.
   (C) state that you cannot do more than spot check the work of your subordinates.
   (D) advise him that such mistakes are inevitable when emergencies arise and subordinates are under pressure.

63. After a reprimand for a violation of the rules, a subordinate corrects himself and appears to perform his work acceptably. For the supervisor to remind the subordinate occasionally of his past violation would be

   (A) bad; it suggests that the supervisor is devoting too much time and effort to one individual.
   (B) good; it is an indication of the use of positive discipline on a continuing basis.
   (C) bad; the original corrective action appears to have served its purpose.
   (D) good; the supervisor has the best interests of the subordinate in mind.

64. In an attempt to be completely impartial in issuing necessary reprimands to subordinates, a police supervisor uses the same degree of personal forcefulness for all reprimands. This procedure is

(A) good; unfairness in imposing discipline can seriously lower the morale of a police agency.

(B) poor; the more serious error, when committed, should result in a stronger reprimand.

(C) good; effective discipline is best achieved when the supervisor always maintains a uniform supervisory manner.

(D) poor; there will be a tendency on the part of the supervisor to generally use less forcefulness than is required.

65. Lieutenant Mullins, while delivering a lecture to a group of newly promoted sergeants at the police academy, made the statement, "When possible, you should praise in public and punish in private." For the sergeants to adhere to such advice would be

(A) undesirable, because it would demonstrate a high degree of insensitivity by the supervisors.

(B) desirable, because praise must always be given in public if it is to be effective.

(C) desirable, because praise and/or punishment should be given immediately.

(D) desirable, because by punishing in public there is a risk of the group directing a certain amount of sympathy toward the subordinate and hostility toward the superior.

ANSWERS TO QUESTIONS ON DISCIPLINE AND TRAINING

31. **The correct answer is (C).** Supervisors must try to get as much from each officer as that officer is capable of giving. Maximum service cannot be realized if personnel are not encouraged to fully utilize their abilities.

32. **The correct answer is (B).** Getting the job done through people is the objective. The main objective of ratings, communication, and discipline is usually consistent with getting people to provide better service by developing and improving needed skills. Remember, training means changing attitudes, improving skills, and imparting knowledge.

33. **The correct answer is (A).** Joint effort directed at a common goal is a conference advantage and is consistent with the participative management approach.

34. **The correct answer is (B).** "The principal responsibility for maintaining an appropriate level of discipline (training) should rest upon the immediate line supervisor."

35. **The correct answer is (B).** Police personnel as well as personnel in the private sector must be kept abreast of changes that may impact on the manner in which they carry out assigned tasks.

36. **The correct answer is (D).** The (A), (B), and (C) suggested answer choices allow for active participation by those receiving the training. Choice (D) utilizes the lecture (inefficient) coupled with taking comprehensive notes.

37. **The correct answer is (B).** This is a learning principle clearly and accurately stated. (Don't fight it!)

38. **The correct answer is (A).** The subordinates would obviously not be able to remember that which they didn't hear. The lieutenant was accentuating the positive.

39. **The correct answer is (B).** Learning is often interrupted by what is referred to as a learning plateau or leveling-off period during which the student seems to be standing still rather than making progress. At such times morale may suffer and supervisors should be ready to counterattack with encouragement.

40. **The correct answer is (B).** Look at some of the words in the other answer choices: (A), cannot; (C), justification; and (D), assures. Choices (A) and (D) are too positive and exclusive, because justification is never a good reason.

41. **The correct answer is (C).** This is more of a reading interpretation question. Basically, in choice (C) we are accepting that human relationships are more complex than the "re-

lationship" that may exist between a worker and a "thing." This question is easy if you read it carefully!

42. **The correct answer is (A).** As in giving orders, the *why* is extremely important in the learning process.

43. **The correct answer is (D).** This kind of situation allows for face-to-face interaction and immediate feedback—an ideal kind of script for inclusion in the training process.

44. **The correct answer is (B).** Getting subordinates to consider solutions is part and parcel of good training.

45. **The correct answer is (A).** The explaining and asking "provocative" questions would be much better than to "order the group," choice (B); "stay out of the discussion," choice (C); or "postpone," choice (D).

46. **The correct answer is (C).** "Reasonable certainty" is about the best choice.

47. **The correct answer is (A).** Wouldn't you be?

48. **The correct answer is (C).** If you read the question carefully, then the answer is obvious.

49. **The correct answer is (A).** People in any group, such as an assistant supervisor group, vary in learning rate.

50. **The correct answer is (A).** We can draw a parallel between incentive and motivation. The motivated employee who has a reason to learn will learn at a faster rate than the nonmotivated student.

51. **The correct answer is (B).** Emphasizing the correct things is a form of praise and/or recognition and is a positive motivator.

52. **The correct answer is (A).** Punishment for similar breaches should be uniform. But uniformity does not mean equal. Uniformity considers intentions and conditions. Uniformity is closer to fairness, which is a requisite of punishment. It would be difficult to say a penalty was fair if conditions and intentions had not been considered.

53. **The correct answer is (C).** Standard penalties for infractions would preclude the evaluation of conditions and/or intentions. Standard penalties (automatic two days' fine for lost shield, etc.) is an approach known as a "price list" and is not a good policy.

54. **The correct answer is (A).** Once decided upon, discipline should be swift. This is one of the requisites of punishment.

55. **The correct answer is (D).** Prolonging the actual penalty does aggravate the situation and violates the requisite of swiftness. Do not put the person who is to receive the discipline in a position of "waiting for the other shoe to drop."

56. **The correct answer is (C).** "Nip it in the bud" when possible and set the tone.

57. **The correct answer is (C).** If you were tempted to select choice (A) as your answer, think about the following: Would you, as a boss, punish someone who has inadvertently committed an error (in judgment)? This is actually a reading interpretation question. An error could be an accident; a breach of duty is an infraction.

58. **The correct answer is (C).** Actually, this is another reading interpretation question. But if you, as a boss, take punitive action while you are "hot under the collar," fairness may give way to unnecessary severity.

59. **The correct answer is (B).** Criticize the act, not the actor!

60. **The correct answer is (B).** The phrase, "fund of information," is just another way of saying "documentation." Such documentation is great when it comes time for evaluations and/or suggestions to improve performance. (It takes out much of the subjectivity inherent in rating systems.)

61. **The correct answer is (C).** The question tells us that the sergeant believes she is "unable to maintain an objective attitude because of anger . . ." In such a situation, allow a cooling-off period.

62. **The correct answer is (A).** When you indicate that "you will check on it," you are telling your supervisor that you will get the facts in order to prevent a situation. Perhaps the error was a result of inadequate training.

63. **The correct answer is (C).** The reprimand was obviously effective. For how long a time should a boss remind an employee of an old transgression?

64. **The correct answer is (B).** Fairness requires that the punishment fit the crime. Would the same degree of forcefulness be applied for someone caught smoking in uniform as for someone who violated a person's civil rights?

65. **The correct answer is (D).** The crowd usually favors the underdog. Don't make the erring employee into a martyr.

COMMUNICATION AND GIVING ORDERS

It has been argued that the ability to communicate is one of the most important characteristics of a good supervisor. It is not difficult to identify the relationship that exists between communicating and giving orders. Before we look at a series of questions based on these topics, let's review some basic concepts that may serve to help us answer some applicable and job-related questions.

Some basics of effective communication are the following:

- Clarify ideas in your own mind before attempting to communicate them to others.

- Study the real purpose of each communication.

- When appropriate, consult with others to plan your communications.

- Be a good listener.

- Be sure your actions support your communicative efforts.

- Follow up on your communications.

- Obtain feedback.

- Practice empathy.

Some barriers to effective communication are the following:

- Failure to listen

- Language barriers

- Filtering (distorting or diluting content)

- Status differences

- Intentional withholding of information

- Overloaded communications channels

Types of orders are the following:

1. Request—Most often used.

2. Implied Order—Used for well-motivated employees.

3. Direct Command—Used in emergencies and for lazy and/or indifferent employees.

4. Request for Volunteers—Sometimes used for dangerous and/or distasteful jobs.

Note: The boss who too often resorts to the call for volunteers may be guilty of trying to be "Mr. Nice Guy" when the situation demands that he be the boss and consider the concept of equal and fair distribution of the workload.

QUESTIONS ON COMMUNICATION AND GIVING ORDERS

> **Directions:** Read each question and choose the best answer. Circle the letter of your choice.

66. "The supervisor whose subordinates never have any complaints about anything should probably reappraise his or her role as a supervisor." Upon such a reappraisal the supervisor is most likely to discover that

    (A)   supervision is too strict.
    (B)   the officers are afraid.
    (C)   the officers are very satisfied with everything.
    (D)   communication is poor.

67. Provision for effective communication between superior and subordinate levels of command will have a number of valuable results. Of the following, the one that is *least* likely to be a result of an effective communication system is

    (A)   the development of policy decisions at all levels.
    (B)   the dovetailing, rather than overlapping, of separate police activities.
    (C)   the execution of directives in the manner intended.
    (D)   the identification of failures or "sore spots" in the department.

68. A newly appointed sergeant made a special effort to learn the names of all the officers in the squad and to address them by name whenever possible. In general, this practice is considered

    (A)   good, since people like to feel that they are regarded as individuals.
    (B)   poor, since it requires time and effort which could be put to better use.
    (C)   good, since the officers will be encouraged to bring their problems to the sergeant.
    (D)   poor, since it fails to maintain the proper reserve between the ranks.

69. "Some of the most persistent and acute problems of administration, especially in a large or decentralized organization, such as a large urban police department, stem from deficiencies in horizontal communication." Of the following methods, the one that will tend to diminish this problem the most is

    (A)   the provision for more face-to-face contacts on policy between subordinate and superior officers.
    (B)   the greater use of conferences to exchange information between officers of the same rank.
    (C)   the greater emphasis on the use of clear, concise language in the issue of commands or orders.
    (D)   the provision for a more orderly downward flow of information that increases knowledge of the organization and its work.

70. "Crosswise relationships exist between personnel in one unit and personnel of equal, lower, or superior status in other units. Direct communications between them substitutes for having a message follow the chain of command upward through one or more superiors, horizontally across a level of organization, and thus downward to the particular recipient. "Direct or crosswise communication rather than communication through the chain of command is generally a

 (A) good idea, primarily because it affords a subordinate an opportunity to enlarge his knowledge of relationships in a horizontal organizational unit.

 (B) good idea, whenever communication time should be reduced and quality of understanding should be increased.

 (C) poor idea, since it enables incompetent subordinates to transmit hazy, incorrect, and unauthorized communications to persons in other units.

 (D) poor idea, since superiors will generally refuse to permit such crosswise communications and can rarely agree on the need for such communication.

71. "To decrease the possibility of communication blockages and distortions, it is recommended that the span of control in a department be large." Which of the following best explains why a large span of control may improve communications?

 (A) More organizational levels facilitate communications through intervening layers of officers.

 (B) There is a tendency toward group discussions that eliminates the need to communicate through organizational levels.

 (C) There are direct lines to key officers although the department may have many organizational levels.

 (D) Fewer organizational layers are necessary and subordinates can communicate more directly with superiors.

72. According to one text, the greatest obstacle to effective communication is

 (A) the failure to realize that precision of expression depends mostly on developed vocabulary skills.

 (B) that employees write and speak without double-checking facts that they assume to be correct.

 (C) the basic inability of the communication receiver to read and understand or to listen and understand.

 (D) the length of written materials and the duration of oral presentations.

73. A sergeant assigned as the commanding officer of a small police unit has become aware that one particular patrolman usually acts as the spokesman for other police officers in matters affecting their day-to-day work routine. For the sergeant to permit this officer to continue to act in this way is

 (A) desirable; the sergeant is spared the burden of having to deal with each police officer individually.

 (B) undesirable; the police officers are probably developing an unofficial leader of their own because of the deficiencies of the sergeant.

 (C) desirable; a channel of communications has been established with those subordinates who ordinarily would not express their views to the sergeant.

 (D) undesirable; the sergeant cannot be sure that the spokesman presents the views of the other police officers in an accurate and complete manner.

74. The most valid generalization regarding praise by supervisors as an incentive for employees is that such praise must be

 (A) given to all if it is given to any.

 (B) bestowed privately.

 (C) fitted in type and amount to the individual employee.

 (D) given at regularly scheduled intervals.

75. Assume that a certain supervisor has developed the practice of handing the sergeants, without comment, brief written notes that are generally concerned with matters of routine operations. Ordinarily, this kind of information is given to the sergeants verbally and informally. The supervisor's procedure is generally

    (A) desirable; the sergeants are less likely to misinterpret such information when it is given in written form.
    (B) undesirable; the supervisor should take advantage of such opportunities for establishing and maintaining good personal relationships with subordinates.
    (C) desirable; the superior is able to avoid unnecessary conversation and can devote more time to desk duties.
    (D) undesirable; giving information to subordinates in a written form encourages them to ask many clarifying questions.

76. The captain observes that when a police officer is telling a certain sergeant something, the sergeant often interrupts before the police officer has completed the message and says, "I know what you are going to say. The answer is no." Which of the following choices is both the best evaluation the captain should make of this habit and also the most important reason for that evaluation?

    (A) The habit is bad; it includes an element of discourtesy to the police officer.
    (B) The habit is good; a considerable amount of valuable time can be saved by the sergeant's interruptions.
    (C) The habit is good; it helps the sergeant to establish a reputation for being "on top of the job."
    (D) The habit is bad; whether or not the sergeant has understood the message, the police officer is likely to become discouraged and to stop trying to communicate information to the sergeant.

77. Assume that you have been asked to present a speech on crime prevention before a local civic group. After having received permission to make the address, the one of the following that you would consider *first* in preparing the speech would be the

    (A) facts that may be presented.
    (B) purpose of the talk.
    (C) level of knowledge of the audience.
    (D) amount of time allotted for the presentation.

78. An authority on public administration has said, "Good news ascends the hierarchy much more easily than bad news." Which one of the following is the most likely explanation of why this filtering process almost always occurs?

    (A) Many a police chief is unbelievably blind as to what is really going on in the agency.
    (B) Most police organizations do not want an upward communications system to exist or to work.
    (C) Management officials, designing a good upward communications system, deliberately add a filtering process to that system.
    (D) Problems are disturbing and subordinates tend to edit upward communications to present a brighter picture than really exists.

79. Of the following statements concerning subordinates' expressions to a supervisor of their opinions and feelings concerning work situations, which is most correct?

    (A) By listening and responding to such expressions, the supervisor encourages the development of complaints.
    (B) The lack of such expressions should indicate to the supervisor that there is a high level of job satisfaction.
    (C) The more the supervisor listens and responds to such expressions, the more he or she demonstrates a lack of supervisory ability.
    (D) By listening and responding to such expressions, the supervisor will enable many subordinates to understand and solve their own problems on the job.

80. A police commander should be keenly aware of the differences between the formal communication networks of the department (usually written) and the informal communication networks (usually verbal). Which of the following statements concerning informal communications should a police commander recognize as being most accurate?

(A) People resent talking about "business" in friendly, after-work discussions.

(B) People often distort verbal communications transmitted through informal channels.

(C) People are usually unwilling to communicate outside of officially designated channels.

(D) Higher levels in the police organization cannot take cognizance of, or act on, information received informally.

81. Assuming that the "grapevine" in any organization is virtually indestructible, which of the following is the most important for management to understand?

(A) What is being spread by means of the grapevine and the reason for spreading it.

(B) What is being spread by means of the grapevine and how it is being spread.

(C) Who is involved in spreading the information on the grapevine.

(D) Why those who are involved in spreading the information are doing so.

82. A police department's informal communication networks can be very harmful, but they can also benefit management and the department generally. The following are four possible uses of the networks that might be appropriate and beneficial:

I. Valuable information, which a subordinate would not want to communicate officially, may be rapidly transmitted to his superior officers through the networks.

II. Management may use informal communication to clear up the ambiguities of a police operating procedure of importance to the entire department.

III. A superior officer may use the informal communication networks to give a subordinate personal advice that he believes he cannot give in his official capacity.

IV. The kind of information being transmitted through the networks discloses to management which subjects formal communications are not addressing as efficiently as possible.

Which of the following choices lists all of the uses of informal communications that are appropriate and beneficial and none that are not?

(A) Statements I, III, and IV are appropriate and beneficial uses, but II is not.

(B) Statements I, II, and IV are appropriate and beneficial uses, but III is not.

(C) Statements II and IV are appropriate and beneficial uses, but I and III are not.

(D) Statements III and IV are appropriate and beneficial uses, but I and II are not.

83. "No matter how elaborate a formal system of communication exists in an organization, the system will always be supplemented by informal channels of communication, such as the grapevine. Although such informal channels of communication are usually not highly regarded, they sometimes are of value to an organization." Of the following, the chief value of informal channels of communication is that they serve to

(A) transmit information that management has neglected to send through the formal system of communication.

(B) confirm information that has already been received via the formal channels.

(C) hinder the formation of employee cliques in the organization.

(D) revise information sent through the formal system of communication.

84. Which of the following statements should be considered *least* accurate as it applies to methods of reporting?

(A) When a written report is required to be forwarded, the best general rule is "the shorter the better."

(B)   It is more likely that one may get credit for ideas submitted in a written than in an oral report.

(C)   Oral reports are easier to use in passing on information accurately to others.

(D)   The time taken to prepare a written report may be less in the long run than the time needed to make an oral report in some situations.

85.   It would be most desirable to prepare a written order when the

(A)   order is temporary.

(B)   order is relatively simple.

(C)   accountability of the supervisor or the police officer receiving the order is a factor.

(D)   order will be carried out relatively soon after it is issued.

86.   The repeated use by a superior officer of a call for volunteers to get a job done is objectionable mainly because it

(A)   may create a feeling of animosity between the volunteers and the nonvolunteers.

(B)   may indicate that the supervisor is avoiding the responsibility to make assignments that will be most productive.

(C)   indicates that the supervisor is not familiar with the individual capabilities of his subordinates.

(D)   is unfair to officers who, for valid reasons, do not or cannot volunteer.

87.   In giving an order to a subordinate to perform a job, it is important for the police supervisor to decide upon the amount of explanatory detail that should be included in the order. Such a decision should be based mainly on the

(A)   complexity of the job as well as on the extent to which the subordinate is likely to resent detailed explanations.

(B)   complexity of the job as well as on the previous experience of the subordinate in performing this kind of work.

(C)   extent to which the subordinate is likely to resent detailed explanations as well as on the experience of the subordinate in performing this kind of work.

(D)   supervisor's own ability to explain orders clearly as well as on the complexity of the job.

88.   Some superior police officers frequently issue orders to subordinates in such a way that the order appears to be a request to perform a certain act rather than a direct order to perform it. This practice is generally

(A)   undesirable; this method of issuing orders never carries the same weight as a direct command and implies a lack of self-confidence on the part of the superior officer.

(B)   desirable; this method of issuing orders carries almost the same weight as a direct command and is less likely to antagonize subordinates.

(C)   undesirable; this method of issuing orders leaves it up to the subordinate to establish his own priority of performance when several tasks are involved.

(D)   desirable; this method of issuing orders allows the subordinate to determine for himself the precise method of carrying out the order.

89.   Continuously calling for volunteers for an unpopular assignment within the station house is generally a

(A)   good practice, chiefly because it encourages interaction and a spirit of cooperation among the subordinates.

(B)   poor practice, chiefly because this is actually an abdication by the supervisor of his or her role as a leader.

(C)   good practice, chiefly because relations within the station house should be relatively informal and nonauthoritarian.

(D)   poor practice, chiefly because it may induce an unhealthy rivalry in subordinates to compete for the supervisor's favors.

90. As opposed to the direct command, the implied order involves practically no directions. It is more of a suggestion. For example, instead of saying, "Tune up the motor," the supervisor might observe, "That motor didn't sound quite right on the last run." Of the following, the situation in which the implied order would be most appropriately used is the one in which

    (A) haste is important.
    (B) the order is intended for one specific person in a group.
    (C) satisfactory completion of the job requires high standards of performance.
    (D) it is desirable to encourage initiative and resourcefulness.

91. The good leader has the capacity not only to accept responsibility and to exercise initiative, but also to develop these traits in his or her subordinates. Of the following, the best method for a sergeant to use to encourage police officers to use initiative and assume responsibility is to

    (A) rotate routine assignments equally among all members of the squad.
    (B) employ suggestions or implied commands rather than direct commands in other than emergency situations.
    (C) encourage police officers to read books and take courses in leadership.
    (D) ask for volunteers to perform necessary duties.

92. "When issuing an order assigning a task to a subordinate, it is advisable for the supervisor to point out the facts or conditions that have made the order necessary." Of the following, the *least* valid justification for telling a subordinate "why" an order is being issued is to

    (A) avoid giving the subordinate the impression that the order is an arbitrary one.
    (B) give the subordinate a sense of responsibility in connection with the task to be done.
    (C) show the subordinate how the task fits the work of the unit.
    (D) delegate to the subordinate final responsibility for seeing that the work is done properly.

93. Of the following, the best general rule for a supervisory officer to follow is to assign work, whenever possible, on the basis of

    (A) individual abilities.
    (B) previous assignments.
    (C) the probable impact on morale.
    (D) seniority.

94. When assigning work to a subordinate, it is *least* essential for a supervisor to issue written instructions when the

    (A) supervisor will be on hand to check the work.
    (B) instructions are to be passed on to other employees.
    (C) assignment involves many details.
    (D) subordinate is to be held strictly accountable for the work performed.

95. Some management authorities propose that work assignments be made by assigning a varied set of tasks to a group of employees and then allowing the group to decide for itself how to organize the work to be done. This method of assigning work is called "job enlargement." Which of the following is considered the chief advantage of job enlargement?

    (A) Employees are encouraged to specialize in the work they are assigned to accomplish.
    (B) The amount of control that employees have over their work is reduced.
    (C) The employees' job satisfaction is increased.
    (D) The number of skills that each employee is required to learn is reduced.

ANSWERS TO QUESTIONS ON COMMUNICATIONS AND GIVING ORDERS

66. **The correct answer is (D).** The reappraisal may well indicate that the supervisor is not a good listener, or has little appreciation of the fact that employees are "persons" who have needs and aspirations.

67. **The correct answer is (A).** Policy is not, nor should it be, developed at all levels. Policy comes down from the very top of the agency.

68. **The correct answer is (A).** Yes, absolutely! The "Hey you" approach is demeaning, impersonal, and often leads to justified resentment by the officer.

69. **The correct answer is (B).** This is a good question that should not cause a problem for the careful reader. The question concerns itself with "horizontal communication." Answer choices (A), (C), and (D) are concerned with vertical (up-down) communications. Only choice (B) talks about an exchange of information between officers of the same rank.

70. **The correct answer is (B).** Tough question, but the word "should" in choice (B), if properly assessed, should have made it a little easier. It's difficult to argue with a statement that supports reducing time and improving quality of understanding.

71. **The correct answer is (D).** The larger the span of control, the fewer the organizational layers. For example, if a large department store had just one boss (no intermediate managers, section chiefs, etc.), then communication would be direct because there would be no intermediaries. Each supervisory layer increases the distance between the top boss and those involved at the level of execution.

72. **The correct answer is (C).** There will be no effective communication without the presence of an ability and willingness to listen.

73. **The correct answer is (D).** The question relates to the "day-to-day work routine." The sergeant should not permit one individual, possibly with his own agenda, to act as spokesman.

74. **The correct answer is (B).** An easy one! Look at some of the words in the other choices: (A), "all," (B), "privately," and (D), "regularly." Remember, we are talking about praise.

75. **The correct answer is (B).** The supervisor is not taking advantage of an opportunity to engage in face-to-face communication, to get to know his people, and to create a positive tone between himself and the sergeants.

76. **The correct answer is (D).** No one could accuse this sergeant of being a good listener or of encouraging healthy communications.

77. **The correct answer is (B).** This one factor should determine the structure and content of the speech.

78. **The correct answer is (D).** This is a good question that very pragmatically tells us what "filtering" is all about. In years gone by, if the news was bad, then the messenger was killed.

79. **The correct answer is (D).** Yes, by listening and responding, the good supervisor will enable many (not all) to understand and solve their own job-related problems.

80. **The correct answer is (B).** Look for the most accurate statement. Distortion does often occur in messages carried through the "grapevine" or informal network.

81. **The correct answer is (A).** By determining what is being said and why, management is then in a position to respond. Remember, the antidote to rumor is fact!

82. **The correct answer is (A).** A time-consuming but easy question. Look at the language in some of the choices: "may be rapidly transmitted," (I), "may use," (III), and "can be useful," (IV). *Can* and *may* are "safe" words. Information that is important to the entire department should be formally communicated.

83. **The correct answer is (A).** The grapevine exists to the extent that the formal system has failed to give sufficient information to satisfy the reasonable curiosity of the employees.

84. **The correct answer is (C).** Oral reports may save time, but are not overly reliable in passing accurate information to others.

85. **The correct answer is (C).** Choices (A), (B), and (D) indicate the order is simple, temporary, and immediate. Choice (C) considers the holding of someone "accountable" for carrying it out.

86.	**The correct answer is (B).** The "repeated" use of the call for volunteers may be an avoidance of responsibility to be the boss. Supervisors are duty-bound to fit the officer to the job and to assign work fairly.

87.	**The correct answer is (B).** The complexity of the task coupled with the ability of the subordinate would be controlling factors. Remember, treat workers as individuals who have different skills and different needs.

88.	**The correct answer is (B).** The request is the most frequently used kind of order. A request is a courteous approach and is almost always enough to get the job done.

89.	**The correct answer is (B).** The boss should "be the boss" and get things done through people. It is the supervisor's job to direct, coordinate efforts, and issue appropriate orders.

90.	**The correct answer is (D).** Implied orders should be given to employees who readily accept responsibility. These kinds of orders encourage initiative and the acceptance of responsibility.

91.	**The correct answer is (B).** See the explanation for question 90; the reasoning is the same.

92.	**The correct answer is (D).** "Responsibility" remains with the boss. A supervisor may hold a subordinate accountable for a delegated assignment but final responsibility cannot be delegated.

93.	**The correct answer is (A).** "Fit the officer to the job."

94.	**The correct answer is (A).** Follow-up will be immediate and, if needed, corrections can be made promptly.

95.	**The correct answer is (C).** Group participation, joint effort, and "participative management" all increase job satisfaction.

QUESTIONS ON EVALUATIONS AND RATINGS

> **Directions:** Read each question and choose the best answer. Circle the letter of your choice.

96. Lieutenant Connolly has just completed evaluating the performance of Sergeant Mullins. Mullins, who is very popular with his peers, has been found below standard in two areas. Lieutenant Connolly, in his evaluation interview with Mullins, should

    (A) tell Sergeant Mullins that other sergeants were also below standard and he should not get upset over the situation.
    (B) go over the evaluation informally so as to downgrade the importance of the rating.
    (C) ask Sergeant Mullins, at the end of the interview, to sum up his understanding of the evaluation and what is expected of him in the future.
    (D) encourage Sergeant Mullins to improve his value to the department by concentrating on those areas in which he seems to do best.

97. You are conducting a performance appraisal interview with an officer under your direct supervision. The officer vehemently disputes a critical comment you make about his past performance. Of the following, the most appropriate action for you to take in this situation would be to

    (A) support your comment with a specific example documented in the employee's work record and make constructive suggestions on how the officer can improve.
    (B) stop discussing the matter and direct remaining comments to the officer's strong points.
    (C) apologize to the officer for making the comment and explain that making such observations is a necessary part of your job.
    (D) avoid further discussion of the matter but make an entry in the officer's personnel record about his sensitivity to criticism.

98. The most common rating error is

    (A) central tendency.
    (B) leniency.
    (C) the halo effect.
    (D) the error of subjectivity.

99. Lieutenant Nunno is in the process of preparing a required evaluation report for Sergeant Ryan, one of his subordinates. The lieutenant is favorably impressed with the amount of enthusiasm displayed by the sergeant in accepting job assignments. Based on this, the lieutenant assumes that the sergeant has a great deal of job knowledge and rates him "above standards" in that trait. The rating error committed by the lieutenant would be most properly referred to as

   (A) critical incidents.
   (B) the halo effect.
   (C) a logical error.
   (D) error of overweighting.

100. A useful performance evaluation procedure should include a discussion between the superior and the subordinate about that evaluation. The following are three techniques that may or may not be desirable in such discussions:

   I. The subordinate's strong points should be acknowledged initially and his or her weaknesses discussed in specific and objective terms.

   II. A comparison should be made between the performance of the subordinate and that of the other members of the unit.

   III. The superior should apologize for any problems that may have been caused by his supervisory methods.

   Which of the following choices best classifies the above techniques?
   (A) Statement I is generally desirable, but II and III are not.
   (B) Statements I and II are generally desirable, but III is not.
   (C) Statements I and III are generally desirable, but II is not.
   (D) Statements II and III are generally desirable, but I is not.

101. On February 15, 1990, P.O. Ruth McLoughlin arrested one John Loftus for the crime of murder. Loftus had been wanted by this department, the F.B.I., and several other police departments throughout the country. The arrest was effected while Officer McLoughlin was performing routine patrol under the supervision of Sergeant Rutledge. As a result of the arrest, a great deal of positive publicity and recognition was directed at the officer, the sergeant, and the command. For several months before the date of the arrest, P.O. McLoughlin's performance had been average. On March 7, 1990, Sergeant Rutledge submitted a semiannual evaluation report on Officer McLoughlin and, mindful of her outstanding arrest, evaluated her more on the basis of the arrest than on her actual long-term contribution to the work unit and the department. Sergeant Rutledge is guilty of the rating error known as the error of

   (A) subjectivity.
   (B) leniency.
   (C) central tendency.
   (D) overweighting.

102. It is a formal procedure that identifies characteristics or dimensions in a person who has applied for a position or is interested in administrative advancement. The procedure incorporates group and individual exercises where the participant's behavior is evaluated by trained personnel. It is called

   (A) a diagnostic forced choice evaluation.
   (B) an assessment center.
   (C) role playing.
   (D) a personnel conference.

103. "The error of leniency is by far the most common of all errors in the rating of personnel." Evaluate the following statements about the error of leniency:

   I. This tendency to overrate has a damaging effect on the morale of the truly outstanding workers.

II. The error of leniency has a tendency to spread rapidly from one supervisor to another that feels compelled to overrate his subordinates so that they may compete favorably with others who have been rated too highly by an overly lenient supervisor.

III. A supervisor is likely to "overrate" his subordinates if they will see their ratings, or if the supervisor is defensive and feels that he is protecting a deficient employee.

(A) All the statements are valid.
(B) None of the statements are valid.
(C) Statement I is valid, but II and III are not.
(D) Statements I and II are valid, but III is not.

104. You are conducting a periodic performance evaluation interview with one of your subordinates. Without being asked, the officer defensively describes his own shortcomings and then states that he believes these problems are due to your poor supervisory methods. Which of the following is the best action for you to take in this situation?

(A) Tell the officer that your supervisory methods can best be discussed at a later time since this discussion is being held to assess his performance.
(B) Apologize to the officer for any part your methods may have played in causing his problems, but gently return the focus of the discussion to his performance.
(C) Ask the officer to explain what he means, since his comments may give you a better insight into the effect of your supervisory methods.
(D) State that you are sorry that you may have been the cause of some of the officer's problems and seek his aid in improving your supervisory methods.

105. Captain Farrell is in the process of formally rating Sergeant Peterman. The captain knows that Sergeant Peterman is a good worker and consequently groups all the ratings for Sergeant Peterman at the high end of the scale. Captain Farrell is guilty of the rating error known as the

(A) error of related traits.
(B) halo effect.
(C) error of subjectivity.
(D) error of central tendency.

106. As a supervisor, you are continually evaluating the performance of your subordinates. Of the following choices, the major objective of such performance evaluation should be to

(A) serve as the basis for the assignment of duties to subordinates.
(B) aid in the improvement of employee effectiveness.
(C) provide data upon which to decide who is eligible.
(D) furnish standards against which the performance of all employees may be compared.

107. Of the following, the most important reason for a supervisor to have private, face-to-face discussions with subordinates about their performance is to

(A) help employees improve their work.
(B) give special praise to employees who perform well.
(C) encourage the employees to compete for higher performance ratings.
(D) discipline employees who perform poorly.

108. The one of the following methods that would best ensure that employees perform up to their capacity is for the supervisor to

(A) encourage workers to keep their ideas to themselves.
(B) avoid insisting upon absolute truthfulness about the job because no one is perfect.
(C) demand "hard" details from your subordinates about their performance in order to get the most accurate information.
(D) keep a "hands-off" policy if workers come to you with suggestions in order to avoid the appearance of favoritism.

109. After her first contact with a new employee, the best way for a supervisor to maintain further contact with the employee during the initial period of employment is to

    (A) meet with him as often as with established employees, no more and no less.
    (B) discuss the employee's work with him when he is doing good work, but not when he is doing bad work.
    (C) avoid contact with the new employee.
    (D) make provisions for frequent conferences with the new employee.

110. Suppose that you are approached by a usually reliable fellow lieutenant, "Smith," who informs you that one of your subordinates, "Jones," is doing a generally poor job. The *first* action you should take is to

    (A) tell Smith you will check the matter yourself.
    (B) go to the floor and reprimand Jones immediately.
    (C) call Jones to your office as soon as possible to discuss the problem with both Jones and Smith.
    (D) chastise Smith for his action, but investigate Jones's performance.

111. A certain sergeant has difficulty in effectively performing a particular portion of his routine assignments, but his overall productivity is average. As the direct supervisor of this individual, a lieutenant's best course of action would be to

    (A) attempt to develop the sergeant's capacity to execute the problematical facets of his assignments.
    (B) diversify the sergeant's work assignments in order to build up his confidence.
    (C) reassign the sergeant to less difficult tasks.
    (D) request in a private conversation that the sergeant improve his work output.

112. Assume that you are a supervisor in charge of a subordinate who may be abusing sick leave. Under the circumstances, the *first* thing you should do is to

    (A) interview the subordinate to find out what is wrong.
    (B) prepare a calendar of sick leave used by the subordinate to see if a pattern develops indicating abuse.
    (C) warn the subordinate against any further malingering.
    (D) institute corrective disciplinary action the very next time the subordinate reports sick.

113. Assume that you are in charge of a squad. One officer has been performing ineffectively, although he has been working hard. All attempts to improve his performance have failed and he is nearing the end of his probationary period. In these circumstances, it is best to

    (A) reschedule assignments so that the rest of the squad takes over a greater share of the workload.
    (B) recommend separation on the grounds that improvement cannot be achieved.
    (C) leave the officer alone, since he seems to be doing the best he can.
    (D) assign only the simplest cases to the officer.

114. If, as a rater, you especially favor one or two characteristics and, as a result, subordinates who demonstrate those characteristics are rated higher by you, then you have committed the error known as

    (A) central tendency.
    (B) the halo effect.
    (C) subjectivity.
    (D) personal bias.

115. As a rater, you give a higher rating to those subordinates who think like yourself. You have committed the error known as

    (A) central tendency.
    (B) the halo effect.
    (C) subjectivity.
    (D) personal bias.

ANSWERS TO QUESTIONS ON EVALUATIONS AND RATINGS

96. **The correct answer is (C).** There must be a meeting of the minds about what the lieutenant expects and the sergeant's understanding of that expectation.

97. **The correct answer is (A).** Documentation of incidents is one way to reduce subjectivity and, at the same time, to shift the burden from the evaluator to the person being evaluated.

98. **The correct answer is (B).** Leniency is the most common rating error.

99. **The correct answer is (C).** The lieutenant appears to be equating enthusiasm with knowledge. These attributes are not necessarily related. This kind of error is also known as an error of related traits or association error.

100. **The correct answer is (A).** Statement I is right on the money. Statement II, where you compare the work of one person to that of another, is not acceptable. The focus should be on the one being rated and not someone else. Statement III, "apologize for any problems…" is not appropriate.

101. **The correct answer is (D).** A good practical description of the error of overweighting (undue influence on the basis of an action, good or bad, which occurs near the end of the rating period).

102. **The correct answer is (B).** A textbook definition of an assessment center. Assessment centers may, and often do, last for several days.

103. **The correct answer is (A).** These are three well-stated reasons that support the position that leniency is the most common rating error and explain why. Another reason is, "If the people I rate receive low ratings, might it not reflect poorly on my ability to train and provide proper leadership?"

104. **The correct answer is (C).** A typical kind of question that allows the boss to take a look at the boss; a kind of self-inspection.

105. **The correct answer is (B).** The question states that the sergeant "knows." A good inference is that this is a general impression.

106. **The correct answer is (B).** This is the major objective of evaluations *as well as* of good communication, training, and discipline. The objective is to "get the job done through people."

107. **The correct answer is (A).** Look at the preceding question and its answer.

108. **The correct answer is (C).** Should you settle for "soft" details in order to obtain accurate information?

109. **The correct answer is (D).** Remember, you should treat employees according to their needs, strengths, and weaknesses (not equally). During the "initial period of employment," the new employee may be in need of frequent contacts with the supervisor.

110. **The correct answer is (A).** In effect, you are taking the position of "thanks for your interest, but they are my people and I'll take a look at it. " (You steer your ship and Smith can steer his ship.)

111. **The correct answer is (A).** Keep trying. This is an average employee who is having a problem in a certain area.

112. **The correct answer is (B).** Do your homework before the interview. If you like choice (A) as an answer, you are assuming something is "wrong."

113. **The correct answer is (B).** This describes a "probationary" employee who is ineffective and "all attempts to improve performance have failed." The police force cannot retain an ineffective officer.

114. **The correct answer is (C).** One or two characteristics you favor translates into the error of subjectivity.

115. **The correct answer is (D).** The statement, "who think the way you do" is easily equated with "subscribe to the same platform."

QUESTIONS ON CONFERENCES

> **Directions:** Read each question and choose the best answer. Circle the letter of your choice.

116. A conference is defined as an interchange of views between persons with common problems. In view of this definition, which of the following is the *least* accurate of the following statements?

(A) A conference is a problem-solving device.

(B) Conference makeup should be a randomly selected cross section of the organization.

(C) A conference utilizes the collective knowledge of well-qualified persons.

(D) Solutions to problems that affect an organization can often be found by means of a conference.

117. A conference is a mutual consultation involving the pooling of ideas and experiences of selected individuals for the purpose of analyzing problems and seeking solutions to them. Consider the following three statements about conferences, which may or may not be correct:

I.   Conference participants from the same organization should range in rank from the highest to the lowest within the organization so as to obtain a well-rounded view of problems.

II. Conference participants should have had some common experiences with the kind of problem selected for discussion.

III. A conference that results in clearly understood disagreement may by just as fruitful as a conference in which all agree.

Of the following choices, which most accurately describes the above statements?

(A) All three statements are correct.

(B) Only statement I is incorrect.

(C) Only statement II is correct.

(D) Only statement III is correct.

118. Which of the following statements is *least* accurate as it relates to conferences?

(A) A conference is one of the most efficient and effective ways of imparting new knowledge and developing skills.

(B) A serious conference limitation is the dearth of skillful conference leaders.

(C) Most reasons for conference failure can be eliminated by practice.

(D) The expert conference leader will conduct the conference in an informal, impersonal manner.

119. Which statement below is *least* accurate as far as the conference leader is concerned?

(A) He should realize that group knowledge of the subject under discussion is superior to his own.

(B) He must summarize contributions and crystallize opinions.

(C) He should realize that if the conferees believe the problem at hand has already been solved, the conference may fail.

(D) He should act as the expert when strong disagreement takes place among conferees.

120. The degree of success of a conference is closely related to the planning done by the leader. Good planning maximizes accomplishment. Consider the following three statements, which may or may not be correct:

I. The most important element in conference planning is the discussion plan.

II. A conference plan should not suggest the objectives to be accomplished since this is within the realm of the conferees.

III. Probable questions from the conferees should be anticipated so that the leader can research them and decide on correct answers to them.

Which of the following choices most accurately describes the above statements?

(A) All three statements are correct.

(B) Statements I and III are correct, but II is not.

(C) Statements I and II are correct, but III is not.

(D) Statements II and III are incorrect, but I is correct.

121. Which of the following statements is *least* accurate?

(A) In planning for a conference, the leader should list possible conclusions with suitable alternatives.

(B) The conference problem should be clearly stated by the conference leader.

(C) The conference problem should be stated in positive rather than negative terms.

(D) As the conference progresses, the leader should evaluate and summarize the contributions made by conferees.

122. A good conference leader can be distinguished from a poor one by the quality of his or her follow-up questions and the timing with which they are employed. When a conference leader directs a question to an entire group that might be answerable by any member by voluntary response, the question is called

(A) an overhead question.

(B) a directed question.

(C) a reverse question.

(D) a relay question.

123. Most experts would agree that

(A) the conference leader should not appraise the conferees prior to the conference being held.

(B) an over-talkative conference member may be utilized positively by giving him the task of summarizing contributions.

(C) the conference leader should force the reticent conference member to take part in discussion by directing difficult questions to him so that he is forced to think.

(D) it is never a good practice to ignore remarks made by a conferee.

124. Consider the following four statements:

I. The subject matter is poorly selected.

II. A poorly introduced subject fails to state the real problem.

III. The discussion of the problem has been exhausted.

IV. Improperly selected participants lack appropriate backgrounds in the subject matter.

The statements above that are the predominant cause of a lack of interest in the conference discussion are

(A) Statements I, II, III, and IV.
(B) Statements I, II, and III, but not IV.
(C) Statements III and IV, but not I and II.
(D) Statements I and II, but not III and IV.

125. Of the following statements, which is the most inaccurate as it relates to conferences and conference procedures?

(A) The conference leader may find it necessary to represent conferees' interests to management.
(B) Statements made in the conference setting usually should be treated as confidential.
(C) Each member of a conference group has a responsibility to participate in achieving the conference objectives.
(D) Physical facilities are not important to the success of a conference.

126. Which of the following statements concerning staff meetings is *least* accurate?

(A) They do not generally provide an opportunity for training subordinate personnel.
(B) They are useful in passing on new information and in solving problems within the organization.
(C) When properly handled they are without equal as a means of developing coordination and integrating efforts.
(D) Every supervisor should take advantage of staff meetings for training.

127. The most effective staff meeting is

(A) an autocratically controlled assembly.
(B) a democratically led conference.
(C) the one held as a training session.
(D) the one held as a benevolent dictatorship.

128. As a superior officer you may find it necessary to conduct meetings with your subordinates. Of the following, which would be most helpful in assuring that a meeting accomplishes the purpose for which it was called?

(A) Give notice of the conclusions you would like to reach at the start of the meeting.
(B) Delay the start of the meeting until everyone is present.
(C) Write down points to be discussed in proper sequence.
(D) Make sure everyone is clear on whatever conclusions have been reached and on what must be done after the meeting.

129. Assume that you are a training conference leader and that you have just begun a series of conferences on supervisory techniques for new supervisors. Each is scheduled for 3 hours. A thorough discussion of all the material planned for the first session, which you had estimated would last until 4 P.M., is completed by 3:30 P.M. For you to summarize the points that have been made and close the meeting would be

(A) advisable; the participants will lose interest in the conference if it is permitted to continue merely to occupy the remaining time.
(B) inadvisable; the participants should be asked if there are any other topics they would like to discuss.
(C) advisable; the participants in a training conference should not be kept from their regular work for long periods of time unless necessary.
(D) inadvisable; material scheduled for discussion at future sessions should be used for the remainder of this session.

130. During a staff conference being held to help solve an important problem, it becomes apparent to the superior officer conducting the conference that one particular officer is talking too much and is discouraging the other officers present from participating actively in the conference. The one of the following actions that the superior officer should take at this time is to

(A) allow this officer to talk freely at this conference, but later take him aside and inform him that the other participants are entitled to a chance to express their views.

(B) allow this officer to talk freely at this conference but later point out to the other participants individually that they should participate more fully in future conferences.

(C) interrupt this officer as politely as possible and summarize what he has been talking about.

(D) interrupt this officer as politely as possible and ask the other participants for their views.

131. Captain Connolly, a precinct commander in a racially mixed neighborhood, is desirous of instituting some new and innovative programs in an effort to alleviate police-community tensions. The captain conducts a meeting with all available sergeants and lieutenants assigned to the command. During the meeting the captain directs rapid-fire questions (for which he demands spontaneous answers) at the sergeants and lieutenants. All of the answers that are offered are reduced to writing by a clerical person. The most important result of the captain's approach is that

(A) the captain will be able to identify those supervisors who have the ability to "think on their feet."

(B) the approach may elicit thoughts and ideas that might not otherwise be verbalized by the supervisors concerned.

(C) it will ensure that the problem is the center of focus during the meeting.

(D) the approach provides training in a participative climate.

132. "Conferences should be conducted in a businesslike manner in order to utilize the time of all members to best advantage. Participants should leave the meeting with a feeling of accomplishment and renewed interest in their work." Of the following, which set of practices is most likely to achieve the objectives of the above quotation?

(A) Conferences should be formal, wherever possible, with compulsory attendance, and every item should be clearly outlined and resolved by the chief.

(B) An agenda should be prepared in advance, the discussion of divergent views encouraged, and a clearly understood conclusion reached on each item of business.

(C) Discussion should be under control and related only to the agenda items, with each item resolved to a conclusion without discussion of divergent opinions.

(D) The membership of the conference should be given ample time and occasions to air their grievances and to discuss other matters in which they have an interest.

133. It has been proposed that members of a conference should be provided with an agenda prior to the convening of the conference. Such a procedure would be

(A) advisable; all participants will be intimidated if the agenda is hidden.

(B) inadvisable; only spontaneous responses are consistent with acceptable problem-solving techniques.

(C) advisable; the conferees will have time to give thought to the items that need to be discussed.

(D) inadvisable; secrecy of the agenda is a prerequisite for a successful conference.

134. A certain district, under the command of Captain Piacquadio, has been changing ethnically. At the same time, crime rates have risen steadily. Police officers in the district, who had always gotten along well with civilians, are experiencing ugly encounters and civilian complaints. Everyone in the district is aware of the problem. The problem reaches a crisis when Captain Piacquadio is summoned to headquarters for a lengthy meeting. Departmental rumors report that the captain has been told very strongly that his district must shape up or else. When he returns from the meeting he says nothing about the meeting, but the next day calls a staff meeting of lieutenants and sergeants. Without heat, he tells them that the district has a serious and difficult problem to handle, but that he is confident that together they have the brains and leadership to work out the solution. He proceeds to conduct a discussion of how to solve the problem.

Which one of the following choices most correctly indicates whether the situation was handled properly and gives the best reason?

(A) His handling is improper because he is falsely creating a feeling of calmness and confidence that cannot exist.

(B) His handling is proper because his calmness and confidence are more likely to help the lieutenants and sergeants solve the problem than any other attitude.

(C) His handling is improper because he has failed to create in his subordinates the atmosphere of tension that is necessary to step up performance.

(D) His handling is improper because, by his calmness and lack of emotion, he has failed to convey to his subordinates the full urgency of the situation.

135. One of the tools of the administrator in the performance of his varied functions involving planning and direction is the conference. Of the following choices, which is the *least* important criterion in determining the effectiveness of a conference after it has been held?

(A) Amount of disagreement with the decisions reached at the conference
(B) Positive results achieved at the conference
(C) Ability to arrive at a full solution to the problem at hand
(D) Satisfaction of participating members with the conference

ANSWERS TO QUESTIONS ON CONFERENCES

116. **The correct answer is (B).** The conferees should be carefully selected. One of the reasons conferences fail is the "improper or careless selection of conference members."

117. **The correct answer is (B).** When conference participants are from the same organization they should be at or about the same rank. If not, the discussion could easily become stifled. *Reminder*: Read the answer choices carefully.

118. **The correct answer is (A).** A conference is time-consuming and is not a good device for training and imparting new knowledge. *Note*: There is a big difference between "effective" and "efficient." This question demands both.

119. **The correct answer is (D).** The conference leader should not be the "expert" at the conference. It is the group's knowledge from which the expertise is drawn.

120. **The correct answer is (D).** The conference plan should suggest the objectives to be accomplished, and probable questions from the conferees should be anticipated, but *answers* should come from the group.

121. **The correct answer is (D).** Be careful here. If the conference leader "evaluates" a contribution, then he or she is abandoning a neutral position. It is important to summarize, not to evaluate.

122. **The correct answer is (A).** Choice (A) describes an overhead question. A directed question is aimed at a specific person for a response. A reverse question is a situation wherein the conference leader gives back the question to the person who asked it. A relay question is directed to the leader, who then relays it to another in the group.

123. **The correct answer is (B).** Choice (B) is the only acceptable statement and the question could be answered based on the notes preceding these questions.

124. **The correct answer is (B).** This is a tough question. Statements I, II, and III may correctly be categorized as predominant causes of lack of interest. Statement IV, however, would more likely result in shallow conclusions and a general lack of interest.

125. **The correct answer is (D).** This is an easy, common-sense question. It would be difficult to support a position that "Physical facilities are not important. "

126. **The correct answer is (A).** A well-conducted meeting with one's subordinates provides a great opportunity for training.

127. **The correct answer is (B).** This should have been an easy question. Do not allow this opportunity for training and sharing to degenerate into a "show and tell" where the boss merely tells or directs.

128. **The correct answer is (D).** The decisions and/or conclusions must be followed up.

129. **The correct answer is (A).** The question tells us that a "thorough" discussion of "all" the material planned has been completed. Prolonging discussion will lead to loss of interest and may even hinder follow-through.

130. **The correct answer is (D).** The purpose of a conference is to obtain input from all of the participants. The views of the other participants are essential and the conference leader must allow them to be heard.

131. **The correct answer is (B).** This effective technique is known as "brainstorming."

132. **The correct answer is (B).** This question should not have been difficult for you. Choice (A) suggests "resolved by the chief," choice (C) suggests "without discussion," and choice (D) suggests "discuss other matters."

133. **The correct answer is (C).** Participants who have time to think about problems will not arrive at the meeting cold.

134. **The correct answer is (B).** This question is an easy one and tells us that the captain believed in a democratic style and participative management.

135. **The correct answer is (C).** A "full" solution to the problem may not be possible. But the seriousness of the problem may be highlighted and the need for additional effort brought to the attention of those in positions of authority.

QUESTIONS ON PATROL

> **Directions:** Read each question and choose the best answer. Circle the letter of your choice.

136. Patrol is an indispensable service that plays a leading role in the accomplishment of the police purpose. In keeping with this statement, which of the following choices is *correct*?

    (A) Patrol aids in crime suppression by reducing the criminal's desire to commit the crime or misdeed.
    (B) The maintaining of patrol in unmarked vehicles is of great assistance in the projection of the omnipresence of patrol.
    (C) The police purpose referred to in the above is the supervision of public gatherings and affairs.
    (D) Crime is reduced by the projection of the threat of apprehension and subsequent prosecution.

137. Since police patrol activity is not able to eliminate all opportunities for criminal behavior, the patrol force procedure that is generally regarded as most desirable is to

    (A) assign the entire available patrol force to those areas that have the greatest incidence of crimes.
    (B) attempt to give an impression of omnipresence at every hour and in all sections of the community.
    (C) devote its major efforts to the creation of wholesome influences in a community.
    (D) keep a substantial patrol force in reserve to answer specific complaints received from the public.

138. The basic purpose of patrol is most effectively implemented by police activity that

    (A) influences favorably individual and group activities in routine daily associations with the police.
    (B) intensifies the potential offender's expectation of apprehension.
    (C) lessens the potential offender's desire to commit a crime.
    (D) provides for many types of specialized patrol with less emphasis on routine patrol service.

139. It has been said that police patrol should aim at giving the impression of omnipresence. Which of the following is the primary reason for this statement?

    (A) Planning for successful theft must be prolonged by the potential offender's expectation of apprehension.
    (B) The potential thief's desire to steal is diminished by the presence of a uniformed officer.
    (C) The potential thief's belief in the opportunity for successful theft is diminished by his expectation of apprehension.
    (D) The potential thief's desire to steal is diminished by his expectation of apprehension.

140. When properly performed, patrol plays a leading role in the accomplishment of the police purpose of crime prevention chiefly by

    (A) apprehending offenders and impressing them with the omnipresence of the police.
    (B) being the only form of police service that directly attempts to eliminate the opportunities for crime.
    (C) gaining public support by the prompt investigation of offenses and recovery of stolen property.
    (D) influencing public attitudes against crime in its routine daily associations with the public.

141. The theory of police patrol which, if properly applied, should be the greatest deterrent to crime favors patrolling

    (A) all areas so as to make the police officers as inconspicuous as possible.
    (B) all areas so to attract the maximum of attention to the police.
    (C) areas of high incidence of crime in an obvious manner and on a frequent and fixed schedule.
    (D) areas of low incidence of crime obviously and irregularly and areas of high incidence of crime on an irregular schedule and attracting a minimum of attention.

142. "Specialization in the performance of administrative planning duties is not an example of an undesirable specialization of duty being made at the expense of the patrol force." This statement is generally

    (A) false; specialization of any kind inevitably results in some depletion of the patrol force.
    (B) true; specialization is desirable to the extent that it efficiently performs part of the actual patrol duty.
    (C) false; this type of duty can be performed efficiently by the individual patrol sergeant.
    (D) true; these duties cannot be performed by police officers in the course of their regular patrols.

143. In order to provide the smoothly running law enforcement program essential to the accomplishment of the total police purpose, police experts generally agree that the best organized police force

    (A) considers policing to be a task for specialists with patrol duties being a specialized service on a par with any other specialized service.
    (B) uses the force on patrol primarily to assist the special services to perform their crime prevention and detection duties more expeditiously.
    (C) gives joint and equal responsibility for the accomplishment of each phase of the total police job to both the force on patrol duty and the special services.
    (D) considers policing to be essentially a patrol service with specialized activities developed as aids to this service.

144. It has been said that the plans and tactics devised by administrators to solve police problems depend heavily on the patrol force. This is true chiefly because the patrol force

    (A) serves as the principal source of trained manpower for the special services units.
    (B) contains the largest number of officers assigned to any one specific function.
    (C) serves as the eyes and ears of the administrator in the gathering and reporting of essential information.
    (D) bears the ultimate responsibility for safeguarding the community from criminals.

145. Whenever new tasks and duties are assigned to the police force, the question arises whether they should be assigned to the regular patrol force or to a specialized unit. It would be most desirable in such a situation for the new tasks and duties to be assigned to give the

    (A) regular patrol force all tasks and duties that it can perform substantially as well as if done by specialists and that do not interfere with regular patrol duties.
    (B) specialized units all tasks and duties that they can perform as efficiently as the regular patrol force.
    (C) regular patrol force only those tasks and duties that are clearly in keeping with patrol duties and that are of a nonspecialized nature.
    (D) specialized units all those tasks and duties that are of a specialized nature regardless of their relationship to regular patrol duties.

146. The importance of the patrol force and the innumerable variety of the tasks it performs for the public cannot be overemphasized. However, from the point of view of the administration of a department, the patrol force has specific obligations. Evaluate the following statements:

    I.   It must function as the "eyes and ears" of the administrator.
    II. It is the backbone of the department, the frame around which all other units are arranged in subordinate postures.
    III. Patrol is responsible for the total police job, and in small departments having no specialization, it actually performs all police tasks.
    (A) Only statements I and II are correct.
    (B) Only statements II and III are correct.
    (C) All three statements are correct.
    (D) Only statements I and III are correct.

147. It has been recommended that police officers perform many tasks in connection with the preliminary investigation of a crime primarily because

    (A) the police officers can conserve the time and energy of detectives for duties that require their special skill and abilities.
    (B) they are generally better qualified to conduct preliminary interrogations of suspects and witnesses.
    (C) preliminary investigation provides an ideal training ground for developing crime-detecting techniques.
    (D) such practice aids considerably in promoting needed coordination between the patrol and detective branches of police service.

148. Statistical studies usually reveal a slump in police activity just before the end of a tour of duty. This seeming slump is likely, however, to reflect a decrease in police activity at this time rather than an actual decrease in the need for police service. The *least* likely explanation for the decrease in police activity just before the end of a tour of duty is

    (A) a tendency on the part of the individual police officer not to initiate action just before going off duty if it might interfere with his reporting back to the station house at the termination of his tour.

    (B) an awareness on the part of law violators as to the time and manner of police officers reporting to and from duty.

    (C) a tendency on the part of the dispatcher to assign cases or complaints received during the last hour of his shift to the detail of officers about to go on duty.

    (D) fatigue at the end of a tour of duty that probably results in a diminution of activity.

149. "Setting aside the actual issue of legality and the highly emotional issue of discrimination, the public at large receives substantial benefits when a carefully articulated, well-conceived field interrogation program is executed with discretion by patrol force personnel." Select the choice that is *not* a value of this practice.

    (A) A written field interrogation report may be valuable later to disprove an alibi.

    (B) Traffic violations may be uncovered.

    (C) Criminals may be discouraged.

    (D) Shabbily dressed persons can be questioned and made to feel welcome in the community.

150. "The police officer is the ultimate in the decentralization of municipal service." Of the following, the chief justification for this statement is that

    (A) the police officer plays a leading role in the accomplishment of the police purpose.

    (B) the police officer provides an unfavorable influence for the potential violator.

    (C) the availability and mobility of the police officer makes his services useful to other city agencies as well as to the police department.

    (D) the patrol force is practically without limit in its responsibility for police service.

151. The police officer performs a wide variety of public services while on duty. Most requests for these services originate

    (A) with citizens who request such services in person.

    (B) from the actions of alert officers who observe conditions and situations requiring attention.

    (C) with citizens who telephone headquarters.

    (D) with local pressure groups who fail to see the true functions of the police in a democratic society.

152. The development of effective police canine programs in this country has been a slow process "because of probable adverse public reaction to dogs in police work." The sensitive police administrator should recognize the inherent limitations of dogs in police work and plan canine patrol operations accordingly. The sensitive police administrator should realize that canine patrols should *not* be used

    (A) in crowd control or riot situations.

    (B) for search purposes.

    (C) to detect contraband.

    (D) to track down missing or wanted persons.

153. Erroneously, officers see the concept of community oriented policing as being a social work program and not real police work. The strength of community oriented policing and of solving crimes lies in:

I.   the overall improvement of communities.

II. citizen involvement not only with the police department but also with their own well-being.

III. officers being able to autonomously deal with social issues and obtain results, improving the quality of life in the community.

(A) Only statement I is correct.

(B) Only statements I and II are correct.

(C) Only statements II and III are correct.

(D) All three statements are correct.

ANSWERS TO QUESTIONS ON PATROL

136. **The correct answer is (D).** The desire by one so inclined to commit a crime is not diminished by the omnipresence concept. What is diminished is the potential criminal's belief that he will not be detected. Unmarked cars do not enhance the sense of omnipresence.

137. **The correct answer is (B).** Trying to give the impression of omnipresence ("they're all over the place") at all times and in all places is consistent with preventive patrol.

138. **The correct answer is (B).** One who has a high expectation of detection and apprehension is less likely to commit a crime.

139. **The correct answer is (C).** See the two preceding questions.

140. **The correct answer is (B).** This choice does not say that patrol "eliminates," but it merely points out that it attempts to eliminate opportunities for crime.

141. **The correct answer is (B).** This approach is consistent with the concept of omnipresence.

142. **The correct answer is (D).** Administrative planning is a must and specialization for this kind of function is a good way to go.

143. **The correct answer is (D).** Patrol is the backbone of the total force and most specialized units are in place to aid the patrol force.

144. **The correct answer is (C).** This is a major function of patrol.

145. **The correct answer is (A).** Note that choice (A) indicates duties "it can perform substantially as well," but it does not say "performs better" or even "as well as."

146. **The correct answer is (C).** Once again, look at the notes that precede this series of questions. The statements are all correct.

147. **The correct answer is (A).** Choices (B), (C), and (D) may be reasons, but the primary reason is contained in choice (A).

148. **The correct answer is (B).** This is primarily a reading question. The question actually asks, "Why are the men slowing down?" Choice (B) talks about the law violators. Choices (A), (C), and (D) address the officers and/or dispatchers.

149. **The correct answer is (D).** If you had trouble answering this question, review the materials once more.

150. **The correct answer is (C).** The police are always available. Most departments do not close for the holidays; availability and mobility are inherent to the police service.

151. **The correct answer is (C).** An information-giver and something you should know.

152. **The correct answer is (A).** Dogs are not able to distinguish "good guys" from "bad guys" and some neighborhoods believe the use of dogs is discriminatory. Public relations should *always* be a concern when it comes to the utilization of dogs. Dogs are very useful for the purposes of the other three choices.

153. **The correct answer is (D).** Community oriented policing has a base philosophy that by allowing officers to go into a community and work with the citizens of that community, it will not only improve the living conditions, but also reduce deviant behavior. Most serious property crimes are reduced in communities that have a high quality of life.

QUESTIONS ON COMPLAINTS AGAINST POLICE PERSONNEL

> **Directions:** Read each question and choose the best answer. Circle the letter of your choice.

154. Lieutenant Connolly, upon entering the station house, sees Sergeant Mullins put an open can of beer in a desk drawer. Drinking in the station house is a violation of department regulations, but the lieutenant is aware that Sergeant Mullins is a knowledgeable, hardworking, and loyal employee. The lieutenant is also aware that it is lunchtime, and the sergeant was probably having a beer with a sandwich. Lieutenant Connolly decides to ignore the situation, but does make his presence known to Sergeant Mullins. This action by the lieutenant is

   (A) proper, because it would be counterproductive to punish the sergeant for such a minor matter.
   (B) improper, because a supervisor should never ignore an observed breach of discipline.
   (C) proper, because to do otherwise would have a detrimental effect on the sergeant's morale.
   (D) improper, because everyone would assume that drinking in the station house is not prohibited.

155. In the situation described in the preceding question, it would have been proper for the lieutenant to

   (A) speak to the sergeant promptly and in private, but refrain from making any record of the incident.
   (B) make a record of the incident, and refrain from speaking to the sergeant about it.
   (C) speak to the sergeant and make a record of the incident.
   (D) take steps to determine if the sergeant was having a drinking problem.

156. Of the following, the *least* advisable action for a police supervisor to take when investigating a complaint made by a citizen against a police officer is to

   (A) record the statement of a bystander who claims to have seen nothing.
   (B) follow up on a complaint made by a second party at the request of the alleged victim.
   (C) bring the complainant and the accused officer together immediately to discuss the complaint.
   (D) listen to a complaint made by someone who is obviously intoxicated.

157. An intoxicated suspect who has just been arrested by one of the officers under your command and is being detained is complaining that the officer has stolen his wallet. In this situation, which one of the following actions should you take *first*?

    (A) Wait until the suspect is sober and determine if he still wishes to make the complaint at that time.
    (B) Search the areas where the suspect has been detained to see if the wallet can be found.
    (C) Interview the suspect immediately to get any additional facts that he may remember.
    (D) Disregard the complaint entirely since the person arrested is probably attempting to evade further criminal action.

158. A complaint involving serious misconduct on the part of P.O. Dillinger has been forwarded to you through channels from the chief's office. As a supervising officer, you have been directed to investigate and make appropriate recommendations. Of the following, the best course of action for you to take is to

    (A) record information in your investigative report from witnesses who were in a position to observe the incident but who say they saw or heard nothing, even though such evidence usually has little probative value.
    (B) interview the accused employee at the very beginning of the investigation.
    (C) inform the complainant at the conclusion of the investigation of the disposition of the matter, and if the charges are sustained, of the specific penalty imposed or recommended.
    (D) avoid scrutinizing the accused employee's personnel records for evidence that he has previously been the subject of similar complaints in order not to prejudice the investigation.

159. Sergeant Perry is assigned to the Civilian Complaint Review Board. While lecturing to a group of probationary police officers at the police academy, the sergeant was asked if, during the course of a police personnel investigation, he would check the personnel record of an officer under investigation. Sergeant Perry replied, "No, I try to conduct investigations which are as objective as possible and a personnel check may cause me to prejudge the officer." The response by Sergeant Perry was

    (A) appropriate, because a prejudiced investigation often leads to improper conclusions.
    (B) inappropriate, because scrutiny of the personnel record may reveal clues to the accused employee's pattern of behavior.
    (C) appropriate, because department morale would suffer if personnel records were scrutinized by investigators.
    (D) inappropriate, because it would be impossible to fully investigate without checking such records.

160. Lieutenant Galvin was interviewing a civilian in a New York City police station. The civilian, a visitor from Los Angeles, stated that he was verbally abused by a police officer from whom he had asked travel directions. The complaining civilian also stated that the officer referred to him as "a dope" who should have remained in Los Angeles if he did not know how to find Times Square in New York City. The complainant was assured by the lieutenant that an investigation would be conducted and the officer would be disciplined if the facts were as stated by the complainant. The complainant stated that he was not interested in "hurting" the officer and that an apology would end the matter. Under these circumstances the lieutenant should

    (A) order the officer to apologize to the complainant.
    (B) interview the officer and, if he admits to being rude, ask him if he would consent to ending the matter by offering an apology.

     (C)   not allow an apology to settle the matter because to do so would establish a dangerous precedent. Other personnel would soon come to believe that all they need to do to escape punishment for their misdeeds is to apologize.

     (D)   allow the apology, if to do so would preclude an unnecessary investigative effort.

161. A man enters a precinct station house, approaches a station house officer, and tells the officer that he has a complaint against a precinct patrol officer. The man is obviously intoxicated. The lieutenant assigned to investigate citizen complaints in this precinct is on duty, and the matter is turned over to him. The lieutenant takes the complainant's name and address. Without questioning him further, he suggests that the complainant go home and that he will be contacted later. After the complainant leaves, the lieutenant checks the complainant's record and finds that he has made three similar complaints against police officers. The next day the lieutenant contacts the complainant and arranges for an interview at his home. During the interview, the lieutenant asks the complainant to describe the incident in his own words. He then tactfully has the complainant repeat the story several times. Which of the following, if any, is the most serious error or omission made by the lieutenant in handling the situation up to this point?

     (A)   He should have called the complainant back to the station house after he was sober instead of going to his home.

     (B)   He should not have checked the complainant's background since that might possibly have affected his objectivity.

     (C)   He should have interviewed the complainant at the time the complaint was made, as well as interviewing him at a later date.

     (D)   None of the above, since no serious error or serious omission was committed in this situation.

162. Sergeant Jones, a patrol supervisor, is approached by several of his subordinate police officers who inform him that Officer Smith, a co-worker, is prejudiced towards members of minority groups. They claim that on several occasions, during normal police contacts with the public, Officer Smith has manifested his prejudices. The officers have indicated their reluctance to work with Smith. In this situation, which one of the following actions should Sergeant Jones take *first*?

     (A)   Take disciplinary action against Officer Smith before his conduct creates bigger problems.

     (B)   Disregard the issue, since no official complaint has been lodged.

     (C)   Discuss the matter with Officer Smith to determine to what extent, if any, there is a problem.

     (D)   Reassign Officer Smith to someone who shares his views and will work with him.

163. On a cold winter day, two police officers on radio motor patrol observe a crowd gathered on a main intersection. They investigate and discover a male weighing about 140 pounds standing in the middle of the crowd dressed only in long underwear. He is shouting and waving his arms about, bragging that no one is going to take him anywhere. He threatens violence to anyone who approaches him, especially police officers. In this situation, the most appropriate action for the officers to take is to

     (A)   call for assistance and stay with the man until help arrives.

     (B)   approach the man immediately to bring him under control.

     (C)   assess the situation carefully and resist the impulse to do something immediately.

     (D)   talk to the persons on the scene to determine if there are any relatives, friends, or others who may be able to assist the officers.

164. In your department there is a rule against police officers taking their meal periods inside the patrol car. Without exception, at least on late tours from 12 P.M. midnight to 8 A.M., every officer in the jurisdiction, including the supervisor, has a ham and cheese and a cola in the patrol car. Official meal periods are not taken, and once the meal is eaten, patrol is resumed. As a unit supervisor concerned about the meal restriction, the most constructive action you should take with regard to the rule is

   (A) set a good example by following the rule rigidly.
   (B) insist that all your subordinates follow the rule.
   (C) find out whether the original reason for the rule still exists.
   (D) find out what other unit supervisors are doing about the rule.

165. Marginal employees will do only enough work so that the department has no cause of action against them. There are many reasons why a police officer may be a marginal employee. Which one of the following approaches is likely to be *least* effective in dealing with this type of officer?

   (A) Hear out any of his real or imagined grievances.
   (B) Provide sources for additional training.
   (C) Transfer the officer to a place where he will have a better job match.
   (D) Give him the most undesirable assignments to motivate him to work.

ANSWERS TO QUESTIONS ON COMPLAINTS AGAINST POLICE PERSONNEL

154. **The correct answer is (B).** This is obviously an observed breach of discipline and cannot be ignored by a supervisor. The word "ignore" in the answer choice should serve as a red flag.

155. **The correct answer is (C).** The making of a record is part and parcel of documentation. A record is good to have when ratings and evaluations are due. Fairness and avoidance of the behavior in the future require talking to the sergeant.

156. **The correct answer is (C).** This would probably be a good idea if you wanted to make a bad situation worse.

157. **The correct answer is (B).** There are many things that may properly be done in this kind of situation. But the question asked, "Which of the following would you do *first*?" If the wallet is found as a result of a search, the other actions would be unnecessary.

158. **The correct answer is (A).** With regard to the other suggested answers, consider the following: (B) Do not interview the accused employee at the very beginning. Get facts concerning the allegation first.
(C) Complainant should not be advised of the exact penalty.
(D) Personnel record of the accused should be examined.

159. **The correct answer is (B).** The word "may" in choice (B) should have directed you to the answer. And the word "impossible" in choice (D) should have caused you to reject it as an answer.

160. **The correct answer is (C).** The correct answer accurately states the reason for not allowing an apology to close a civilian complaint.

161. **The correct answer is (C).** The answer to this question was clearly indicated in the notes preceding this series of questions.

162. **The correct answer is (C).** Always get the facts before taking action.

163. **The correct answer is (B).** Two officers should be able to subdue a 140-pound male standing in his underwear.

164. **The correct answer is (C).** If the reason for the enactment of the rule no longer exists, it would be consistent with good management and supervisory procedure to get rid of it. If everyone is ignoring the rule, then its purpose should be questioned.

165. **The correct answer is (D).**
It would be hard to argue that undesirable assignments would be consistent with motivating a marginal employee. *Note*: Choice (C) suggests that transfer may be a solution. Ordinarily, we do not transfer our problems, but a transfer to a better job match in which the capabilities of a worker are more fully utilized is acceptable.

QUESTIONS ON INTERVIEWING AND EMPLOYEE GRIEVANCES

Directions: Read each question and choose the best answer. Circle the letter of your choice.

166. A supervisor in a unit is faced with a number of tasks to be performed. Of the following tasks, for which would the interview be *least* suitable?

(A) To obtain information from a suspected employee about alleged criminal activity

(B) To try and improve the performance of an employee whose work performance has slipped

(C) To communicate to an employee a new policy of the organization

(D) To advise an employee with respect to his career potential

167. As a sergeant you find that one of your subordinates has reported to work late on an excessive number of occasions during the past few months. You decide to conduct a disciplinary interview with this officer to attempt to rectify the situation. Which of the following is the *least* useful type of information to obtain from the officer at the interview?

(A) The attitudes of his fellow officers toward his latenesses

(B) The officer's current level of motivation to perform his job well

(C) Whether or not the officer is experiencing any personal problems at home

(D) Whether or not the officer has had problems performing his duties

168. In conducting an interview with a police officer concerning the officer's low productivity, Captain Lydon asks, "Don't you feel it would be better for the department and your own future if you improved your productivity?" In this situation, a question of this type can best be described as

(A) proper; it will allow the police officer to think through his problem and arrive at his own solution.

(B) improper; it is less directive than an overt, straightforward statement that would be more appropriate in this situation.

(C) proper; the police officer is treated like an adult by this appeal to reason, department loyalty, and self-interest.

(D) improper; questions like this usually permit only one answer and are often actually thinly veiled forms of advice or censure.

169. P.O. Barbella, a very capable officer, approaches Captain Juliano and informs him that he intends to resign because of family pressures. Captain Juliano is not convinced that the reason advanced for leaving the service by P.O. Barbella is the real reason. At a subsequent separation interview attended by P.O. Barbella, the Captain tries to determine, as specifically as possible, the real reason P.O. Barbella is leaving. Captain Juliano's action can best be described as

    (A) proper; if the circumstances surrounding an employee's separation from the service are not discussed, it could have a short-term adverse effect upon the organization's image.
    (B) improper; the captain should accept the reason advanced by the police officer for resigning and use this opportunity to express his gratitude for a job well done.
    (C) proper; the true reason for Police Officer Barbella's action could be adverse working conditions, or a capricious supervisor, either condition being correctable.
    (D) improper; separation interviews should not pry into personal matters that could be embarrassing to the officer.

170. Captain Sekarski is sitting on a board with other members of the service to interview police officers for designation as community affairs specialist. In order to assess each candidate's reaction to frustration and pressure, he deliberately asks highly complex questions and feigns dissatisfaction with the candidate's responses. In this situation, the captain's action can most appropriately be viewed as

    (A) proper; the interviewer has the right to attempt to penetrate the candidate's defenses to catch a glimpse of the "real person" under stress.
    (B) improper; in this situation the creation of a relaxed, informal atmosphere is essential to comprehensively assess the qualifications of the candidate.
    (C) proper; stress can legitimately be introduced in an interview, but only after a sincere effort has been made to put the candidate at ease.
    (D) improper; good interviewing technique should not include a deliberate tactic to raise the tension level of the interview.

171. Officer Patrick Cortright, having been the subject of numerous disciplinary proceedings, is being "terminated for cause." Relative to such a dismissal, it would be most *incorrect* to state that

    (A) Cortright's probable poor attitude towards the organization justifies not conducting a separation interview in this case.
    (B) a separation interview should be held regardless of the cause for separation.
    (C) in voluntary separations, such interviews are particularly valuable to learn the true reason for the separation rather than the expressed reason.
    (D) besides helping to identify useful or harmful hiring practices, the separation interview can also pinpoint such other correctable conditions as undue work pressure or capricious supervisors.

172. Supervisors, whether interviewing or interrogating, will find questions a valuable tool. However, unless caution is exercised, questions may work at cross-purposes to the aims of the interviewer-interrogator. Evaluate the following statements:

    I. Questions may be used in starting the conversation or delving deeper into a specific area.
    II. Studies have shown that questions framed in negative terms have a tendency to elicit inaccurate responses more frequently than positive questions.
    III. The best questions are those that can be answered with a simple "yes" or "no" reply.
    IV. Leading questions such as, "Don't you like the graveyard shift?" should be avoided.

(A) All the preceding statements are correct.

(B) None of the statements are correct.

(C) Statements I and II are correct, but III and IV are not.

(D) Statements I, II, and IV are correct, but III is not.

173. During the course of an interview, Officer Mullins indicates to Lieutenant Connolly that if he, Connolly, will keep the information confidential, then Mullins will reveal information of an important nature to the organization. The lieutenant desires to obtain the information. Of the following, it would be most appropriate for the lieutenant to

(A) agree to keep the information confidential, but if the officer reveals information implicating himself and others in criminal behavior, promptly arrest him.

(B) under no circumstances should the lieutenant agree to such confidentiality.

(C) inform the officer that such a request on his part is unethical and that he, the officer, is not to broach the subject again.

(D) keep the information confidential if he agrees to do so.

174. A police officer interviewed a witness in the morning at the witness's home. He asked the witness to bring some information to the station house in the afternoon, at which time he conducted a follow-up interview. In recording this follow-up interview, it is *least* important for the police officer to include which one of the following?

(A) The name of the officer interviewing the witness

(B) The name of the witness being interviewed

(C) The address of the witness being interviewed

(D) The place where the interview is being conducted

175. The following are three statements that may or may not be valid concerning the interview of two or three victims at the same crime scene:

I. The victims should be interviewed together since speedy development of information at this point in the investigation is crucial.

II. Taking notes or making tape recordings should be avoided since this tends to upset the victims and may make them reluctant to answer certain questions.

III. The interviewing of all the victims should be done by one investigator rather than by two or more.

Which one of the following best classifies the above statements?

(A) Statement I is generally valid, but II and III are not.

(B) Statement III is generally valid, but I and II are not.

(C) Statements I and II are generally valid, but III is not.

(D) Statements I and III are generally valid, but II is not.

176. Sergeant Smith arrives on the scene of a wife beating. Officers Jones and White, who are already on the scene, have separated the couple and Officer Jones is interviewing the wife who stops frequently during her narrative. She is a woman in her early forties and appears to have sustained only minor injuries, although her appearance is unsightly from her ordeal and she is in an almost hysterical state. Sergeant Smith notes the following actions on the part of Officer Jones. Which of the following actions taken by Officer Jones in this situation is *least* appropriate?

(A) Aware that the victim's appearance is unsightly, Officer Jones respectfully diverts his eyes to avoid embarrassing her.

(B) When the victim stops during her narrative, Officer Jones often repeats her last phrase in a questioning tone instead of asking a direct question.

(C) Officer Jones spends several minutes at the beginning of the interview assuring the victim that she is now safe.

(D) After the victim tells of her experience, Officer Jones asks clarifying questions and then summarizes her statement.

177. A supervising lieutenant responds to the scene of a robbery that has just occurred. The robbery victim, a 27-year old school teacher, is emotionally upset but uninjured. When interviewing the victim, the lieutenant should avoid doing which of the following?

(A) Use phrases such as, "I am here to help you," or, "You are safe now," in an effort to calm the victim.

(B) Attempt to communicate to the victim the feeling that the lieutenant is able to understand and help with the victim's problem.

(C) Ask rapid-fire questions in order to get quickly a complete description of the perpetrator and thereby facilitate an arrest.

(D) If, during the interview, the lieutenant determines that the investigation appears to be blocked by lack of information, the lieutenant should tell the victim this frankly.

178. The primary purpose of a disciplinary interview is to

(A) change employee behavior to make it more acceptable.

(B) inform the employee of his progress.

(C) air any grievances the employee may have.

(D) justify the negative discipline that was administered.

179. Evaluate the following three statements as they relate to grievances and complaints:

I. An enlightened supervisor should know that employee dissatisfactions, if not expressed, will not have an adverse impact on morale.

II. Grievances, even though imaginary, should be recognized by the supervisor as being real in the mind of the employee who feels he has been wronged.

III. If a supervisor is indifferent to grievances (real or imaginary), then resentment and hostility will occur.

(A) All of the statements are accurate.

(B) Only statement I is accurate.

(C) Only statements II and III are accurate.

(D) None of the statements are accurate.

180. Physical factors in the working environment give rise to a large part of employee dissatisfaction. For example, bad lights and uncleanliness are factors that usually require capital outlay to correct. Evaluate the following statements as they relate to the above statement:

I. In these kinds of cases the supervisor is often powerless to make the necessary corrections directly, but should call such deficiencies to the attention of higher management.

II. Adequate physical facilities and equipment do contribute to the maintenance of a high level of production and do affect employee morale.

(A) Both statements are accurate.

(B) Neither statement is accurate.

(C) Only statement I is accurate.

(D) Only statement II is accurate.

181. Select the *incorrect* statement of the following:

(A) Most law enforcement personnel remain in public service because they like the work.

(B) Studies indicate that the greatest concern of police officers (with regard to rules of conduct) is that such rules and regulations place undue restrictions on their personal rights.

(C) Police officers who have the strongest opinions about organizational controls of their moral conduct (personal debts, alcohol off-duty, etc.) believe control of these matters is an invasion of their right to privacy and is none of the department's business.

(D) Failures of supervisors to follow the same rules that officers are expected to follow do not usually cause strong negative reactions.

182. Assume you are a sergeant and one of your subordinates tells you that he is dissatisfied with his work assignment and that he wishes to discuss the matter with you. The employee is obviously very angry and upset. Of the following, the course of action that you should take *first* in this situation is to

(A) postpone discussion of the employee's complaint, explaining to him that the matter can be settled more satisfactorily if it is discussed calmly.

(B) have the employee describe his complaint, correcting him whenever he makes what seems to be an erroneous charge against you.

(C) permit the employee to present his complaint in full, withholding your comments until he has finished describing his complaint.

(D) promise the employee that you will review all the work assignments in the unit to determine whether or not any changes should be made.

183. Police Officer Joan Wilson, a most dependable and knowledgeable employee, complains at every opportunity about "preferential assignments for men and racial minorities." A thorough investigation concludes that her complaint is entirely without merit. The officer continues to verbalize her complaint and you are aware that her actions are having an adverse impact on the morale of other squad members. Your most proper course of action would be to

(A) delegate to her the task of assigning squad members to perform required tasks.

(B) request that she be transferred to a more desirable assignment.

(C) speak with her in a one-on-one setting, point out the harmful effects of her comments, and request that she refrain from such comments in the future.

(D) speak with other squad members and tell them to disregard her complaints.

184. Evaluate the following statements:

I. Recent extensions, by the courts and legislatures, of constitutional guarantees to protect public officers' rights have further restricted organizations in exercising management controls once considered commonplace.

II. Generally, courts have rules that an employee cannot be penalized for his acts unless it can be proved that the conduct is related to his performance of duty and that it has impaired his efficiency.

(A) Both statements are accurate.

(B) Neither statement is accurate.

(C) Only statement I is accurate.

(D) Only statement II is accurate.

185. Evaluate the following statements:

I. When dealing with behavior that is not job related, the supervisor must be aware that his or her options are limited in the eyes of the law.

II. Transfer in order to solve a personnel problem is never an acceptable procedure.

III. Once a supervisor recognizes the symptoms that strong feelings of discontent are growing among his subordinates, he should try to determine the cause.

(A) All of the statements are accurate.

(B) Only statement I is accurate.

(C) Only statements II and III are accurate.

(D) Only statements I and III are accurate.

186. You are a supervising officer in charge of a unit. You have received numerous grievances from your subordinates. You have handled all of these grievances as they should be handled, and yet many grievances continue to be made. The probable cause is

    (A) you have failed to act promptly on the grievances that have been made.
    (B) the subordinates have not been notified of the successful disposition of their grievances.
    (C) the grievances have not been acted upon at the proper level within the organization.
    (D) the grievances are an indication of the existence of some other problem.

187. A police officer under your supervision comes to you to complain about a decision you have made in assigning him to duty. You consider the matter unimportant, but it seems to be very important to him. He is excited and angry. The best way to handle the case is to

    (A) tell him to take it up with the captain.
    (B) refuse to talk to him until he has cooled down.
    (C) show him at once how unimportant the matter is and how absurd his argument is.
    (D) let him talk until "he gets it off his chest" and then explain the reasons for your decision.

188. Which one of the following things is it best for a sergeant to do *first* if the constant complaining of one police officer in her command is hurting the morale of the organization?

    (A) Ask the captain to talk to this police officer.
    (B) Talk to this police officer and try to find out the trouble.
    (C) Tell this police officer to "snap out of it."
    (D) Give this police officer a more difficult assignment.

189. Assume that, under a proposed procedure for handling employee grievances in a public agency, the aggrieved employee is to submit his grievance as soon as it arises to a grievance board set up to hear all employee grievances in the agency. The board, consisting of representatives of management and of rank and file employees, is to consider the grievance, obtain all necessary pertinent information, and then render a decision on the matter. Thus, the first-line supervisor would not be involved in the settlement of any of his or her subordinates' grievances except when asked by the board to submit information. This proposed procedure would be generally undesirable chiefly because

    (A) the board may become a bottleneck to delay the prompt disposition of grievances.
    (B) the aggrieved employees and their supervisors will not have been given the initial opportunity to resolve the grievances themselves.
    (C) employees would be likely to submit imaginary as well as real grievances to the board.
    (D) the board will lack first-hand, personal knowledge of the factors involved in grievances.

190. The principal purpose of a formal employee grievance procedure should be to

    (A) demonstrate that top management is interested in staff morale.
    (B) prevent employee grievances from building up to a point where they may receive undesirable publicity in the public press.
    (C) provide a safety valve for employees who would otherwise resort to quite serious misconduct.
    (D) reveal the existence of inequitable situations and afford an opportunity for their correction.

ANSWERS TO QUESTIONS ON INTERVIEWING AND EMPLOYEE GRIEVANCES

166. **The correct answer is (A).** Choice (A) would more properly indicate that an interrogation of the suspect, and not an interview, would be the appropriate vehicle for an "alleged criminal activity."

167. **The correct answer is (A).** This is a good example of a question that could be answered by a careful reading of the suggested answers. After all, you are interviewing the officer: (A), fellow officers; (B), the officer; (C), the officer; and (D), the officer.

168. **The correct answer is (D).** This kind of question begs for a "yes" or "no" answer and the officer would almost be forced to reply in the affirmative. This kind of question does not allow for a great deal of exchange of views between the interviewer and interviewee and does not elicit information.

169. **The correct answer is (C).** Remember, a separation interview should *always* be conducted when an officer leaves the department. And the captain who utilizes it to identify deficiencies that are correctable is acting in a manner that is consistent with the best interests of the department.

170. **The correct answer is (A).** The question tells us that a purpose of the interview is to "assess the candidate's reaction to frustration and pressure." Consequently, choice (A) would appear to be appropriate.

171. **The correct answer is (A).** We are looking for a most incorrect statement and we have already established that a separation interview should be conducted "in all cases."

172. **The correct answer is (D).** Regarding statement III, the purpose of the questioning is to "get" information. "Yes" and "no" answers do not allow for elaboration. Regarding statement IV, the practice is wrong, but the statement is correct.

173. **The correct answer is (D).** A tough question! The concept is that certain ground rules should be established prior to an agreement to keep the exchange confidential. Corruption, violations of law, etc., cannot be tolerated and/or kept in confidence. But once that is understood the supervisor should honor an agreement to maintain confidentiality.

174. **The correct answer is (C).** The address of the person (probably already recorded in the morning interview) would be *least* important of those listed for the follow-up interview.

175. **The correct answer is (B).** Victims should not be interviewed together. One witness may unduly influence the response of others. Choices (A), (C), and (D) all indicate that statement I is valid.

176. **The correct answer is (A).** The object is to maintain eye contact. Expressions of sympathy, understanding, interest, and compassion are difficult to achieve without eye contact.

177. **The correct answer is (C).** Rapid-fire questions would not be appropriate to direct at an emotionally upset robbery victim. Do not shy away from choice (D); if the investigation does not appear to be going anywhere, then it is acceptable to tell the witness.

178. **The correct answer is (A).** Remember, discipline means training, and training implies changing attitudes, improving skills, and imparting knowledge.

179. **The correct answer is (C).** An easy question to answer because statement I is obviously not a good statement; a dissatisfied employee will not be one with high morale. Statements II and III are accurate.

180. **The correct answer is (A).** Both statements are accurate. In statement I, the word "often" does not make the statement unacceptable. And the phrase "do contribute" in the second statement does not preclude a broad interpretation of that statement whether the contribution is small or large.

181. **The correct answer is (D).** View the question as an information-giver. Choices (A), (B), and (C) are correct. Choice (D) merely points out that supervisors who take the "do as I say" approach as opposed to the "do as I do" approach cause strong negative reactions among employees.

182. **The correct answer is (C).** Ventilation or verbal catharsis is most important in solving grievances. Let the man talk and talk. Let him get it "off his chest."

183. **The correct answer is (C).** An effective supervisor uses face-to-face communication to solve many of the personnel problems that confront him or her.

184. **The correct answer is (A).** Both statements are accurate and could be inferred from the information contained in prior questions.

185. **The correct answer is (D).** We have seen that officers' rights have constitutional guarantees, which makes I a correct statement. As for statement II, we know that sometimes a transfer may be appropriate if it will cause a better job match. And with regard to statement III, it is *always* good for a supervisor to "attempt to determine the cause."

186. **The correct answer is (D).** The question tells you that "*all* have been handled as they should be handled." Therefore, (A), (B), and (C) are eliminated as answers. Logic dictates that choice (D) is the answer.

187. **The correct answer is (D).** Yes, let him talk and let him engage in a catharsis, talking it out in a permissive atmosphere. Real or imagined, it is real to him, and it is his turn to let you know how he feels.

188. **The correct answer is (B).** An easy one! Get the facts before you take any action.

189. **The correct answer is (B).** Whenever possible, grievances should be resolved by first-line supervisors.

190. **The correct answer is (D).** The question concerns itself with the purpose of a formal grievance procedure, and choice (D) is the proper response.

QUESTIONS ON TACTICS

Directions: Read each question and choose the best answer. Circle the letter of your choice.

191. Select the *incorrect* statement as it relates to police dogs.

(A) Police canines are not "attack" dogs; they are trained to stop and immobilize suspects.

(B) The patrol officer should remain with the canine officer at all times when the police dog is unleashed.

(C) It is extremely difficult to utilize police dogs in cases where a search and seizure warrant is being executed in a drugs dealer or user.

(D) Police dogs are trained to follow human scent from clothing worn or objects touched by a person, but in some cases the dog is able to follow the movement of an individual without being given a presented article.

192. Evaluate the following statements as they relate to crime prevention:

I. Burglary, car stripping, and street assaults are examples of offenses that lend themselves to more control through alert aggressive patrol operations.

II. The offense over which police have the least control is homicide.

III. The job of the police in crime prevention is twofold: reducing the desire on the part of an individual to commit an offense and reducing the opportunity to commit the offense.

(A) All of the statements are accurate.

(B) Only statements I and II are accurate.

(C) Only statements II and III are accurate.

(D) Only statement II is accurate.

193. All departments engage in some form of criminal intelligence activity. There are two principal ways in which information is obtained: overtly and covertly. With regard to criminal intelligence, select the *incorrect* statement.

(A) The great bulk of information collected by a police agency is by overt means and an important source of information is the patrol officer.

(B) Information obtained covertly should be directed toward a primary objective; the arrest of the person involved.

(C) Undercover agents are rarely able to penetrate the upper echelons of organized criminal groups.

(D) Both tactical and strategic intelligence are ordinarily developed from information collected over a period of time and deal with patterns or emerging trends of criminal activity.

194. Select the *incorrect* statement as it relates to tactics when interrogating juveniles.

    (A) It is desirable for the interrogating officer to relate personal experiences that demonstrate that he or she understands the juvenile's position.

    (B) The officer should point out the futility of resistance to telling the truth.

    (C) The officer should not push the juvenile into a situation where he must lose his self-respect in order to cooperate.

    (D) The officer should discontinue the questioning temporarily if the juvenile begins to cry.

195. You are the commanding officer of a precinct in which a jail is located. A hostage situation with the potential for violence has erupted in the jail and some prisoners are rioting. It has been recommended that local police be utilized to intervene. You should evaluate such a recommendation as

    (A) appropriate; the facility is within your geographical area of command and you are ultimately responsible for restoring order.

    (B) inappropriate; the assigned correctional personnel that are supplemented, if necessary, by state police, should be utilized to correct the situation.

    (C) appropriate; a potentially violent confrontation between correctional personnel and inmates may permanently damage future working relationships in the jail.

    (D) inappropriate; civil liability actions may be lodged against the municipality and individual officers.

196. An officer caught in an ambush cannot afford to react normally. If there is any general rule about what police officers should do when ambushed, it is to defend themselves first and think of counterattack second. Select the *incorrect* statement as it relates to ambush attacks.

    (A) The initial reaction of a police officer on foot to a short-range firearm attack is to make himself as small a target as possible and to avoid the assailant's direct line of fire. By throwing himself to the ground, the officer may force the assailant to momentarily stop firing.

    (B) If the firearm attack is close-in, the probability of the officer's being hit by a second or third round is so great that he will usually have no choice but to return fire immediately after taking a simple evasive step.

    (C) While returning fire, the officer should seek cover, moving rapidly, at an uneven pace, toward the attacker.

    (D) In ambush situations, cover is practically *always* available.

197. Evaluate the following statements as they relate to ambush and ambush countermeasures:

    I. Most of those who attack police officers are mentally disturbed and only a small percentage have criminal records and/or convictions.

    II. Suddenness, surprise, and lack of provocation are the identifying features of an ambush.

    III. The target of most ambush attempts is the uniformed officer in or near his marked vehicle.

    (A) All of the statements are accurate.

    (B) Only statements I and II are accurate.

    (C) Only statements II and III are accurate.

    (D) Only statement II is accurate.

198. Police Officer John Dempsey is testifying as a witness for the prosecution in a racially charged murder trial. The defense attorney has asked the officer to respond to a relevant and important question. Police Officer Dempsey should

    (A) initially face the defense attorney, but then seek to obtain eye contact with the prosecutor while answering.

(B)   initially face the defense attorney and maintain eye contact with him or her while responding to the question.

(C)   initially face the prosecutor and then face the defense attorney while responding.

(D)   initially face the defense attorney and then turn to the jurors or judge to direct the answer.

199.   Select the *incorrect* statement as it relates to hostage incidents.

(A)   The terrorist poses the greatest of threats because he is often fanatical to the point of murder and suicide.

(B)   Most terrorists will react to the reality of the situation and negotiate.

(C)   Armed felons who take hostages when trapped often imitate the behavior of political terrorists.

(D)   It is not recommended that police officers suggest that a felon who has taken a hostage "cool off," analyze his position, and reflect on the consequences of his acts.

200.   When interviewing the victim of a wife beating, the police officer concerned should be governed by certain guidelines. Evaluate the following statements as to whether they describe appropriate or inappropriate actions on the part of the officer:

I.   The victim should be permitted to wash and care for other needs before being interviewed.

II.   The officer should allow the victim to "ventilate" to help relieve her emotional tension.

III.   Eye contact should be avoided when the victim is describing a traumatic or humiliating experience.

(A)   All of the statements are appropriate.

(B)   None of the statements are appropriate.

(C)   Only statements I and II are appropriate.

(D)   Only statements II and III are appropriate.

ANSWERS TO QUESTIONS ON TACTICS

191.   **The correct answer is (C).** Dogs may be utilized with ease in this kind of situation.

192.   **The correct answer is (B).** The police have no control over a person's desire to commit a criminal offense. (We have seen this before.)

193.   **The correct answer is (D).** "Tactical" usually refers to a specific event.

194.   **The correct answer is (D).** The officer concerned should use the opportunity to demonstrate friendliness. Furthermore, the subject may be ready to "get it off his chest" at this moment of weakness.

195.   **The correct answer is (C).** The correctional guards will still be working at the jail when the situation is terminated. Outside, local police personnel will resume regular duty somewhere else when the condition is corrected.

196.   **The correct answer is (C).** Most suggest that he move laterally from the attacker, not toward the attacker.

197.   **The correct answer is (C).** Contrary to I, most do have criminal records. Statements II and III are accurate.

198.   **The correct answer is (D).** Try to make sure the judge and/or the jurors hear what you have to say. Defense attorneys and prosecutors do not decide cases.

199.   **The correct answer is (D).** This course is strongly recommended by most authorities.

200.   **The correct answer is (C).** Eye contact should be maintained. The officer concerned may more readily indicate concern or compassion when eye contact is present.

THE POLICE AND CONSTITUTIONAL LAW

Constitutional law—the term sounds dry, boring, and static. Yet in actuality, to the practical police officer, constitutional law is quite dynamic and interesting.

When the United States Constitution was originally written, the framers realized that the Constitution by itself left something to be desired. Although it spelled out the law of the land, it truly did not provide sufficient protection for individuals against the power and might of the newly formed federal republic. This lack of protection for individuals led to the first ten amendments to the Constitution. As a unit, these ten amendments are referred to as the Bill of Rights. As originally written, this Bill of Rights served as protection only against action of the new federal government. It was not applicable against actions of the individual state governments. Over the years, by way of the Due Process Clause of the Fourteenth Amendment to the Constitution, the Supreme Court has decreed that all of the protections against federal governmental action provided for in the Bill of Rights also operate to protect individuals from state governmental action.

The Bill of Rights is now part of the law of the land and protects all individuals from unconstitutional acts of federal, state, or local governments.

The portions of the Bill of Rights that have special applications to police work are as follows.

THE FIRST AMENDMENT

Congress shall make no law respecting an establishment of religion, or prohibiting the free exercise thereof; or abridging the freedom of speech, or of the press; or the right of the people peaceably to assemble, and to petition the Government for a redress of grievances. (Effective date November 3, 1791.)

FIRST AMENDMENT RESTRICTIONS

FREEDOM OF SPEECH

Although the First Amendment guarantees freedom of speech (among other freedoms), this guarantee is not absolute. A person is not free to shout "fire" in a crowded theater. Common sense dictates that there be some restrictions on the right of free speech contained in the First Amendment.

The following kinds of speech may be regulated by the government and such regulations will not be considered as unreasonable.

SPEECH THAT INCITES VIOLENCE

There must be clear and present danger of violence. Language or speech that incites others to riot may be prohibited.

Brandenburg v. Ohio, 395 U.S. 444. Speech advocating use of force or crime is prohibited when (1), the advocacy is "directed to inciting or producing imminent lawless action," and (2), the advocacy is also "likely to incite or produce such action."

Language that can be construed as "fighting words." Speech which is spoken only to provoke a fight maybe prohibited. In most states, statutes dealing with disorderly conduct or harassment will prohibit this kind of speech. If fighting words, obscene language, or speech designed solely to provoke a fight are based on race, religion, or national origin (and in some states sexual preference), various local civil rights laws may be violated as well. The recent flag-burning cases present interesting questions with regard to protected speech.

FREEDOM OF ASSEMBLY

Here too, there is no *absolute* right of assembly. If a narrowly tailored significant government interest is involved, then the freedom to assemble can be restricted. If the right to assemble is restricted, then the restrictions must be reasonable.

The regulation must be content neutral. This means the assembly (or demonstration) cannot be prohibited simply because of the ideas being expressed.

Clark v. Community for Creative Nonviolence, 468 U.S. 288 (1984). In addition to the "regulation must be content neutral," it also must be "narrowly tailored" to serve a significant government interest.

The regulations must allow for ample alternative means of communication. The alternative means must be reasonable with respect to time, place, and manner. For example, a demonstration in front of the local city hall cannot be moved to a park on the other side of town.

Consider the following situation:

In New York City, the Russian Embassy, a police station house, a church, a synagogue, and numerous apartment buildings are all located on the same street—East 67th Street. Needless to say, East 67th Street is the scene of daily demonstrations of people who are exercising their right of free speech. It is obvious that New York City has a significant interest in what occurs on East 67th Street and the police may reasonably restrict the place of demonstration, the number of demonstrators, signs to be carried (could be used as weapons), time of demonstration, etc.

Even in a troublesome situation such as the Russian Embassy, the government cannot prohibit completely the citizens from assembling and trying to seek redress.

There are a number of common areas of assembly and demonstration. Obviously, the purpose of assembly and demonstration is to be seen and heard. Therefore, locations with high visibility are most often targeted. Subject to safety considerations, the more public the area, the greater the citizens' right to assemble and/or demonstrate. Demonstrating citizens have greatest access to public streets and to public property which is regularly open to the public. This latter category includes areas such as public parks and transportation facilities.

Restrictions multiply with respect to demonstrations on public property that is not open to the general public such as jails, schools, and government offices. There is no absolute right to demonstrate on these premises. Local policy dictates police action against demonstrations on this type of public property. Police action may include arrests for criminal trespass or for obstructing governmental administration.

Some private property, such as commercial or residential buildings and privately owned shopping malls, offer ideal visibility to citizens with agendas or grievances to air. However, there is no *right* to assemble or demonstrate on these premises. Federal rules allow owners of private shopping malls to prohibit demonstrators from gathering, speaking, handing out leaflets, etc. Public relations and an appearance of fairness are important to private owners. Labor disputes on private property may be a different matter.

PORNOGRAPHY AND OBSCENITY

According to the dictionary, pornography is defined as writings, pictures, etc., intended *primarily* to arouse sexual desire. Obscenity is that which is offensive to one's feelings or to prevailing notions of modesty or decency that are lewd, disgusting, and repulsive. Pornography and obscenity are not protected by the First Amendment. Unfortunately for both police officers and for judges, the tests (or standards) for obscenity are confusing and are subject to various interpretations.

The following elements are used to determine if materials such as books, magazines, and films, or a performance (live on stage) are obscene:

■ Is the predominant appeal to a "prurient interest" (lustful craving) in sex? Contemporary community standard must be used.

■ In a patently offensive manner, does it depict actual or simulated acts such as sexual intercourse, sodomy, and bestiality? Again, contemporary community standard must be used.

■ As a whole, does it lack serious literary, artistic, political, or scientific value? A reasonable person standard is used rather than a contemporary community standard.

Brockett v. Spokane Arcades, Inc. 472 U.S. 491 (1985). Prurient interest defined means "material having a tendency to excite lustful thoughts."

ENFORCEMENT OF OBSCENITY LAWS.

In most instances, only a judge can make the initial decision that material is obscene. The police are usually required to purchase a copy of the material in question and bring it to a judge. The judge, if he or she decides it is obscene, may further direct action by the police. In the case of a live performance, prior judicial review may not be necessary, but the actions of the performers must clearly fall within the definition of obscenity. When the material involves children the offenders are held to a stricter standard and it is more likely that the judge will consider borderline material as obscene.

THE FOURTH AMENDMENT

The right of the people to be secure in their persons, houses, papers, and effects, against unreasonable searches and seizures, shall not be violated, and no warrants shall issue, but upon probable cause, supported by oath or affirmation, and particularly describing the place to be searched, and the persons or things to be seized. (Effective date November 3, 1791.)

HISTORICAL BACKGROUND

Weeks v. United States, 232 U.S. 383 (1914). The Supreme Court held that in a prosecution in a federal court the Fourth Amendment prohibits the use of evidence obtained through the use of an illegal search and seizure. This is the federal exclusionary rule, which bars the use of evidence unconstitutionally seized by federal law enforcement officials.

Wolf v. Colorado, 338 U.S. 25 (1949). The Supreme Court held that in a state court prosecution unlawfully obtained evidence is admissible. The Supreme Court refused to use the Due Process Clause of the Fourteenth Amendment to make the Fourth Amendment applicable against the states for the purpose of excluding illegally obtained evidence. In this case, the Supreme Court emphasized other avenues of redress for the offended party other than exclusion of the evidence (private law suits, internal police discipline, etc.). The Court seemed to consider the federal exclusionary rule from *Weeks v. United States* to be a judicially created rule of evidence that Congress could negate and not a command of the Fourth Amendment.

Elkins v. United States, 364 U.S. 206 (1960). In this case, the Supreme Court discarded what had come to be known as the Silver Platter Doctrine, which stated that evidence of a federal crime, seized by state police in the course of an illegal search conducted during the investigation into a state crime, could be handed to federal officers "on a silver, platter" and be admissible in a federal court prosecution.

Mapp v. Ohio, 367 U.S. 643 (1961). Cleveland police unlawfully entered Mapp's house without a warrant and conducted an unlawful search of the entire house. Officers claimed they were conducting an investigation regarding a bombing and wanted to enter the defendant's house to find a person who they thought was hiding there. The police forcibly entered the house and showed a false warrant. The search uncovered various items of obscene and pornographic material for which Mapp was placed under arrest. The Ohio state courts convicted Mapp using the prior court decisions, which held that even though unlawfully obtained, evidence could still be used against a defendant in a state prosecution, the Supreme Court of the United States changed the rule in this case and brought the full weight of Fourth Amendment protection against the state through the Due Process Clause of the Fourteenth Amendment. It decreed that evidence that is obtained as the result of an illegal search and seizure may not be used against a defendant in a state court prosecution.

Note: Reference is sometimes made to Justice Cardozo's remark that under the exclusionary rule, "… the criminal is to go free because the constable has blundered." It is apparent, however, that the Supreme Court's thrust is not to allow a wronged defendant some avenue of redress against unlawful governmental action but to prevent such action in the first instance.

FOURTH AMENDMENT DISCUSSION

Only *unreasonable* searches and seizures are prohibited by the Fourth Amendment. The Supreme Court of the United States has interpreted the meaning of this amendment and has concluded that there are many warrantless searches and seizures that are not unreasonable.

SEARCH INCIDENT TO A LAWFUL ARREST

Weeks v. United States, 232 U.S. 383 (1914). The Supreme Court made its first reference to the right of police to search the person as incident to a lawful arrest.

Carroll v. United States, 267 U.S. 132 (1925). The Supreme Court stated that the person arrested may be searched as well as whatever is found upon his person or in his control.

Agnello v. United States, 269 U.S. 20 (1925). The Supreme Court stated that the person arrested may be searched without a warrant and so may the place where the arrest is made be searched for fruits of the crime, weapons, and means of escape.

Harris v. United States, 331 U.S. 145 (1947). The Supreme Court extended the search incident to a lawful arrest (for cashing forged checks) to include every room of a four-room apartment occupied by Harris at the time of his arrest.

United States v. Rabinowitz, 339 U.S. 56 (1950). The Supreme Court took the position that a search incident to lawful arrest may extend to the area in possession of or under the control of the person arrested.

Chimel v. California, 395 U.S. 752 (1969). The Supreme Court reversed the direction of the prior decisions and, in this landmark case, took the position that a search incident that a *warrantless* search incident to a lawful arrest must be limited to a search of the following:

1. The person arrested

2. Anything found on the arrested person

3. The area into which the arrested person might reach in order to grab a weapon or an evidentiary item is unknown as the "grabbable" area. Under federal cases, this would include items such as pocketbooks and packages being carried

Note: Specifically, this case overruled *Harris v. United States* and *United States v. Rabinowitz*. With some minor variations, such as the grabbable area becoming the "lungeable area," the rule in *Chimel v. California* is still the rule today. In *Chimel v. California*, the Court reiterated the rule that no warrant is required to search a person who is the subject of a custodial arrest. This rule is known as a bright line rule, meaning that it is clear to all that no warrant is required for such a case. It is not necessary to look at a case-by-case assessment. If the arrest is lawful, then the search is authorized. This bright line rule even applies when there are no exigent circumstances such as danger to police or danger to evidence (*United States v. Robinson*). And in *United States v. Edwards*, the Supreme Court held that no warrant was required to search an arrested person's clothing 10 hours after the arrest was made and while the defendant was still in custody. The rationale of the Court seems to be that there is a "diminished expectation" of privacy when a person has become the subject of a custodial arrest. This diminished expectation is also used by the Court to justify searches of vehicles and searches based on third-party consent. For example, if A leaves a locked suitcase with B for safekeeping, then B may consent to a police search of the suitcase.

Maryland v. Buiei, 494 U.S. 325 (1990). Modified the *Chimel* case by stating "fruit of the protective sweep is admissible against defendant."

THE PLAIN VIEW DOCTRINE

This doctrine stands for the rule that if a police officer, during the course of a reasonable intrusion, sees evidence or contraband in plain view, he may seize it.

In order for evidence or contraband to be seized under the Plain View Doctrine, the following three conditions must be met:

1. The officer must be in a place where he has a lawful right to be when he makes the observation.

    a. However, if a police officer is on the sidewalk and, through a window, sees contraband on a table in a street-level apartment, he may not enter to seize by way of the Plain View Doctrine.

    b. Automobiles present an exception to the above. Whenever a police officer lawfully stops an automobile he or she may look into it and immediately seize any evidence in plain view.

2. The incriminating nature of the seized item must be immediately apparent to the officer.

    a. In *Arizona v. Hicks,* (1987), the Supreme Court stated that it was not reasonable for a police officer to move a piece of stereo equipment to locate the serial number when he suspected it might be stolen.

    b. In *Stanley v. Georgia,* 394 U.S. 557 (1969), police found reels of obscene film while searching for gambling paraphernalia. They viewed the film on a projector and screen. The Supreme Court suppressed the evidence because the obscene nature of the reels was not immediately apparent.

3. The discovery of the item must be inadvertent. If the police are searching for the item in question, it does not come within the Plain View Doctrine.

THE CONSENT SEARCH

If an individual freely and voluntarily consents to a search, then the search is constitutionally permissible. Neither probable cause nor a search warrant is required to conduct the search. When a prosecutor seeks to rely upon consent to justify the lawfulness of a search, he has the burden of proving that the consent was, in fact, freely and voluntarily given.

Whether or not the consent was freely and voluntarily given is determined by the court after an examination of the totality of the circumstances. Consent does not turn on the presence or absence of a single controlling criterion. No one factor is a *sine qua non* (required element) in establishing consent. The following factors must be considered:

1. The age, intelligence, and criminal background of the person who is consenting. In *United States v. Elrod,* (1971), the Court held that if the consentor lacks mental capacity, although he seems normal, there was no consent.

2. Was coercion used, or were threats involved? In *Bumper v. North Carolina,* (1968), police falsely announced they had a search warrant and then asked if they could search. Reliance on consent as a means of justifying the search failed.

3. What was the period of police contact before the consent was obtained?

4.   Was the person under arrest, or was he free to leave?

5.   Was the person cooperative or uncooperative?

6.   Was the person advised of his right to refuse consent? In the case of *Schneckloth v. Bustamonte,* 412 U.S. 218 (1973), it was firmly established that failure to so advise the person does not by itself vitiate the consent. Consent need merely be voluntary, not necessarily knowledgeable. A consenter's ignorance of his or her right to refuse does not invalidate consent.

Third-party consent raises other issues. The third party must halve legitimate control over the area to be searched. This control may be joint access and control. If a true joint occupant properly consents to a search, the consent is valid even if the other party objects to the search.

In *Frazier v. Cupp,* (1969), two persons were using the same duffel bag. One consented to a search and incriminating evidence against the other was found. Court held that the third-party consent was valid.

United States v. Matlock, 415 U.S. 164 (1974). The court held that a warrantless search is valid, even if the officers obtained consent from a third party who possesses common authority over the premises. Here, a woman consented to the search of a room that she shared with the defendant, thus there was no violation of defendant's rights.

The following represent the most common third-party consent situations:

- *Husband—Wife.* A spouse may consent to a search of any property over which there is joint control. This rule applies to common-law as well as ceremonial marriages. In Coolidge v. New Hampshire, (1971), police visited home of defendant who was at a police station in connection with a murder investigation. Police asked the wife if she kept guns in the house and if they could have clothing worn by the husband on night in question. She said "yes" and consented. The Supreme Court said it was valid consent.

- *Parent—Child.* Age can become a factor here. Usually a parent can consent to a search of a part of the premises occupied by a minor child. But, the reverse would not be true. Older children (age being a relative term) may consent to search of a family residence if they have joint access and control of the area in question.

- *Hotel—Guest.* Hotel personnel cannot consent to the search of a room of a guest who is up-to-date in his rent payments. See *Stoner v. California,* (1964), where the Supreme Court held that the search of a defendant's hotel room without his consent and without a warrant, but with the consent of the hotel clerk violated the defendant's constitutional rights.

- *Boyfriend—Girlfriend.* It is not necessary that the person giving consent be a full-time resident of the premises in question. If he or she has keys and is free to come and go as he pleases, the consent will be valid.

- *School Official—Student.* The usual rule is that a student's locker may be searched with consent of school authorities, but not a student's dormitory room.

- *Employer—Employee.* If an employee is assigned a desk for his or her exclusive use, the supervisor cannot validly consent to a search of that desk by police to find evidence.

- *Employee—Employer.* If the employee is of high rank or authority, he may sometimes validly consent to a search of employer's premises.

- *Bailor—Bailee.* If the first party leaves a locked suitcase with a second party for safekeeping, the second party may validly consent to a search of the suitcase by police.

ARREST IN THE HOME

A person's right to privacy in his home is one of the most fundamental rights in our society. It is also one of the rights most closely protected by the courts.

Consider the following arrest statute that appears in the New York State Criminal Procedure Law in Article 140, Section 140.15, Subdivision 4.

> *Sub. 4.* In order to effect such an arrest (without a warrant), a police officer may enter premises in which he reasonably believes such person to be present, under the same circumstances and in the same manner as would be authorized, by the provisions of subdivision four and five of section 120.80, if he were attempting to make such arrest pursuant to a warrant of arrest.

This section of law purports to give police authority to enter any premises in any situation where they are seeking to make a probable cause arrest without a warrant. However, in the case of *Payton v. New York*, 445 U.S. 573 (1980), the Supreme Court held that the Fourth Amendment prohibits the police from making a warrantless, and nonconsensual entry into a suspect's home in order to make a routine felony arrest. The Court further stated that if exigent circumstances (not further defined) were present, then such an entry to make a warrantless arrest would be permissible.

Experts maintain that exigent circumstances include the following:

■ *Hot pursuit.* If the defendant flees into his home or the home of a third party after committing a crime, then the police may enter without a warrant to make the arrest. But if police knock on a door and the defendant opens the door, then flees into the apartment when he sees police, this is not hot pursuit.

■ *Emergency situations.* These are based on reasonable cause to believe that any of the following conditions are present:

1. There is danger to the life or safety of the officer or another.
2. The defendant may escape.
3. Evidence may be damaged, destroyed, or concealed.
4. Response to an emergency.

ARREST IN A THIRD-PARTY RESIDENCE

If a person sought by the police is in the home of a third person, then the police can enter that home only if they can show exigent circumstances, consent, or a search warrant. Without one of these three conditions, the police officer's entry into the third-party residence is a violation of the third party's constitutional rights for which the police may be held civilly liable.

Unless the police have reasonable cause to believe that the wanted defendant is inside the third-party residence at the time, exigent circumstances will not give police authority to enter such residence in order to search for the defendant.

CRIME SCENE SEARCHES

The Supreme Court has held that there is no crime scene exception to the search warrant requirement. This means that the general rule with regard to crime scenes is, "Get a search warrant." See *Mincey v. Arizona*, 437 U.S. 385 (1978).

There are numerous exceptions to this general rule and several are listed as follows:

■ When the defendant does not possess a reasonable expectation of privacy in the premises, a search warrant is not necessary. When the defendant is a trespasser, no warrant is required.

■ When the search is conducted for the purpose of finding dead or injured crime victims or rendering aid to a victim, no warrant is required.

■ When evidence is being protected or photographed during the time it takes to obtain a search warrant, no warrant is required to enter the crime scene.

■ No warrant is required to enter the crime scene in order to find the perpetrator who may still be present on the scene.

A crime scene search may be made without a warrant if:

1. it is an emergency and there is a reasonable belief that there is imminent danger to persons. In an emergency crime scene search, contraband in plain view may be seized. If evidence is seen that is not contraband, it is best to get a warrant before seizing it.

2. a homicide victim is the sole occupant.

3. the scene is a public place.

AUTOMOBILE SEARCHES

The three generally accepted bases for the searching of vehicles are listed as follows:

1. The vehicle emergency that arises because of the vehicle's mobile capability; the possibility that the suspect will drive away.

2. A reduced expectation of privacy regarding a vehicle. This reduced expectation is based on such things as regulations, licensing requirements, and inspections, all of which are somewhat intrusive.

3. A search of the vehicle "incident" to the arrest of an occupant of the vehicle.

VEHICLE EMERGENCY CASES

Carroll v. United States, 267 U.S. 132 (1925). This case established the rule that permits a search of a vehicle based on probable cause to believe that it contains contraband. It was a prohibition era case involving the warrantless search of an automobile for illegal liquor.

Chambers v. Maroney, 399 U.S. 42 (1970). Following an armed robbery of a gas station in Pennsylvania, the robbers were arrested and their blue compact station wagon in which they were riding was seized. The car was driven to the station house where it was thoroughly searched. Weapons were found, and property belonging to the gas station attendant was found. The Court could not justify the search of the vehicle as being incident to the arrest because the arrest was made prior to the search and at another location. The Supreme Court justified the search on the grounds that at the time the vehicle was stopped and the occupants arrested, the police had probable cause to believe the vehicle contained fruits of the crime and weapons. The Court stated that it saw no difference between seizing a car and holding it until a search warrant based on probable cause could be obtained and carrying out an immediate search (based on probable cause) without a warrant.

United States v. Ross, 456 U.S. 798 (1982). The Supreme Court reiterated its position that when the police have probable cause to believe the vehicle contains contraband, the entire vehicle may be searched in an effort to locate the contraband, and no search warrant is required.

California v. Acevedo, 500 U.S. 565 (1991). On May 30, 1991 the Supreme Court overruled a 1979 decision (*Arkansas v. Sanders*) and ruled that police may make a warrantless search of a container found in a vehicle if they have probable cause to believe the container contains contraband. This warrantless search is permitted even though the police do not have probable cause to search the vehicle itself as in *United States v. Ross*.

REDUCED EXPECTATION OF PRIVACY CASES

United States v. Chadwick, 433 U.S. 1 (1977). The Supreme Court stated that there is a reduced expectation of privacy in an automobile because it travels public thoroughfares where both its occupants and its contents are in plain view. Although the *Chadwick* case noted the reduced expectation of privacy regarding vehicles, the Court held that a foot locker seized from the trunk of a vehicle could not be searched without a warrant.

Texas v. Brown, 460 U.S. 730 (1983). A police officer lawfully stopped an automobile, questioned the driver, saw what appeared to be containers usually used to carry narcotics (opaque balloons) in plain view, seized them and arrested the occupant. The Supreme Court said that the search was valid under the Plain View Doctrine.

But in *United States v. Bradshaw* and *New York v. Class*, the Court held that a car's interior is subject to protection under the Fourth Amendment when an intrusion is required to see the inside.

New York v. Class, 475 U.S. 106 "A citizen does not surrender all the protections of the Fourth Amendment by entering an automobile."

ARREST OF AN OCCUPANT OF THE VEHICLE

New York v. Belton, 453 U.S. 454 (1981). The Supreme Court established a bright line rule that obviates the necessity for a case-by-case analysis. The rule is that if an occupant of a vehicle is validly arrested, the police may make a contemporaneous search of the passenger compartment of the vehicle and any containers found therein as incident to the arrest. The search is valid even if the arrested person has been removed from the vehicle and placed in handcuffs. However, on remand to the New York State Court of Appeals, the New York court rejected the argument of the Supreme Court and opted to decide the case under the New York State Constitution. The New York Court of Appeals takes the position that, in addition to the valid arrest, there must be some reason to believe that the vehicle contains a weapon or evidence related to the crime for which the arrest was made, or a means of escape. None of these is required under the federal rule. It is imperative to know your own state's position. This case also ruled on the definition of a container, which is any object capable of holding another object.

INVENTORY SEARCHES, VEHICLES

Cooper v. California, 386 U.S. 58 (1967). The Supreme Court allowed an inventory search of a vehicle impounded a week earlier following the arrest of the operator for using the vehicle in transporting narcotics.

Harris v. United States, 390 U.S. 234 (1968). The Supreme Court allowed an inventory search of an automobile about to be entered by a person arrested for robbery. The automobile had been seen at the place of the robbery and was impounded and brought to the precinct where its contents were inventoried.

Cady v. Dombrowski, 413 U.S. 1074 (1973). The Supreme Court allowed an inventory search of the automobile of a Chicago police officer that had been arrested for driving while intoxicated following an accident. The vehicle was towed to a repair shop. The arrested policeman did not have his gun on him and local police searched the car to find the gun. They found items that were later linked to an unreported murder. The police went to look for the gun since it was "standard police procedure" because the gun could have been stolen from the car.

Dyke v. Taylor Implement Mfg. Co., 391 U.S. 216 (1968). An arrest was made for reckless driving. The defendant's vehicle was parked by police outside the courthouse and an inventory search was conducted. Supreme Court said search was not valid. There was no basis upon which to support the search.

Colorado v. Bertine, 479 U.S. 367 (1987). This is the latest case decided by the Supreme Court concerning an inventory search of a vehicle. In this case the Court permitted a full inventory search of a seized or impounded vehicle. It ruled that the search may extend to a locked trunk as well as to containers found in the trunk or passenger compartment. (Do not do more than minimum damage to open unless exigent circumstances are present.)

The reasons for an inventory search under the federal rules are the following:
Standard department procedures must be followed

1. to protect personal property in the vehicle.

2. to protect the police from accusations that property is missing.

3. to protect the public from harm if contraband or weapons should be found in the vehicle.

Note: The states are permitted to adopt stronger protective measures concerning police action than may be indicated in federal decisions. Frequently the Supreme Court has permitted a search, but when the case is remanded to a state Court of Appeals, the state court declares the search as unreasonable under the State Constitution. Keep informed of rulings in your own state.

INVENTORY SEARCHES, NO VEHICLES INVOLVED

The leading case is *Illinois v. La Fayette*, 462 U.S. 640 (1983). In this case, the defendant was arrested and at the time was carrying a duffel bag. At the station house, the arresting officer dumped the contents of the duffel bag onto a table to inventory the contents. Contraband was discovered. The Supreme Court stated that the search was reasonable as an inventory search. Probable cause is not needed to take inventory of personal effects of defendant at the police station. Inventory is proper at a police station for reasons that include safety, deterrence of false claims, and identity.

FRISK ON LESS THAN PROBABLE CAUSE

Terry v. Ohio, 392 U.S. 1 (1968). In this case, a Cleveland detective with 30 years' experience observed what he suspected to be three men about to rob a store they were casing. The detective stopped the men and frisked them by external patting. A gun was found on Terry and he was arrested. The Supreme Court said, " . . . there must be a narrowly drawn authority to permit a reasonable search for weapons for the protection of the police officer where he has reason to believe that he is dealing with an armed and dangerous individual, regardless of whether he has probable cause to arrest the individual for a crime. The sole justification of the search … is the protection of the police officer and others nearby."

Sibron v. New York, 392 U.S. 41 (1968). In this case, a police officer had observed Sibron for several hours and had seen him in numerous conversations with known drug addicts and dealers. None of the conversations were overheard and nothing was seen passing between Sibron and the other persons. The officer approached Sibron and said, "You know what I want." Sibron reached into his trouser pocket and the officer grabbed his hand and emptied Sibron's packet of what turned out to be heroin. The Supreme Court refused to use the rule in *Terry v. Ohio* in this case and decided that the heroin was inadmissible.

Note: The New York court had permitted the intrusion under its "stop and frisk statute," but the Supreme Court said such statutory application to these facts was improper.

BODILY EXTRACTIONS OF EVIDENCE

Rochin v. California, 342 U.S. 165 (1952). In this case Rochin, at the time of police entry into his home and in full view of the police, picked up and swallowed two capsules from a night table. The police brought Rochin to a hospital where an emetic solution was forced into his stomach to cause him to vomit. The capsules were recovered and found to contain morphine. The Supreme Court held that the police conduct violated the Due Process Clause of the Fourteenth Amendment. In its opinion, the Court likened this to a forced confession and said that it would be wrong to " . . . hold that in order to convict a man the police cannot extract by force what is in his mind, but can extract what is in his stomach."

Breithaupt v. Abram, 352 U.S. 432 (1957). In this case, the police took a sample of blood from an unconscious person who had been involved in a fatal automobile accident. The blood sample showed the man to be intoxicated, and he was later convicted of manslaughter based on the blood alcohol reading. The Supreme Court distinguished this case from the *Rochin* case and took the position that the antiseptic circumstances (hospital, doctor in attendance, etc.) and the interest of society in ridding the road of intoxicated drivers outweighed the slight intrusion into the person's body.

Schmerber v. California, 384 U.S. 757 (1966). Schmerber was placed under arrest for driving while intoxicated. Over his objections, a blood sample was taken from him by a doctor at a hospital. The blood sample was analyzed and Schmerber was found to be intoxicated. The Supreme Court used the same reasoning in this case (the defendant conscious and objecting) as it did in the *Breithaupt* case and found the bodily intrusion under the circumstances not to be unreasonable.

One of the circumstances considered by the Court was that "time" was important. The blood alcohol level would diminish with the passage of time. If the blood sample taken from a person is not to test for blood alcohol level, but is to determine a constant such as blood type, then a warrant would be required.

Note: in all three of the cases cited, the defendants were in a hospital, the conditions were antiseptic, a doctor was in attendance, and yet the results were not the same. The difference seems to be that in the *Breithaupt* and *Schmerber* cases, there was a strong societal interest in prosecuting drunken drivers.

Some states have codified the rule in *Schmerber* and have enacted laws that require the taking of blood from a suspect involved in a serious motor vehicle accident who refuses to submit to a chemical test (as in *Schmerber*) or who is unable to consent to a chemical test (as in *Breithaupt*).

New York State Vehicle and Traffic Law, Section 1194, Subdivision 3, that is reprinted below is typical. Consult the laws of your own state for the specifics as they apply to you.

3. Compulsory chemical tests. (a) Court-ordered chemical tests. Notwithstanding the provisions of subdivision two of this section, no person who operates a motor vehicle in this state may refuse to submit to a chemical test of one or more of the following: breath, blood, urine, or saliva, for the purpose of determining the alcoholic and/or drug content of the blood when a court order for such chemical test has been issued in accordance with the provisions of this subdivision.

(b) When authorized. Upon refusal by any person to submit to a chemical test or any portion thereof as described above, the test shall not be given unless a police officer or a district attorney, as defined in subdivision thirty-two of section 1.20 of the criminal procedure law, requests and obtains a court order to compel a person to submit to a chemical test to determine the alcoholic or drug content of the person's blood upon a finding of reasonable cause to believe that: (1) such person was the operator of a motor vehicle and in the course of such operation a person other than the operator was killed or suffered serious physical injury as defined in section 10.00 of the penal law; and

(2) a. either such person operated the vehicle in violation of any subdivision of section eleven hundred ninety-two of this article; or

b. breath test administered by a police officer in accordance with paragraph (b) of subdivision one of this section indicates that alcohol has been consumed by such person; and

(3) such person has been placed under lawful arrest; and

(4) such person has refused to submit to a chemical test or any portion thereof, requested in accordance with the provisions of paragraph (a) of subdivision two of this section or is unable to give consent to such a test. (c) Reasonable cause; definition. For the purpose of this subdivision reasonable cause shall be determined by viewing the totality of circumstances surrounding the incident which, when taken together, indicate that the operator was driving in violation of section eleven hundred ninety-two of this article. Such circumstances may include, but are not limited to, evidence that the operator was operating a motor vehicle in violation of any provision of this article or any other moving violation at the time of the incident; any visible indication of alcohol or drug consumption or impairment by the operator; the existence of an open container containing an alcoholic beverage in or around the vehicle driven by the operator; any other evidence surrounding the circumstances of the incident which indicates that the operator has been operating a motor vehicle while impaired by the consumption of alcohol or drugs, or intoxicated at the time of the incident. (d) Court order; procedure. (1) An application for a court order to compel submission to a chemical test or any portion thereof, may be made to any Supreme Court justice, county court judge or district court judge in the judicial district in which the incident occurred, or if the incident occurred in the city of New York before any Supreme Court justice or judge of the criminal court of the city of New York. Such application may be communicated by telephone, radio or other means of electronic communication, or in person. (2) The applicant must provide identification by name and title and must state the purpose of the communication. Upon being advised that an application for a court order to compel submission to a chemical test is being made, the court shall place under oath the applicant and any other person providing information in sup-

port of the application as provided in subparagraph three of this paragraph. After being sworn, the applicant must state that the person from whom the chemical test was requested was the operator of a motor vehicle and in the course of such operation a person, other than the operator, has been killed or seriously injured and, based upon the totality of circumstances, there is reasonable cause to believe that such person was operating a motor vehicle in violation of any subdivision of section eleven hundred ninety-two of this article and, after being placed under lawful arrest, such person refused to submit to a chemical test of any portion thereof; in accordance with the provisions of this section or is unable to give consent to such a test or any portion thereof. The applicant must make specific allegations of fact to support such statement. Any other person properly identified, may present sworn allegations of fact in support of the applicant's statement. (3) Upon being advised that an oral application for a court order to compel a person to submit to a chemical test is being made, a judge or justice shall place under oath the applicant and any other person providing information in support of the application. Such oath or oaths and all of the remaining communication must be recorded, either by means of a voice-recording device or verbatim stenographic or verbatim longhand notes. If a voice-recording device is used or a stenographic record made, the judge must have the record transcribed, certify to the accuracy of the transcription and file the original record and transcription. with the court within 72 hours of the issuance of the court order. If the longhand notes are taken, the judge shall subscribe a copy and file it with the court within twenty-four hours of the issuance of the order. (4) If the court is satisfied that the requirements for the issuance of a court order pursuant to the provisions of paragraph (b) of this subdivision have been met, it may grant the application and issue an order requiring the accused to submit to a chemical test to determine the alcoholic and/or drug content of his blood and ordering the withdrawal of a blood sample in accordance with provisions of paragraph (a) of subdivision four of this section. When a judge or justice determines to issue an order to compel submission to a chemical test based on an oral application, the applicant therefor shall prepare the order in accordance with the instructions of the judge or justice. In all cases the order shall include the name of the issuing judge or justice, the name of the applicant, and the date and time it was issued. It must be signed by the judge or justice if issued in person, or by the applicant if issued orally…"

THE FIFTH AMENDMENT

No person shall be held to answer for a capital, or otherwise infamous crime, unless on a presentment or indictment of a Grand Jury, except in cases arising in the land or naval forces, or in the militia, when in actual service in time of War or public danger; not shall any person be subject for the same offence to be twice put in jeopardy of life or limb; nor shall be compelled in any criminal case to be a witness against himself, nor be deprived of life, liberty, or property, without due process of law; nor shall private property be taken for public use, without just compensation. (Effective date November 3, 1791.)

HISTORICAL BACKGROUND

We saw in our opening paragraphs of "The Police and Constitutional Law" that the Bill of Rights, as originally enacted, was considered to be protection only against actions of the newly created federal government.

In 1897, in the case of *Gram v. United States*, the Supreme Court held that in criminal trials in courts of the United States, the question of whether or not a confession is incompetent because it was not voluntarily given is governed by the Fifth Amendment to the United States Constitution.

The rationale supporting the exclusion of involuntary confessions, historically, was based on whether or not the method used to extract the confession would cause a person to make a false confession. If the confession made by a defendant was considered to be the truth, then the method used would not necessarily result in the confession's being excluded.

In the case of *Brown v. Mississippi*, 297 U.S. 278 (1936), the Supreme Court used the Fourteenth Amendment's Due Process Clause to bring Fifth Amendment protections against self-incrimination to bear against state governmental action. In this case, a confession was beaten out of a black defendant by police deputies using whips. Since this method obviously made the confession "untrustworthy," the confession was excluded. Subsequent to *Brown v. Mississippi*, the cases involving physical abuse and threats were not difficult for the courts to decide. But when cases involving psychological pressures (long hours of continuous interrogation, etc.) began to arise, it was not easy for the courts to conclude that these subtle pressures resulted in confessions that were unreliable as evidence of guilt.

In the case of *Watts v. Indiana*, 338 U.S. 49 (1949), the Supreme Court held that the Due Process Clause bars police procedures which violate basic decencies of civilized conduct. In 1952, in the case of *Rochin v. California*, supra, the stomach-pumping case, the Supreme Court pointed out that the unreliability of a coerced confession is not the sole ground for its exclusion. Coerced confessions offend society's sense of fair play and decency.

Note: There is an overlap between cases involving self-incrimination, interrogation, and right to counsel. The self-incrimination/interrogation cases are based, on Fifth Amendment rights, while the "right to counsel" cases are based can Sixth Amendment rights. Frequently, the two rights overlap and both may be applicable to a particular case.

Consider *Escobedo v. Illinois*, 378 U.S. 478 (1964). In this case, Danny Escobedo was arrested without a warrant. While in custody, but prior to arraignment, Escobedo asked to confer with his attorney and was refused this right. Escobedo's attorney was present at the police facility where Escobedo was being held and questioned and saw Escobedo for a moment but was denied access to his client. During this period of custody, Escobedo admitted complicity in a murder. He was tried and convicted in the state court. On appeal to the Supreme Court of the United States, the conviction was reversed and the Court held as follows: " . . . where the investigation is no longer a general inquiry into an unsolved crime but has begun to focus on a particular suspect, the suspect has been taken into police custody, the police carry out a process of interrogations that lends itself to eliciting incriminating statements, the suspect has requested and been denied an opportunity to consult with his lawyer; and the police have not effectively warned him of his absolute constitutional right to remain silent; the accused has been denied the assistance of counsel in violation of the Sixth Amendment to the Constitution as made obligatory upon the states by the Fourteenth Amendment, and that no statement elicited by the police during the interrogation may be used against him at a criminal trial .... [W]e hold . . . that when the process shifts from investigatory to accusatory, when its focus is on the accused and its purpose is to elicit a confession, our adversary system begins to operate, and, under the circumstances here, the accused must be permitted to consult with his lawyer."

Two years after the decision in *Escobedo v. Illinois*, the Supreme Court decided the landmark case of *Miranda v. Arizona*, 384 U.S. 436 (1966). In this case, the Supreme Court held that when a person has been taken into custody, or otherwise deprived of his freedom of action in any significant way and is subjected to custodial interrogation, the prosecution may not use any statements obtained during this interrogation unless it demonstrates the use of procedural safeguards to secure the privilege against self-incrimination. The safeguards are the following:

1. Prior to any questioning, the person must be warned that:

    a. he has a right to remain silent; and
    b. any statement he does make may be used as evidence against him; and
    c. he has the right to the presence of an attorney, either retained or appointed.

2. The defendant may waive these rights if he does so voluntarily, knowingly, and intelligently. If the defendant indicates in any manner and at any stage of the process that he wishes to consult with an attorney, there can be no questioning. If the defendant is alone and indicates in any manner that he does not want to be interrogated, he may not be questioned. The mere fact that he may have answered some questions or volunteered some statements on his own does not deprive him of the right to refrain

from answering any further inquiries until he has consulted with an attorney and thereafter consents to be questioned.

In *Harris v. New York*, 401 U.S. 222 (1971). The Court held that a confession obtained in violation of *Miranda* may be used at trial for impeachment purposes. Also of special interest is the 1987 Supreme Court decision in *Colorado v. Springs* in which Springs, while under arrest on a weapons charge, was interrogated by federal officers after waiving his Miranda rights. During this interrogation, Springs was asked if he ever killed anyone. Springs answered in the affirmative. Three months later, state officers interrogated Springs about the murder and obtained a confession. The Colorado Court suppressed the confession because of improper "trickery." The Supreme Court allowed the confession to stand maintaining that mere silence as to the subject matter of the interrogation does not amount to impermissible trickery. Another permissive decision is *Connecticut v. Barrett* where in 1987 the Supreme Court allowed a waiver to take place orally even though the defendant stated that he would not waive in writing without consulting his lawyer.

Note: The Supreme Court of the United States has frequently taken the position that when an emergency exists (searching for a possible crime victim, trying to locate a kidnap victim who may still be alive, location of a weapon, etc.), then the emergency will take precedence over the safeguards. However, once the emergency is over all constitutional safeguards must be adhered to.

THE SIXTH AMENDMENT

In all criminal prosecutions, the accused shall enjoy the right to a speedy and public trial, by an impartial jury of the state and district wherein the crime shall have been committed, which district shall have been previously ascertained by law, and to be informed of the nature and cause of the accusation; to be confronted with the witnesses against him; to have compulsory process for obtaining witnesses in his favor, and to have assistance of counsel for his defense. (Effective date November 3, 1791.)

HISTORICAL BACKGROUND

In the case of *Powell v. Alabama*, 287 U.S. 45 (1932), the Supreme Court held that in a capital case where the defendant is unable to employ counsel and is incapable of making an adequate defense of himself because of ignorance, illiteracy, or the like, it is the duty of the court, whether requested or not, to assign counsel for him as a necessary prerequisite of due process of law.

Ten years later in *Betts v. Brady,* 316 U.S. 455 (1942), the Supreme Court declined to extend the right to have appointed an assigned counsel in all criminal cases. The Court took the position that in a noncapital case the state courts were free to decide on their own whether or not failure to appoint or assign counsel to an indigent defendant would result in an unfair trial.

It took almost twenty more years for the Supreme Court to reverse and to decide that assigned counsel for any indigent defendant was a constitutional guarantee applicable to the states through the Fourteenth Amendment.

In the case of *Gideon v. Wainwright*, 372 U.S. 335 (1963), the Supreme Court reviewed the decision in *Betts v. Brady* and concluded that the decision was improper. The court referred to the language used in the earlier case of *Powell v. Alabama* that said that the right to counsel is a fundamental constitutional right. Unfortunately, in the *Powell* case the Court limited its decision to capital crimes because the case before it was a capital crime. The *Gideon* Court's opinion was that the Court in *Betts v. Brady* erred in stating that right to counsel is not a fundamental right essential to a fair trial. *Betts v. Brady* was overruled and the current file was established.

Note: It should be apparent to all that there is overlap between the Fifth Amendment and Sixth Amendment rights. The decision in *Miranda v. Arizona* mandates that a person who is to be subjected to custodial interrogation be informed of his "right to counsel" and of the fact that if he cannot afford counsel, counsel will be provided for him.

Douglas v. California, 372 U.S. 353 (1963), says that the state must appoint counsel to assist an indigent defendant for the first appeal as a right from a conviction.

THE SEVENTH AMENDMENT

In suits at common law, where the value in controversy shall exceed twenty dollars, the right of trial by jury shall be preserved, and no fact tried by a jury, shall be otherwise reexamined in any Court of the United States, than according to the rules of the common law. (Effective date November 3, 1791.)

HISTORICAL BACKGROUND

In the case of *Duncan v. Louisiana*, 391 U.S. 145 (1968), the Supreme Court concluded that the provisions of the Seventh Amendment were applicable against state action through the Fourteenth Amendment in any prosecution for a "serious" crime. The Court did not define what it meant by a serious crime, but its direction pointed toward any crime where it was possible to be sentenced to more than six months in jail.

In the case of *Baldwin v. New York*, 399 U.S. 66 (1970), in a decision without an opinion, the Supreme Court decided that no offense can be deemed a "petty" offense for purposes of the right to trial by jury where imprisonment for more than six months is authorized.

In *Williams v. Florida*, 399 U.S. 78. (1970), the Supreme Court decided that the size of the jury is not part of the constitutional guarantee of jury trial. The Court took the position that a six-person jury could operate just as effectively in determining a case as can a twelve-person jury.

Note: In most states, juries that decide felony cases are twelve in number, while those that decide less than felony cases have six persons.

THE EIGHTH AMENDMENT

Excessive bail shall not be required, nor excessive fines imposed, nor cruel and unusual punishments inflicted. (Effective date November 3, 1791.)

HISTORICAL BACKGROUND

In the recent past, when people have spoken of "cruel and unusual" punishment, almost always they have been referring to the death penalty. At the time the Eighth Amendment became effective, the death penalty was not considered to be cruel and unusual. In the case of *Furman v. Georgia*, 408 U.S. 238 (1972), decided by the Court, *per curiam*, along with two other cases, the Supreme Court held the death penalty to be cruel and unusual punishment. Each member of the Court contributed his own opinion as to why it was cruel and unusual. The statutes that permitted the death penalty left it up to the discretion of the jury, and Justice Douglas stated that they were "pregnant with discrimination." The issue of whether or not a mandatory death sentence would not be cruel and unusual was not reached. Following the *Furman* case, other cases came before the Supreme Court and the death penalty was declared not to be cruel and unusual punishment. As it stands now, each state devises its own death penalty law, and the Supreme Court decides whether that law, as applied, is "cruel and unusual."

The best that can be said for the death penalty currently is that it is still a controversial issue that is approached differently in each of the states.

THE FOURTEENTH AMENDMENT

Section 1 (of 5). All persons born or naturalized in the United States, and subject to the jurisdiction thereof, are citizens of the United States and of the State wherein they reside. No State shall make or enforce any law which shall abridge the privileges or immunities of citizens of the United States; nor shall any State deprive any person of life, liberty, or property, without due process of law; nor deny to any person, within its jurisdiction the equal protection of the laws. (Effective date July 28, 1868.)

(Please note the effective date of the Fourteenth Amendment, which came into being about 3 years after the Civil War. It has been used, mainly in the last 35 to 50 years, as the vehicle that brings the protections of the Bill of Rights to bear against unconstitutional actions of the states and the various political subdivisions of the states.)

Section 5. The Congress shall have power to enforce, by appropriate legislation, the provisions of this article.

QUESTIONS ON CONSTITUTIONAL LAW

> **Directions:** Read each question and choose the best answer. Circle the letter of your choice.

1. While Sergeant Connolly is supervising patrol within his jurisdiction, he receives a call to meet a patrol unit at a large, downtown, privately owned shopping mall. Upon his arrival, Sergeant Connolly determines that a group of people representing an animal rights organization are distributing leaflets calling for a ban of the use of animals in medical experiments. They are interfering with the other users of the mall. The mall manager has asked them to leave and they have refused to do so, claiming that their activity is an exercise of free speech protected by the First Amendment to the United States Constitution. Under these circumstances, Sergeant Connolly would be best advised to

   (A) ignore the situation as it is not a police matter.
   (B) inform the mall manager that the group has a constitutional right to demonstrate and distribute leaflets.
   (C) inform the group that this kind of activity on private property is not constitutionally protected.
   (D) direct the patrol officers on the scene to arrest the members of the group for trespassing on private property.

2. Lieutenant Mullins is assigned to supervise a police detail that is present at the scene of a political rally. The sponsors of the rally have obtained all required permits. An opposing political party is on the scene and wishes to demonstrate against the party sponsoring the rally. The location is a public square within the town covered by Lieutenant Mullins' department. Lieutenant Mullins, after conferring with the leaders of both parties, decides to allow the opposing political party to demonstrate, but in the interest of public safety informs them that the number of demonstrators will be limited, that they will not be able to carry signs with handles that could be used as weapons, and that they must remain at least one hundred feet away from the planned rally. Lieutenant Mullins' decision could best be characterized as

   (A) improper; he should have banned the opposing protest.
   (B) proper; while the opposing party has a right to demonstrate on public property, that right can be limited, reasonably, in the interest of public safety.
   (C) improper; the opposing party should not have had its activity limited.
   (D) proper; since Lieutenant Mullins could have, at his discretion, banned the opposing protest altogether.

3. You are a police officer on patrol. A robbery has taken place in your jurisdiction. Shortly thereafter, you observe an automobile that fits the description of the getaway car, and the occupants fit the description of the wanted persons. You stop the vehicle and arrest the occupants. You are convinced that proceeds from the robbery will be found inside the car, but the location is very dark and will not permit a thorough search. You have the car removed to the station house where there is more light. You search the interior of the car and find the robbery proceeds. At trial, the defendants claim that the search without a warrant under these circumstances was an unreasonable search prohibited by the Fourth Amendment to the United States Constitution, and they move to suppress the evidence. The probable outcome of the motion is that the evidence will

   (A) be suppressed since the search of the vehicle was not made contemporaneously with the arrest.

   (B) be suppressed because once the vehicle is moved from the scene, any search for evidence would require a search warrant.

   (C) not be suppressed because an inventory search of the vehicle at the police facility would have had the same result.

   (D) not be suppressed since the police had probable cause to believe the vehicle contained contraband or evidence, and moving the automobile to a more well-lighted location was not unreasonable.

4. You are in command of a detective unit. You have obtained a warrant of arrest for Roger, who is a dealer in counterfeit coins and stamps. Roger is at work right now, but you decide to wait until he comes home from work so that you can arrest him in his house. Your objective is to search Roger's house "incident to the arrest" on the warrant. When Roger arrives home you enter his house, place him under arrest in the ground-floor living room, and search the entire house incident to the arrest. You seize numerous items of incriminating evidence from an upstairs bedroom. At trial, Roger claims that the search of his home under these circumstances was unreasonable and in violation of his Fourth Amendment rights. Roger's claim is

   (A) valid, since a search incident to a lawful arrest is limited to the person arrested and the grabbable (or lungeable) area surrounding him.

   (B) valid, since any search following an arrest can be justified only if a search warrant is obtained.

   (C) invalid, since it is a long-standing law that a search incident to a lawful arrest is not unreasonable.

   (D) invalid, since Roper's objection was not timely; it should have been made at the time that his house was searched.

5. You are the watch commander in your police jurisdiction when Police Officer Lucille Nunno enters the station house with a prisoner. P.O. Nunno informs you that she arrested the person for a traffic infraction because the person was not properly identified and a traffic citation would be improper. You agree with P.O. Nunno and, as part of the arrest processing, you direct that a search of the violator be made. Your direction to search would be considered

   (A) proper; when an arrest is made, a search of the person arrested is always valid, even if only a traffic offense is involved.

   (B) proper; a search would be proper even if you determined that P.O. Nunno should dispose of the matter by the issuance of a summons or citation.

   (C) improper; searches incident to an arrest are only justified when the arrested person has committed a crime.

   (D) improper; a felony or high misdemeanor was not involved, therefore no search was authorized.

6. During an investigation into a burglary of commercial establishment, a police investigator develops probable cause to believe that that Roger is the burglar. He arrests Roger and, pending arraignment in court, lodges him in a detention cell at the local police facility. About 10 hours later, the police investigator determines that there is probably some trace of evidence on Roger's clothing that was transferred from the scene during the burglary. The investigator returns to the police facility, directs Roger to remove his outer clothing, and he searches the clothing. Traces of evidence from the burglary scene are discovered. At trial, Roger moves to suppress this evidence claiming that the search of his clothing without benefit of a search warrant was unreasonable. Roger's claim is

   (A) valid; the time lapse between arrest and the search was too great for the search to be considered as incident to the arrest.
   (B) invalid; under the circumstances, since Roger was still in local police custody, the substantial time lapse did not vitiate the search.
   (C) valid; once a suspect is transferred from the scene to a police facility, searches of his person are no longer considered to be contemporaneous with the arrest.
   (D) invalid; until the criminal proceeding is commenced by the filing of an accusatory instrument with the proper court, all searches of the arrested person may be conducted without a search warrant.

7. Detective Connolly is investigating a series of burglaries. He suspects that one Judy Milowe is involved, but he has been unable to reach her to speak with her. Detective Connolly leaves one of his calling cards at Ms. Milowe's home with a request that she call him at the local police facility. Ms. Milowe calls the next day, and Detective Connolly says, "I would appreciate it if you could find the time to come to my office so that I can speak with you." Ms. Milowe replies, "I can come over right now." Ms. Milowe shows up at the police facility. The meeting is friendly, but Detective Connolly advises Ms. Milowe that she is a suspect in the burglaries. He also tells her that she is free to leave if she so desires. Then Detective Connolly uses a subterfuge and tells Ms. Milowe that her fingerprints were found at the scene of several burglaries. This is not true. When Ms. Milowe hears this false statement, she breaks down and confesses to her part in the burglaries. Detective Connolly advises her of her rights, tapes the confession, permits Ms. Milowe to leave, and turns the taped confession over to the prosecutor. At her trial, Judy Milowe moves to have the confession suppressed. Her motion will

   (A) not be granted since she was not in custody when she was questioned and was free to leave at any time.
   (B) be granted because investigators are not permitted to trick suspects into confessing.
   (C) not be granted because even though she was confined in a police facility, she did not request an attorney.
   (D) be granted because she was the focus of the investigation and should have been advised of her rights prior to being questioned.

8. Police Officers Mullins and Connolly have been conducting an investigation into the illegal drug activities of Tondelayo. During the investigation, they establish probable cause to arrest Tondelayo and they do so as she exits from a passenger train at the local railroad station. P.O. Mullins escorts Tondelayo to the local police facility, but P.O. Connolly takes Tondelayo's suitcase and brings it to a forensic lab where it is searched inside and out and drugs are found. This search is conducted without benefit of a search warrant. At her trial, Tondelayo moves to suppress the drug evidence found in the suitcase. Tondelayo's motion should be

   (A) successful because Tondelayo could not have reached into the suitcase to alter or destroy the evidence, and it should not have been searched without consent or a search warrant.
   (B) unsuccessful because this was a search incident to a lawful arrest and the fact that the suitcase was no longer in Tondelayo's possession has no effect on the validity of the search.
   (C) successful because containers being carried by an arrested person can never be searched without consent, a search warrant, or exigent circumstances.
   (D) unsuccessful, because public policy demands that the full weight of legal authority be brought to bear against drug dealers.

9. Detective Mullins responds to the scene of a suspected homicide. Apparently, Roger and Tondelayo, tired of caring for their aged aunt and anxious to inherit her money, have conspired to kill the aunt and have given her arsenic with her warm milk. Detective Mullins enters the apartment where all three lived. He announces that this is a crime scene and he is going to search it for evidence. Roger objects and says, "This is our home. You can't search unless one of us consents or you have a search warrant." Detective Mullins replies, "The rule is different with a crime scene. Now stand aside, or I will have you arrested for obstructing an investigation." Detective Mullins searches the scene without a warrant and finds the milk glass with traces of arsenic still in the glass. Detective Mullins' actions could best be described as

   (A) proper; a crime scene is a recognized exception to the search warrant requirement.
   (B) proper; only because a homicide was involved and public policy demands that homicide crime scenes be fully open to police.
   (C) improper; absent special circumstances, a crime scene in private premises is constitutionally protected against unreasonable searches.
   (D) improper; unless consent is given, a crime scene in private premises may not be searched in the absence of a search warrant.

10. Captain Milowe advises her police officers to conduct a series of vehicle stops at random in an attempt to locate stolen cars and to enforce equipment requirements concerning automobiles. P.O. Connolly asks, "But Captain, aren't random vehicle stops to check out the operators prohibited?" Captain Milowe answers, "Of course not. When someone drives a car on our public highways he gives up his right to privacy." Captain Milowe's statement is

   (A) incorrect; random vehicle stops to check licenses, etc., are improper.
   (B) correct; a vehicle, in and of itself, is an emergency.
   (C) incorrect; unless some traffic offense is involved, vehicle stops for inspections are improper.
   (D) correct; public policy demands such safety inspections.

11. Police Officer Mullins has arrested Roger on a warrant. He has given Roger his Miranda warnings and has asked him to waive his rights. Roger does not respond verbally, but by his actions indicates that he will consent to being questioned. He refuses to sign a waiver, but says that he will talk and it is apparent that he understands the Miranda warnings. When asked if he wants a lawyer he does not respond. Of course, at the trial Roger wants his statements suppressed, claiming he did not waive his rights. The probable decision by the court on the above facts will be that Roger

   (A) waived his rights by his actions.
   (B) did not waive his rights because he did not sign a waiver.
   (C) waived his rights specifically when he said he would talk, but would not sign a waiver.
   (D) did not waive his rights because when an arrest warrant has been issued the defendant's right to counsel becomes absolute and cannot be waived in the absence of counsel.

12. While on foot patrol in a densely populated area, Police Officer Connolly sees Judy Milowe, a resident on his post, coming out of a doctor's office with bandages on her face and with an obviously swollen lip. P.O. Connolly inquires as to how she received the injuries, and Judy replies that her current boyfriend, Roger, beat her when she refused to have a drink with him at the local bar. P.O. Connolly asks Judy if she would be willing to press charges, and Judy says "yes." Judy tells P.O. Connolly where Roger lives and says, "He has lived there for about a year and has 2 years to go on his lease." P.O. Connolly goes to Roger's apartment, knocks on the door, and announces his purpose and authority. Roger refuses to admit P.O. Connolly and says, "Leave me alone. That woman is always trying to get me into trouble." P.O. Connolly calls for backup and when it arrives he forcibly enters Roger's apartment and arrests him for the assault on Judy. P.O. Connolly's actions could best be characterized as

   (A) proper; the arrest was based on probable cause, he had the right person, and he was refused admittance.
   (B) improper; absent consent or exigent circumstances, a person's home may not be entered to make a routine, arrest unless an arrest warrant has been obtained.
   (C) proper; since a felony had obviously occurred, P.O. Connolly had a legal right to forcibly enter and arrest Roger.
   (D) improper; when a person is in his home, he may not be arrested unless the arresting officer has an arrest warrant.

13. Tondelayo was on trial for murder. She stated that although she killed Roger, she acted in self-defense. The facts in the case established that Tondelayo did not surrender until two weeks after the killing and during that period did not mention the killing to anyone. The prosecutor commented adversely on Tondelayo's prearrest silence in order to impeach her credibility. Tondelayo objected stating that this adverse comment violated her constitutional rights. The decision of the court should be

   (A) in Tondelayo's favor since she was not obliged to comment on the matter to anyone.
   (B) against Tondelayo because, while she was not obligated to speak, it was not unreasonable to expect her to make known her problem.
   (C) in Tondelayo's favor because this impacts on her reputation and unless she puts her reputation in issue the prosecutor may not address it.
   (D) against Tondelayo because she is obligated under law to deny criminal accusations made against her.

14. Roger was placed under arrest for the armed robbery of a taxi driver. A shotgun had been used in the robbery, but it was not recovered. On the way into the police station in a patrol car, after Roger had said he wanted a lawyer, P.O. Mullins made the following comment to his partner, "There are a lot of handicapped children in this area because one of their schools is nearby. I hope to God one of them doesn't find that shotgun." When Roger heard this comment, he told the police officers where to find the gun. Evaluate the following statements:

   I.   When Roger said he wanted a lawyer, his right to counsel was triggered and became absolute.
   II.   The "off-hand" remark by P.O. Mullins was not interrogation.
   III. If P.O. Mullins had made the remark in the hope of getting a response from Roger, his remark would be considered interrogation and therefore improper.
   (A)   All three statements are correct.
   (B)   Only statement I is correct.
   (C)   Only statements I and II are correct.
   (D)   Only statements I and III are correct.

15. Judy was in jail under indictment and awaiting trial. Federal agents arranged for a paid informant to be placed into the same cell as Judy to overhear Judy's comments, to engage her in conversation, and to ask her questions about her alleged crime. The informant had a conversation with Judy and Judy made incriminating statements.

   Evaluate the following statements based on the preceding facts:

   I.   Although the police engaged in trickery, it was good police work and Judy's statements will not be suppressed.
   II.   Since Judy was in jail awaiting trial on an indictment, she already must have been arraigned; therefore her right to counsel was absolute.
   III. The actions of the police in placing the informant into Judy's cell violated Judy's right to counsel.
   (A)   All three statements are correct.
   (B)   Only statements I and II are correct.
   (C)   Only statement I is correct.
   (D)   Only statements II and III are correct.

16. Federal officers obtained a warrant of arrest for Frank. They had information that led them to believe that Frank was inside George's house. They went to George's house with the arrest warrant and, after George told them that Frank was not there, they forced their way into George's house and searched for Frank. Frank was not in the house, but during the search for Frank the police saw, in plain view, contraband possessed by George. The police seized the contraband and arrested George for its possession. Evaluate the following statements:

   I.   The police violated George's right to privacy.
   II.   If Frank had been in George's house and had been placed under arrest, his arrest would have been lawful.
   III. Before the police could lawfully search George's house for Frank, absent consent or exigent circumstances, they would need a search warrant for George's house.
   (A)   All three statements are correct.
   (B)   Only statements I and II are correct.
   (C)   Only statements II and III are correct.
   (D)   Only statement II is correct.

17. Police Officer Connolly had obtained a search warrant to search the home of Roger. When P.O. Connolly arrived at Roger's home there were several people present. The people were detained, and P.O. Connolly searched the premises. Contraband was found on the premises and Roger was arrested for its possession. Evaluate the following statements:

I. P.O. Connolly had no right to detain the persons while he searched the premises.

II. If P.O. Connolly reasonably suspected that any of the persons present were armed, then he would have been justified in patting them down for his own protection.

III. On the basis of the search warrant for the premises, P.O. Connolly would have been authorized to search all the persons in the premises when the search warrant was executed.

(A) All three statements are correct.
(B) Only statements I and II are correct:
(C) Only statements II and III are correct.
(D) Only statement II is correct.

18. You are a police officer, and you have developed Roger as a previously reliable confidential informant who has always met the "two pronged Aguilar-Spinelli test" of reliability. Roger comes to you and informs you that one of his associates is planning to "kill a cop" and has an illegally possessed 357 Magnum somewhere in his automobile. Roger tells you that he saw the weapon placed into the automobile. Roger also informs you that the automobile is currently packed at the curb in front of a local bar and grill. Which of the following statements is *correct*?

(A) Roger's information is not sufficient to give you the probable cause needed to support a search warrant application.
(B) You may search the suspect automobile without a warrant, but only if you verify that, in fact, the weapon is inside.
(C) You may not search the suspect vehicle for the weapon unless you have either consent or a search warrant.
(D) You may search the entire automobile, trunk included, and any and all containers that could contain the weapon and you do not need a search warrant to do so.

19. Police Officer Dolores Izzo, while checking the driver's license of a driver, shined her flashlight into the car and saw an opaque party balloon knotted at the end. Based on P.O. Izzo's experience, she was aware that narcotic substances are frequently carried this way. While the driver was reaching into the glove compartment for his license, P.O. Izzo saw other indications of narcotics. The driver had no license and P.O. Izzo ordered him from the car, picked up the knotted balloon, saw that it contained a powdery substance, and arrested the driver. A forensic test later on established that the powder on the balloon was, in fact, heroin. Which of the following is *not* correct?

(A) P.O. Izzo did not exceed her authority when she shined her flashlight into the car.
(B) P.O. Izzo did not exceed her authority when she asked the driver to step out of the car.
(C) P.O. Izzo, when she saw the knotted balloon, did not know at that point that it contained contraband.
(D) Since P.O. Izzo only had probable cause to believe that the knotted balloon contained narcotics, she was not authorized to seize it under the plain view exception to the need to have a search warrant.

20. While on patrol, Police Officer Anthony Nunno has occasion to arrest Roger for a minor offense. At the time, Roger is in possession of a shoulder bag that was not searched as incident to the arrest. While at the station house where the arrest is being processed, P.O. Nunno conducts an "inventory" search of Roger's shoulder bag. He finds a cigarette case that he opens and inside the cigarette case he finds ten amphetamine pills. Roger is charged, additionally, with the unlawful possession of the pills. Which of the following statements is *not* correct?

(A) Under federal rule concerning searches incident to an arrest, the shoulder bag could have been searched by P.O. Nunno at the time of arrest.

(B) As long as the inventory search is not a subterfuge to find evidence, and if department procedures are followed, the courts will permit an inventory search.

(C) While P.O. Nunno had the authority to search the shoulder bag, generally, he did not have the authority to open the cigarette case without consent or a search warrant.

(D) P.O. Nunno did not heed a search warrant to conduct any portion of this inventory search.

21. Police Officer Judy Milowe is on foot patrol in a densely populated area. An excited robbery victim runs up to her and says, "Officer, that man in the black jacket running into the supermarket just robbed me at gunpoint. He forced me to give him my wallet, showed me a gun, and said he would shoot me if I didn't comply." P.O. Milowe chases the suspect and overtakes him in the supermarket. Prior to being overtaken, the suspect hides the gun in a food container. P.O. Milowe overpowers the suspect, sees that he doesn't have a gun and says, "Where is the gun?" The suspect replies, "I put it into that food container." P.O. Milowe handcuffs the suspect, retrieves the gun, and arrests the suspect. Evaluate the following statements:

I. The suspect was "in custody" when P.O. Milowe questioned him about the gun.

II. The trial court's position was that this was "'custodial interrogation" and Miranda warnings should have preceded the question concerning the gun.

III. The Supreme Court of the United States concluded that there was a public policy exception to the Miranda requirements and this was an emergency.

(A) All three statements are correct.

(B) Only statements I and III are correct.

(C) Only statement III is correct.

(D) Only statement I is correct.

22. A federal drug agent is working in North Carolina not far from South Carolina. He sees a heavily laden camper-type pickup truck followed by a Pontiac automobile. He reasonably suspects that the vehicles are involved in smuggling narcotics and he starts to pursue the vehicles. In South Carolina, he gets assistance from the state police. The federal agent overtakes and stops the Pontiac, and the state trooper overtakes and stops the camper farther south. The South Carolina trooper detains the camper and its occupants for 20 minutes until the arrival of the federal police. When the federal police officer arrives, he detects an odor of marijuana coming from the camper. An arrest is made and the marijuana is seized. Based on the above information, evaluate the following statements:

I. The initial stop by the federal police, based on reasonable suspicion, was not improper.

II. The stop of the camper by the South Carolina police was not improper.

III. Since probable cause to arrest the camper's occupants was not developed by the South Carolina police, detaining the camper and its occupants amounted to an unauthorized arrest.

(A) All three statements are correct.

(B) Only statements I and II are correct.

(C) Only statement III is correct.

(D) All three statements are incorrect.

23. Roger has been placed under arrest and has been given Miranda warnings. As a matter of fact, he has been given "Miranda" on three occasions and each time his response his been "I have no problem making an oral statement to you, but if you want me to sign anything or put anything into writing, I won't do it unless my attorney is present." Police continue to question Roger, who makes oral, incriminating statements to them. Based on the federal rule with regard to this set of facts, evaluate the following statements:

I. When Roger mentioned "my" attorney the questioning should have been terminated.

II. Simply mentioning "my" attorney should be considered as a request for an attorney.

III. Roger's incriminating oral statements will be suppressed.

(A) All three statements are correct.

(B) Only statements I and II are correct.

(C) Only statement III is correct.

(D) All three statements are incorrect.

24. Police Officers George Mullins and Judy Milowe respond to the scene of a sniper incident. They determine that the shots probably came from a fourth-floor apartment facing the street. Using their "emergency" authority, the police officers enter the apartment looking for the sniper, or evidence that he was in that apartment. The apartment is very shabby. The furniture is old and decaying. But along one wall there is a full set of brand-new, very valuable stereo components. P.O. Mullins says, "Hey Judy, that doesn't look right to me. I bet this equipment is stolen." P.O. Milowe replies, "It looks that way to me too. See if you can find some serial numbers and we'll call it in. We may get a hit." P.O. Mullins lifts up and turns one of the units, locates a serial number, gives it to P.O. Milowe, and P.O. Milowe calls it in to their stolen property inquiry section. In a matter of minutes a return call is made, and the equipment is positively identified as stolen property. Evaluate the following statements:

I. The two police officers lawfully entered the suspect apartment.

II. The stereo equipment observed by the two officers was in plain view and was sighted inadvertently.

III. P.O. Mullins had no authority to move the stereo equipment to locate the serial number.

(A) All three statements are correct.

(B) Only statements I and II are correct.

(C) Only statement I is correct.

(D) Only statement II is correct.

25. Tondelayo is suspected of being a member of a gang of thieves that regularly steals and then disposes of any valuable property they can get their hands on. Tondelayo is known to be a "neat freak" that is always cleaning her house and disposing of any clutter for pick-up by the local refuse truck. Tondelayo puts her garbage out at the curb and, before it is picked up, P.O. Connolly searches through the garbage and finds evidence that connects Tondelayo to the ring of thieves. Evaluate the following statements:

    I.   It was not a violation of Tondelayo's Fourth Amendment rights when the officer searched her garbage.

    II. If Tondelayo's garbage had been on her property rather than of the curb, then a search warrant would have been required.

    III. If there was no immediate need to seize the garbage (no collection until next week), then a search warrant would probably be required.

    (A) All three statements are correct.
    (B) Only statement I is correct.
    (C) Only statements I and II are correct.
    (D) All three statements are incorrect.

ANSWERS TO QUESTIONS ON CONSTITUTIONAL LAW

1. **The correct answer is (C).** The federal courts have held that this kind of speech on private property may be restricted. Be careful about choice (A), which suggests that Sergeant Connolly should ignore the situation. In civil service examinations, a supervisor who "ignores" something is almost always going to be wrong.

2. **The correct answer is (B).** Generally, on public property the exercise of free speech is constitutionally protected, but reasonable restrictions to accomplish a legitimate governmental interest may be imposed.

3. **The correct answer is (D).** See *Chambers v. Maroney* (Supreme Court U.S., 1971).

4. **The correct answer is (A).** See *Chimel v. California* (Supreme Court U.S., 1971).

5. **The correct answer is (A).** See *United States v. Robinson* and *Gustafson v. Florida* (Supreme Court U.S., 1974).

6. **The correct answer is (B).** See *United States v. Edwards* (Supreme Court U.S., 1974).

7. **The correct answer is (A).** See *Oregon v. Mathiason* (Supreme Court U.S., 1977).

8. **The correct answer is (A).** See *United States v. Chadwick* (Supreme Court U.S., 1977).

9. **The correct answer is (C).** See *Mincey v. Arizona* (Supreme Court U.S., 1978). Searches of crime scenes without a warrant may be conducted in an emergency, or when evidence or contraband is in plain view, or when a homicide victim is the sole occupant, or if it's a public place.

10. **The correct answer is (A).** See *Delaware v. Prouse* (Supreme Court U.S., 1979). Road-blocks and nonarbitrary checkpoints are allowed. For example, stopping every fifth car at a roadblock. Stops based on an articulated reason are also permitted.

11. **The correct answer is (A).** See *North Carolina v. Butler* (Supreme Court U.S., 1979). Please note that under the federal rule right to counsel becomes absolute when the defendant is arraigned. In many of the states, absolute right to counsel is triggered when a criminal proceeding is commenced by the filing of an Information with the court.

12. **The correct answer is (B).** See *Payton v. New York* (Supreme Court U.S., 1980). Exigent circumstances would include such situations as the following:
    1. Hot pursuit
    2. An emergency where:
       a. evidence will be destroyed, or
       b. police or others will be endangered, or
       c. the suspect may escape.

13. **The correct answer is (B).** See *Jenkins v. Anderson* (Supreme Court U.S., 1980).

14. **The correct answer is (A).** See *Rhode Island v. Innis* (Supreme Court U.S., 1980).

15. **The correct answer is (D).** See *United States v. Henry* (Supreme Court U.S., 1980).

16. **The correct answer is (A).** See *Steagald v. United States* (Supreme Court U.S., 1981). There are those who argue that statement II is incorrect. But Frank would not have a right to privacy in George's house and the arrest would be valid. However, George's civil rights were violated and the officers involved could be sued for such violation.

17. **The correct answer is (D).** See *Michigan v. Summers* (Supreme Court U.S., 1981). The people could be detained, but they could not be searched unless the warrant authorized a search of all persons present.

18. **The correct answer is (D).** See *United States v. Ross* (Supreme Court U.S., 1982). This is a true vehicle emergency search, and the "probable cause" from Roger gives you the authority to search without a warrant. In the case of *Illinois v. Gates* (1983), the Supreme Court established the "totality of the circumstances" test to determine probable cause where an anonymous informant is involved. Although the two-pronged Aguilar-Spinelli test is still useful when dealing with a known informant, the court, in granting a search warrant, may look at all the facts supplied in judging whether or not probable cause exists.

19. **The correct answer is (D).** See *Texas v. Brown* (Supreme Court U.S., 1983). Under prior rulings, the seizing officer using the Plain View Doctrine had to know that the item observed was in fact contraband. This case relaxes the standard from knowledge to probable cause.

20. **The correct answer is (C).** See *Illinois v. La Fayette* (Supreme Court U.S., 1984). In this case, the court "refused to write a manual" on how and when inventory searches could be conducted. The Court recited many interests that support the inventory process such as protect the property, protect the police, and verify identity.

21. **The correct answer is (A).** See *New York v. Quarles* (Supreme Court U.S., 1984). Believe it or not, the trial court said that Miranda was required.

22. **The correct answer is (B).** See *United States v. Sharpe* (Supreme Court U.S., 1985). The Court said that the duration of detention based on reasonable suspicion depends on the circumstances, and in this case 20 minutes was not unreasonable.

23. **The correct answer is (D).** See *Connecticut v. Barrett* (Supreme Court U.S., 1987). In this case, the Supreme Court said there was a knowing, intelligent waiver regarding the oral statements. Please note that many other state courts have not followed this decision. For example, New York State's position is that reference to "my" lawyer means he has a lawyer, and when police know that a defendant is represented by counsel he cannot be requested to waive counsel in the absence of counsel.

24. **The correct answer is (A).** See *Arizona v. Hicks* (Supreme Court U.S., 1987). Most of you probably chose choice (B) as the answer because it seems to make the most sense. But remember, in 1983 in *Texas v. Brown*, the Court relaxed the plain view standard from knowledge to probable cause. In the case at hand (*Arizona v. Hicks*), the police merely suspected the property was stolen. This standard does not support a seizure under the Plain View Doctrine. The Court held the moving of the stereo equipment to be an unlawful seizure. If the serial number could have been obtained without moving the equipment, the court would have allowed the police action to stand.

25. **The correct answer is (A).** See *California v. Greenwood* (Supreme Court U.S., 1988), which states that there is no need to procure a search warrant for garbage if it is on the curb because there is no "expectation of privacy in trash left for collection in an area accessible to the public."

EVIDENCE

DEFINITION

Evidence is a system of rules and standards by which the admission of proof at a trial or hearing is regulated. In its broad sense, it is the means or method by which any disputed or necessary fact is proved or disproved. It can be said that proof is the result of evidence.

Example:

George is indicted for murder. At his arraignment he pleads "not guilty." We now have a disputed fact. The prosecution maintains that George is guilty, and George maintains that he is not guilty. At George's trial for murder the prosecution must offer evidence to prove that George committed the crime and is guilty. The burden of proof is on the prosecution to prove beyond a reasonable doubt that George is guilty. George may (but he doesn't have to) offer evidence to rebut the prosecutor's evidence. This is an example of the use of evidence to attempt to prove or disprove a disputed fact.

TYPES OF EVIDENCE

There are three types of evidence: testimonial evidence, real evidence, and documentary evidence.

Testimonial evidence may be defined as an oral statement made under oath with a right of cross-examination by the adverse party. In some states, there are exceptions to the "under oath" rule in certain criminal cases. The most common exception is with regard to a witness who is young (usually less than 12) or a witness who is mentally impaired and who, in the opinion of the judge, does not understand the nature of an oath but whose intelligence is adequate to justify his or her use as a witness. Such witness may be permitted to give unsworn evidence yet still be subject to cross-examination. However, this unsworn evidence by itself is generally not sufficient to convict a defendant. There must be corroboration by a witness who gives sworn testimony.

There are two kinds of testimonial evidence: direct evidence and circumstantial evidence.

Direct evidence is actual knowledge of the facts through the use of the senses. Direct evidence tends to prove the fact in issue without the intervention of other facts.

Example:

Frank sees George shoot and kill Tondelayo. George is arrested and tried for murder. At the trial Frank says under oath, "I saw George shoot and kill Tondelayo." This is testimonial direct evidence. The fact in issue is: "Did George kill Tondelayo?" Frank's testimony tends to prove the fact in issue without the intervention of other facts.

Circumstantial evidence is testimony concerning a fact not in issue by which the fact in issue may be inferred.

Example:

A ballistics expert testifies that the gun found at the scene is registered to George and that the bullet that killed Tondelayo came from this gun. The fact in issue is: "Did George kill Tondelayo?" The expert's testimony has established a fact not in issue by which the fact in issue may be inferred. This is an example of testimonial circumstantial evidence. In this case, it is probably not sufficient in itself to prove George guilty beyond a reasonable doubt.

The second type of evidence, *real evidence*, is that evidence furnished by objects, things, or persons themselves. Real evidence can be seen, heard, or otherwise observed by the court and the jury. It is frequently referred to as "demonstrative evidence" and sometimes (though rarely) referred to as "autoptic proference."

Example:

At George's trial for murder, the gun that fired the fatal bullet is presented for inspection by the jury. This is real evidence. By the same token, if an assault victim shows his wounds to the jury, this too is real evidence.

The third type of evidence, documentary evidence, is evidence in the form of writing, typing, or printing. It is real evidence of a particular type. This kind of evidence is the basis for a rule known as "the best evidence rule." When the contents of a written document are in issue, the best evidence of what the document contains is the original document.

RULES OF EVIDENCE

Separate rules of evidence are established by each state individually. However, there are some constants that leave almost universal application. We will refer to these constants as: "the cardinal rules of evidence" and "the ordinary rules of evidence." Let's start with the cardinal rules of evidence.

CARDINAL RULES

There are three cardinal rules that are listed as follows:

1. All relevant material and competent proof of all facts is admissible unless excluded by a specific rule of law.

   - Evidence is relevant when it has a direct bearing on a fact worth consideration by the jury.
   - Evidence is material when it is of sufficient importance or influence and when it is not trivial or unimportant. All material evidence is at least relevant.
   - Evidence is competent when it is not subject to exclusion by any of the ordinary rules of evidence and when it is legally adequate and sufficient.

2. Specific rules of law may exclude evidence.

   - The evidence itself may be inadmissible—for example, hearsay.
   - The witness seeking to give the evidence may not be a competent witness. For example, there may be a confidential relationship such as between a husband and wife or a doctor and patient.

3. The specific rules of law that exclude evidence may apply automatically or only when an objection is made. Whenever you are faced with a problem concerning the admissibility of evidence, consider all three cardinal rules. Take the following scenario: George shoots Tondelayo. Frank sees this action and tells Roger that George shot Tondelayo. George is on trial for murder and Roger is called as a witness. The prosecutor begins to question Roger about what Frank told him. George's lawyer objects. Will Roger's testimony be admitted? Don't jump at an answer—check it out against the three cardinal rules.

   Consider Rule 1: All relevant, material, and competent proof of facts is admissible in evidence unless excluded by a specific rule of law. Roger's testimony is relevant and material (frequently the case with hearsay); it deals directly with the fact in issue: "Did George shoot Tondelayo?" But is Roger's testimony competent? Roger's testimony is not competent because under one of the ordinary rules of evidence, the "hearsay evidence rule," it is not admissible. (We will discuss the hearsay evidence rule shortly.)

Consider Rule 2: Specific rules of law may exclude evidence because the evidence itself is inadmissible, or because the witness is incompetent. In the scenario above a specific rule of law, the hearsay evidence rule, declares the evidence to be inadmissible even though Roger, as a witness, is competent.

Consider Rule 3: The specific rules of law that exclude evidence may apply automatically or only when an objection is made. The hearsay evidence rule must be triggered by an objection. George's counsel has objected, so Roger's testimony will not be admitted. If George's counsel had experienced a mental lapse and had not objected, Roger's testimony (even though hearsay) could have been admitted into evidence. There are three ordinary rules of evidence: the hearsay evidence rule, the best evidence rule, and judicial notice. We shall discuss each of these in turn.

1. THE HEARSAY EVIDENCE RULE

Hearsay is evidence not from personal knowledge of the witness, but a mere repetition of what the witness heard others say. It is testimony regarding something said outside the court and offered as true by someone other than the actual witness.
Example:

In our earlier scenario where Frank told Roger that George shot Tondelayo, Roger's testimony that George shot Tondelayo would be hearsay. But suppose the fact in issue was not "Did George shoot Tondelayo?" but instead was, "Did Frank tell Roger that George shot Tondelayo?" In this case, Roger's testimony would be direct evidence.

The reason why hearsay will be excluded when an objection is made is because the original source of the information (Frank in our scenario) cannot be cross-examined. Remember our definition of testimonial evidence: "An oral statement made under oath with a right of cross-examination in the adverse party."

Not all hearsay is inadmissible. Over the years, several universally recognized exceptions to the hearsay exclusionary rule have developed. The reason for these exceptions is a very practical one—they are probably true. The recognized exceptions are the following:

1. Confessions

2. Admissions

3. Dying declarations

4. *Res gestae* (thing done)

5. Business entries

6. Prior testimony

7. Reputation

8. Pedigree

9. Certificate or affidavit of a public officer

Now let's look in depth at each one of these exceptions to the hearsay exclusionary rule.

CONFESSIONS

Police Officer Connolly arrests George for murder. Wishing to question George, P.O. Connolly first gives George his "Miranda" warnings as follows:

▪ George has a right to remain silent.

▪ Any statement George makes may be used against him in evidence.

■ George has a right to presence of an attorney retained by George.

■ George has a right to the presence of an attorney appointed for him if he wants one.

George makes a voluntary, knowing, and intelligent waiver and under P.O. Connolly's questioning George confesses orally. At the trial, P.O. Connolly may testify as to what George said, and an objection to hearsay will be overruled. Remember, a confession is a statement which directly and expressly acknowledges guilt of a crime charged against the defendant.

ADMISSIONS

In a criminal prosecution, any act or declaration of the accused inconsistent with his innocence is admissible against him as an admission.

Example:

George is on trial for murder and is offering as an alibi that at the time of the crime he was elsewhere than at the crime scene. Frank is called to testify that, after the crime was committed, George admitted to Frank that he, George, was in the area of the crime scene. An objection to hearsay will be overruled.

Be sure to know the difference between confession and admission. Admissions and confessions are *not* the same. The above is an admission because it is "inconsistent with George's innocence." However, it is not an admission of guilt. Had George said to Frank, "I'm the one who killed Tondelayo," that would have been an acknowledgment of guilt, and would have constituted a confession.

Besides the admission described in the preceding paragraph that may be oral, written, or by conduct, there is another type of admission that is sometimes called "adoptive admission" or "failure to deny." Adoptive admission or failure to deny occurs when someone is accused by any person of an offense, in the accused's presence and hearing, and the accused remains silent when it would be proper for him to speak. Testimony as to the accusation and as to the accused's silence is admissible.

Note: This rule (adoptive admission-failure to deny) does not apply to persons under arrest or a criminal charge.

DYING DECLARATIONS

Dying declarations constitute another exception to the hearsay rule. Necessity for the use of such declarations is found in the unavailability of the declarant due to death. Many times the declarant and the defendant were the only witnesses to the event in issue.

Example:

Tondelayo, bleeding from multiple wounds, is found lying in the street. P.O. Connolly ascertains that Tondelayo is near death, and Tondelayo herself states she believes she is about to die. P.O. Connolly says, "What happened?" Tondelayo replies, "George shot me." Tondelayo later dies, and at George's trial for murder P.O. Connolly is called to testify. P.O. Connolly is asked, "What did Tondelayo tell you?" George's attorney objects claiming hearsay. The objection will be overruled. This statement is hearsay, but will be admitted. Why? Because considering the circumstances under which Tondelayo made the statement (she believed she was about to die) it is probably true, and since Tondelayo has died, there may be no other witness. The principle upon which dying declarations are admitted is the "probable truth" of the statement because of the declarant's sense of impending death.

Certain essentials must be shown for a dying declaration to be admissible.

1. The declarant was *in. extremis.* That is, death was certain. It is not necessary that the declarant die immediately. What is necessary is the impression of almost immediate death and not the actual rapid succession of death. In one case, the declarant died five months after making the dying declaration and it was admitted. But remember—the declarant must actually die before the statement can be used in court.

2. The declarant sensed impending death and had no hope of recovery. In the foregoing example it would have to be shown than Tondelayo truly believed she was about to die. If it could be shown that Tondelayo said to a doctor, who responded to the scene, "Pull me through, Doc!" then this would effectively defeat this element and the declaration would be inadmissible. Conversely, if Tondelayo said to the doctor, "It's no use, Doc, I'm through," then this would buttress the validity of the dying declaration.

3. The declarant, if living, would be competent as a witness. If the defense could show at the trial that at the time of the incident Tondelayo was a mental defective, the declaration would be inadmissible.

Remember, all three of the foregoing elements must be established.

There are two further points on the subject of dying declarations. Firstly, a dying declaration need not be in writing. The dying declaration may be oral, written, or even indicated by signs. There are no formalities requited. Police procedures will suggest a certain format to be followed, but under law all that is necessary is that the three essentials spelled out above be established.

Secondly, be aware that the dying declaration is not given the same value and weight as the sworn testimony of a witness in open court. The court, upon request, must so instruct the jury.

RES GESTAE

This fourth exception to the hearsay evidence rule is Latin for "things done." For example, a pedestrian named Anne saw a truck careening down a narrow, crowded street and heard the driver exclaim as the truck passed by, "My God, the brakes failed!" If the incident led to a trial for criminally negligent homicide, Anne (the pedestrian) could be called to testify as to what the driver said and an objection to hearsay would be overruled. The reason for the exception would be that since the statement was made spontaneously, during or immediately after the incident, it's probably true. There was no time to think and to contrive a false answer.

BUSINESS RECORDS

In the regular course of business, if a writing or record is made at the time of the transaction or within a reasonable time thereafter, the information contained therein is admissible as an exception to the hearsay evidence rule. Why? Because the records are probably true.

PRIOR TESTIMONY

When, because of death, sickness, or insanity, a witness cannot be produced, or when, after a diligent search, the witness cannot be found in the state, his testimony at a prior trial may be read into evidence by either the prosecution or the defense in two situations that are of interest with reference to criminal proceedings.

Prior testimony may constitute admissible hearsay if it was given in a preliminary examination before a judge provided that on a charge against the present defendant, a witness has

■ been examined before a judge, and

■ his or her testimony was reduced to a deposition in the defendant's presence, and

■ the defendant, either in person or through counsel, cross-examined the witness, or had an opportunity to cross-examine the witness, then the witness's deposition may be read into evidence by either side.

Prior testimony may also be admitted if the defendant had previously been tried on the same charge (and the trial resulted in a mistrial or the verdict is under appeal, for example). Specifically, if the defendant, on an indictment or an information, was previously tried on the same charge, then the testimony of any witness who testified at such prior trial may be read into evidence by either the prosecution or the defense.

REPUTATION

If the defendant calls someone as a character witness in the defendant's behalf, this person may testify as to the defendant's good character. Reputation is based mostly on hearsay—what people say about him—but is admissible as an exception.

In a criminal trial, the prosecution cannot introduce evidence relative to the defendant's bad character unless the defendant presents evidence of his good character as noted above.

PEDIGREE

Pedigree refers to ancestors such as parents or grandparents, or a line of succession (children, grandchildren, etc.). Suppose that pedigree is an issue in a case. For example, "Is Kevin the son of Eleanor?" Kevin, to establish his pedigree, may call on Chris who will testify that Eleanor, (now deceased) had told Chris that Kevin was her son.

CERTIFICATE OR AFFIDAVIT OF A PUBLIC OFFICIAL

If a public officer is required or authorized by law to make a certificate or affidavit of a certain fact or facts, or if an act or acts performed by him in his official duty is filed or deposited in a public office of the state, the certificate or affidavit is *prima facie* evidence of the facts stated therein. Although it is hearsay, it is admissible as an exception to the hearsay exclusionary rule.

2. THE BEST EVIDENCE RULE

The best evidence rule requires that whenever a party seeks to prove the contents of a writing, he or she must either produce the original writing, or satisfactorily account for its absence.

Example:

At a trial a question arises as to the language used in a contract. The "best evidence" is an original copy of the contract. The same theory can be applied to any writing the contents of which are in issue.

The reasons for the best evidence rule are the following:

- To prevent fraud

- To guard against copying errors

- To guard against mistakes in reading

- To guard against faulty recollection

The use of the best evidence rule is limited to certain specific instances and the regulations concerning the rule are quite stringent. The best evidence rule may be used to prove the contents of a writing. It does not apply to facts that have an existence independent of the writing.

Example:

The payment of money or the receipt of goods are facts that may be established orally—even though a receipt may be involved. But a divorce comes about only by judicial decree. Therefore, the decree is the best evidence of the divorce.

The best evidence rule applies only when the contents of the writing are in issue. If the contents of the writing are not in issue but are only collateral to the issue, the best evidence rule does not apply. Whether or not a writing is collateral to the issue may not be easily determined. It will be collateral if it is of such minor importance that no useful purpose is served by producing the writing.

Under certain circumstances, copies of public documents may be produced as best evidence. However, if a duplicate of an original (a photocopy) is offered in evidence, then it will not be admitted until the absence of the original is satisfactorily explained.

If a contract is executed in duplicate (if both copies were signed as originals), then both copies are treated as originals and both copies must be produced to qualify as best evidence.

An exception to the rules concerning copies and duplicates occurs in the case where the original writings are voluminous. In such cases, a qualified person may testify as to a summary of the documents.

3. JUDICIAL NOTICE

Judicial notice is the notice that a judge will officially take of a fact, even though no evidence to prove that fact has been introduced. It is a judicial shortcut taken when there is no need for evidence to be introduced to prove the fact. A judge may take judicial notice of the following:

■ Notorious facts that are common knowledge within the court's jurisdiction.

■ Facts that can be immediately and accurately demonstrated by resort to easily accessible sources of indisputable accuracy. For example, the time the sun rose or set last Tuesday.

■ Commonly known facts, although the judge may be precluded from taking such notice of facts that he or she personally observed.

■ Matters of law, in which case the law of the forum will be judicially noticed (courts may take judicial notice of foreign law).

■ Matters of fact that include the following:

1. Public officers and their authority
2. Seals and signatures of public officers
3. Political subdivisions
4. Existence of foreign governments
5. Course and laws of nature (for example, the seasons of summer and winter or that the sun rises and sets)
6. Course of agriculture
7. Qualities and properties of matter
8. Generally known scientific facts
9. Facts relating to human life (for example, that coal dust is bad for the lungs)
10. Common beliefs
11. Geographical facts, etc.

Judicial notice precludes the introduction of evidence to establish a fact that may be in issue. Some state courts have taken judicial notice of the general reliability of certain instruments and scientific procedures. This makes it unnecessary to prove their reliability by expert testimony. Radar speedometers, ballistic evidence, X-ray pictures, and fingerprint identification are subject to judicial notice. Polygraphs and voicegraphs usually have not been treated the same way. The reliability of these measures must be defended.

PRIVILEGED COMMUNICATIONS

There are certain privileged communications that are not admissible in evidence unless the person holding the privilege consents to their admission.

COMMUNICATION

1. Husband to wife or wife to husband (communication made during the marriage)

2. Client to attorney

3. Patient to physician, dentist, or nurse

HOLDER OF PRIVILEGE

1. Husband or wife against whom the communication is to be used

2. Client

3. Patient

4. Penitent to clergyman

5. Client to psychologist

6. Client to social worker

7. Confessor

8. Client

Exceptions are the following:

- A dentist can be compelled to disclose information needed for identification of a person.

- A physician, dentist, or nurse can be compelled to disclose information that a patient under 16 has been the victim of a crime.

- A doctor must report certain kinds of wounds.

- A physician may be required to testify concerning certain narcotics matters.

- Information given to a doctor or dentist by someone trying to procure narcotics unlawfully is not privileged.

Police officer's confidential informant will have to be disclosed if the informant is the only one who can "make the case."

MISCELLANEOUS PROVISIONS REGARDING EVIDENCE

The following miscellaneous provisions apply to evidence:

▪ In any criminal prosecution the defendant is presumed innocent until he is proved guilty "beyond a reasonable doubt."

▪ A criminal prosecution must prove the *corpus delecti*, which includes the body of the crime and the identity of the offender.

Example:

Assume that Tondelayo walks into a police station and confesses to a murder. The proper warnings are given and Tondelayo waives her right freely and intelligently. Tondelayo may not be convicted of the crime solely on the basis of her confession. The state must establish the *corpus delecti*, which means that it must do the following:

1. Prove that the crime was committed

2. Prove that the event was criminal

3. Establish the identity of the offender

A confession by itself is never sufficient to establish both the *corpus delecti* and the identity of the offender.

▪ Direct evidence is not necessarily always given more weight than circumstantial evidence.

▪ A conviction can be obtained solely on the basis of circumstantial evidence?as long as it establishes guilt beyond a reasonable doubt.

▪ It is a good general rule that witnesses testify to facts and not to opinions or conclusions that are to be drawn from those facts. However, there are exceptions to this rule and the exceptions are listed under the following headings.

OPINIONS NOT PERMITTED

The following are situations about which ordinary witnesses cannot give opinions:

▪ That more force than was necessary was used to remove a passenger from a common carrier

▪ Whose negligence caused an accident

▪ Whether a plaintiff acted in a careful or careless manner

▪ Whether the condition of the highway was dangerous

▪ Whether a fire was of incendiary origin

▪ How long a fire had been burning

▪ Whether blood is of human or animal origin

OPINIONS PERMITTED

The following are situations about which ordinary witnesses can give opinions:

- Whether a red stain is blood or paint

- Year and make of a car

- Matters of color, weight, size, light, darkness, race, language, smell, touch, taste, etc.

- Apparent physical condition

- That a photo is a good likeness

- Voice identification of a person

- Whether a person seemed intoxicated

- Speed of trains, cars, etc.

- Estimated age of a person

- Rational or irrational nature of a person's acts

- Value of property and services

- Genuineness of another's handwriting (must show that he or she knew handwriting)

EVIDENCE QUESTIONS

Directions: Read each question and choose the best answer. Circle the letter of your choice.

---

1. *Prima facie* evidence is best defined as evidence that

    (A) is based on the personal observation of a witness.
    (B) suffices to establish a fact in issue until rebutted by contrary evidence.
    (C) is presumed from the existence of other known facts and its connection therewith.
    (D) is inferred as circumstantial evidence by a jury.

2. Evidence is direct and positive when

    (A) given by a witness under oath.
    (B) the facts in dispute are communicated by those who have the actual knowledge of them by the use of their senses.
    (C) it tends to prove one or more facts in issue.
    (D) the facts in issue may properly be inferred from other facts shown.

3. Evidence that does not tend directly to prove the controverted facts, but to establish collateral facts from which the facts in issue will follow as a logical inference is called

    (A) circumstantial evidence.
    (B) hearsay evidence.
    (C) corroborative evidence.
    (D) opinion evidence.

4. Evidence furnished by the things themselves exhibited to the court for inspection is known as

    (A) positive evidence.
    (B) *prima facie* evidence.
    (C) real evidence.
    (D) partial evidence.

5. Such evidence as it relates to or bears directly upon the point in issue and tending to prove it is known as

    (A) real evidence.
    (B) competent evidence.
    (C) presumptive evidence.
    (D) relevant evidence.

6. The term "autoptic proference" is sometimes used to refer to

   (A) oral evidence.
   (B) circumstantial evidence.
   (C) state's evidence.
   (D) real evidence.

7. Real evidence is also commonly known as

   (A) demonstrative evidence.
   (B) second-hand evidence.
   (C) substantive evidence.
   (D) positive evidence.

8. Which of the following statements constitutes hearsay evidence?

   (A) "I was told not to take the chance."
   (B) "The defendant reported the crime to me."
   (C) "The boy's mother told me that her son committed the crime."
   (D) "He told me that I would be sorry if I reported the crime."

9. In a prosecution for disorderly conduct, a police officer testifies that he heard the defendant say, "American soldiers are blustering cowards." This testimony of the police officer is *not* hearsay evidence because

   (A) it relates to an offense and not to a crime.
   (B) the person who made the statement has an opportunity to deny it.
   (C) the hearsay rule does not apply to police officers under oath.
   (D) the truth or falsity of the statement is not in issue.

10. Hearsay evidence is generally *not* admissible in a criminal trial because it

    (A) proves nothing.
    (B) is generally false.
    (C) is not subject to the test of cross-examination.
    (D) usually is irrelevant.

11. The burden of proof required to convict in a criminal trial is

    (A) a fair preponderance of evidence.
    (B) beyond a reasonable doubt.
    (C) the testimony of the greatest number of credible witnesses.
    (D) the quantum of convincing evidence.

12. A confession made by an accused is not deemed circumstantial evidence because

    (A) a confession proves the fact in issue directly.
    (B) a confession will not stand alone without additional proof of the crime charged.
    (C) it is documentary.
    (D) it is demonstrative.

13. The prosecution may not introduce evidence of a criminal defendant's bad character unless the

    (A) crime is an infamous one.
    (B) defendant was previously convicted of other crimes.
    (C) defendant is permitted to introduce evidence of his good character.
    (D) the court rules otherwise.

14. At the trial of Tondelayo for murder, Tondelayo is asked on cross-examination if she has ever been previously convicted of any crime. This mode of questioning is

(A)   improper if the particular crime charged differs from her previous convictions.
(B)   allowed as a means of testing her credibility.
(C)   improper unless Tondelayo has already testified as to her good character.
(D)   permitted to show her general criminal disposition (she took the stand).

15.   Judicial notice is best defined as

(A)   the recognition that a judge will officially take of a fact of common knowledge without proof thereof.
(B)   a rule of law that courts and judges shall draw a particular inference from particular facts or evidence unless and until the truth of the evidence is disproved.
(C)   a mandate issued by the court during the course of a trial requiring one of the parties to produce certain evidence in his possession.
(D)   the knowledge of a fact in issue that is imputed to one of the parties to the litigation.

16.   A presumption is best defined as a rule of law that

(A)   requires that a particular inference trust be drawn from an ascertained state of facts.
(B)   is given to explain, repel, or disprove facts given in evidence.
(C)   is plain, obvious, and conclusive as to its certainty.
(D)   admitted as a substitute for what would be the primary instrument of evidence.

17.   An inference drawn by a jury from circumstantial evidence is sometimes termed

(A)   a presumption of law.
(B)   presumption of fact.
(C)   a conclusive presumption.
(D)   judicial notice.

18.   Which of the following statements is *not* correct?

(A)   All relevant, material, and competent proof of facts is admissible in evidence unless excluded by a specific rule of law.
(B)   Documentary evidence is real evidence of a particular type.
(C)   Evidence is relevant when it has a direct bearing on a fact worth consideration by the jury.
(D)   Hearsay evidence is always inadmissible.

19.   The recent and exclusive possession of the fruits of a crime justifies the inference of guilt provided that

(A)   the possession is proved by direct evidence.
(B)   the possession is explained or explained falsely.
(C)   the nature of the guilt of the possessor is certain.
(D)   it is applied only to larceny.

20.   Burden of proof is best defined as

(A)   the burden of trying to persuade the jury of the facts of the truth of the allegations contained in the pleadings.
(B)   the coming forward with evidence.
(C)   taking the initiative in establishing guilt or innocence.
(D)   the sum total of all the evidence necessary to establish innocence.

21.   Which of the following terms is normally within the province of the court rather than the jury to decide?

(A)   Rejecting a confession because it was not made voluntarily
(B)   Whether the witness was the common-law wife of the defendant
(C)   Credibility of witnesses
(D)   Admissibility of evidence

22. An ordinary witness (not an expert) may give an opinion concerning any of the following *except*

 (A) that a photograph is a good likeness of a person he or she knows.
 (B) the estimated age of a person.
 (C) that a person seemed to be intoxicated.
 (D) that a fire was of incendiary origin.

23. Tondelayo was charged with murder. At her trial, Tondelayo, claiming self-defense, introduced evidence that the deceased had the general reputation of a quarrelsome, vindictive, and violent man. Such evidence is

 (A) not admissible, unless supported by specific acts of violence toward other persons.
 (B) admissible, to prove that the deceased was the aggressor.
 (C) not admissible, since the deceased cannot cross-examine the character witnesses.
 (D) admissible, if such a reputation had come to Tondelayo's attention prior to the homicide.

24. The best evidence rule has application mainly to

 (A) direct as opposed to circumstantial evidence.
 (B) questions concerning the contents of documents.
 (C) the use of evidence that will not be held inadmissible.
 (D) the use of nonhearsay as the best way to establish a fact.

25. If a witness to a fatal accident testifies that he heard the driver of the car say at the time of the accident that his brakes failed, then this statement, though hearsay, is admissible because it is

 (A) a confession.
 (B) part of the *res gestae*.
 (C) direct, testimonial evidence.
 (D) relevant, material, and competent.

ANSWERS TO QUESTIONS ON EVIDENCE

1. **The correct answer is (B).**
2. **The correct answer is (B).** There are two types of testimonial evidence: direct and circumstantial. Choice (B) is a good definition of direct evidence.
3. **The correct answer is (A).** This is a good working definition of circumstantial evidence.
4. **The correct answer is (C).** Real evidence is one of the three kinds of evidence.
5. **The correct answer is (D).**
6. **The correct answer is (D).**
7. **The correct answer is (A).**
8. **The correct answer is (C).** This is a classic example of inadmissible hearsay.
9. **The correct answer is (D).** In this case, the "fact in issue" is not whether soldiers are cowards, but whether the defendant made the statement.
10. **The correct answer is (C).** The true witness is not giving the testimony.
11. **The correct answer is (B).** Criminal conviction is a serious matter and guilt must he proven beyond a reasonable doubt.
12. **The correct answer is (A).** Be careful. The question deals with circumstantial as opposed to direct testimony.
13. **The correct answer is (C).**
14. **The correct answer is (B).** When a defendant elects to take the stand, he or she swears to tell the truth and credibility becomes a factor to consider. Admission of previous convictions on record is a test of truthfulness.
15. **The correct answer is (A).** A judicial notice preludes the need to introduce evidence to prove a fact.
16. **The correct answer is (A).** A good definition of a presumption of law, which requires that a particular inference be draw.
17. **The correct answer is (B).** This inference is frequently referred to as a "presumption of fact." This is theoretically erroneous because the inference drawn is not mandatory. A true presumption requires that a certain inference be drawn. In theory, there are only presumptions of law and not presumptions of fact.
18. **The correct answer is (D).**
19. **The correct answer is (B).**
20. **The correct answer is (A).** The burden of proof is almost always on the prosecution. In some states, if the defendant raises an affirmative defense, he must prove the affirmative defense. Burden of proof refers to proving guilt. Choice (D) refers to proving innocence.
21. **The correct answer is (D).** Questions of fact are for the jury to decide. Questions of law are for the court to decide.
22. **The correct answer is (D).**
23. **The correct answer is (D).** If it is it relevant, material, and competent, then it is admissible.
24. **The correct answer is (B).**
25. **The correct answer is (B).**

CRIMINALISTICS AND INVESTIGATION

INTRODUCTION

The material contained in this chapter has been taken from various "experts" in the field of criminalistics and investigation. It begins with an easy-to-understand textual coverage of firearms identification, glass fractures, gunpowder residue, blood, semen, and fingerprints. It also contains an up-to-date explanation of the current state of DNA (deoxyribonucleic acid) processing as a means of identifying a person through blood, semen, or body tissue.

On almost every police promotion examination, and certainly on examinations for the job title "Investigator" there will be some questions based on this material.

We have tried to be very practical and instead of presenting you with a doctoral dissertation that may be accurate but complicated we have simplified the subject matter so that even a person with no investigative background should find is easy to understand.

The seventy multiple-choice questions that follow the text represent the kinds of questions used by civil service examiners in the past. Not all of the questions are based on the textual material in this chapter. Some of the questions deal with general knowledge that you should have acquired through experience working as a police officer.

We, the authors of this publication, have been in the police promotion field for more than twenty-three years and are familiar with the kinds of job-related questions used by examiners throughout the country. Our mail-order and in-house students have included police personnel nationwide. Our students have almost always topped the list and finished "in the money."

PRINCIPLES OF FIREARMS IDENTIFICATION

For many years, firearms have been the predominant weapon used in murders throughout the United States. Civil service examiners are aware of this and frequently direct exam questions toward firearms.

Most firearms have rifled bores. The rifling in the bore of the firearm is cut in so that the "grooves" and the "lands" will cause the bullet to rotate. This rotation gives the bullet a spiral motion and prevents it from turning end over end. As the bullet begins to lose velocity and spin, it starts to turn end over end. If the bullet strikes someone at this point, then it may leave a gaping wound referred to as a "keyhole" wound.

The bullet that fits any particular rifled bore firearm is larger than the bore of the barrel. Because if is larger and fits the entire diameter of the barrel, then it prevents gases from leaking when the bullet is traveling inside the barrel. Thus, the bullet gets speed and spin when the gunpowder explodes.

In addition to speed and spin, the bullet also takes onto itself some of the minute imperfections and markings from inside the barrel. These markings are called striae. When a technician compares striae from a suspect bullet with striae on a test-fired bullet, the technician can get a positive identification of the gun from which the bullet was discharged. However, statistics show that in only about fifty percent of lead bullets a postmortem examination will result in a positive identification.

Striae (or markings) may also be found on the cartridge case (shell) when a semiautomatic or automatic firearm has been used. These striae on the cartridge case may be caused by the following:

1. The firing pin

2. The breech face

3. The extractor

4. The ejector

It is important to know that these striae can be used to identify a weapon. Therefore, when either cartridge cases or bullets are found, care must be exercised in marking them for identification. The rules are as follows:

1. Mark bullets on the base.

2. Mark shells on the side.

If these rules are followed, there is less chance of damaging the striae and the integrity of the evidence is preserved.

Note: It is also permissible to mark a bullet on its ogive, the downward slope of the nose of the bullet.

BULLETS PASSING THROUGH GLASS

It is possible to determine the direction of travel of a bullet that has passed through a pane of glass.

There are several points of identification to be considered:

1. Radial fractures

2. Concentric fractures

3. Flakes

4. Crater

The sequence of events is as follows:

1. When the bullet strikes the glass, radial fractures (the somewhat straight lines running out from the hole) form on the side opposite the entry.

2. Concentric fractures (the circular cracks in the glass) form on the same side the bullet entered.

3. Flakes of chipped and broken glass will be blown away as the bullet passes through the glass.

4. A crater is formed on the side opposite the point of entry.

A code word (invented by the authors in 1968, but now used liberally by everyone) is *corn flakes*.

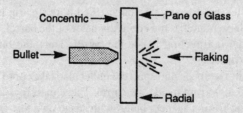

As the bullet strikes it causes the following:

- *Concentric fractures* on the side of entry.

- *Radial fractures* on the exit side (but these form first).

- *Flaking* on the side opposite the entry.

Note: If there is more than one bullet hole in a pane of glass, then it is possible to determine which occurred first by studying the fractures. The radial fractures from the second hole will end when they meet the fractures from the earlier hole.

GUNPOWDER RESIDUE

It is sometimes important to determine the answers to the following two questions:

1. Did this person recently fire a gun?

2. How far from the victim was the barrel of the gun? This is important if there is a claim of self-defense or suicide.

The following are several tests that have been used in the past to determine whether or not someone recently fired a gun:

The Dermal Nitrate or Paraffin Test

The dermal nitrate of paraffin test is not conclusive. Many other substances give the same reaction.

The Neutron Activation Analysis

The neutron activation analysis is not conclusive, but is better than the paraffin test. Two elements, barium and antimony, are components of primer mixture. They don't occur together in nature. If a suspect's hand contains traces of both barium and antimony, then there's a good chance he fired a gun.

Gunpowder Residue

In order to determine how far the barrel of the gun was from the victim at the time the gun was fired, the investigator must determine the size of the powder pattern residue around the bullet hole.

Sometimes this can be done by inspection; as when the powder residue is on a white shirt. It is not so easy when the residue is on a blue uniform. Some of the techniques used in this case are the following:

1. The Walker or C-Acid Test

2. Infrared Photography

3. Soft X-Ray Photography

Once the investigator knows the size of the powder pattern, he then conducts trial firings using the gun in question with similar ammunition. Once he almost duplicates the size of the pattern, he can state how far the muzzle of the gun was from the victim. Obviously, the wider the pattern, the farther away the muzzle must have been.

BLOODSTAINS

The most positive thing that can be said about bloodstains is that they can *exclude* suspects. They do not positively identify a suspect. *Note:* DNA testing may be able to positively identify a suspect.

SEARCHING FOR BLOODSTAINS

Quite often bloodstains are not red in color and many times they are not readily visible. In searching for bloodstains, the following are the various techniques that can be used:

1. A chemical known as luminol may be sprayed over the suspected area. If blood is present, the luminol will give off a bluish-white luminescence.

2. Artificial light (flashlight) can be used, even in the daytime. Under artificial light a dried bloodstain on a dark background will appear as a glossy varnish.

TESTING FOR BLOOD

When suspected bloodstains or samples are discovered, there are several tests that might be used to confirm the presence of blood. Some of these tests are field tests used by the investigator and others are laboratory tests used by a chemist or technician.

Field Tests

1. The benzidine test is a nonspecific field test for the presence of blood (human or animal). A positive reaction is a blue or green color. If the reaction does occur, the stain might be blood.

2. The leuco-macachite test is also a nonspecific (but more specific than benzidine) field test for blood. A positive reaction is a green stain that becomes a greenish blue in about one minute.

Laboratory Tests

1. The phenolphthalein test is a fairly specific preliminary test for blood. If the test results are positive, then the lab technician might use the precipitin reaction test.

2. The precipitin reaction test is a specific laboratory test for human blood. The test tube reaction is the formation of a white ring (or precipitate) at the point in the test tube where the suspected material and the chemical reagent meet.

3. A microspectroscope is used in some cases to aid the lab technician in testing for blood.

BLOOD GROUPINGS

Human blood can be divided into definite groups because of the ability of the blood of one person to agglutinate with the blood of another. The agglutination process is not the same as coagulation. Agglutination is a process of the blood serum clumping or bringing together the red blood cells of another individual. Coagulation is the process of scab formation that heals wounds.

The four broad classes or groupings of blood are as follows: O, A, B, and AB. These groupings are permanent and hereditary. If you are born with blood group A, then you will die with blood group A.

Remember, for identification proposes, blood groupings have negative value. They can exclude a suspect, but they can't be used to positively identify a person.

DNA processing may greatly expand the usefulness of blood analysis in the future. DNA processing holds out promise for positive identification.

SEMEN

Semen stains may be important evidence in rapes, sex murders, etc. Special care must be taken when gathering semen as evidence. Semen contains spermatozoa, or small living cells with an egg-shaped head and a long, thin tail. These spermatozoa die when the semen dries, but they maintain their shape. They become brittle when dry and can be broken. Therefore, clothing containing suspected semen stains should not be rolled up in order to transport it. This may be done with bloodstained clothing but *not* with semen. In order to preserve the semen as evidence, the full spermatozoa must be present, head and tail.

SEARCHING FOR SEMEN

The most effective way of determining the presence of semen is to use an ultraviolet lamp. If semen stains are present, they will give off a white or bluish-white color under the lamp.

SEMEN TESTS

1. The florence reaction test is a nonspecific laboratory test for semen. A positive reaction is the formation of brown, rhombic-shaped crystals.

2. The puranen reaction test is also a preliminary nonspecific laboratory test for semen. The positive reaction involves the formation of a yellow precipitate in the test tube.

3. The microscopic identification of semen depends on the detection of at least several spermheads with necks attached.

GROUPING SEMEN AS WITH BLOOD

Some people are known as secretors. Eighty percent of the people who have A, B, or AB blood groupings are secretors (blood group O people are not secretors). If you are a secretor, then the antigens that are characteristic of your blood group are secreted with other body fluids such as semen or saliva. These other fluids can then be grouped and can be used to exclude persons as suspects. Again, remember that DNA processing may result in positive identification.

DNA TESTING

DNA is deoxyribonucleic acid. It is an organic substance found primarily within the chromosomes. Chromosomes are structures within cell nuclei.

The nucleus of almost every cell in the human body contains 23 pairs of chromosomes for a total of 46. The exceptions are the male sperm cell and the female egg cell. Each of these cells contains 23 unpaired chromosomes. When the sperm cell fertilizes the ovum, the resulting zygote will have 46 chromosomes; 23 from the father and 23 from the mother.

The DNA within any chromosome is composed of two strands. Each of these strands is a polymer composed of molecules called nucleotides. There are four different nucleotides found in DNA. The chemical names for these four nucleotides are as follows:

1. Deoxyadenosine Monophosphate (A)

2. Thymidine Monophosphate (T)

3. Deoxycytidine Monophosphate (C)

4. Deoxyguanosine Monophosphate (G)

The scientists who work with DNA have as much of a problem with these terms as you do, so they conveniently renamed them as follows: A, T, C, and G.

The chemicals named above, represented by their letter symbols, appear on chromosomal strands in an infinite variety of letter sequences. The presence in DNA of multiple repeats of letter sequences is the foundation of one of the methods by which body fluid and tissue specimens can be genetically characterized. The procedures used to analyze the DNA in the various fluids or specimens are very complicated and cannot he done by many forensic laboratories. As a matter of fact, the Federal Bureau of Investigation (F.B.I.) has had to conduct DNA training courses for lab technicians in order to assist the various state and local laboratory personnel to become proficient in their DNA analysis.

As a practical matter, controlled studies in the laboratory have shown that necessary patterns can be discerned with as little as one-tenth of a drop of blood from an eyedropper and one fiftieth of a drop of semen. But, because the environment can adversely affect the sample being used, the recovery of DNA from actual case evidence will undoubtedly be less than that which will result from a controlled sample.

Some of the environmental factors that can negatively impact on the success of the DNA lab analysis are sunlight, bacterial growth heat, moisture, and chemicals.

Note: In light of the above, it is no wonder that the year's delay in the DNA testing in the now infamous Central Park jogger case in New York City resulted in nonpositive findings.

The sequence of the DNA testing process that holds out the hope of being able to identify a biological specimen (blood, semen, tissue, etc.) as having come from a single individual is as follows:

1. The extraction of the DNA from the biological specimen

2. Cutting the DNA with restriction enzymes, Restriction Fragment Length Polymorphisms (RFLP).

3. Electrophoretic separation of the fragments by pulling them through a molecular sieve gel with an electrical field

4. Transfer of the DNA from the gel to a nylon membrane (called Southern blotting)

5. Probing the transferred DNA with radioactive probes to get a reaction

6. Using X-ray film to visualize the location of the radioactive probes

7. Finally, reading the developed X-ray film called an "auto-radiogram," which provides the pattern of nucleotides that may allow positive identification of the individual from whom the specimen came

FINGERPRINTS

Fingerprints, palmprints, and footprints are the most accepted form of identification. DNA testing may someday become as accurate, but fingerprinting is so much simpler.

The characteristics that make prints the best means of personal identification include the following:

1. They are permanent. The prints one is born with are the prints one will die with.

2. They are unique to one person. No two sets of identical prints have ever been found. Some researchers have said that if only twenty characteristic points in each pattern were recorded (more are used), the possibility of getting the same pattern would occur once in every 4.5 million centuries. That's unique! When DNA testing is done in a lab, under lab conditions, it may be possible to say that the chances of two people having the same match are once in ten billion people.

FINGERPRINT PATTERNS

There are three broad categories of fingerprint patterns as follows, although all fingerprints have friction ridges.

1. Loops have only one delta.

2. Whorls have two or more deltas.

3. Arches have no delta and no core.

Note: A delta is the triangular-shaped portion of a fingerprint pattern that is found in all patterns except arches. It is formed by the bifurcation (splitting) of a friction ridge, or by the separation of two friction ridges that had been running side by side. The core is the center of the pattern. Both the delta and the core are important in ridge counting. An imaginary line is drawn connecting. the delta and the core and all friction ridges that cut this line are counted. This ridge count can serve as the basis for fingerprint classification.

LOOPS

Loops are the most common pattern, occurring in 60 percent of all fingerprints. They may be divided into two categories:

1. The radial loop occurs where the openings of the ridges that form the pattern point to the radius (the forearm bone on the same side as the thumb).

2. The ulna loop occurs where the opening of the loop points to the ulna (the forearm bone on the same side as the little finger).

Note: It is not possible to determine from a single print whether or not the loop is radial or ulna unless you know which hand it came from.

WHORLS

There are many kinds of whorls, which occur in 30 percent of fingerprints. The whorls comprise all patterns with two deltas and patterns that are too irregular to classify, but the following are a few:

1. The simple whorl

2. The central pocket loop

3. The lateral pocket loop

4. The twin loop

5. The accidental whorl

Note: Although some of the above are called loops, they are in the whorl category.

ARCHES

There are two categories of arch patterns that occur in 10 percent of fingerprints.

1. The plain arch occurs when the ridge line goes from one side of the pattern to the other, never turning back to make a loop.

2. The tented arch occurs when the ridge line enters from one side, rises sharply in the center, and then continues to the other side of the pattern.

SEARCHING FOR FINGERPRINTS

The following are the three different kinds of chance impressions that may be left at a crime scene:

1. The plastic print is left in wax, putty, tar, butter, etc.

2. The visible print is left by dirty hands, etc. These are seldom clear and frequently look like stains. They should be photographed.

3. The latent print is usually not visible, but can sometimes be seen on a smooth surface by the use of oblique indirect light. Various forms of fine powders (light on a dark surface, dark on a light surface) can be used to make latent prints visible. Latent prints are usually the most valuable. Once they are made visible, they should be photographed. No attempt to lift a latent print should be made until after it is photographed.

METHODS TO MAKE LATENT PRINTS VISIBLE

1. Dusting has been mentioned previously and requires photographing before dusting to preserve the print.

2. The use of silver nitrate for prints on bank notes, etc.

3. The use of iodine fuming for prints on paper.

4. The use of osmium chloride for prints on porous material.

5. The use of ninhydrin for very old fingerprints.

Important: As a general rule, the courts require 12 points of identification to establish an indisputable identification when using fingerprints.

QUESTIONS ON CRIMINALISTICS AND INVESTIGATIONS

Directions: Read each question and choose the best answer. Circle the letter of your choice.

---

1. Most modern small arms have rifled bores. The *chief* reason for these grooves is to

   (A) cause the bullets to rotate around their longitudinal axis in order to prevent their turning end over end in flight.

   (B) cut longitudinal markings into the bullets for purposes of permanent identification.

   (C) increase the velocity of the bullet at the point of ejection from the barrel by giving it a spinning motion.

   (D) protect the barrel of the gun by enabling the expanding gases caused by the explosion to leave rapidly.

2. A comparison of the caliber of a bullet with that of the bore of the gun from which it is to be fired indicates that, generally, the bullet has a caliber

   (A) absolutely equal to the bore of the gun.

   (B) slightly larger than the bore of the gun.

   (C) slightly smaller than the distance between the lands of the bore of the gun.

   (D) equal to the distance between the two opposite grooves in the bore of the gun.

3. Experts generally agree that the best of the following methods of determining whether Bullet A was fired from a certain gun is to

   (A) chemically analyze Bullet A and compare it with the residue taken from the barrel of the gun.

   (B) make a direct visual comparison of Bullet A and the parts of the gun barrel.

   (C) compare the markings made by the ridges and grooves of the gun barrel on another bullet with those found on Bullet A.

   (D) analyze the gunpowder residue in the barrel of the gun to determine the time elapsed since the firing of the gun in question.

4. "Comparisons of bullets in order to establish if they were fired from the same gun may at times lead to hopeful expectations that are not based on fact." This statement is borne out principally by the fact that

    (A) most bullets recovered by autopsies have proved to be unidentifiable, regardless of their metal content.
    (B) full hard metal-jacketed bullets generally can be identified positively in only a very small percentage of cases.
    (C) only about half of the lead bullets recovered by postmortem examinations can be identified.
    (D) most bullets being used today are lead and only a small fraction of these can be identified after recovery.

5. An expended bullet that is needed as important physical evidence is found at the crime scene by a police officer. For the purpose of being able to identify the bullet positively at some later date, the police officer scratches his initials on the nose of the bullet. This method of marking such a bullet is

    (A) poor; the nose of the bullet will probably be flattened and will therefore be difficult to mark legibly.
    (B) good; the important impressions on the side of the bullet made by the gun barrel will then not be destroyed.
    (C) good; the actual marking of the nose of the bullet may reveal the presence of minute amounts of important physical evidence.
    (D) poor; important bits of physical evidence that may have adhered to the nose of the expended bullet could be destroyed.

6. When a bullet is fired at fairly close range through a glass window, the direction from which it has been fired can be determined. Of the following, the statement that is *correct* concerning such determination is that

    (A) radial fractures will form first on the side opposite the one from which the bullet was fired.
    (B) the hole is wider on the side facing the source of the bullet.
    (C) numerous small flakes are found blown away from the side from which the bullet was fired.
    (D) the more acute the angle, the fewer flakes will be blown away.

7. P. O. Connolly, at the scene of a crime where two bullets have been shot through a glass window, asks Sgt. Mullins whether or not it is possible to determine which shot was fired first. Which of the following responses by Sgt. Mullins would be most accurate?

    (A) "No. The various cracks in the glass prohibit coming to any conclusion."
    (B) "Yes. You can use the luminol test to do so."
    (C) "No. But it could have been done if the calibers were not the same."
    (D) "Yes. The radial fractures of the second bullet terminate when they meet such fractures of the first bullet."

8. Items required by the laboratory technician in his effort to determine the distance between the muzzle of the fatal gun and the victim at the instant the fatal shot was fired include all but one of the following. The one that would *not* be useful in determining this wanted information is

    (A) test ammunition of the type used in the weapon firing the fatal shot.
    (B) the fatal weapon.
    (C) the clothing of the suspect particularly if it contains powder residue.
    (D) the clothing of the victim.

9. The maximum distance at which a firearm will leave powder deposits or residue on the object at which it is fired

    (A) is invariably 18 inches.
    (B) depends entirely upon the kind of gunpowder used.
    (C) is directly related to the degree of twist of the rifling in the gun barrel.
    (D) depends mainly on the type of gunpowder used, the caliber, and the length of the gun barrel.

10. A police investigator must not overlook the possibility of various types of fingerprint traces or impressions that may be found on objects at the scene of a crime. Such impressions formed by the pressure of the finger upon comparatively soft or pliable surfaces such as wax, putty, or soap are called

    (A) visible impressions.
    (B) fixed imprints.
    (C) latent traces.
    (D) plastic impressions.

11. "Every effort should be made to obtain a photograph of a fingerprint impression found at a crime scene before the fingerprint is developed with powder." The main reason for following this precaution is that

    (A) the surrounding atmosphere may dry up the impression if it was produced by perspiration from the sweat pores.
    (B) significant details of the imprint may be obliterated in the powdering process.
    (C) better contrast is obtained with photography.
    (D) the photograph will show surrounding details in addition to the fingerprint pattern.

12. An experienced police investigator will be aware that an automobile that has been used in connection with a crime may contain valuable fingerprint impressions on the

    (A) front door windows.
    (B) areas near the door handles.
    (C) steering wheel.
    (D) rearview mirror.

13. Fingerprint experts have classified the prints made by human fingers into groups based on the general patterns or characteristics of which each individual print is composed. According to these experts, it would generally be correct to state that an individual fingerprint that has

    (A) the lines going from one side to the other in a more or less straight line, without curving back, is called an arch.
    (B) the lines curving back in a horseshoe turn is called a whorl.
    (C) a number of lines making a complete circle is called a loop.
    (D) a mixture of arches, loops, and whorls is called a complex.

14. In fingerprint identification, a delta is rarely found in which of the following groups?

    (A) Arches
    (B) Whorls
    (C) Accidentals
    (D) Loops

15. A method to develop very old fingerprints is to use

    (A) iodine fumes.
    (B) silver nitrate.
    (C) ninhydrin.
    (D) fixed-focus camera.

16. A specific test for human blood is the
    (A) benzidine test.
    (B) reduced phenolpthalein test.
    (C) precipitin test.
    (D) luminol test.

17. The body of a man is found in the river. The body is fully clothed but badly mutilated, waterlogged, and swollen. The clothing contains no identifying papers. The one of the following means of identification of the body that is *least* reliable is
    (A) fingerprints.
    (B) measurements of the body.
    (C) examination of the teeth.
    (D) scars on the body.

18. Vehicle A has crashed into Vehicle B while being driven at considerable speed. Immediately prior to the crash, the driver of Vehicle A realized what was about to happen and jammed on his brakes. The impact caused the driver of Vehicle A to crash into his vehicle's speedometer, crushing its glass cover and leaving the needle pointing permanently at a certain speed. The one of the following facts which would be of *least* value to the police in attempting to determine the minimum speed at which Vehicle A could have been traveling at the time the brakes were first applied is the
    (A) braking distance of Vehicle A.
    (B) length of the skid marks made by Vehicle A.
    (C) reaction time of the driver of Vehicle A.
    (D) speed indicated by the needle of the smashed speedometer in Vehicle A.

19. It is considered desirable for a police officer who is to testify at a criminal trial to discuss the case with the prosecuting assistant district attorney before the trial begins. The one of the following that is the most likely reason for this practice is that
    (A) during the trial, the police officer may unwittingly reveal prejudice towards the defendant.
    (B) the police officer should be briefed as to how the prosecutor intends to develop the detailed presentation of the case in court.
    (C) the prosecutor and the police officer should agree as to the amount of information to be revealed during the trial.
    (D) there may have been developments in the case of which the prosecutor is unaware.

20. "A police officer who is testifying in court in a criminal trial should rarely volunteer information, but should trust the prosecutor to ask the key questions." This statement is generally
    (A) false; the ends of justice may be defeated if important testimony is not presented.
    (B) true; the prosecutor may be waiting for the proper psychological moment when the police officer's response will have the greatest effect on the jury.
    (C) false; the police officer's opinion as to the value of evidence should be expressed clearly and forcefully in court.
    (D) true; the prosecutor may feel that information possessed by the police officer will adversely affect his or her case.

21. At the scene of a homicide, the *first* of the following steps taken by the officer in charge, after clearing the room of unnecessary persons, should be to
    (A) interrogate witnesses present before they have time to forget or collaborate with each other.
    (B) have photographs and detailed sketches made of the premises, the body, weapons, etc.

(C)   secure and properly mark all items of evidence.

(D)   ascertain whether the homicide was accidental or deliberate.

22.   "Moulage" is a

(A)   system of personal identification.

(B)   special process used for making casts of objects.

(C)   narcotic drug.

(D)   criminal parlance for money.

23.   Assume that you are questioning a holdup victim in order to obtain a description of the gunman. Of the following, the best example of a type of question to be *avoided* is

(A)   "Did you notice any scars or unusual features?"

(B)   "Did he wear a brown or black coat?"

(C)   "What color were his shoes?"

(D)   "Approximately how tall was he?"

24.   The *easiest* way to discover latent fingerprint impressions is to view the area

(A)   directly.

(B)   in a mirror.

(C)   at a distance of about one-half inch.

(D)   obliquely.

25.   In checking for latent fingerprints, which one of the following surfaces would be *least* likely to show a good print?

(A)   White paper envelope

(B)   Cardboard box

(C)   Unpolished bureau drawer

(D)   Checkered pistol grip

26.   A good method of developing fingerprints on paper is by the use of

(A)   copper powder.

(B)   ultraviolet rays.

(C)   infrared rays.

(D)   silver nitrate.

27.   In addition to their use in developing secret writing, iodine fumes can be used to

(A)   determine if erasures have been made on a document.

(B)   develop gunpowder patterns.

(C)   distinguish blood from other substances.

(D)   develop latent fingerprints.

28.   In police investigations, the paraffin test was formerly used to

(A)   detect whether a witness was telling the truth.

(B)   discover whether a deceased person had been poisoned.

(C)   estimate the approximate time of death of a deceased person.

(D)   determine whether a suspect had fired a revolver recently.

29.   Of the information obtained from examining a piece of glass in connection with a shooting, it is most accurate to state that

(A)   it is difficult to determine the direction from which a shot was fired.

(B)   a craterlike appearance of the hole indicates the exit side of the bullet path.

(C)   the side of the pane with the radial fractures indicates the side of entry of the bullet.

(D)   concentric fractures indicate the side from which the bullet emerged.

30. Whenever circumstances require a police officer to mark a cartridge or spent bullet, it would be most correct for him to mark the

    (A) cartridge by scratching his initials, on the base where the primer is located and not on the side of the cartridge.
    (B) spent bullet by scratching his initials on the bearing surface (side) and not on the base.
    (C) cartridge by scratching his initials on the side of the cartridge and not on the base where the primer is located.
    (D) spent bullet by scratching his initials on either the base or on the bearing surface (side).

31. Suppose that, while on patrol, you find the victim of a knife attack lying unconscious in the street. Nearby, a bloodstained handkerchief is found. A suspect with a bleeding nose is picked up by a police officer several blocks away. Of the following, the inference that can be established most accurately on the basis of the blood grouping is that the

    (A) blood on the handkerchief is not the blood of the victim.
    (B) blood on the handkerchief is probably the blood of the suspect.
    (C) person whose blood was found on the handkerchief is not of the same race as the victim.
    (D) person whose blood was found on the handkerchief is of approximately the same age and physical condition as the suspect.

32. The heaps of dust and dirt thrown up by a car on either side of its tracks indicate

    (A) its speed.
    (B) its direction of travel.
    (C) its weight.
    (D) the width of its tires.

33. The major responsibility for the police response to crime and the conducting of a preliminary investigation rests *primarily* with

    (A) the Detective Division, in conjunction with plainclothes units.
    (B) the office of special services assigned to the office of chief of police.
    (C) the patrol force.
    (D) the Crime Scene Unit assigned to the nearest forensic laboratory.

34. If reddish-brown or yellow smoke is present at the scene of a possible arson fire, the arson investigator should consider that which of the following substances is involved?

    (A) Gasoline
    (B) Heating oil
    (C) Nitrates
    (D) Phosphorous

35. Which of the following tests might be used to determine whether or not a substance is marijuana?

    (A) Precipitin reaction test
    (B) Duquenois test
    (C) Florence test
    (D) Leuco-malachite test

36. When someone says, "He deals in kilo weight cocaine," the weight referred to is

    (A) one thousand pounds.
    (B) one pound.
    (C) two and two-tenths pounds.
    (D) 370 milligrams.

37. Which of the following statements about marijuana is *not* correct?

    (A) Sudden abstinence after prolonged use causes severe withdrawal symptoms.
    (B) It is a weed that can be grown in many climates.
    (C) There is usually an odd number of serrated leaflets.
    (D) It is no more than one-tenth as strong as hashish.

38. When barbiturates are combined with alcohol, the effect on the human body is geometric and not arithmetic. This effect is known as the

    (A) synergistic effect.
    (B) multiple causative effect.
    (C) Stockholm syndrome.
    (D) symbiotic effect.

39. When a prostitute decides to "slip a mickey to a John" in order to knock him out so that he or she can steal his wallet, it is probable that the substance that is used is

    (A) amphetamine.
    (B) chloral hydrate.
    (C) heroin.
    (D) nitrous oxide.

40. A "voyeur" is a

    (A) world traveler.
    (B) travel agent.
    (C) peeping Tom.
    (D) child molester.

41. The pickpocket who is considered by other pickpockets to have reached the top of the profession is the

    (A) fob worker.
    (B) pants-pocket worker.
    (C) inside worker.
    (D) lush worker.

42. At the scene where a dead body has been discovered, little blood is present and yet there are massive injuries. Which of the following is the most logical conclusion?

    (A) It was a murder and not a suicide.
    (B) It was a suicide and not a murder.
    (C) A blunt instrument was used.
    (D) The injury was inflicted elsewhere.

43. With respect to blood in the investigation of a crime, which of the following statements is *not* correct?

    (A) When blood from a fleeing suspect strikes the ground at an angle, the droplets will point in the direction of travel.
    (B) When a dead body rests upon the ground, the blood still inside the body will settle into the lowest parts of the body.
    (C) The dark-blue color formed by the process in choice (B) is known as postmortem lividity.
    (D) If a body is found with postmortem lividity on the upper surface of the body, it can be assumed that the person was alive when he hit the floor.

44. A *modus operandi* file can be useful to a criminal investigator in that it

    (A) will single out the person who committed the crime.
    (B) will buttress the court testimony and make a conviction easier to obtain.
    (C) may reduce the number of suspects to be considered initially.
    (D) will eliminate the need to conduct a preliminary investigation.

45. The best time to conduct a raid the purpose of which is to apprehend a wanted fugitive is

    (A) early dawn.
    (B) early evening.
    (C) high noon.
    (D) between midnight and 4 A.M.

46. The major weakness of photographs of a crime scene as compared with a crime scene sketch is that

    (A) experts are required to take the photographs.
    (B) there may not be enough light to take a proper photograph.
    (C) photographs do not accurately show relative distances between objects.
    (D) sketches are more valuable as evidence because the sketchmaker had to observe the scene for a longer period of time.

47. While fleeing from police, a criminal suspect entered a five-story loft building. The most appropriate way for the police to conduct a search of this building for the suspect is to

    (A) start at the bottom and secure each floor in turn, flushing the suspect onto the roof.
    (B) start at the top and secure each floor downward in turn, flushing the suspect to the lowest point.
    (C) remain outside the building, blockading it, and making public address announcements for the suspect to surrender.
    (D) flood the building with tear gas and then have a trained team of experts, wearing gas masks, enter to conduct the search.

48. You are investigating a robbery of a supermarket. The manager of the store has wisely asked the shoppers who were witnesses to await your arrival. When you arrive, you engage in certain investigative techniques. Of the following, which action taken by you would be inappropriate?

    (A) Take the witnesses one at a time into the manager's office to be interviewed, allowing the remainder of the witnesses to talk over what they saw.
    (B) Separate the witnesses and then interview them separately.
    (C) Advise the witnesses not to speak with each other about the robbery prior to being interviewed by you.
    (D) Interview each witness separately.

49. When you, as a criminal investigator, arrive at the scene of a crime, the *first* thing you should do is

    (A) survey the scene and make an estimate of the situation.
    (B) photograph those areas that contain physical evidence.
    (C) aid any injured victims.
    (D) sketch the crime scene.

50. Cadaveric spasm is the stiffening of body muscles that occurs almost instantaneously with death. It is not a form of rigor mortis that starts a few hours (2.5) after death and lasts for about 24 to 36 hours. If a dead body is found to have a very tight grasp on a gun, then the criminal investigator might logically conclude that the death was caused by

    (A) suicide.
    (B) murder.
    (C) poison.
    (D) accident.

51. When a long-term narcotic user finds that he needs more and more of the narcotic in order to produce the same effect, it would be most correct to state that he is experiencing

    (A) tolerance.
    (B) physical addiction.
    (C) emotional dependence.
    (D) withdrawal.

52. During a criminal investigation, certain procedures used by the investigator in handling evidence are acceptable and others are not. Evaluate the following procedures:

    I.   Bullets should be marked for identification purposes on the base or the ogive.
    II.   If a bloodstained garment is found, ship the entire garment to the lab for testing.
    III. Firearms at the scene can be picked up by inserting a pencil through the trigger guard or by grasping the knurled handle.
    IV. Burglar's tools found at a crime scene should be placed against suspected tool marks to establish a match.

    (A) Statements I, II, III, and IV are correct.
    (B) Only statements I, II, and III are correct.
    (C) Only statements I and II are correct.
    (D) Only statements I, II, and IV are correct.

53. As a general rule, the important points to be looked for in most fingerprint patterns for the purpose of classification are

    (A) the delta and the core.
    (B) the direction of the friction ridges.
    (C) deformities that might be present.
    (D) unique characteristics.

54. When a police officer is checking a building at night and he is required to open a door, he should push it open all the way. The *best* reason for doing this is

    (A) he can be sure no one is hiding behind the door.
    (B) he can get a better view of the room.
    (C) it widens his area of entry in the event of an emergency.
    (D) light from behind him can be allowed to filter into the room.

55. In the event that you find it necessary to interview a person who is known to be unreliable as a witness, a good procedure would be for you to

    (A) ask leading questions.
    (B) seek" yes" or "no" answers.
    (C) convince him of the importance of his information.
    (D) allow him to talk as much as he wants.

56. During an interrogation of a suspect and after receiving a proper waiver of Miranda rights, you succeed in obtaining a confession. The problem is that the suspect is confessing not only to the crime under investigation, but to three other independent, unrelated crimes. You want to reduce the confessions to writing. It would be best for you to

    (A) use two writings, one for the original crime under investigation and the other for the remaining three crimes.
    (B) use one writing, include all four crimes confessed to, and have the suspect sign it.
    (C) use four separate writings, one for each of the crimes confessed to, and have the suspect sign each one.
    (D) permit the suspect to write out one confession covering all of the crimes to which he has confessed.

57. You have responded to the scene of an armed robbery. When you arrive, you see that no one is injured and there is no immediate danger to the victim. The perpetrator hasn't seen you and he is still inside the premises in question. Under these circumstances, it would be most appropriate for you to

    (A) enter the premises from the rear, confront the robber, and take him into custody.
    (B) stay outside, wait for help, and try to arrest the suspect after he leaves.
    (C) call to the suspect and let him know that he doesn't have a chance to get away.
    (D) try to get the attention of the victims in order to relieve their anxiety.

58. In the collection or search for evidence, it is important for the criminal investigator to be aware of the transfer theory. This theory holds that

    (A) when evidence is being transferred from the scene to the lab, extra care must be taken.
    (B) the transfer of evidence from one investigator to another must not break the chain of custody.
    (C) the scene may transfer evidence to the suspect and the suspect may transfer evidence to the scene.
    (D) only that amount of evidence that can be handled properly should be transferred to the lab.

59. You have been directed to respond to the scene of a possible D.O.A. Upon arrival, your *first* concern should be

    (A) if there are witnesses.
    (B) the identity of the victim.
    (C) the cause of death.
    (D) to confirm whether or not the person is dead.

60. In a recent examination, the examiner wanted to know what the most important element in fingerprint classification is. If you were asked this question, you would choose

    (A) delta.
    (B) core.
    (C) whorls.
    (D) pattern.

61. As a general rule, before evidence will be admitted at a criminal trial, it must meet a triple standard of admissibility. Which of the following is *not* part of that triple standard?

    (A) Beyond a reasonable doubt
    (B) Relevant
    (C) Material
    (D) Competent

62. An interrogation is different from an interview. In an interrogation, the dominant role

    (A) must be assumed by the interrogator.
    (B) must be shared that there is a free flow of information.
    (C) may fluctuate between the interrogator and the person being interrogated.
    (D) is not important.

63. The greatest danger faced by a police officer when responding to a robbery call is

    (A) superior fire power.
    (B) complacency.
    (C) lack of familiarity with the location.
    (D) lack of communication between units and headquarters.

64. The hallmark of a professional burglary is

   (A) an obviously well-planned crime.
   (B) the property stolen is of great value.
   (C) only one person is involved.
   (D) that it usually occurs at night in an occupied dwelling,

65. You have responded to a burglary at the ABC Assembly Plant. The office safe has been opened and there is no evidence of forced entry. The most likely explanation is that

   (A) the safe was left open.
   (B) the management was in on it.
   (C) the burglar knew the combination.
   (D) it is probably an insurance scam.

66. The single most important factor contributing to motor vehicle theft is the

   (A) number of vehicles from which to choose.
   (B) ease with which the vehicles can be disposed of.
   (C) careless motorist who leaves the car unlocked with keys in ignition.
   (D) demand for such vehicles.

67. When interviewing a rape victim, it is a good procedure to allow the victim to ventilate. This most nearly means

   (A) trying to get the victim to talk about the rape.
   (B) trying to get the victim to laugh instead of cry.
   (C) getting the victim to discuss the matter unemotionally.
   (D) a verbal release of tension.

68. The abnormal sexual desire of an adult toward children is known as

   (A) acrophobia.
   (B) pedophilia.
   (C) necromancy.
   (D) fetishism.

69. Which of the following would *not* be considered an effective deterrent to robbery for business people?

   (A) Maintaining firearms on the premises
   (B) Keeping only small amounts of cash on hand
   (C) Locking all but customer entrances
   (D) Keeping front windows clear of obstructions

70. The most important element in a polygraph examination is the

   (A) examiner.
   (B) emotional state of the suspect.
   (C) galvanic resistance of the skin.
   (D) respiration response ratio.

ANSWERS TO CRIMINALISTICS REVIEW QUESTIONS

1. The correct answer is (A).
2. The correct answer is (B).
3. The correct answer is (C).
4. The correct answer is (C).
5. The correct answer is (D).
6. The correct answer is (A).
7. The correct answer is (D).
8. The correct answer is (C).
9. The correct answer is (D).
10. The correct answer is (D).
11. The correct answer is (B).
12. The correct answer is (D).
13. The correct answer is (A).
14. The correct answer is (A).
15. The correct answer is (C).
16. The correct answer is (C).
17. The correct answer is (B).
18. The correct answer is (C).
19. The correct answer is (D).
20. The correct answer is (B).
21. The correct answer is (B).
22. The correct answer is (B).
23. The correct answer is (B).
24. The correct answer is (D).
25. The correct answer is (D).
26. The correct answer is (D).
27. The correct answer is (D).
28. The correct answer is (D).
29. The correct answer is (B).
30. The correct answer is (C).
31. The correct answer is (A).
32. The correct answer is (B).
33. The correct answer is (C).
34. The correct answer is (C).
35. The correct answer is (B).
36. The correct answer is (C). Referred to as a *key*.
37. The correct answer is (A). It is not physically addicting.
38. The correct answer is (A).
39. The correct answer is (B). It depresses the central nervous system and the victim falls asleep. If too much is used, the victim never wakes up.
40. The correct answer is (C).
41. The correct answer is (B).
42. The correct answer is (D).
43. The correct answer is (D). It can be concluded that the body was moved after death.
44. The correct answer is (C). Please note the words *will*, *will*, *may*, and *will*. This is similar to *apples*, *pears*, *screwdrivers*, and *peaches*.
45. The correct answer is (A).
46. The correct answer is (C).
47. The correct answer is (B). Please note that (A) and (B) are opposite choices and, since they both relate to the stem of the question, one of them is probably the answer.
48. The correct answer is (A). Note that (A) and (B) are opposite choices, so one of them is most likely the answer.

49. **The correct answer is (A).** Be careful here. Some competitors will jump at choice (C). But remember, before you can "aid the victim," you must have made an estimate of the situation. If choice (A) were not offered, then choice (C) would be the answer.

50. **The correct answer is (A).** It is almost impassible to simulate the tight grasp that occurs through cadaveric spasm.

51. **The correct answer is (A).** As you use more, your body tolerates more.

52. **The correct answer is (B).**

53. **The correct answer is (A).** Arches don't have deltas and cores, but arches only make up about ten percent of the fingerprint patterns.

54. **The correct answer is (A).**

55. **The correct answer is (D).**

56. **The correct answer is (C).** This way, if there is a problem with one, it may not affect the others. Furthermore, it is a good procedure to include some minor errors for the suspect to correct and initial. This can go a long way if the suspect brings a motion to suppress saying that the confession was coerced

57. **The correct answer is (B).**

58. **The correct answer is (C).**

59. **The correct answer is (D).** An obvious answer frequently missed by many competitors.

60. **The correct answer is (D).** The configurations of the friction ridges account for the patterns. In fingerprint classification, the ridges between certain points of the pattern are counted.

61. **The correct answer is (A).** "Beyond a reasonable doubt" is the standard for conviction, not for admissibility.

62. **The correct answer is (A).**

63. **The correct answer is (B).**

64. **The correct answer is (B).**

65. **The correct answer is (C).**

66. **The correct answer is (C).**

67. **The correct answer is (D).** Some jurisdictions now send a criminal investigator and a rape counselor because it is so important for the victim to experience a release of tension.

68. **The correct answer is (B).**

69. **The correct answer is (A).**

70. **The correct answer is (A).**

THE IN-BASKET EXERCISE

INSTRUCTIONS FOR THE IN-BASKET EXERCISE

Assume that you have been appointed as the acting chief of the city of Orange police department. The permanent chief, Terry Quinn, has broken his leg and cannot be contacted for at least three weeks. Therefore, you are in command.

THE IN-BASKET EXERCISE

It is now 0800 hours on Friday, February 16. You are on duty as of 0800 hours, but must leave for reserve military duty at 1200 hours. You will be gone for two weeks and will be unavailable during that time. You will return to work at 0800 hours on March 2.

The desk officer working today is newly assigned, and the patrol supervisor was promoted to his current rank yesterday.

You are to go through the chief's in-basket and deal with all items contained therein. Answer the related questions pertaining to the in-basket items by utilizing the following background information:

- The city of Orange police department headquarters is a four-story brick building located at 1234 Donegal Street. The building is bounded by Belfast Avenue on the south, Cork Boulevard on the west, Tyrone Avenue on the east, and Dublin Avenue on the north.

- The population of 120,000 is 70 percent white, 20 percent African American, 7 percent Hispanic, and 3 percent other.

- There is a mix of businesses along Donegal Street and Cork Boulevard. The southern end of the jurisdiction has a public park, a skating pond, and a new shopping mall that attracts numerous people from adjacent towns and villages. The city also contains some luxury cooperative apartments.

- There is a private hospital that contains a teaching facility. There is one public school, one Christian church, and one synagogue.

The questions that follow the items are to be answered based on the data provided, the map, the organization chart, the personnel profiles, the calendars, and your knowledge of department policies, procedures, and applicable laws.

Page A

LIST OF PAGES IN ADMINISTRATIVE TEST PACKET

This list does NOT include the actual questions.

Instructions	Page A
List of Pages	Page A-1
Personnel Profiles	Page B-1
	Page B-2
	Page B-3
Department Profile	Page C
Organizational Chart	Page D
Calendar (February)	Page E
Calendar (March)	Page F
Map	Page G
	Item 1
	Item 2
	Item 3
	Item 4
	Item 5
	Item 6
	Item 7
	Item 8
	Item 9
	Item 10
	Item 11
	Item 12
	Item 13
	Item 14
	Item 15
	Item 16
	Item 17
	Item 18
	Item 18A
	Item 19
	Item 20
	Item 21
	Item 22
	Item 23
	Item 24
	Item 25
	Item 26
	Item 27
	Item 28
	Item 29
	Item 30
	Item 31
	Item 32

Page A-1

PERSONNEL PROFILES

Chief Terry Quinn

In command of the city of Orange police department for the past eighteen months. A dynamic leader and a college graduate who attended the F.B.I. Academy, he is highly respected by most of his ranking subordinates. He is fair but firm and sets high standards for himself and his subordinates.

Captain Martin Harding

This planning officer is a twenty-four-year veteran of the department. He has been a captain for the past four years, two of which have been in his present assignment. He often disagrees with decisions made by the chief, but once a decision is finalized he supports it. He works steady tours of 1000 hours to 1800 hours from Monday to Friday.

Lieutenant Patrick McMahon

A youthful, conscientious member of the staff, he is the integrity control officer and has been in this assignment for the past eight months. Members of the command find him to be very approachable and often come to him with personal problems. He has identified numerous corruption hazards, and has been most instrumental in improving the level of integrity in the department. In addition, he is working closely with a special state prosecutor concerning a problem of corruption within the department. He works an undisclosed schedule submitted in advance to the chief.

Lieutenant 1—John MacDougall

A newly appointed lieutenant, he has been assigned to desk duty since his promotion. He does not like this assignment. As a sergeant he worked for many years in the Detective Division and he believes that he is not being properly utilized in his current job.

Lieutenant 2—Anthony Nunno

A quiet, low-key supervisor; he is a very competent desk officer. He is single and does not mind changing tours of duty to oblige other lieutenants. He is well-liked by his colleagues and is loyal, conscientious, and dependable, but he has been on sick report frequently for the past two years.

Lieutenant 3—Hector Mendoza

A young officer, he coaches the department softball team. He often socializes with his subordinates and enjoys being known as the police officers' champion who consistently takes their side in disciplinary matters. He has the reputation of being a lenient rater.

Lieutenant 4—William Nugent

A veteran desk officer who has the respect of his fellow lieutenants, sergeants, and police officers, he has a circulatory problem and cannot stand for long periods of time. His report writing is excellent, and he is very knowledgeable about conditions in the community. He has not reported sick in two years in spite of his infirmity. His last three evaluations were above standard.

Sergeant Harry Peterman

The director of Plainclothes and Undercover Operations, he works Saturday through Wednesday and is off every Thursday and Friday. He has an A.A.S. degree in criminal justice from the local community college.

Sergeant Kathy Driscoll

She performs steady midnight tours with Friday and Saturday off. She is intelligent, dependable, and the first female sergeant assigned to the department.

Sergeant 1—Harry Grobe

An energetic sergeant, he has a reputation for getting the job done.

Sergeant 2—Sam Sherrid

Promoted on August 4 of last year. He has adjusted extremely well to his position as a patrol supervisor. He is intelligent, a hard worker, and has above average potential. He gets the job done.

Sergeant 3—Luis Gonzalez

He speaks Spanish fluently and has a good relationship with the Hispanic community. He was promoted to sergeant yesterday.

Sergeant 4—Calvin Moore

He has been a sergeant for three years. He appears to be a good prospect for promotion. He is the first African American police officer promoted to the rank of sergeant.

Sergeant 5—Robert Fitzgerald

An older sergeant who is content with his assignment. He has been a sergeant for ten years.

Sergeant 6—Al Goodman

He has a high level of energy. He likes to tackle new and difficult assignments.

Sergeant 7—Frank Bornholdt

He had retired to sell cars, but has since returned to the department. He may have a drinking problem.

Sergeant 8—Arthur Gescheidel

He has been a sergeant since last October. He is reliable and takes a hands-on approach, but does not like to delegate.

Sergeant 9—Joseph Dunne

He likes varied assignments. He has been in Plainclothes, Headquarters, and Detective Division positions.

Police Officer James Bible

The community affairs officer, he is a very effective public speaker and has a great many contacts in the community.

Detective John Kilroy

The crime prevention officer, he has good rapport with the community. He frequently shows slide presentations at schools and gatherings.

Police Officer Edmond Baccaglini

The department training officer, he is a former schoolteacher. He knows the job thoroughly and keeps abreast of the latest department trends. He also attends St. Joseph's law school.

Page B-2

Police Officer Henry Ackerman

The traffic safety officer, he is an "old timer" who has done this job diligently throughout the years.

Police Officer Julian Chait

He is very active. He makes many quality arrests based upon observation and has an outstanding conviction record.

Police Officer Michael Fenty

The youth officer, he is a young, dependable, highly motivated officer who enjoys a good reputation with the youngsters. He drives a motorcycle.

Steady midnight tours are filled by the following officers:

Police Officer Carlos Monroe

He has a good attitude. He acts as a translator when needed.

Police Officer Gloria Brown

She is active and reliable. She is one of the few female officers assigned to the department.

Page B-3

DEPARTMENT PROFILE

The headquarters building is located at 1234 Donegal Street and was completed in 1978. It is a four-story brick building with an underground garage. Before the budget cutbacks, the building housed a complement of 200 uniformed police personnel on the first and second floors. This complement has since been reduced to 150 uniformed personnel. The third floor is occupied by the Detective Squad and the Training Unit. The Plainclothes, Undercover, and Internal Affairs Units occupy the fourth floor.

Page C

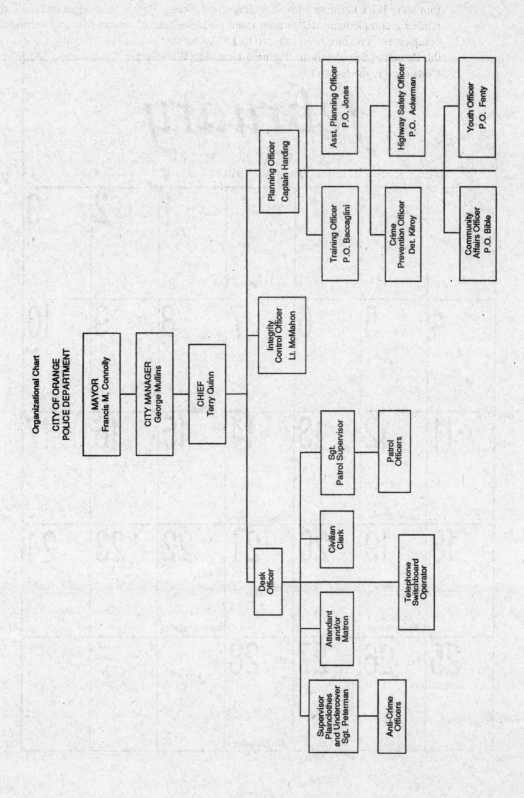

Organizational Chart
CITY OF ORANGE POLICE DEPARTMENT

MAYOR
Francis M. Connolly

CITY MANAGER
George Mullins

CHIEF
Terry Quinn

Integrity Control Officer
Lt. McMahon

Planning Officer
Captain Harding

Asst. Planning Officer
P.O. Jones

Highway Safety Officer
P.O. Ackerman

Youth Officer
P.O. Fenty

Training Officer
P.O. Baccaglini

Crime Prevention Officer
Det. Kilroy

Community Affairs Officer
P.O. Bible

Desk Officer

Sgt. Patrol Supervisor

Patrol Officers

Civilian Clerk

Telephone Switchboard Operator

Attendant and/or Matron

Supervisor Plainclothes and Undercover
Sgt. Peterman

Anti-Crime Officers

Page D

february

S	M	T	W	T	F	S
				1	2	3
4	5	6	7	8	9	10
11	12	13	14	15	16	17
	Lincoln's Birthday		Valentine's Day			
18	19	20	21	22	23	24
	Washington's Birthday Observed			Washington's Birthday		
25	26	27	28			
			Ash Wednesday			

Page E

march

S	M	T	W	T	F	S
				1	2	3
4	5	6	7	8	9	10
11	12	13	14	15	16	17 St. Patrick's Day
18	19	20	21	22	23	24
25	26	27	28	29	30	31

Page F

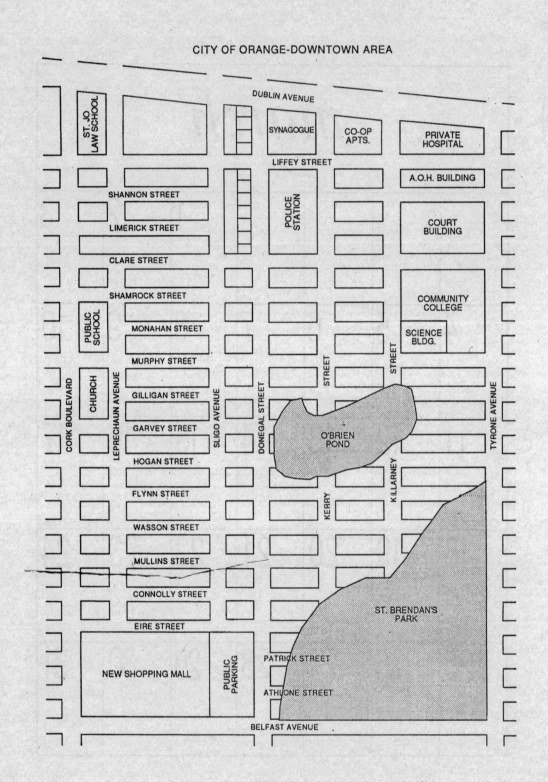

CITY OF ORANGE-DOWNTOWN AREA

Page G

CITY MANAGER'S OFFICE

CITY OF ORANGE

February 14

FROM: City Manager

TO: Chief of Department

SUBJECT: TEMPORARY ASSIGNMENT OF SERGEANT GROBE TO MAYOR'S TASK
            FORCE

---

1. Sergeant Harry Grobe has been temporarily assigned to the
    mayor's office for the months of March and April. He will
    report to said office at 0900 hours, Thursday, March 1.

2. For your information.

                              George Mullins

                              City Manager

Item 1

CURRENT VACATION SELECTIONS

SUPERVISORS

Planning Officer

Captain Harding November 19 to November 30 and December 17 to January 4

Lieutenants

MacDougall	1	June 16 to July 6 and December 11 to December 24
Nunno	2	August 20 to September 22.
Mendoza	3	July 12 to July 23 and October 2 to October 20
Nugent	4	July 24 to August 12 and October 29 to November 16

Integrity Control Office

McMahan		January 1 to February 3

Sergeants

Grobe	1	March 3 to March 15 arid. August 30 to September 19
Sherrid	2	September 12 to October 1 and November 11 to November 23
Gonzalez	3	April 5 to April 24 and June 11 to June 23
Moore	4	February 10 to February 28 and November 29 to December 10
Fitzgerald	5	January 9 to January 28 and July 7 to July 18
Goodman	6	June 19 to July 8 and September 2 to September 14
Bornholdt	7	July 24 to August 12 and September 29 to October 11
Gescheidel	8	August 13 to September 9
Dunne	9	March 21 to April 9 and November 9 to November 20
Driscoll (Kathy)	Steady Late	November 11 to December 7
Peterman (Harry)	Plainclothes	February 4 to March 7

Item 2

MAYOR'S OFFICE

CITY OF ORANGE

February 12

FROM: Mayor's Office

TO: Chief of Department

SUBJECT: SPECIAL ASSIGNMENT

1.   This office is finalizing a request for a grant from the
     federal government. The request, if approved, will provide a
     substantial amount of financial aid to be utilized in the
     furtherance of police/community relations programs.

2.   You are directed to submit the name of a supervisory officer,
     currently assigned to your department, to assist in the
     drafting of the final written request.

3.   Respond no later than February 18.

                              Francis M. Connolly

                              Mayor

Item 3

February 13

Chief Quinn:

Our block has been the scene of many muggings, assaults, and burglaries aver the past three months and finally your department gives us attention! Everyday, promptly at 8 A.M., your Officer Fortugno arrives on Connolly Street and puts parking tickets on our cars. In fact, yesterday he erroneously put a summons on my auto,which was parked on the proper side of the street. Enclosed is a copy. Is this your answer to our crime wave?

It would be another thing if we could count on Officer Fortugno to remain on the street to offer protection to us after getting his quota for the day, but no, your man disappears, visiting his friends down in Sammy's Garage on the corner of Connolly Street and Leprechaun Avenue.

We demand service, not summonses!

A Tax Payer,

Rhonda Fleming

18 Connolly Street

Item 4

February 13

Memorandum to Chief Terry Quinn

From: Captain Handing, Planning Officer

Subject: PLAINCLOTHES CANDIDATES

As you requested, the following information concerns personnel who submitted requests for plainclothes assignments. This data is for the past twelve-month period.

Officer	Arrests Fels.	Arrests Misds.	Summons Moving	Summons Parking	Time Sick	Civilian Complaints*	Supervisory Warnings**
Miller	38	20	105	200	1	2	0
Flores	34	20	20	140	2	0	0
Blue	37	15	95	190	0	0	0
Jackson	24	26	90	114	2	1	0
Kelly	17	16	36	72	1	0	1
Pinkett	50	11	70	111	0	1	1
Holmes	11	4	48	100	0	1	0
Fortugno	5	5	114	1485	1	3	0
Rios	32	17	90	140	0	0	0

* Formal complaints of misconduct lodged by civilians.

** Supervisory warnings indicate a warning by a supervisor that did not require formal disciplinary action.

Item 5

February 10

FROM: Mayor's Office

TO: Chief of Department

SUBJECT: QUALIFIED SUPERIOR FOR MAYOR'S TASK FORCE

1.   You are directed to submit the name of a qualified sergeant
      for assignment to the mayor's task force on crime. This is in
      addition to the assignment of Sergeant Grobe.

2.   Respond no later than February 18.

                                    Francis M. Connolly

                                    Mayor

Item 6

PERFORMANCE EVALUATION—SERGEANT/LIEUTENANT

1.

SURNAME	FIRST	M.I.	RANK	DEPARTMENT
Sherrid	Sam		Sgt.	City of Orange P.D.

SOCIAL SECURITY NUMBER	TAX REGISTRY NUMBER	DATE ASSIGNED TO COMMAND
106-36-1666	986420	08/04

PRESENT ASSIGNMENT	DATE OF PRESENT ASSIGNMENT
Supervise Patrol	08/04

2.

ANNUAL ( )   INTERIM (x)   PROBATION ( )
                                TRANSFER ( )

DATE PREPARED _____

OVERALL EVALUATION

Should be consistent with the pattern of rating on the interior of the form. A member's overall rating should not be affected by his/her relative standing in the group.

3.

WELL ABOVE STANDARDS [X]   ABOVE STANDARDS [ ]   MEETS STANDARDS [ ]   BELOW STANDARDS [ ]   WELL BELOW STANDARDS [ ]

RECOMMENDATION

Remember that recommendations for assignment are subject to accountability standards.

4.

CONTINUE IN PERSON ASSIGNMENT (X)
NOT RECOMMENDED FOR DETAIL ( )
TRANSFER ( )   Specify _____
ADDITIONAL TRAINING ( )   Specify _____
OTHER ( )

5. RATER COMMENTS – Indicate your general assessment of the individual's overall performance. This should reflect the standards on the interior of the form, which are derived from the specific dimensions in the Evaluation Guide. Include comments as to strengths, weaknesses and career potential.

The sergeant, since his promotion has adjusted well to his position. He undertakes and completes some very difficult tasks intelligently. His squad has shown a considerable increase in productivity. With no significant weaknesses, the sergeant has very high career potential. He has not reported sick during this rating period.

I have shown this performance evaluation to the ratee and have fully discussed its contents _____ *PB*

RATER INITIALS

I wish to appeal this performance evaluation _____

RATEE'S INITIALS

6.

Name (typed)	Rank	Command	Date Assigned to Command
Frank Bornholdt	Sgt.	City of Orange	August 1

Rater Signature	Tax Registry Number	Social Security Number
	851887	131-22-7771

7.

Name (typed)	Rank	Command	Date Assigned to Command

Reviewer Signature	Tax Registry Number	Social Security Number

8. REVIEWER: Comments and recommendations

Item 7

```
                    Professional Type Security

                       420 Cork Boulevard

                        City of Orange


                                             February 12

Chief Quinn:

     Police Officer James Wassori, while employed by me in a secu-
rity capacity, made an excellent arrest of two robbers on February
9 at Acme Warehouse. While checking the premises as a part of his
function for me, he observed two men inside the building and cap-
tured them single-handedly. I believe this arrest deserves depart-
mental recognition.

                                       Sincerely,


                                       Kevin Mullins

                                       President

                                       P.T.S.




Chief,

     I have investigated this as you directed.

Good arrests and within department guidelines.

He has permission for off-duty employment.

                                     . Capt. Harding
```

Item 8

February 14

Chief Quinn:

    I have noticed that many prisoners arrested by Police Officer Jack Dempsey have sustained cuts and bruises about the head and face that required medical treatment. Perhaps there is a pattern here?

Sergeant Fitzgerald

Item 9

February 14

FROM: Training Officer

TO: Chief of Department

SUBJECT: ROLE CALL TRAINING INSTRUCTIONS

1.   Please review the attached memo that I have prepared for roll
     call instructions at outgoing platoons beginning Monday,
     February 19.

Edmond Baccaglini

Training Officer

Item 10

ROLL CALL INSTRUCTIONS FOR WEEK OF FEBRUARY 19 THROUGH FEBRUARY 24

In conformance with CONSTITUTIONAL SAFEGUARDS, the following procedures will be followed:

1.   No crime scene shall be searched without a search warrant.

2.   No arrests will be made of a person inside his home without first obtaining an arrest warrant.

3.   Under no circumstances will interrogation continue once a defendant in custody requests to see an attorney.

Item 11

SUPERVISOR'S COMPLAINT REPORT   SERIAL NO. __66__

From: Sgt. Harry Grobe,

To: Chief of Dept.,

Subject: REPORT OF VIOLATION OF THE RULES AND PROCEDURES.

Member Complained Of:	Rank	Full Name		Shield No.	Command
	P.O.	CYNTHIA SMITH		1851	P.D.

Location where violation occurred		Time	Date	Day of Week
Headquarters		1045 hrs. 1050 hrs.	2/9	FRIDAY

Complainant (if any):	Name and Address	Telephone Number
N/A		N/A

Details of Violation:

While assigned to clerical and telephone duty, above officer failed to answer the telephone for a period of five minutes. The undersigned attempted to call into headquarters, and the phone rang continuously.

The Officer was ☐ was not ☑ warned and admonished, and

was ☐ was not ☑ instructed in the proper performance of duty and /or procedure.

Signature of superior preparing report	Rank	Command	Date
Sgt. Harry Grobe	Sgt.	P.D.	2/9

FOLLOW-UP

☐ Unsubstantiated   ☐ Command Discipline Accepted

☐ Charges and Specifications   ☐ Command Discipline Review
   Precinct Ser. No. _____

Final Disposition	Rank	Signature of C.O.	Command

Instruction:

Commanding Officers must investigate and report disposition under FOLLOW-UP.

Item 12

City of Orange

Department of Highways

220 East Fermi Street

February 11

Chief Terry Quinn

1234 Donegal Street

City of Orange

Dear Chief Quinn:

This letter is to advise you that it will be necessary for the Department of Highways to close Liffey Street for major emergency regains from March 5 to March 9.

During this period the street will be impassable and all vehicle and pedestrian traffic will be excluded. Suitable signs and detours will be constructed and the public will be advised to use alternate routes.

I anticipate that the closing of Liffey Street will cause some traffic problems. To address these problems I have scheduled a meeting at 0900 hours on Thursday, March 2 at the Department of Highways office. I have also invited representatives from the bus company, the Department of Parks, and the Fire Department to attend.

Please advise my office whether or not you will attend.

Yours truly,

Anthony Maloney

Deputy Commissioner

Mayor's office called concerning this matter.

States you should attend.

Capt. Harding

Item 13

February 14

Memo to Chief Quinn:

It is my opinion that Police Officer Robert White of the Undercover Unit might possibly be drinking too much.

Sgt. Harry Peterman

Item 14

Private Hospital

2101 Dublin Avenue

Office of Security

February 15

Chief Terry Quinn

Dear Chief:

I wish to inform you of an impending labor problem at our hospital. Negotiations with various unions representing a majority of our personnel have broken down. As a result, we now anticipate a large-scale strike to take place at the beginning of the day shift on March 25.

We will need coverage by police personnel. In previous strikes by these groups 130 to 150 wooden barriers were also required to provide access to and from hospital facilities. A meeting with you is requested, at your headquarters if possible, on March 2 or 3 to discuss tactics in dealing with the problem.

Yours truly,

Dave Sackman

Director of Security

Item 15

From: Integrity Control Officer

To: Chief of Department

Subject: DISCIPLINARY MATTER

1.   Chief, a disciplinary report was referred to us by the mayor's task force. The original charges occurred as a result of a family problem between Civilian Clerical Employee Bill Bailey and his wife.

2.   Bill Bailey has been in this department for the past seven years. During this period he has performed "well above standards" and has assumed increasing responsibility. As you know, he is seldom late and has reported sick only once in the past year. I suggest that we impose the minimum penalty based on his excellent record. Apparently the mayor's office did not consider this a serious matter either.

Patrick McMahon

Lieutenant

Item 16

RANK P.O.	SOCIAL SECURITY NO. 113-12-7711	COMMAND City of Orange PD	
SHIELD 716	SURNAME WASSON	INITIAL(S) J.	SQD./~~CHT.~~ 9

DATE ENTERED DEPT. 11-1-72			DATE PRESENT RANK		

		FROM		TO	HRS.	MIN
TIME ACTUALLY WORKED	DATE	2/9	DATE	2/10		
	TIME	2200	TIME	1430	16	30

		FROM		TO	HRS.	MIN
TIME SCHEDULED TO WORK	DATE	DAY	DATE	OFF		
TOUR NO.	TIME		TIME		—	—

OVERTIME PERFORMED	16	30
PLUS TRAVEL TIME (IF APPLICABLE)		
TOTAL OVERTIME	16	30
COMPENSATION OPTION: (INDICATE HRS. & MIN.) ~~TIME~~ CASH	16	30

CMD./LOCATION WHERE DUTY PERFORMED

INCIDENT TIME (Actual time of Occurrence) 2200 HRS. 2/9
REASON FOR LOST TIME: (Identify incident specifically)

ARREST OF 2 ROBBERS

I hereby certify that this report is accurate:

Date 2/10	Rank/Signature of Requesting Member P.O. *Jann Wasson*

SUPERVISORY OFFICER'S CERTIFICATION

MEMBER DIRECTED TO RETURN TO COMMAND?

☐ YES–Do not sign
form. Advise member
to submit at command.

☐ NO–Time dismissed:
_____ Hours
(Forward form to member's C.O.)

Log Entry : Date 2/10	Time 1500	Page No. 130

Date 2/10	Supervisor's Name Printed WILLIAM NUGENT	Command PD
	Rank Signature of Supervisor *Lt. William Nugent*	

INSTRUCTIONS: Submit one copy to stationhouse officer or supervisor at
time of FINAL dismissal. Form must be certified by a supervisor and then
forwarded to member's Command Officer without delay

OVERTIME REPORT

Item 17

February 10

Chief:

I must attend a meeting at 1100 hours on February 28 re: robbery problems within our city. I want you to have a statistical report on my desk by 0800 hours on February 17 re: robbery. The attached statistical raw material must be used to come up with the information.

I want the following answers:

1. The percentage of increase and decrease in each category for the six-month period ending December 31 last year as compared to the same period the year before.

2. The total number of J.D. offenses during the last six months of last year.

Francis M. Connolly

Mayor

Item 18

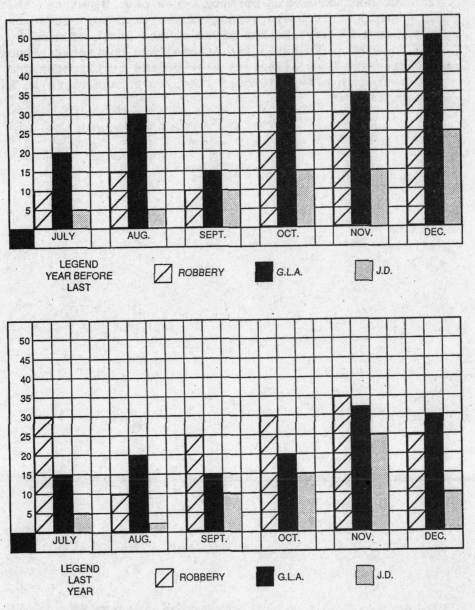

CRIME

STATISTICS

LAST SIX MONTHS YEAR BEFORE LAST
compared to
LAST SIX MONTHS LAST YEAR

LEGEND
YEAR BEFORE
LAST

⬜ ROBBERY   ⬛ G.L.A.   ⬜ J.D.

LEGEND
LAST
YEAR

⬜ ROBBERY   ⬛ G.L.A.   ⬜ J.D.

NOTE: G.L.A.=GRAND LARCENY of an AUTOMOBILE

Item 18A

February 15

From: Police Offices Jose Morales, Undercover

To: Chief of Department

Subject: M.A.D. (Minorities Against Discrimination)

On this date, while performing undercover duty in civilian clothes, I was contacted by a citizen who has proven to be a reliable information source on many occasions. He stated that M.A.D. was engaging in subversive activities from Apt. 52 at 24 Watson Street in the city. He has given me the names of numerous perpetrators together with dates, locations, and businesses involved in robberies and burglaries. In view of the complicated and extensive information involved, I would like you to assist me in handling this matter.

Jose Morales

Undercover

Item 19

February 14

From: Patrol Sergeant

To: Chief of Dept. Quinn

Subject: ARREST OF A MINOR AFTER APPARENT SALE OF NARCOTICS
             INSIDE A BAR AND GRILL

1.   At 2000 hours on this date Police Officer Virgilo Moretti
     arrested one Janet Wells, FW, 17 years old, of 150 Bayview
     Terrace, Apt. 10C, for possession of narcotics (heroin).

2.   At time of occurrence, Officer Moretti and I observed Ms.
     Wells exit from Angie's Cabaret, 125 Cork Boulevard. She
     seemed intoxicated and as we approached she threw a glassine
     envelope containing alleged heroin to the sidewalk. She
     stated she had purchased it from Sal the bartender. Sal is
     known to be Sal LoPiparo.

3.   For your information.

                              Luis Gonzalez

                              Sergeant

Item 20

RESIGNATION AND EXIT INTERVIEW					Date 2/15	

		Rank P.O.	Name (Last, First, M.I.) Shay Marvin J.		

Shield # 40205	Tax Registry No. 911286	Command		Date of Appointment

Eff. Time of Resignation 1000 hrs.	Eff. Date of Resignation	Reasons Educational Opportunity

1. Is This Act Voluntary And Of Your Own Free Will And Not Caused By Any Threat Or Act Of Coercion On The Part Of Any Person Connected With The Police Department? (✓) Yes ( ) No

2. Are You Presently A Respondent In A Disciplinary Proceeding In This Department? ( ) Yes (✓) No

3. Are You Presently Under Investigation By Any City, County, State Or Federal Investigating Body Or Agency? ( ) Yes (✓) No

4. Are You Presently Under Subpoena And Have Been Summonsed To Testify Before Any City, County, State Or Federal Investigating Body Or Agency? ( ) Yes (✓) No

(If Answer To Question 2, 3, Or 4 is "Yes," Attach A Report Describing The Circumstances.)

Signature of Applicant P.P.O. *Marvin Shay*	Rank P.O.	Signature of Witness *Harrison Grant*	Pct.
( ) Approved ( ) Disapproved Chief Of Personnel	( ) Approved ( ) Disapproved Police Commissioner		

NOTE: Resignation of a member of the department permanently appointed bars reinstatement except upon the approval of the Police Commissioner within one year from the date of resignation. Resignation of a member of the department during probation bars reinstatement.

EXIT INTERVIEW

PART 1 (To Be Conducted By Commanding Officer, If On Duty, Otherwise By The Supervisory Officer Receiving This Application.)

A. If Applicant is Accepting Other Employment Complete This Section

Name of Agency or Firm (Include Address If Applicable)	Title of Position or Nature of Work

Starting Salary	Maximum Salary	If Own Business, State Nature of Business

Benefits or Advantage of New Employment Stated By Applicant

B. If Other Than "A" Explain

C. Disadvantages Of Police Work Stated By Applicant

D. Reasonable Recommendations Or Suggestions Made By Applicant

E. What, In Your Opinion, Are The Basic Reasons Why This Employee Is Resigning?

Rank	Signature	Command

PART 2 (To Be Completed By Commanding Officer Only)

Are Charges Pending Or Is Applicant The Subject Of Any Investigation Which May Result In Charges Being Preferred?	( ) Yes ( ) No (If Yes, Attach Report.)
Based Upon Information Available, Is Applicant Presently Under Investigation, Or Been Summonsed To Testify Before Any City, County, State, Or Federal Investigating Body?	( ) Yes ( ) No (If Yes, Attach Report.)

State Your Evaluation Of The Conduct And Duty Performance Of The Member Concerned.

Rank	Signature Of Commanding Officer

DISTRIBUTION:
1. White - Pension Section
2. Blue - Member's C.O. If Other Than In Person
3. Pink - Employee Mgt. Division
4. Buff - Member's Command
5. Green - To Member If He/She Resigns In Person

Item 21

February 15

Chief:

Police Officer Marvin Shay of our command called and stated that he wishes to resign for a period of three months. He wants to complete a degree program at a local school after which he antici-pates being reinstated to the department. He will come in tomorrow to be interviewed.

Capt. Harding

Captain

Item 22

February 14

From: City Manager's Office

To: All Department Heads

Subject: OFF-DUTY EMPLOYMENT

1. Any activity performed by city employees while engaged in a secondary (noncity) employment situation will not be recognized as "job related."

2. This relates to injuries, court appearances, overtime, etc.

3. Department heads requiring further information concerning this matter will direct all inquiries to Mr. John Walsh at the city manager's office.

George Mullins

City Manager

Item 23

From: Planning Officer

To: Chief of Department

Subject: PEDDLER PROBLEMS NEAR ST. BRENDAN'S PARK AT WASSON,
          CONNOLLY, AND MULLINS STREETS

---

1.   I wish to advise you of a seasonal problem with food vendors
     near St. Brendan's Park and O'Brien Pond.

2.   Every winter numerous food vendors conduct business on the
     street, attracted by the crowds of people attending the
     Winter Festival and ice skating in the park and at the pond.
     In the past we have used various methods to deal with this
     condition. The following are some actions concerning these
     vendors that you may consider effective:

     a.   Have uniformed members of the service serve summonses
          when they observe a vendor who is operating in
          violation of law.

     b.   Notify the Property Clerk Division when a large amount
          of property is seized.

     c.   Designate sufficient number of supervisory members to
          inspect perishable goods (food and nonfood) frequently
          so that such items may be condemned and disposed of
          when necessary.

     d.   Direct a supervising officer to forward perishable
          foods or goods to the Property Clerk Division.

                         Martin Harding

                         Captain

Item 24

February 15

Chief Quinn:

The following is my schedule for the month of March:

1.	2400-0800	17.	RDO
2.	600-2400	18.	0300-1100
3.	200-2000	19.	2400-0800
4.	1100-1900	20.	1600-2400
5.	RDO*	21.	1600-2400
6.	1000-1800	22.	RDO
7.	RDO	23.	Excused Lost Time
8.	2400-0800	24.	Excused Lost Time
9.	RDO	25.	1500-2300
10.	RDO	26.	1200-2000
11.	0800-1600	27.	1000-1800
12.	0800-1600	28.	RDO
13.	1200-2000	29.	RDO
14.	0800-1600	30.	RDO
15.	1600-2400	31.	0800-1600
16.	RDO		

Lt. Patrick McMahon

I.C.O.

*RDO Regular Day Off

Item 25

<u>MEMO FROM CHIEF TERRY QUINN</u>

February 9

To: Sergeant Peterman

        I did a 4-12 last night and spent a considerable amount of time observing your operation. Your units were very active and a lot of good police work was being done, but unfortunately I also observed the following:

1.   One team spent half the tour doing a follow-up investigation of a past burglary.

2.   Photo line-ups were not being performed properly.

3.   A great deal of time was being spent studying crime statistics and reports.

4.   Units were not informing the radio dispatcher that they were present at the scene of police incidents.

You are the supervisor. Where were you?

                        Chief Quinn

                        Chief of Department

Item 26

February 13

From: Sergeant Harry Peterman

To: Chief Quinn

Subject: PROPOSED GUIDELINES FOR ALL PLAINCLOTHES PERSONNEL

---

1.   In response to your observations and comments on February 9, attached, I believe that these deficiencies are not deliberate, but are the result of some new members not fully understanding all the guidelines of our units. I am thinking of instituting a training session for new personnel, if you approve, during the week of February 19. I will emphasize the following points:

    a.   Unit personnel will not conduct follow-up investigations in excess of 2 hours without the approval of a supervisor.

    b.   Unit personnel will not conduct photo or other line-ups but will limit themselves to show-ups.

    c.   Analysis of crime reports other than burglaries is to be prohibited.

    d.   Unit personnel will inform the radio dispatcher when responding to, or being present at, the scene of a police incident and in addition will include a description of clothing worn, vehicle used, etc.

2.   For your information.

                                   Sergeant Harry Peterman

Item 27

February 15

Chief:

Police Officer John Kelly is asking for a vacation from February 18 to February 28. It is from last year when he was ill and nonline of duty. He was hospitalized during this time. If we grant him this request, we will exceed the 12 percent vacation quota. Does this meet with your approval?

Clerical Staff

Item 28

February 14

Chief Quinn:

As you know, I have a vacancy of one police officer in the Plainclothes Unit. After careful consideration, I wish to propose Police Officer Jane Rios for the position. Although young, in her short time in the department she has amassed an impressive arrest record. Her other police activities are also above standards. She now performs patrol duty in the fourth squad. With your approval, I will arrange her assignment to my unit as soon as possible.

Harry Peterman

Sergeant

Item 29

February 13

Chief:

    This year, as in past years, our department's softball team is being sponsored by Police Tutorial Service. They have supplied us with jerseys with the name of the business printed on the back. The proprietor, Kevin Mullins, has no criminal record and his business is legitimate. I have researched the matter and found that the mayor's guidelines and general regulations state that we should not publish advertisements without the permission of the mayor's office. I believe the jerseys might be considered as a form of advertising. Should we try to obtain the necessary permission? How do we go about it?

                  Lt. McMahon

Item 30

February 13

From: Mayor's Office

To: Police Chief

Subject: PATROL STRENGTH

---

1. As you know, we have been experiencing a great deal of
    community pressure to keep our uniform patrol as visible as
    possible. Furthermore, our contractual agreements with the
    Police Union permit us to restrict the number of officers on
    vacation at any one time to 121 of the total force.

2. Departures from this vacation restriction will not be
    tolerated.

Francis M. Connolly

Mayor

Item 31

POLICE DEPARTMENT

CITY OF ORANGE

February 11

From: Police Officer Aurora Garcia

To: Chief of Department

Subject: CONFRONTATION SITUATION

---

1. At approximately 1530 hours on Monday, February 5, while on duty in uniform, I observed a white male, dressed in business attire, loitering in the vicinity of a public school on my post. When I confronted him, he stated he was a detective. However, he refused to show me any identification and stated I should know all the local detectives. He went on to make remarks about the competence of female police officers in general. At that point, I called for the patrol sergeant over my walkie-talkie.

2. The sergeant immediately recognized the male as Detective Thomas Wilson, ascertained that he was on duty, was present on police business, and told us both to "forget about it." Because neither Detective Wilson nor I was satisfied with the sergeant's handling of the incident, we all went into your office at the precinct station house.

3. I was impressed with the investigation you conducted. I know you telephoned the mayor's office and forwarded all the necessary reports. At that time, I accepted your explanation of Detective Wilson's conduct. However, I still feel dissatisfied with your final determination that there was no intent by Detective Wilson to belittle female police officers.

4. Please advise me as to my next step to appeal your decision.

Aurora Garcia

Item 32

IN-BASKET EXERCISE QUESTIONS

> **Directions:** Read each question and choose the best answer. Circle the letter of your choice. The questions are to be answered solely on the basis of the information contained in the in-basket exercise instructions. We suggest that a careful reading of the items and utilization of the index be your first order of business. Remember, in these kinds of exercises *organization* is the name of the game.

1. With respect to Item 3, the directive from the mayor's office, and any related items, it would be most appropriate for you to select which one of the following supervisors?

   (A) Patrick McMahon
   (B) William Nugent
   (C) Anthony Nunno
   (D) Flurry Grobe

2. With respect to Item 4, the letter from Miss Fleming, and any related items, it would be most appropriate for you to

   (A) ignore this relatively unimportant communication because you are leaving for military duty today.
   (B) make an appointment to speak with Miss Fleeting within the next week.
   (C) direct this to the patrol supervisor concerned and to Lt. McMahon.
   (D) personally investigate the matter.

3. With respect to Item 7, the performance evaluation, as the reviewing officer you should

   (A) sign in the space indicated because it is your function in this situation to "review" the evaluation.
   (B) speak with Sergeant Bornholdt prior to signing the evaluation.
   (C) speak with Sergeant Sherrid and the rater prior to signing the evaluation.
   (D) do not sign the evaluation, but refer the matter for appropriate investigation.

4. With respect to Item 17, the overtime request, and any related items, which of the following actions should you take?

   (A) Approve the request, but only if the facts as stated on the request form are verified by the desk officer.
   (B) Disapprove the request because the overtime was not authorized in this instance.
   (C) Approve the request after Lieutenant McMahon has reviewed the records relating to the court appearance.
   (D) Disapprove the request because a typed copy of a supervisor's off-duty arrest report must be attached.

5. With respect to Item 9, the memo from Sergeant Fitzgerald, and any related items, the most appropriate action for you to take to check for a possible pattern of prisoner abuse would be to direct

    (A) a check of the central repository of civilian complaints.
    (B) a check of the admitting desks of the local hospitals.
    (C) that a supervisor check with the Mayor's task force.
    (D) a check of any prisoner treatment records maintained in the department.

6. With respect to Items 10 and 11, the roll call instructions prepared by Police Officer Baccaglini, and any related items, it would be most appropriate for you to approve which paragraphs as *correct*?

    (A) Paragraphs 1, 2, and 3
    (B) Paragraphs 2 and 3, but not 1
    (C) Paragraphs 1 and 2, but not 3
    (D) Approve neither paragraph 1, 2, nor 3, as they are all incorrect.

7. With respect to Item 12, the supervisor's complaint report, serial number 65, and any related items, you are informed by Sergeant Grobe that he had interviewed Police Officer Smith, who stated she had been unable to answer the telephone during the period mentioned in the report because she had been recording a serious allegation of police brutality against Police Officer Dempsey. In addition, department records indicate that Police Officer Smith did record a civilian complaint during this time period. Considering these facts, the *most* appropriate action for you to take relative to the supervisor's complaint is to find the matter

    (A) unsubstantiated because there was no intent to violate department regulations.
    (B) substantiated because Police Officer Smith should have put the civilian caller on hold and continued to answer incoming calls.
    (C) unsubstantiated because Police Officer Smith's delay in answering the phone was justified.
    (D) substantiated because Police Officer Smith should have referred the complainant to another officer.

8. With respect to Item 14, the memo to Chief Quinn from Sergeant Peterman, and any other related items, your *most* appropriate action concerning this matter would be to

    (A) confer with the personnel officer regarding a possible limited duty assignment.
    (B) request additional information from Sergeant Peterman.
    (C) interview other members of the Plainclothes Unit to verify the existence of a problem.
    (D) place Officer White on restricted duty.

9. With respect to Item 5, the letter from Private Hospital, and any other related items, what is the next action you should take after meeting with hospital authorities?

    (A) Direct a survey of the affected area and ascertain personnel and equipment needed.
    (B) Order additional barriers.
    (C) Advise picket leaders that they cannot picket because of a street closing.
    (D) Advise Mr. Sackman that hospital security is his problem.

10. With respect to Item 16, discipline for Mr. Bailey, and any related items, assuming that you agree with Lieutenant McMahon, you should

    (A) warn and admonish Mr. Bailey orally.
    (B) warn and admonish Mr. Bailey in writing.
    (C) fine Mr. Bailey an undetermined amount of vacation or accrued time.
    (D) fine Mr. Bailey five days' vacation or accrued time.

11. With respect to Item 15, the letter regarding the anticipated strike at Private Hospital, and any other related items, you decide to conduct a subordinate supervisor conference. The agenda for this conference should include all of the following, with the exception of

(A) location of entrances, exits, and loading platforms.

(B) employees arrival and departure times, as well as transportation facilities most frequently used.

(C) a determination as to the racial composition of the picketers.

(D) parking lots and routes used by employees, as well as the time of meal periods and locations of premises where meals are taken.

12. With respect to Item 19, the memo concerning M.A.D., and any other related items, it would be *most* appropriate for you to

(A) direct Captain Harding to interview Police Officer Morales and make a detailed report concerning the matter to forward to the city manager's office.

(B) direct Police Officer Morales to prepare a report for Sergeant Bornholdt.

(C) arrange for an interview between Police Officer Morales and a member of the appropriate Intelligence Unit.

(D) arrange for a meeting between the citizen involved and Sergeant Peterman to determine the reliability of the informant.

13. With respect to Item 28, Police Officer Kelly's request for vacation, and any other related items, which one of the following actions should you take?

(A) Disapprove this request and reschedule it, as it exceeds the 12 percent quota.

(B) Approve the request as lost vacation time should be available at any subsequent time if the member was hospitalized.

(C) Disapprove the request because such vacations should be taken prior to March 31 of the succeeding year.

(D) Approve the request because it indicates an interest in the well-being and morale of subordinates.

14. Regarding the problem presented by Item 18, statistics, and any related items, which month showed the greatest percentage decrease in robberies from the year before last to last year during the last six months?

(A) July

(B) August

(C) September

(D) October

15. The answer to question 2 on Item 18 is most nearly

(A) 68

(B) 75

(C) 85

(D) 90

16. Regarding Item 26, and any related items, Sergeant Peterman's response to the chief's question should be

(A) "My responsibilities with paperwork keep me inside most of the time."

(B) "I was interviewing Police Officer Morales about his communication concerning M.A.D."

(C) "I left Police Officer Chait in charge."

(D) "I was on my day off."

ANSWERS TO IN-BASKET EXERCISE QUESTIONS

1. **The correct answer is (B).** See the personnel profiles. Harry Grobe is already temporarily assigned to the mayor's office (see Item 1). Patrick McMahon is currently involved with the state prosecutor. Anthony Nunno's frequent sick reports make him a poor choice for the mayor's office. The job for which he is selected should not require Lt. Nugent to stand for prolonged periods.

2. **The correct answer is (C).** It is "relatively unimportant," but must *not* be totally ignored. You should not personally investigate, you should delegate. You'll be gone for the next two weeks; therefore an appointment to speak with her "within a week" is impossible.

3. **The correct answer is (D).** In this situation we have a sergeant with a possible drinking problem evaluating another sergeant. An investigation would appear to be the way to go.

4. **The correct answer is (B).** Look at Item 23 wherein overtime as a result of secondary employment is prohibited. This memo from the city manager leaves no room for doubt.

5. **The correct answer is (D).** The best answer. If another item had indicated that prisoners requiring treatment, etc., were, as a matter of procedure, handled and recorded in a specific manner, then a check of those particular records would be appropriate. But there is no such item.

6. **The correct answer is (D).**
   1. Crime scenes in public places may be searched without a warrant (as well as other crime scenes).
   2. Arrests in the home without a warrant are acceptable if there is consent or exigent circumstances.
   3. In an emergency, questioning may continue. For example, a kidnapping victim has not yet been found. See chapter four on constitutional law.

7. **The correct answer is (C).** Spending time on a department telephone accepting a "serious allegation of police brutality" would be an action that should not merit the application of punishment. The investigation did not reveal any information that indicated malfeasance by P.O. Smith.

8. **The correct answer is (B).** This kind of allegation, "might possibly be drinking too much," is very subjective. What is too much to Sergeant Peterman may be perfectly all right to someone else. More objective data needed prior to a decision in this matter.

9. **The correct answer is (A).** This should have been an easy one. You would be hard pressed to justify the ordering of "additional barriers" without taking a look at the area concerned. Furthermore, picketing is considered a constitutional right under the First Amendment.

10. **The correct answer is (A).** Nobody else seems to be particularly excited about Mr. Bailey's domestic problem. Do not turn a grounder into a line drive.

11. **The correct answer is (C).** For what justifiable reason?

12. **The correct answer is (C).** The questions you need to ask are as follows: Choice (A), Why to the city manager? Choice (B), What item justifies a report to Sergeant Bornholdt? Choice (D), What purpose is served by Sergeant Peterman's determining the reliability of an informant described in the item as "reliable . . . on many occasions."

13. **The correct answer is (A).** See Item 31, wherein the mayor has specifically directed the police chief not to exceed the 12 percent limit.

14. **The correct answer is (B).** August! Each of the other months in the choices given showed an increase during the period concerned.

15. **The correct answer is (A).** If you added the J.D. columns in the "Last Year" chart, you arrived at the number 68. But if you used the chart for "Year Before Last," you would have arrived at 75, which is a wrong answer.

16. **The correct answer is (D).** See the personnel profile for Sergeant Peterman, which indicates he is off every Thursday and Friday. This item is dated February 9 (a Friday) and refers to "last night," a Thursday.

PART FOUR

Model Examinations

INTRODUCTION TO THE MODEL EXAMINATIONS

The trial examinations that follow are similar to official police promotion examinations conducted throughout the country. There are questions dealing with supervisory and administrative principles, reading comprehension, statistics (graphs and charts), criminalistics, investigation, judgment, and constitutional law. All of the questions are based on concepts that civil service examiners nationwide have used in prior examinations.

In a publication such as this, we cannot be specific for every state and every jurisdiction. Local laws and ordinances, internal rules, regulations, and guides must be your responsibility. However, we have found that the material we have highlighted will benefit you regardless of your jurisdiction.

When answering the trial examination questions, try not to mark the answers in the booklet. If you do not, then you will be able to reuse the examination booklet. Use the answer sheet provided to record your answers. It is a good idea to make a photocopy of the blank answer sheet so that you can use it at another time.

MODEL EXAMINATION 1: ANSWER SHEET

1. Ⓐ Ⓑ Ⓒ Ⓓ Ⓔ   31. Ⓐ Ⓑ Ⓒ Ⓓ Ⓔ   61. Ⓐ Ⓑ Ⓒ Ⓓ Ⓔ   91. Ⓐ Ⓑ Ⓒ Ⓓ Ⓔ
2. Ⓐ Ⓑ Ⓒ Ⓓ Ⓔ   32. Ⓐ Ⓑ Ⓒ Ⓓ Ⓔ   62. Ⓐ Ⓑ Ⓒ Ⓓ Ⓔ   92. Ⓐ Ⓑ Ⓒ Ⓓ Ⓔ
3. Ⓐ Ⓑ Ⓒ Ⓓ Ⓔ   33. Ⓐ Ⓑ Ⓒ Ⓓ Ⓔ   63. Ⓐ Ⓑ Ⓒ Ⓓ Ⓔ   93. Ⓐ Ⓑ Ⓒ Ⓓ Ⓔ
4. Ⓐ Ⓑ Ⓒ Ⓓ Ⓔ   34. Ⓐ Ⓑ Ⓒ Ⓓ Ⓔ   64. Ⓐ Ⓑ Ⓒ Ⓓ Ⓔ   94. Ⓐ Ⓑ Ⓒ Ⓓ Ⓔ
5. Ⓐ Ⓑ Ⓒ Ⓓ Ⓔ   35. Ⓐ Ⓑ Ⓒ Ⓓ Ⓔ   65. Ⓐ Ⓑ Ⓒ Ⓓ Ⓔ   95. Ⓐ Ⓑ Ⓒ Ⓓ Ⓔ
6. Ⓐ Ⓑ Ⓒ Ⓓ Ⓔ   36. Ⓐ Ⓑ Ⓒ Ⓓ Ⓔ   66. Ⓐ Ⓑ Ⓒ Ⓓ Ⓔ   96. Ⓐ Ⓑ Ⓒ Ⓓ Ⓔ
7. Ⓐ Ⓑ Ⓒ Ⓓ Ⓔ   37. Ⓐ Ⓑ Ⓒ Ⓓ Ⓔ   67. Ⓐ Ⓑ Ⓒ Ⓓ Ⓔ   97. Ⓐ Ⓑ Ⓒ Ⓓ Ⓔ
8. Ⓐ Ⓑ Ⓒ Ⓓ Ⓔ   38. Ⓐ Ⓑ Ⓒ Ⓓ Ⓔ   68. Ⓐ Ⓑ Ⓒ Ⓓ Ⓔ   98. Ⓐ Ⓑ Ⓒ Ⓓ Ⓔ
9. Ⓐ Ⓑ Ⓒ Ⓓ Ⓔ   39. Ⓐ Ⓑ Ⓒ Ⓓ Ⓔ   69. Ⓐ Ⓑ Ⓒ Ⓓ Ⓔ   99. Ⓐ Ⓑ Ⓒ Ⓓ Ⓔ
10. Ⓐ Ⓑ Ⓒ Ⓓ Ⓔ   40. Ⓐ Ⓑ Ⓒ Ⓓ Ⓔ   70. Ⓐ Ⓑ Ⓒ Ⓓ Ⓔ   100. Ⓐ Ⓑ Ⓒ Ⓓ Ⓔ
11. Ⓐ Ⓑ Ⓒ Ⓓ Ⓔ   41. Ⓐ Ⓑ Ⓒ Ⓓ Ⓔ   71. Ⓐ Ⓑ Ⓒ Ⓓ Ⓔ   101. Ⓐ Ⓑ Ⓒ Ⓓ Ⓔ
12. Ⓐ Ⓑ Ⓒ Ⓓ Ⓔ   42. Ⓐ Ⓑ Ⓒ Ⓓ Ⓔ   72. Ⓐ Ⓑ Ⓒ Ⓓ Ⓔ   102. Ⓐ Ⓑ Ⓒ Ⓓ Ⓔ
13. Ⓐ Ⓑ Ⓒ Ⓓ Ⓔ   43. Ⓐ Ⓑ Ⓒ Ⓓ Ⓔ   73. Ⓐ Ⓑ Ⓒ Ⓓ Ⓔ   103. Ⓐ Ⓑ Ⓒ Ⓓ Ⓔ
14. Ⓐ Ⓑ Ⓒ Ⓓ Ⓔ   44. Ⓐ Ⓑ Ⓒ Ⓓ Ⓔ   74. Ⓐ Ⓑ Ⓒ Ⓓ Ⓔ   104. Ⓐ Ⓑ Ⓒ Ⓓ Ⓔ
15. Ⓐ Ⓑ Ⓒ Ⓓ Ⓔ   45. Ⓐ Ⓑ Ⓒ Ⓓ Ⓔ   75. Ⓐ Ⓑ Ⓒ Ⓓ Ⓔ   105. Ⓐ Ⓑ Ⓒ Ⓓ Ⓔ
16. Ⓐ Ⓑ Ⓒ Ⓓ Ⓔ   46. Ⓐ Ⓑ Ⓒ Ⓓ Ⓔ   76. Ⓐ Ⓑ Ⓒ Ⓓ Ⓔ   106. Ⓐ Ⓑ Ⓒ Ⓓ Ⓔ
17. Ⓐ Ⓑ Ⓒ Ⓓ Ⓔ   47. Ⓐ Ⓑ Ⓒ Ⓓ Ⓔ   77. Ⓐ Ⓑ Ⓒ Ⓓ Ⓔ   107. Ⓐ Ⓑ Ⓒ Ⓓ Ⓔ
18. Ⓐ Ⓑ Ⓒ Ⓓ Ⓔ   48. Ⓐ Ⓑ Ⓒ Ⓓ Ⓔ   78. Ⓐ Ⓑ Ⓒ Ⓓ Ⓔ   108. Ⓐ Ⓑ Ⓒ Ⓓ Ⓔ
19. Ⓐ Ⓑ Ⓒ Ⓓ Ⓔ   49. Ⓐ Ⓑ Ⓒ Ⓓ Ⓔ   79. Ⓐ Ⓑ Ⓒ Ⓓ Ⓔ   109. Ⓐ Ⓑ Ⓒ Ⓓ Ⓔ
20. Ⓐ Ⓑ Ⓒ Ⓓ Ⓔ   50. Ⓐ Ⓑ Ⓒ Ⓓ Ⓔ   80. Ⓐ Ⓑ Ⓒ Ⓓ Ⓔ   110. Ⓐ Ⓑ Ⓒ Ⓓ Ⓔ
21. Ⓐ Ⓑ Ⓒ Ⓓ Ⓔ   51. Ⓐ Ⓑ Ⓒ Ⓓ Ⓔ   81. Ⓐ Ⓑ Ⓒ Ⓓ Ⓔ   111. Ⓐ Ⓑ Ⓒ Ⓓ Ⓔ
22. Ⓐ Ⓑ Ⓒ Ⓓ Ⓔ   52. Ⓐ Ⓑ Ⓒ Ⓓ Ⓔ   82. Ⓐ Ⓑ Ⓒ Ⓓ Ⓔ   112. Ⓐ Ⓑ Ⓒ Ⓓ Ⓔ
23. Ⓐ Ⓑ Ⓒ Ⓓ Ⓔ   53. Ⓐ Ⓑ Ⓒ Ⓓ Ⓔ   83. Ⓐ Ⓑ Ⓒ Ⓓ Ⓔ   113. Ⓐ Ⓑ Ⓒ Ⓓ Ⓔ
24. Ⓐ Ⓑ Ⓒ Ⓓ Ⓔ   54. Ⓐ Ⓑ Ⓒ Ⓓ Ⓔ   84. Ⓐ Ⓑ Ⓒ Ⓓ Ⓔ   114. Ⓐ Ⓑ Ⓒ Ⓓ Ⓔ
25. Ⓐ Ⓑ Ⓒ Ⓓ Ⓔ   55. Ⓐ Ⓑ Ⓒ Ⓓ Ⓔ   85. Ⓐ Ⓑ Ⓒ Ⓓ Ⓔ   115. Ⓐ Ⓑ Ⓒ Ⓓ Ⓔ
26. Ⓐ Ⓑ Ⓒ Ⓓ Ⓔ   56. Ⓐ Ⓑ Ⓒ Ⓓ Ⓔ   86. Ⓐ Ⓑ Ⓒ Ⓓ Ⓔ   116. Ⓐ Ⓑ Ⓒ Ⓓ Ⓔ
27. Ⓐ Ⓑ Ⓒ Ⓓ Ⓔ   57. Ⓐ Ⓑ Ⓒ Ⓓ Ⓔ   87. Ⓐ Ⓑ Ⓒ Ⓓ Ⓔ   117. Ⓐ Ⓑ Ⓒ Ⓓ Ⓔ
28. Ⓐ Ⓑ Ⓒ Ⓓ Ⓔ   58. Ⓐ Ⓑ Ⓒ Ⓓ Ⓔ   88. Ⓐ Ⓑ Ⓒ Ⓓ Ⓔ   118. Ⓐ Ⓑ Ⓒ Ⓓ Ⓔ
29. Ⓐ Ⓑ Ⓒ Ⓓ Ⓔ   59. Ⓐ Ⓑ Ⓒ Ⓓ Ⓔ   89. Ⓐ Ⓑ Ⓒ Ⓓ Ⓔ   119. Ⓐ Ⓑ Ⓒ Ⓓ Ⓔ
30. Ⓐ Ⓑ Ⓒ Ⓓ Ⓔ   60. Ⓐ Ⓑ Ⓒ Ⓓ Ⓔ   90. Ⓐ Ⓑ Ⓒ Ⓓ Ⓔ   120. Ⓐ Ⓑ Ⓒ Ⓓ Ⓔ

MODEL EXAMINATION 1

> **Directions:** This test contains 120 questions. Circle the correct answers directly on the page. You have three hours to complete this examination. Each question has a relative weight of 1.0.

1. Establishing the priority of work to be performed is an essential part of the police supervisory function. It is required primarily in order to
   (A) plan assignment of work.
   (B) appraise subordinates' performance.
   (C) determine deficiencies in record keeping.
   (D) ascertain the need for disciplinary action.

2. "In practice, perhaps the greatest deficiencies of planning arise from poorly structured plans." Generally, if a supervisor's plans are poorly structured, then it is most likely to be the result of
   (A) ignorance of facts necessary for decision-making.
   (B) lack of incentives to achieve organization goals.
   (C) chance factors over which he has no control.
   (D) lack of appreciation of the need for planning.

3. Superior officers must set up work schedules to plan for the effective use of time, personnel, and equipment. Of the following, the most important factor for the supervisor to consider in setting up a work schedule is the
   (A) seniority of the various personnel assigned to the supervisor.
   (B) standard of performance to be attained by the subordinates.
   (C) cost of job operations.
   (D) availability of personnel necessary for the job.

4. Effective management involves the process of decision making. The following are five steps in decision making:
   1. Analyzing the problem
   2. Deciding upon the best solution
   3. Converting the decision into effective action
   4. Defining the problem
   5. Developing alternate solutions
   Which of the following is generally the proper sequence of these five steps?
   (A) 1—4—5—2—3
   (B) 4—1—5—2—3
   (C) 1—5—2—3—4
   (D) 4—5—2—3—1

5. Superior officers are expected to develop plans to meet squad problems. Which one of the following is the *first* step in developing plans?
   (A) Determine what resources are available for the job
   (B) Decide what methods should be used
   (C) Weigh the cost factors involved
   (D) Establish objectives in specific terms

6. To conform with directions from headquarters, a change is adopted in a certain procedure. A supervisor finds, after a short period, that the old procedure was distinctly superior. Of the following, the best action for him to take is to
   - (A) have one of his experienced subordinates broach the matter by bringing it to the attention of the commanding officer.
   - (B) follow the new procedure without comment because the reasons for doing so will probably become self-evident.
   - (C) follow the new procedure until his superior officers learn of its drawbacks and amend it.
   - (D) follow the new procedure, but assemble definite facts and figures to prove its inadequacy to his superior officer.

7. For a superior officer to permit her subordinates to participate in the decision-making process is generally desirable, when practicable, primarily because
   - (A) it leads to the elimination of grievances.
   - (B) better solutions may be obtained.
   - (C) individual development requires an ever-expanding view of operations.
   - (D) the commander is forced to keep on her toes under the stimulation of the interchange of ideas.

8. A newly appointed superior officer believes that the use of group participation in the decision-making process will improve his squad's morale and productivity. For this officer to make clear to the subordinates the areas in which group participation will not be permitted would generally be considered
   - (A) desirable, chiefly because decisions involving certain areas are beyond the control of both the group and the superior officer.
   - (B) undesirable, chiefly because any restraint on the subordinates' freedom of action will dilute the effectiveness of the program.
   - (C) desirable, chiefly because the subordinates will be unable to take advantage of the officer in any area.
   - (D) undesirable, chiefly because the limitations should be made clear to the group, as it becomes involved in a specific area of decision making.

9. The assignment of tasks to subordinates is a major area of decision-making for superiors. Which of the following would be the *least* appropriate guide for a superior officer to follow when allocating assignments?
   - (A) Assigning work according to the member's ability.
   - (B) Combining related tasks for one member to carry out.
   - (C) Showing a willing member to assume as many tasks as he or she wishes.
   - (D) Distributing the workload among members so that no one's load is too light or too heavy.

10. Your department does not have a policy stating the use of a flashlight to be used as a blunt weapon in affecting the arrest of uncooperative offender. However, it has been a common practice among officers and supervisors to use their flashlights to help subdue an offender. In fact, new recruits are shown this procedure by the field-training officers. Your department is now being sued due to injuries an offender received while being arrested and subdued by being hit with a flashlight. Which of the following statements holds true?
   - (A) The department will not be held accountable for such actions since an individual patrol officer was wholly responsible for the injuries.
   - (B) The department will be held accountable since it has become an unwritten policy that flashlights are considered a blunt weapon.
   - (C) The department will be held accountable because the courts always find in favor of defendants in police abuse cases.
   - (D) The department will not be held accountable since flashlights are not purchased and issued by the department and must be purchased by individual officers.

11. "Periodic training of all police personnel, experienced officers as well as recruits, is a necessary requirement for effective police operations." This statement is generally

   (A) false; methods of police operation are relatively stable and therefore additional training is unnecessary.

   (B) true; experienced personnel and recruits both require continued training at essentially the same level.

   (C) false; such training would undermine the morale of the experienced officers and seriously affect their job performance.

   (D) true; the original training may be forgotten or made obsolete by changing community conditions and improved methods.

12. It has been suggested that a supervisor should strive constantly to develop each of her subordinates to the limit of the latter's ability and skills. This suggestion is generally

   (A) advisable; although basically alike, individuals possess widely different backgrounds and each subordinate must be given training in the specific duties of his or her immediate job.

   (B) inadvisable; individuals differ from each other and urging an unambitious employee to greater effort against his or her will may make him a reluctant and less satisfactory worker.

   (C) advisable; only by full utilization of each subordinate's talents can maximum service be obtained.

   (D) inadvisable; assisting subordinates to develop themselves may result in their dissatisfaction when insufficient opportunities for promotion are available.

13. The main objective of any training program is to

   (A) prepare members for higher responsibilities.

   (B) develop skills needed on the job.

   (C) keep members abreast of the latest professional developments.

   (D) stimulate members to pursue further results.

14. Training often fails to provide the results that departments wish to achieve. The major reason for this failure is that

   (A) training is always conducted at inopportune times when officers are tired from working shifts.

   (B) training officers wholly are responsible for the material they present.

   (C) training is primarily the responsibility of individual officers.

   (D) training is conducted without a purpose.

15. A supervisor should not permit officers who have just been appointed to learn department procedures entirely on the basis of their own experience mainly because they will

   (A) learn more quickly under correct guidance.

   (B) learn quickest when left to their own resources.

   (C) remember best what they learn first.

   (D) lose too much time worrying about learning the proper things in the proper manner.

16. When instructing officers under his supervision, a supervisor should realize that

   (A) after the age of 20, a person's ability to learn decreases progressively at a slow rate.

   (B) learning should be uniform if instruction is uniform.

   (C) learning should be uniform if there is active participation by each learner.

   (D) persons of the same age differ in the amount they can learn in a given time.

17. A supervisor institutes a practice of having his subordinates role-play the technique they would use in affecting an arrest. A newly assigned officer does not give the impression that she is in "command" of the situation. The best explanation the supervisor can offer to the subordinate to motivate her to take command in an arrest situation is that her demeanor

   (A) will not do much to enhance the opinion of the police held by the public viewing the arrest.
   (B) puts the police at a psychological disadvantage by reducing or eliminating the favorable element of surprise.
   (C) would be misinterpreted by an offender as evidence of weakness and thereby provide encouragement to resist.
   (D) is suitable for a role-playing situation, but not for the real-life situation.

18. In a police training program, the group (or conference) method of instruction, in addition to being an acceptable method of teaching facts or skills, is of value chiefly because of the

   (A) stimulation afforded the individual members as the result of joint efforts toward a common goal.
   (B) adaptability of such instruction to the needs of each individual in a group.
   (C) enhancement of department morale resulting from the spirit of cooperation and good fellowship engendered by the use of this method.
   (D) minimization of competition, which is a generally undesirable ingredient in the learning process.

19. The following are basic steps that a supervisor might take in instructing a new officer. If the steps were taken in logical order, the second step would be to

   (A) relate each facet of the job to the officer's experience.
   (B) break down the job into distinct learning units.
   (C) relate the key points of the job to technical procedures used to implement them.
   (D) arrange the learning units of the job in their proper order.

20. The key to effective discipline is in the hands of the police supervisor at all ranks. However, the most important link in the disciplinary chain is the

   (A) sergeant, for he works closely with the officers and must constantly evaluate their competency and integrity.
   (B) lieutenant, for she must consider whether positive or negative discipline is appropriate in the case at hand.
   (C) captain, for he is the precinct commander and is responsible ultimately for the competency and integrity of every precinct officer.
   (D) commissioner, for discipline does not emanate from the bottom of an organization it is only from the top that good discipline flows.

21. Disciplinary action usually will be initiated by the immediate superior of the person to be disciplined. This is true mainly because

   (A) it permits the higher superiors to be able to devote most of their attention and effort to broader and more generalized problems of administration.
   (B) it helps to develop a forceful image of the immediate superior that will serve to prevent other overt acts of misconduct by other subordinates.
   (C) the immediate superior is the one most qualified to make recommendations as to the severity of punishment to be applied.
   (D) the immediate superior is usually in the best position to observe derelictions of duty requiring some kind of corrective action.

22. "Often and early in many supervisory careers, the big compromise is made by a new supervisor and the unpleasant aspects of the job are studiously avoided. The compromising supervisor usually has both his unit and his nervous system in turmoil. Work output goes down and this type of supervisor is often on sick report. No one profits." The words "big compromise," refer to the supervisor's failure to

   (A) familiarize new employees with their job obligations.
   (B) interview privately each member of the unit to determine what the on-the-job problems are.
   (C) take disciplinary action.
   (D) take note of profit from corruption in his unit.

23. When a superior must often take disciplinary action against subordinates, the superior should realize that

   (A) this is normal practice if officers are to be well-disciplined.
   (B) he was probably assigned to this troublesome group because he had the ability to handle it.
   (C) it would be best to ask for a new assignment for the good of the department.
   (D) his methods of supervision may need self-review to determine whether they are faulty.

24. One of the police officers under your supervision presents minor disciplinary problems. Investigation discloses that he has had a good record under several other supervisors. Under these circumstances, the best course of action to follow is to

   (A) discuss this matter with your superior officer him as the other supervisors appear to have been much too lenient.
   (B) ask a supervisor who formerly supervised the officer to advise him to change his attitude.
   (C) exercise strict close supervision until the condition is corrected.
   (D) review your treatment of the officer to determine if the fault lies with you.

25. The one of the following that is the primary aim of discipline is to

   (A) inform the public that compliance is insisted upon from all members of the department.
   (B) apply punishment with a view that the superior officer shares responsibility with the offender.
   (C) provide uniform standards to all offenders regardless of assignment or seniority.
   (D) change the thinking and performance of an officer so that she will work in conformance with department standards.

26. A police commander should recognize that discipline is a major function of command. Which one of the following actions is most properly recognized as being the true essence of discipline?

   (A) Improving morale through conferences and pep talks
   (B) Separating incompetent subordinates from the police service
   (C) Requiring subordinates to conform to the policies and procedures of the department
   (D) Providing department members with a continuing formal training program

27. As a supervisor, you have had repeated problems with one of your officers. This officer has been a constant discipline problem since assigned to your unit. However, once you have informed him of his actions he never repeats that particular act. You have finally reached your limits with his newest infraction. You should

    (A) bring this officer in and review all of his past infractions.
    (B) treat this newest infraction the same as you have all the others and consult with him as to other issues he may be dealing with that could lead to his continual misconduct.
    (C) have him transferred immediately to another division.
    (D) avoid this newest infraction since he corrects his mistakes on his own.

28. Public relations programs of any public agency have a dual function: to make the public aware of what the agency is doing and to

    (A) suppress information that is unfavorable to the agency.
    (B) inform agency officials of the public's response to the services rendered.
    (C) mold public opinion to support the enactment of favorable legislation.
    (D) publicize the executives of the agency.

29. The maintenance of good public relations in a public agency is important mainly because

    (A) the public is naturally hostile to any abrogation of its rights.
    (B) public attitudes affect the efficiency of an agency program.
    (C) public favor will benefit the individuals responsible for the agency's program and activities.
    (D) public attitudes determine the amount of money appropriated for an agency.

30. The relationship between any department and the press is like a two-way street. The press is not only a medium through which the department releases information to the public, but the press also

    (A) is as interested as the department in the success of the department's program.
    (B) can teach the department good public relations.
    (C) makes the department aware of public opinion.
    (D) releases such information from another point of view.

31. When employees constantly engage in poor public relations practices, the cause is most often

    (A) disobedience of orders.
    (B) lack of emotional control.
    (C) bullheadedness.
    (D) poor supervision.

32. You have been asked to answer a request from a citizen in your jurisdiction. You find that it cannot be granted. In your answering letter you should begin by

    (A) saying that the request has been given careful attention.
    (B) discussing in detail the consideration you gave to the request.
    (C) quoting the laws relating to the request.
    (D) explaining in detail why the request cannot be granted.

33. You have been asked to address the needs for a detoxification center in your city. Personally, you believe that drug addiction and alcoholism are major problems in your city and responsible for most of the street crime. Your reaction to this should be to

    (A) absolutely excuse yourself from this assignment.
    (B) assign this to one of your subordinates.
    (C) take the assignment, but profoundly proclaim the errors of such a project.
    (D) take the assignment, but prior to this assignment review the department's assessment of such a project using this as the format for your presentation.

34. You have been assigned, as a sergeant, to assist a local high school principal and initiate a program aimed at the detection of narcotic drug addiction in this school. Of the following courses of action, the one that you should recommend as the *first* one to be taken is for the teaching staff to

    (A) advise and enlighten parents on the effects of narcotic drug addiction on the physical and moral health of juveniles.
    (B) be directed to notify the principal immediately if unauthorized persons are noticed loitering around or in the school.
    (C) become acquainted with the methods of recognizing users of narcotic drugs and the necessity for reporting such information promptly to the police.
    (D) present to their students the facts concerning the social evils resulting from widespread narcotic addition and acquaint the parents with the school program.

35. Evidence introduced at a trial in the form of physical objects or persons themselves to prove or disprove a fact in issue is legally defined as

    (A) material evidence.
    (B) real evidence.
    (C) cumulative evidence.
    (D) personal evidence.

36. Circumstantial evidence has been so often used in a deprecating context that jurors are inclined to shy away from the true meaning of the evidence when they are told that it is "purely circumstantial." The disrepute in which such evidence is sometimes held is attributable mainly to

    (A) case histories where the circumstantial evidence was insufficient to warrant the conclusions that were drawn.
    (B) the belief that testimony based on visual and other sensory experiences is often quite unreliable.
    (C) the fact that circumstantial evidence is not subject to the equivalent of cross-examination.
    (D) the fact that the increased use of scientific methods has weakened the value of circumstantial evidence.

37. "The supervisor whose subordinates never have any complaints about anything should probably reappraise his role as a supervisor." Upon such a reappraisal, the supervisor is most likely to discover that the

    (A) supervisor is too strict.
    (B) officers are afraid.
    (C) officers are well satisfied with everything.
    (D) communication is poor.

38. Effective communication between superior and subordinate levels of command will have a number of valuable results. Of the following, which one is *least* likely to be a result of an effective communication system?

    (A) Development of policy decisions at all levels
    (B) Dovetailing, rather than overlapping, of separate police activities
    (C) Execution of directives in the manner intended
    (D) Improvement of morale and productivity

39. Of the following statements concerning subordinates' expressions to a supervisor of their opinions and feelings concerning work situations, which one is most correct?

    (A) By listening and responding to such expressions, the supervisor encourages the development of complaints.

    (B) The lack of such expressions should indicate to the supervisor that there is a high level of job satisfaction.

    (C) The more the supervisor listens to and responds to such expressions, the more he demonstrates lack of supervisory ability.

    (D) By listening and responding to such expressions, the supervisor will enable many subordinates to understand and solve their own problems on the job.

40. As a supervisor, you believe that a certain police officer under your supervision is responsible for starting several unfounded rumors concerning police matters in the precinct. Which one of the following possible courses of action would be the most effective in dealing with this problem?

    (A) Ignore the situation since none of the rumors contained any elements of truth.

    (B) Provide sufficient facts about police matters in the precinct to establish a basis upon which rumors may be evaluated.

    (C) Institute formal disciplinary action against the suspected officer.

    (D) Speak to your subordinates, as a group, on the undesirable effects of spreading false information.

Directions: Each of the following questions, 41 to 43, is based upon a group of sentences. The sentences may be scrambled, but when they are correctly arranged they form a well-organized paragraph. Read the sentences, and then answer the question by choosing the most appropriate arrangement.

---

41. 1. However, they have one characteristic in common; they are laws that are difficult to enforce because the "victims" are usually willing participants who seldom complain to the police.

    2. The laws against gambling, prostitution, and Sunday sales all contribute to the prevalence of police corruption in differing degrees of seriousness.

    3. Consequently, if a police officer, for whatever motive, decides to condone a violation, he need only fail to report it.

    4. Such a situation is an invitation to corruption.

    (A) 4—3—2—1

    (B) 2—1—3—4

    (C) 3—1—2—4

    (D) 2—4—3—1

42. 1. In addition, more effective procedures must be established with strong controls for insuring that complaints of corruption get immediately recorded no matter where in the department they may originate.

    2. Such complaints must be encouraged by informing the public specifically how and where to make complaints and what details are necessary for action.

    3. A complaint from a citizen or a police officer is one starting point for detecting corruption and apprehending corrupt officers.

    4. These actions are all necessary to insure compliance with department procedures and adequate complaint follow-up.

    (A) 3—4—1—2

    (B) 3—2—1—4

    (C) 3—4—2—1

    (D) 1—2—3—4

43.
1. Some line-ups to identify corrupt officers are conducted with the witnesses in full view of the suspected officers.
2. If the witness is a professional investigator, he will probably not be deterred.
3. However, if the witness is an ordinary citizen, he may be intimidated by such a procedure.
4. Therefore, line-up procedures should insure that a complaining witness could identify an officer in a manner that protects the witness's anonymity.
(A) 2—3—1—4
(B) 3—2—1—4
(C) 4—3—2—1
(D) 1—2—3—4

44.
1. No civilian could be subject to a comparable penalty.
2. A serious defect in a department's disciplinary options is the present law requiring loss of pension upon dismissal regardless of the nature of the offense or the number of years of service.
3. Although a police commissioner should be able to dismiss a corrupt officer, it by no means follows that a single act of corruption justifies what may amount to a fine of several hundred thousand dollars.
4. The end result of the present forfeiture rule has been that the courts have on appeal reinstated patently unfit police officers because the courts could not tolerate the injustice involved in the forfeiture of vested pension rights.
(A) 2—1—3—4
(B) 2—3—1—4
(C) 4—1—2—3
(D) 3—2—1—4

45.
1. Many such improvements have already been made in municipal and county police departments.
2. These situations and others like them can be readily corrected.
3. For example, expense money is inadequate or too slow in being paid, and procedures for handling contraband are too complex and too time-consuming.
4. Police officers sometimes engage in corrupt practices because alternative means of solving problems are not available or are too bothersome.
(A) 4—3—2—1
(B) 1—2—3—4
(C) 2—1—3—4
(D) 4—2—3—1

Directions: Questions 46 to 48 are to be answered solely on the basis of the information contained in the following passage.

Of those arrested in your jurisdiction in 1990 for felonies or misdemeanors, only 32 percent were found guilty of any charge. Fifty-six percent of such arrestees were acquitted or had their cases dismissed, 11 percent failed to appear for trial, and 1 percent received other dispositions. Of those found guilty, only 7.4 percent received any sentences of over one year in jail. Only 50 percent of those found guilty were sentenced to any further time in jail. When considered with the low probability of arrests for most crimes, these figures make it clear that the crime control system in your jurisdiction poses little threat to the average criminal. Delay compounds the problem. The average case took four appearances for disposition after arraignment. Twenty percent of all cases took eight or more appearances to reach a disposition. Forty-four percent of all cases took more than one year to disposition.

46. According to the above passage, crime statistics for 1990 indicate that
    - (A) there is a low probability of arrests for all crimes in your jurisdiction.
    - (B) the average criminal has much to fear from the law in your jurisdiction.
    - (C) over 10 percent of arrestees in your jurisdiction charged with felonies or misdemeanors did not show up for trial.
    - (D) criminals in your jurisdiction are less likely to be caught than criminals in the rest of the country.

47. According to the above passage, the percentage of arrestees in 1990 who were found guilty was
    - (A) 20 percent of those arrested for misdemeanors.
    - (B) 11 percent of those arrested for felonies.
    - (C) 50 percent of those sentenced to further time in jail.
    - (D) 32 percent of those arrested for felonies or misdemeanors.

48. According to the above paragraph, the number of appearances after arraignment and before disposition amounted to
    - (A) an average of four.
    - (B) eight or more in 44 percent of the cases.
    - (C) over four cases that took more than a year.
    - (D) between four and eight for most cases.

Directions: Each of questions 49 to 52 consists of a quotation that contains one word that is incorrectly used because it departs from the meaning that the quotation is intended to convey. For each of these questions, select the incorrectly used word and substitute one of the words lettered (A), (B), (C), or (D) that helps best to convey the meaning of the quotation.

---

49. "The determination of the value of the employees in an organization is fundamental not only as a guide to the administration of salary schedules, promotion, demotion, and transfer; but also as a means of keeping the working force on its toes and of checking the originality of selection methods."
    - (A) Effectiveness
    - (B) Initiation
    - (C) Increasing
    - (D) System

50. "No training course can operate to full advantage without job descriptions that indicate training requirements so that those parts of the job requiring the most training can be carefully analyzed before the training course is completed."
    - (A) Improved
    - (B) Started
    - (C) Least
    - (D) Meet

51. "The criticism that supervisors are discriminatory in their treatment of subordinates is to same extent untrue, for the subjective nature of many supervisory decisions makes it probable that many employees who have not progressed will attribute their lack of success to supervisory favoritism."
    - (A) Knowledge
    - (B) Unavoidable
    - (C) Detrimental
    - (D) Deny

52. "Some demands of employees will, if satisfied, result in a decrease in production. Some supervisors largely ignore such demands on the part of their subordinates and instead concentrate on the direction and production of work, while others yield to such requests and thereby emphasize the production goals and objectives set by higher levels of authority."

    (A) Responsibility
    (B) Increase
    (C) Neglect
    (D) Value

53. Supervisors should know that evaluating a subordinate's work performance should be continuous. The primary purpose of such evaluation by the supervisor is to

    (A) arrive at a method of estimating how well the subordinate is performing his or her assigned duties.
    (B) create a strict working relationship between the supervisor and the subordinate.
    (C) discover new work methods that can be useful to the subordinate in improving his or her job performance.
    (D) enable the supervisor to establish accurate performance standards to use in appraising the work of all the subordinates that are under supervision.

54. A supervisor made a practice of calling in his subordinates every few months to discuss their job performance. During the discussion, he would commend them for the good aspects of their performance, point out weaknesses, and suggest ways of making improvements. This practice is

    (A) desirable; subordinates like to know how they stand with their supervisors.
    (B) undesirable; the supervisor should not start an evaluation program on his own initiative.
    (C) desirable; the supervisor can show his interest in his subordinates and his fair-mindedness.
    (D) undesirable; commendation and criticism should be made whenever appropriate and not at fixed times.

55. As commander of a unit, it has become your responsibility to choose from among your subordinates one officer for the position of detective/investigator. You decide to use the periodic rating forms to assist you in your decision. While studying these forms, in which of the following areas would you be best advised to look for proficiency?

    (A) The ability to interact well with the general public
    (B) Report writing ability
    (C) The ability to interview and interrogate properly, so that crime-solving information can be obtained
    (D) The ability to perform as an undercover operator without being observed and identified

56. Outstanding and heroic police performance in the making of arrests is frequently considered unimportant factor in making special assignments and in promoting to higher rank. A basic weakness of this system is that it

    (A) tends to inspire ambitious young officers to deliberately seek situations in which they can excel and that will enhance their standing in the eyes of their superiors.
    (B) tends to weaken respect for the senior members of the department since the system described favors younger officers.
    (C) overlooks that the rapid growth of suburbs and the tremendous increase in the use of motor vehicles have brought certain police hazards to almost every neighborhood.
    (D) tends to penalize to an unfair extent those officers who are most productive in the area of crime prevention.

57. An essential function of a superior officer is to set objective standards of performance for his subordinates. The greater the number of effective objective standards a superior officer establishes, the

    (A) more time he has to devote to supervising his subordinates work.
    (B) more he can avoid many time-consuming consultations with his subordinates.
    (C) less time he will have available to correct deviations from policies and procedures.
    (D) less likely he will be able to delegate to subordinates functions he would usually perform himself.

58. A superior officer may supervise the members of specialized units most adequately by

    (A) occasionally observing the subordinates at work and periodically evaluating the volume of work produced by each of the subordinates in the unit on a comparative basis.
    (B) personally observing the subordinates at work, but to a much lesser degree than is needed with the regular patrol forces and then comparing the subordinates' completed work with that of other subordinates with similar assignments.
    (C) frequent personal observation of the subordinates and continuing evaluations of the work produced by the subordinates.
    (D) personally observing the subordinates much more closely than is needed with regular patrol forces and then comparing the subordinates' completed work with the general departmental averages of all completed police actions.

59. In evaluating the capability of an officer to use independent judgment, the supervisor should usually give greatest consideration to the

    (A) ability of the officer to establish good relationships with people.
    (B) number of times the officer speaks to the captain.
    (C) officer's record of emotional stability.
    (D) decisions made by the officer in previous work situations.

60. Numerous methods of rating employees' job performance and efficiency are currently being used by different police agencies. In practice, the method to be preferred appears to be a combination of both quantitative marks and qualitative appraisals. However, the abstract character of numerical or alphabetical marks creates some major drawbacks that preclude their exclusive use. The chief drawback of a wholly quantitative rating system, if it were to be applied to the police service, is that

    (A) it does not show the specific defects that the officer being rated should strive to correct.
    (B) the ratings thus produced are more often than not based on inaccurate facts that do not lend themselves to verification.
    (C) it does not make any provision for a review of the rating given should the officer desire to appeal.
    (D) the ratings are usually prepared at fixed yearly intervals without any provision for officers to be informed at amore frequent intervals of their superiors' appraisal of their work.

61. In making periodic reports on platoon operations to your captain, you should bear in mind that the chief value of the report is that it

    (A) clarifies the problems of your captain and suggests the basis for improvement.
    (B) is the basis for his consolidated reports to the chief inspector.
    (C) is an official document that may be the basis for future action or decision.
    (D) enables him to exercise his supervisory and administrative fractions more effectively.

62. Assume that your captain has asked you to present comprehensive periodic reports on the progress that your squad is making in meeting its work goals. For you to give your captain oral reports rather than written ones is

    (A) desirable; it will be easier for her to transmit your oral reports to her superiors.
    (B) undesirable; the oral reports will provide no permanent record to which she may refer.
    (C) undesirable; there will be less opportunity for you to discuss the oral reports with her than the written ones.
    (D) desirable; the oral reports will require little time and effort to prepare.

63. Of the following reasons for requiring that negative reports be submitted, the most valid is that

    (A) report procedures should be uniform throughout the department.
    (B) negative reports sometimes are more important than positive reports.
    (C) the habit of submitting reports regularly is reinforced.
    (D) reports that are late or missing are not counted as negative.

64. Not every police agency uses the same method to evaluate its employees, and not every agency uses an evaluation system. However, regardless of the method used, the primary purpose of a rating/evaluation system is to

    (A) lay the foundation for disciplinary proceedings.
    (B) evaluate training programs instituted by the agency.
    (C) improve employee performance.
    (D) guarantee that employees are adhering to department rules and regulations.

65. "If you use a concrete word when you might use an abstract one, then you are handicapping yourself in your task of preparing comprehensive and understandable reports." This advice is

    (A) good; the use of concrete words prevents effective generalization.
    (B) bad; it is easier to prepare a report whose meaning is clear if the concrete is preferred to the abstract.
    (C) bad; the use of abstract words prevents any effective generalization.
    (D) good; it is easier to prepare a report whose meaning is clear if the abstract is preferred to the concrete.

66. Which of the following is the core of a report based on the results of an investigation?

    (A) Conclusions
    (B) Data
    (C) Sequence
    (D) Analysis

67. In submitting a report, which of the following is *least* essential?

    (A) Speed
    (B) Clarity
    (C) Correctness
    (D) Conciseness

68. In preparing a report aimed at giving information concerning a complex and extensive matter, which of the following devices will, in general, provide the most clarity and ease of reading?

    (A) Personalized style
    (B) Short sentences
    (C) Repetition and paraphrasing
    (D) One idea to a paragraph

69. The chief purpose in preparing an outline for a report is usually to insure that
    (A) the report will be grammatically correct.
    (B) every point will be given equal emphasis.
    (C) principal and secondary points will be properly related to the framework of the whole.
    (D) the language of the report will be of the same level and include the same technical terms.

70. "Leadership ability ranks as the most important quality of a supervisor and so the modern supervisor should be a leader rather than a boss." With reference to a large municipal police department, this statement is
    (A) true; modern accepted theories of leadership are not essentially differentiated in their applicability between a nonpolice and a police setting.
    (B) false; modern accepted theories of leadership do not apply similarly to private and governmental agencies.
    (C) true; it eliminates the use of disciplinary measures.
    (D) false; it fails to give due emphasis to the quasi-military character of law enforcement agencies.

71. The main responsibility of a supervising police officer is to
    (A) see that the required work is done properly.
    (B) insure an atmosphere of mutual trust between his subordinates and himself.
    (C) make certain that all his officers are treated equally as to assigned duties.
    (D) create a receptive attitude towards the objectives of the department.

72. "Although there is a normal disparity between successive ranks of officers in any police department, the greatest disparity and changes occur when a police officer becomes a sergeant."
    This is true chiefly because the sergeant
    (A) must be better formed than his subordinates in all aspects of law enforcement.
    (B) becomes responsible for the first time for the job performance of other officers.
    (C) must learn to assume new and more complex duties.
    (D) has greater responsibility and authority than the subordinates under his supervision.

73. Many newly appointed supervisors develop a form of inner conflict that has been called "status anxiety." The most appropriate description of this type of conflict is that the supervisor
    (A) becomes torn between the responsibilities of newly acquired authority and the need to be liked by persons who were formerly his peers.
    (B) tries to discard the symbols of his status and authority by acting out the role of the "nice guy."
    (C) is prevented from making decisions because his subordinates have stripped his status and authority to the point where he becomes immobilized.
    (D) is reluctant to make decisions because he is fearful of hostile behavior by his subordinates.

74. As a newly appointed supervisor, you will be exercising a two-way relationship in the field of police work. This two-way relationship means that you
    (A) will be equally responsible for law enforcement functions and supervisory duties.
    (B) will exercise supervisory responsibility over your subordinates while continuing to maintain relationships with former colleagues.
    (C) must be prepared not only to discipline your subordinates, but also to give them recognition for well-done work.
    (D) must accept the dual responsibility for the work output of your subordinates and that of representing them to the upper levels of supervision.

75. The sergeant's responsibilities to her subordinates include all of the following *except*

   (A) backing up subordinates caught in misconduct.
   (B) trying to prevent grievances on the part of her subordinates.
   (C) communicating to her superiors the faults she finds in existing practices.
   (D) accepting responsibility for the mistakes of subordinates.

76. Good street supervision by superiors of their subordinate police officers on patrol is essential to high morale among these subordinates chiefly because

   (A) arrests made at some personal effort and perhaps danger to the officers involved may be negated by improper administrative or judicial action.
   (B) officers want to be observed and credited by superiors when an assignment has been properly performed.
   (C) the superior's continual correction of negligent officers for recurrent violations of departmental rules is good procedure.
   (D) the boredom, discomfort, and routine of much of police work requires the stimulus of close and continuous supervision.

77. "Maintenance of discipline depends an the right degree of surveillance." The patrol sergeant should know that the degree of surveillance exercised

   (A) is primarily determined by directives and orders from higher authority.
   (B) is primarily determined by the patrol conditions that exist in a precinct.
   (C) should be uniformly high for all subordinates.
   (D) should be varied according to the individual subordinate.

78. Your superior officer notifies you, the patrol sergeant, that several police officers have complained to her about your harsh supervisory methods. Of the following, the *first* reply you should make is to

   (A) tell her that, in doing your job, you have always considered only the welfare of the department and the citizens it protects.
   (B) ask her what specific acts have been considered harsh.
   (C) ask her to refuse to listen to such complaints and to instruct these officers to observe the chain of command.
   (D) promise to ease up on your subordinates.

79. Assume that you are a sergeant. Another sergeant has been newly assigned to your precinct. For you to tell this new sergeant the strengths and weaknesses of some of the individual officers she will supervise would be

   (A) bad; bias will be introduced unknowingly into the work situation.
   (B) good; the new sergeant will be able to make various assignments of officers more intelligently.
   (C) bad; it will delay the new sergeant's adjustment to new responsibilities.
   (D) good; the abilities of an officer change from day-to-day due to various factors.

80. One of the police officers under your supervision has suddenly become very careless in his personal appearance, and his job performance has fallen below the required standard. Questioning of the officer reveals that this condition is due to a serious personal problem. For you to become involved is

   (A) improper; your police background and training make it unlikely that you could provide any real assistance.
   (B) proper; all personal problems of your officers should be your concern.
   (C) improper; you would be intruding upon the officer's right to privacy in personal matters.
   (D) proper; the officer's personal problem has seriously affected his work.

81. The ability of the body to adapt to progressive increases in the amount of a drug taken is called

    (A) addiction.
    (B) tolerance.
    (C) dependence.
    (D) synergism.

82. Benzedrine is

    (A) an amphetamine.
    (B) a tranquilizer.
    (C) a barbiturate.
    (D) a sedative.

83. Methadone is an addictive drug that is in the same chemical family as

    (A) heroin and morphine.
    (B) cocaine and hashish.
    (C) peyote and morning glory seeds.
    (D) LSD and DMT.

84. Those experts who believe in the theory of reverse tolerance state that it is most likely to develop among marijuana users who

    (A) have a serious, underlying mental disturbance.
    (B) ingest it with food.
    (C) use it in conjunction with other substances.
    (D) use it over a long period of time.

85. A comparison of the number of alcoholics to the number of drug addicts in the United States indicates that the number of alcoholics is

    (A) smaller than the number of drug addicts.
    (B) about the same as the number of drug addicts.
    (C) much greater than the number of drug addicts.
    (D) slightly greater than the number of drug addicts.

86. It's that time of year again, and you, as a supervisor, have been called upon to prepare and submit evaluation reports for all of the subordinates directly supervised by you. You are aware of the fact that if you are not careful, then certain "rating errors" might creep in and taint your ratings. You want to be sure that you are being objective regarding your subordinates. Of the following, the *best* way to insure objectivity in ratings is to

    (A) compare the subordinate's performance during the current period with his performance during the prior rating period.
    (B) analyze your daily thoughts about each officer's performance.
    (C) keep a record of your daily observations of each officer's performance.
    (D) base your rating on specific actions engaged in by each officer that are related to his performance of police tasks.

87. The police officer who understands modern scientific crime detection should know that toxicology involves chiefly the

    (A) analysis of blood.
    (B) study of poisons.
    (C) detection of forgery.
    (D) study of handwriting.

88. A characteristic postmortem symptom of carbon monoxide poisoning is a
    (A) pinkish lividity of all or part of the body.
    (B) bluish tint in the lips and other membrane surfaces.
    (C) waxy texture and appearance of the skin.
    (D) grotesque or contorted position of the body.

89. Which facial characteristic of human beings varies from person to person to the greatest extent, therefore making it the single best feature to use for identification?
    (A) Eye
    (B) Ear
    (C) Nose
    (D) Mouth

90. Which one of the following is a *correct* technique in criminal interrogation?
    (A) There should always be more than one interrogator in the room.
    (B) Complete notes should be taken at the start of the interview.
    (C) The interrogator, if possible, should acquaint himself with all the known facts of the case before attempting to question anyone.
    (D) Questions should be framed so as to be answered in a few words.

91. Most people who are involved in the training of subordinates understand that "feedback," or knowledge of results or progress, is essential to the maintenance of motivation and continued growth. This is one of the basic reasons why periodic performance evaluations must be discussed with subordinates. Based on the above, the most appropriate inference should be that
    (A) in the absence of feedback, erroneous methods of performance will be the result.
    (B) motivation to continue improvement requires periodic feedback of progress.
    (C) feedback insures adequate learning.
    (D) subordinates must be given detailed instructions in order to insure proper performance.

92. Of all the fingerprint patterns, the most common is the
    (A) whorl.
    (B) loop.
    (C) arch.
    (D) accidental.

93. What is the minimum number of handwriting samples that should be obtained from a suspect who has forged checks?
    (A) 1
    (B) 3
    (C) 5
    (D) 6

94. As a supervisor your primary task is to "get the job done" through others. You do not "do," you see that others "do." If you had to classify each of the following statements with regard to its ability to improve employee performance, the one that would be on top of the list would be:
    (A) Everyone wants constructive criticism.
    (B) A guaranteed raise in pay will insure better performance.
    (C) Competition makes everyone better.
    (D) Everyone wants to receive recognition or approval.

95. In examining a knife for prints, the knife should be held
    (A) with the tip of one forefinger placed at the end of the blade and the other at the end of the handle.
    (B) with the handle in the left hand and the index finger of the right hand at the tip of the blade.
    (C) with the handle in the right hand and the index finger of the left hand at the tip of the blade.
    (D) only by a mechanical appliance.

Directions: Questions 96 through 99 are based on the following chart of burglary and robbery incidents in Precinct X during the years 1996 through 2000.

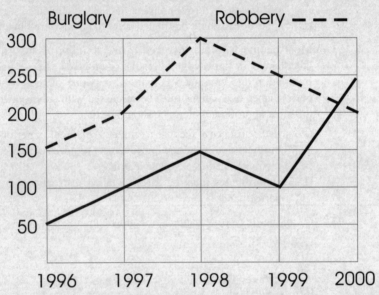

Burglary and Robbery in Precinct X

96. The change in robberies from 1998 to 1999 was most nearly a
    (A) 33 percent decrease.
    (B) 33 percent increase.
    (C) 66 percent decrease.
    (D) 66 percent increase.

97. The decrease in burglary, from 1999 to 2000 was most nearly
    (A) 25 percent
    (B) 30 percent
    (C) 20 percent
    (D) 80 percent

98. The ratio of burglary to robbery in 2000 was most nearly
    (A) 1 to 3.
    (B) 1 to 1.
    (C) 2 to 1.
    (D) 1.25 to 1.

99. If robbery in 2001 will be 10 percent greater than in 2000, and if the ratio of robbery to burglary in 2001 was the same as in 1997, what will most nearly be the number of burglaries in 2001?

    (A) 500
    (B) 550
    (C) 400
    (D) 350

100. You have been directed by a higher authority to institute a special patrol plan that will require that five special posts be covered for three tours every day for one year. Assume that all of your police officers are entitled to two regular days off per week, twenty-four days vacation, ten training days, and each reports sick six days a year. Assume for the solution to this problem that there are three hundred and sixty-four days in the year. Based on the above, how many officers will be required to staff the special posts?

    (A) 23
    (B) 24
    (C) 25
    (D) 26

101. Frank is a sergeant who works for Lieutenant George. George works for you, a captain. Frank comes to you and complains that when George assigns work out to units, his (Frank's) unit gets an unfair share of the workload. Which of the following would be the most appropriate action for you to take *first*?

    (A) Tell Frank that you will discuss the problem with George.
    (B) Tell Frank that you will investigate his complaint and will discuss it with him and George.
    (C) Get all the facts from Frank and then direct George to look into it.
    (D) Ask Frank if he has discussed the problem with George.

102. Lieutenant George gives Sergeant Frank an order. Sergeant Frank personally disagrees with the order and he discusses this with George. George overrules Frank's disagreement. What should Frank do?

    (A) Ask George to put it in writing.
    (B) Try to convince George that he (Frank) is right.
    (C) Ask George to give the order to Frank's unit.
    (D) Give the order to his (Frank's) unit.

103. Lieutenant George is in charge of five units, each one of which is under the direct supervision of a sergeant. Several complaints about Sergeant Frank have come to the attention of Lieutenant George. The complaints allege that Frank's order-giving technique is harsh. Lieutenant George calls Frank to his office to discuss the matter and Frank becomes angry and defensive. It would be best for Lieutenant George to

    (A) tell Sergeant Frank that he had better change his ways or disciplinary action will be taken against him.
    (B) tell Sergeant Frank to come back later when he has cooled off.
    (C) find out from Sergeant Frank whether or not he wants a transfer from his current assignment.
    (D) tell Sergeant Frank about the complaints and ask his advice on how they should be handled.

104. Captain Roger has instituted a new policy that is to be given an eight-week trial period. Not all the units under Roger's command are equally affected by the new policy, but all the employees, in every unit, have voiced considerable resentment. Captain Roger wants to try to eliminate this dissatisfaction. Assuming he has the authority to do any or all of the following, which would be best for Captain Roger to do to reduce hostility?

    (A) Conduct unit meetings with each unit and show how the policy works and why it is needed.
    (B) Post an explanation of the policy, with an indication of its need, onto the bulletin board.
    (C) Conduct meetings with supervisory personnel and try to get them to point out the value of the policy.
    (D) Write and distribute a series of memos that explain the new policy in stages.

105. Captain Roger is about to embark on a special project within his department. He is now at the planning stage. At this stage, of the following, which would be his most important consideration?

    (A) Whether or not he will have to devote his time to the project
    (B) Whether or not the means to accomplish the objectives of the project are available to him
    (C) Whether or not his unit has enough time to carry out the project
    (D) Whether or not his subordinates have the required expertise

106. Absenteeism and lateness are serious problems that must be addressed by an enlightened administration. Rules and policies concerning the problems must be made clear. Some of these rules and policies may be more difficult to enforce than others. Which of the following would be most difficult to set up or enforce?

    (A) Requiring a doctor's approval before returning to work after sick leave
    (B) Making a list of the excuses that will be accepted for lateness
    (C) A statement of working schedules, including starting and ending times
    (D) Requiring that certain absences be arranged in advance with the immediate supervisor

107. Every formal organization has an informal organization contained within it. Every formal communication system has an informal system known as the grapevine. Every organization has formal and informal leaders. Which of the following is the best description of the "informal" organization?

    (A) Spontaneous interpersonal working relationships
    (B) Relationships between staff and line units
    (C) Informal relationships between supervisors and subordinates
    (D) Informal, horizontal relationships between supervisors

108. Sergeant Frank wishes to develop the abilities of one of his subordinates. Frank knows that assigning some special responsibilities to an officer can often have this effect. If Sergeant Frank decides to develop the subordinate in this manner, then it would be most important for Sergeant Frank to tell the subordinate

    (A) how important the job is.
    (B) what is expected from the subordinate.
    (C) when the job is to be completed.
    (D) how the job is to be carried out.

109. Lieutenant George has just received a written suggestion from Sergeant Frank that the sergeant believes will increase productivity of their unit. Upon receipt of the suggestion it would be best for Lieutenant George to

   (A) consider Sergeant Frank's experience in the field before evaluating the suggestion.
   (B) implement the suggestion, but only on a trial basis initially.
   (C) thank Sergeant Frank for the suggestion even if it should not turn out to be valuable.
   (D) accept the suggestion, make no comment, and schedule it for consideration.

110. All individuals have basic needs that, if satisfied, can positively affect morale and performance. Some of these needs can be remembered through the use of the mnemonic device (code word) ROBS, which stands for Recognition, Opportunity, Belonging, and Security. Of the following, which would you consider to be most important in motivation and morale?

   (A) Training courses designed to increase subordinate potential
   (B) Pay grades based on productivity
   (C) Expressed recognition for a job well done
   (D) Job enrichment that increases an officer's freedom to use initiative

111. Change is resisted. Certain steps can be taken to lessen this resistance. Certain things can increase resistance to change. Which of the following is most likely to increase resistance to changes in working procedures?

   (A) The manner in which the change is introduced
   (B) The extent to which the work methods will be affected
   (C) The kind of exchange that is being made
   (D) The way in which employee working relationships will be affected by the change

112. When new employees come into an organization or a unit, it is wise to expose them to some form of orientation program. The major aim of such a program should be to

   (A) eliminate misconceptions about the organization or the unit.
   (B) assist the employee in adjusting to the organization or the unit.
   (C) develop a sense of loyalty to the organization or the unit.
   (D) train the employee to deal with the responsibilities he or she will have to face.

113. Most workers want to do the job properly. Most newly hired employees become anxious about whether or not they will be able to do the required work. This fear of failure is not a minor problem. It is a problem that must be addressed by a supervisor. In dealing with this problem, it is best for the supervisor to recognize that

   (A) this fear can be used to motivate new employees to learn the job.
   (B) employees differ in the amount of encouragement they need.
   (C) mistakes are more an indication of poor training rather than lack of ability.
   (D) new workers require the same amount of help.

114. A supervisor's primary responsibility within the organization is to "get the job done." He or she accomplishes this responsibility through interaction with subordinates. The most appropriate objective of this interaction should be to

   (A) assist subordinates in achieving higher rank.
   (B) aid subordinates in becoming independent in their work.
   (C) train subordinates to follow his or her leadership style.
   (D) train subordinates to handle increasingly difficult work.

115. We have already seen that "planning" is the responsibility of every person within the police agency at every level. Planning can be tactical, strategic, long-range, or short-range. The best reason for a department to include long-range plans in its planning program is to

    (A) define the program in terms of overall department objectives.
    (B) provide a way that future plans can be changed as the need arises.
    (C) set deadlines for achieving department objectives.
    (D) ensure efficiency in the carrying out of department programs.

116. Frequently, there is confusion within an agency about the execution or interpretation of policies laid down by the chief executive. Steps can be taken to minimize this confusion. Which one of the following would best reduce such confusion?

    (A) Seek out department heads and obtain their concurrence prior to the adoption of a policy.
    (B) Consider suggestions of staff before finalizing policies.
    (C) Once the policy is adopted, put it in writing.
    (D) Do not change policies frequently.

117. A chief executive usually has a staff whose responsibility is to advise the chief concerning problems and their solutions. Frequently, staff advice may differ internally and the chief is required to review all the facts presented to her. Having done this, the chief should

    (A) obtain a consensus decision and adopt it.
    (B) make a decision, but leave the door open for administrative reevaluation.
    (C) try to get all members of the staff to agree before making a decision.
    (D) institute a plan that has majority staff acceptance and then try to win over those who disagree.

118. You have detected that there is a natural group leader assigned to your unit. It would be best for you to

    (A) enforce all lines of authority.
    (B) permit this leader to settle grievances and complaints against subordinates.
    (C) give this leader special leadership training.
    (D) use this leader's influence in getting the job done.

119. Sometimes supervisors are faced with difficult work problems. Frequently, supervisors consult with their subordinates concerning these problems. Why is this a good practice?

    (A) It increases understanding and develops cooperation.
    (B) It will permit the supervisor to more quickly reach the best solution to the problem.
    (C) It will train the subordinates in problem-solving techniques.
    (D) It creates a standard way of solving unit work problems.

120. You have been exposed to the concept known as the unity of command. Which of the following best describes this concept?

    (A) Supervisors should assist one another in getting the job done.
    (B) A subordinate should receive orders from only one supervisor.
    (C) A supervisor should give orders to only one subordinate at a time.
    (D) All orders should be brief and clear.

MODEL EXAMINATION 1: ANSWERS AND EXPLANATIONS

1. **The correct answer is (A).** When you establish priority of work, you are deciding what must be done when and by whom. This assists you in assigning the work to the proper subordinate.

2. **The correct answer is (D).** A lack of the proper appreciation for the need to plan will usually result in a poorly structured plan.

3. **The correct answer is (D).** When you are setting up a schedule (a key word in the question), you have to know who will be available to get the job done.

4. **The correct answer is (B).** Some argue that there is an even earlier step than defining the problem determining if there is a need for a decision.

5. **The correct answer is (D).** Although all of the choices deal with factors that must be considered, the objectives are obviously most important.

6. **The correct answer is (D).** It is a given in the question that the old procedure was superior. You owe it to your boss and to your department to make this known and to support your position.

7. **The correct answer is (B).** When the people who do the work have input into the decision-making process, several positive results may be obtained. The decision may be more practical, and they will more readily support the decision.

8. **The correct answer is (A).** They should know at the outset that there will be matters over which neither you nor they will have authority.

9. **The correct answer is (C).** Choices (A), (B), and (D) are words of wisdom. But be careful of choice (C). Your "willing" subordinate may be the only one working.

10. **The correct answer is (B).** Whenever a procedure is taught as part of formal training, then the procedure becomes part of the departments polices, even if it is not a written policy. In this case, since the FTOs show the recruits how to use a flashlight as a blunt weapon, flashlights become blunt weapons for the department and officers must receive formal training on this concept.

11. **The correct answer is (D).** Obviously, this is a true statement. Again, be careful of the choice with the wrong supporting statement. Do you want to train recruits and veterans at the same level?

12. **The correct answer is (C).** The answer is not so obvious this time. But think about it. Would you want your subordinates to give you 90 percent when they are capable of giving you 100 percent? No! You want their best performance.

13. **The correct answer is (B).** This is another way of saying "get the job done," which is the main objective of any supervisory activity by the boss.

14. **The correct answer is (D).** Training must be designed carefully with a purpose. Each training program must be goal specific, enhance specific skills relevant to the goals, and correct deficiencies.

15. **The correct answer is (A).** More quickly and more efficiently. Very few people subscribe to the trial and error method of training.

16. **The correct answer is (D).** Individual differences do occur at any age. Choice (A) is incorrect. The old saying, "You can't teach an old dog new tricks" just isn't right. With motivation, anyone can learn.

17. **The correct answer is (C).** This explanation is both relevant and personal. It should serve to motivate the leader to modify her behavior.

18. **The correct answer is (A).** Remember that teamwork is fostered when people work toward a common goal.

19. **The correct answer is (D).** The sequence would be (B), (D), (A), and (C). The third step is known as using the student's apperceptive base, or going from the known to the unknown. It is somewhat similar to the technique of going from easy to difficult or from simple to complex.

20. **The correct answer is (A).** This is an obvious answer. Remember that the first-line supervisor is in the best position to see training needs and need for discipline and to supply facts necessary to squelch rumors.

21. **The correct answer is (D).** In addition, the first-line supervisor exercises the most influence over the subordinate's social and physical environment.

22. **The correct answer is (C).** One of the most unpleasant aspects of the newly appointed supervisor is the appreciation of negative discipline (punishment). Some supervisors find it difficult to act as a management person rather than as "one of the boys."

23. **The correct answer is (D).** If the supervisor must often take disciplinary action against subordinates, then his or her supervisory methods may very well need to be reviewed and examined.

24. **The correct answer is (D).** This is another version of the same concept.

25. **The correct answer is (D).** Getting the job done is the primary aim of all supervisory action.

26. **The correct answer is (C).** This is yet another way of saying "get the job done."

27. **The correct answer is (B).** Choices A and B sound similar, but by reviewing all the officer's past infractions you make this personal. One of the keys to proper discipline is to avoid making discipline personal.

28. **The correct answer is (B).** The response we get from the public may be a message to mend our ways.

29. **The correct answer is (B).** However, you could go further. It is impossible to accomplish the police function without the support of the community.

30. **The correct answer is (C).** In order to be successful, we must know what the public is thinking.

31. **The correct answer is (D).** You could change the question to deal with any kind of consistent misconduct. Poor practices cannot occur consistently if the supervisor is doing his or her job.

32. **The correct answer is (A).** This is a difficult question. Most people want to start right in by saying that the request cannot be granted. Try to see the difference between: "I cannot grant your request because..." and "After giving your request careful consideration, I find that I must refuse your request because…"

33. **The correct answer is (D).** This should be an obvious answer. As a representative of your department, you should resist advocating your personal views and focus on the mission and policies of the department. If your department does not take a stand on issues of this nature, then review the material available to you via your local library or online and take a neutral stance.

34. **The correct answer is (C).** The question says that the program is aimed at detection.

35. **The correct answer is (B).** After reading our evidence breakdown, this question should be easy.

36. **The correct answer is (A).** The term circumstantial evidence has suffered from bad press and from incomplete understanding on the part of the general public, including members of the jury. The conclusions drawn on the basis of some circumstantial evidence have indeed been unwarranted, but in many cases there are no eyewitnesses to give direct evidence and circumstantial evidence may be all that is available. The judge must explain to the jury that some circumstantial evidence is relevant and admissible.

37. **The correct answer is (D).** He or she is probably unapproachable.

38. **The correct answer is (A).** Policy at all levels? Policy usually comes from a high level in the form of broad guides.

39. **The correct answer is (D).** This is better than giving advice.

40. **The correct answer is (B).** The question asks for the most effective solution. Remember that facts kill rumors.

41. **The correct answer is (B).** Use our techniques outlined in the reading chapter for solving these problems. This is an easy one. Some are much more difficult.

42. **The correct answer is (B).** Sentence 3 is the obvious opening sentence. Sentence 2 is an appropriate second sentence building on the complaint referred to in sentence 3.

43. **The correct answer is (D).** Sentence 1 is the opener and sentence 2 is the obvious second sentence. In this case, the sentences were not scrambled. Be aware that examiners sometimes use this method.

44. **The correct answer is (B).** Here again, the connection between the opening sentence and the second sentence should be plain to all.

45. **The correct answer is (A).** Not quite as easy as the others, but not difficult. Be careful not to be lulled into a false sense of security. Some of these seem to be impossible to handle on occasion, but every question does have an answer.

46. **The correct answer is (C).** It looks like math, but it's reading.

47. **The correct answer is (D).** This is reading by the numbers again.

48. **The correct answer is (A).** This is another easy one.

49. **The correct answer is (A).** Take out "originality" and put in "effectiveness."

50. **The correct answer is (B).** Take out the word "completed" and replace it with "started."

51. **The correct answer is (B).** Take out the word "untrue" and replace it with "unavoidable."

52. **The correct answer is (C).** Take out the word "emphasize" and replace it with "neglect."

53. **The correct answer is (A).** Is he or she getting the job done?

54. **The correct answer is (A).** Sometimes referred to as the sandwich approach; build him up, knock him down, then build him up again.

55. **The correct answer is (C).** Choice (B) looks good too, but a detective/investigator's primary job is to gather information and/or evidence.

56. **The correct answer is (D).** How many times have you heard the story about the police officer who accidentally stumbled into the "big one" when he was going for coffee? The officer who fortuitously makes a spectacular arrest certainly deserves recognition, but not at the expense of the many hardworking officers who are highly effective but less visible. The good supervisor must be aware of the efforts and results of each of the officers.

57. **The correct answer is (B).** When you establish effective, objective standards, everybody knows what he has to do and you are free to engage in higher thinking.

58. **The correct answer is (C).** Couldn't you do the same with any subordinate?

59. **The correct answer is (D).** If you want to determine if he can act independently, then see if he has done so in the past.

60. **The correct answer is (A).** The wholly quantitative system does not consider quality of performance, only quantity of performance.

61. **The correct answer is (D).** If you keep him aware of what is happening, then he can do the job.

62. **The correct answer is (B).** One of the key words in the question is "comprehensive."

63. **The correct answer is (D).** A negative report can be referred to as a "nothing to report" report. Without a report of some sort in hand, a supervisor cannot know whether a report is simply missing, late, or whether there is really nothing to report. The negative report must be filed for the record.

64. **The correct answer is (C).** This is the reason why evaluations must be discussed with employees.

65. **The correct answer is (B).** Abstract words might cloud your meaning. It has been said that a report must not only be capable of being understood, but must also be incapable of being misunderstood.

66. **The correct answer is (B).** The report is based on the results of the investigation. The results themselves are based on the data.

67. **The correct answer is (A).** This is not an easy question. We all know that a report must be timely, but timeliness does not necessarily equate with great speed. Speed in itself is the least essential aspect. The four Cs of report writing are: clear, concise, correct; and complete.

68. **The correct answer is (D).** This makes it easier to read and understand. Remember also that if a report to your boss is a long one, then it is a good idea to summarize it at the beginning so your boss can decide if it must be dealt with now or can wait until after lunch.

69. **The correct answer is (C).** Not difficult as it is presented. If one of the choices included the thought that the outline would tend to prevent you from omitting necessary material, then it would be a much more difficult problem.

70. **The correct answer is (A).** The answer would be the same, even if the question did not refer to a large municipal police department.

71. **The correct answer is (A).** Here it is again, "get the job done."

72. **The correct answer is (B).** Remember the concept of the big change or the big compromise.

73. **The correct answer is (A).** Similar in concept to the last question.

74. **The correct answer is (D).** This is referred to by some as the "ambivalent role" of the first-line supervisor.

75. **The correct answer is (A).** Back individuals when they are right, and discipline them for misconduct.

76. **The correct answer is (B).** Everyone who does a good job wants to be noticed and recognized. This recognition is a positive motivator.

77. **The correct answer is (D).** Each subordinate is an individual; each has different needs. The effective supervisor tailors surveillance to the needs of the individual.

78. **The correct answer is (B).** This is not a difficult question.

79. **The correct answer is (B).** Don't fall into the trap of saying to yourself, "Suppose he has it in for one of the subordinates." Always assume the best of your fellow officers. The new sergeant will find making assignments and supervision much less difficult with some foreknowledge of the strengths and weaknesses of the officers reporting to her. Choice (D) is a good example of gobbledygook.

80. **The correct answer is (D).** There are two occasions when your subordinate's personal problem becomes your problem: when he asks for help, or when his work is being affected adversely.

81. **The correct answer is (B).** When tolerance builds up, it takes more and more substance to reach the same result.

82. **The correct answer is (A).** Just an information giver.

83. **The correct answer is (A).** Another small gem; you should know this and gather a quick point.

84. **The correct answer is (D).** This means that less of the substance will produce the same result.

85. **The correct answer is (C).** Alcohol has been the most serious drug problem in the United States for years.

86. **The correct answer is (D).** This is not an easy question. Choice (C) would seem to overlap somewhat with choice (D).

87. **The correct answer is (B).** Take advantage of questions with obvious answers.

88. **The correct answer is (A).** A frequently asked question involves a dead body found in a car with pinkish skin blotches that are probably a result of carbon monoxide poisoning.

89. **The correct answer is (B).** This is correct, believe it or not.

90. **The correct answer is (C).** It is important to get the facts first.

91. **The correct answer is (B).** This is really a reading question, but it makes a universally accepted point.

92. **The correct answer is (B).** Loops, whorls, and arches; in that order.

93. **The correct answer is (D).** A minimum of 6 samples should be taken. Obviously more would be better. The more a person writes a forged name, address, numbers, etc, the less likely they are to maintain the copied style. In other words, they will more likely revert to their own style of writing.

94. **The correct answer is (D).** Recognition is a positive motivator. Performance evaluations can be used as a form of recognition.

95. **The correct answer is (A).** A more difficult question might be, "How do you pick up a firearm found at the scene of a crime?" The best answer (if there is no lanyard on the butt) is to stick a pencil through the trigger guard behind the trigger.

96. **The correct answer is (A).** In 1998, there were 150 robberies. In 1999, there were 100 robberies. The rule is the following:

    1. Draw a line to make a fraction: –

    2. The bottom number is the place you started from: $\dfrac{1}{150}$

    3. The top number is the distance you traveled away from the starting point: $\dfrac{50}{150}$

    4. Divide the bottom number into the top number: $\dfrac{50}{150} = \dfrac{1}{3} = 33\dfrac{1}{3}$ percent decrease

97. **The correct answer is (C).** In 1999, there were 250 burglaries. In 2000, there were 200 burglaries. Using the rules from the last question, we end up with $\dfrac{50}{250} = \dfrac{1}{5} = 20$ percent decrease.

98. **The correct answer is (B).**   Burglary in 2000 = 200
    Robbery in 2000 = 250
    204 to 250 = 1 to 1.25

99. **The correct answer is (B).** This is the only difficult one. It projects into the future.
    Robbery 2000 = 250
    Robbery 2001 = 250 + 10 percent of 250 = 275
    Ratio of robbery to burglary in 1997 = 1 to 2
    Ratio of robbery to burglary in 2001 = 1 to 2
    Therefore, if robberies in 2001 = 275, then burglaries in 2001 must be 550, a ratio of 1 to 2.

100. **The correct answer is (C).** This is not difficult once you see the technique. Five special posts, 3 times a day, for 364 days means you must cover 5,460 special posts a year. Each police officer is only available to perform 220 tours a year. Why? Because he or she is not available as follows:

    Days off   = 104 (52 x 2)
    Vacation   = 24
    Training   = 10
    Sick   = 6
    144 Days not available
    Days in   =   364 the year
    Days not available   = -144
                                220 Days available

    This means that one police officer can cover 220 special posts during the year.
    Divide 5,460 by 220 and you determine how many police officers are needed: $220\overline{)5460.0}$ with quotient 24.8

    The best answer is 25. Usually the examiners design the problems so you will not be faced with rounding up or down. It's a big problem, however, if the answer is not a whole number. Suppose you need 24.3 officers? Can you do it with 24 officers? No, you would need 25 officers.

101. **The correct answer is (D).** Determine whether or not he has adhered to the chain of command.

102. **The correct answer is (D).** Subordinates owe a duty to their superiors to respectfully disagree when they think it's proper. Having done so, they must carry out the order even if overruled.

103. **The correct answer is (D).** Be careful of choice (B). If the lieutenant is angry, perhaps he should postpone; but not when, as in this case, the subordinate is angry.

104. **The correct answer is (A).** The question wants the captain to take steps to eliminate dissatisfaction. "Explain" is always a good way to go.

105. **The correct answer is (B).** Choice (B) includes choice (D) within it and thus is the better answer.

106. **The correct answer is (B).** How could you possibly cover everything?

107. **The correct answer is (A).** Remember, some people say that without the informal organization, the formal organization could not function.

108. **The correct answer is (B).** We have seen this concept before.

109. **The correct answer is (C).** Also, tell him that his interest is appreciated and to keep up the good work.

110. **The correct answer is (C).** Recognition is a positive motivator.

111. **The correct answer is (A).** We have seen this before.

112. **The correct answer is (B).** A common sense answer to an orientation program.

113. **The correct answer is (B).** Obviously, some need more encouragement than others.

114. **The correct answer is (B).** So that they can get the job done even when the boss is not around.

115. **The correct answer is (A).** Then, the big picture is easier to see.

116. **The correct answer is (C).** This is a not-so-obvious answer. But remember that policies are not usually written.

117. **The correct answer is (B).** As the boss you have to call the shots.

118. **The correct answer is (D).** Of course it is understood that you will use him in a positive way.

119. **The correct answer is (A).** This is another form of participatory management.

120. **The correct answer is (B).** We have seen this concept before.

MODEL EXAMINATION 2: ANSWER SHEET

1. Ⓐ Ⓑ Ⓒ Ⓓ Ⓔ
2. Ⓐ Ⓑ Ⓒ Ⓓ Ⓔ
3. Ⓐ Ⓑ Ⓒ Ⓓ Ⓔ
4. Ⓐ Ⓑ Ⓒ Ⓓ Ⓔ
5. Ⓐ Ⓑ Ⓒ Ⓓ Ⓔ
6. Ⓐ Ⓑ Ⓒ Ⓓ Ⓔ
7. Ⓐ Ⓑ Ⓒ Ⓓ Ⓔ
8. Ⓐ Ⓑ Ⓒ Ⓓ Ⓔ
9. Ⓐ Ⓑ Ⓒ Ⓓ Ⓔ
10. Ⓐ Ⓑ Ⓒ Ⓓ Ⓔ
11. Ⓐ Ⓑ Ⓒ Ⓓ Ⓔ
12. Ⓐ Ⓑ Ⓒ Ⓓ Ⓔ
13. Ⓐ Ⓑ Ⓒ Ⓓ Ⓔ
14. Ⓐ Ⓑ Ⓒ Ⓓ Ⓔ
15. Ⓐ Ⓑ Ⓒ Ⓓ Ⓔ
16. Ⓐ Ⓑ Ⓒ Ⓓ Ⓔ
17. Ⓐ Ⓑ Ⓒ Ⓓ Ⓔ
18. Ⓐ Ⓑ Ⓒ Ⓓ Ⓔ
19. Ⓐ Ⓑ Ⓒ Ⓓ Ⓔ
20. Ⓐ Ⓑ Ⓒ Ⓓ Ⓔ
21. Ⓐ Ⓑ Ⓒ Ⓓ Ⓔ
22. Ⓐ Ⓑ Ⓒ Ⓓ Ⓔ
23. Ⓐ Ⓑ Ⓒ Ⓓ Ⓔ
24. Ⓐ Ⓑ Ⓒ Ⓓ Ⓔ
25. Ⓐ Ⓑ Ⓒ Ⓓ Ⓔ
26. Ⓐ Ⓑ Ⓒ Ⓓ Ⓔ
27. Ⓐ Ⓑ Ⓒ Ⓓ Ⓔ
28. Ⓐ Ⓑ Ⓒ Ⓓ Ⓔ
29. Ⓐ Ⓑ Ⓒ Ⓓ Ⓔ
30. Ⓐ Ⓑ Ⓒ Ⓓ Ⓔ

31. Ⓐ Ⓑ Ⓒ Ⓓ Ⓔ
32. Ⓐ Ⓑ Ⓒ Ⓓ Ⓔ
33. Ⓐ Ⓑ Ⓒ Ⓓ Ⓔ
34. Ⓐ Ⓑ Ⓒ Ⓓ Ⓔ
35. Ⓐ Ⓑ Ⓒ Ⓓ Ⓔ
36. Ⓐ Ⓑ Ⓒ Ⓓ Ⓔ
37. Ⓐ Ⓑ Ⓒ Ⓓ Ⓔ
38. Ⓐ Ⓑ Ⓒ Ⓓ Ⓔ
39. Ⓐ Ⓑ Ⓒ Ⓓ Ⓔ
40. Ⓐ Ⓑ Ⓒ Ⓓ Ⓔ
41. Ⓐ Ⓑ Ⓒ Ⓓ Ⓔ
42. Ⓐ Ⓑ Ⓒ Ⓓ Ⓔ
43. Ⓐ Ⓑ Ⓒ Ⓓ Ⓔ
44. Ⓐ Ⓑ Ⓒ Ⓓ Ⓔ
45. Ⓐ Ⓑ Ⓒ Ⓓ Ⓔ
46. Ⓐ Ⓑ Ⓒ Ⓓ Ⓔ
47. Ⓐ Ⓑ Ⓒ Ⓓ Ⓔ
48. Ⓐ Ⓑ Ⓒ Ⓓ Ⓔ
49. Ⓐ Ⓑ Ⓒ Ⓓ Ⓔ
50. Ⓐ Ⓑ Ⓒ Ⓓ Ⓔ
51. Ⓐ Ⓑ Ⓒ Ⓓ Ⓔ
52. Ⓐ Ⓑ Ⓒ Ⓓ Ⓔ
53. Ⓐ Ⓑ Ⓒ Ⓓ Ⓔ
54. Ⓐ Ⓑ Ⓒ Ⓓ Ⓔ
55. Ⓐ Ⓑ Ⓒ Ⓓ Ⓔ
56. Ⓐ Ⓑ Ⓒ Ⓓ Ⓔ
57. Ⓐ Ⓑ Ⓒ Ⓓ Ⓔ
58. Ⓐ Ⓑ Ⓒ Ⓓ Ⓔ
59. Ⓐ Ⓑ Ⓒ Ⓓ Ⓔ
60. Ⓐ Ⓑ Ⓒ Ⓓ Ⓔ

61. Ⓐ Ⓑ Ⓒ Ⓓ Ⓔ
62. Ⓐ Ⓑ Ⓒ Ⓓ Ⓔ
63. Ⓐ Ⓑ Ⓒ Ⓓ Ⓔ
64. Ⓐ Ⓑ Ⓒ Ⓓ Ⓔ
65. Ⓐ Ⓑ Ⓒ Ⓓ Ⓔ
66. Ⓐ Ⓑ Ⓒ Ⓓ Ⓔ
67. Ⓐ Ⓑ Ⓒ Ⓓ Ⓔ
68. Ⓐ Ⓑ Ⓒ Ⓓ Ⓔ
69. Ⓐ Ⓑ Ⓒ Ⓓ Ⓔ
70. Ⓐ Ⓑ Ⓒ Ⓓ Ⓔ
71. Ⓐ Ⓑ Ⓒ Ⓓ Ⓔ
72. Ⓐ Ⓑ Ⓒ Ⓓ Ⓔ
73. Ⓐ Ⓑ Ⓒ Ⓓ Ⓔ
74. Ⓐ Ⓑ Ⓒ Ⓓ Ⓔ
75. Ⓐ Ⓑ Ⓒ Ⓓ Ⓔ
76. Ⓐ Ⓑ Ⓒ Ⓓ Ⓔ
77. Ⓐ Ⓑ Ⓒ Ⓓ Ⓔ
78. Ⓐ Ⓑ Ⓒ Ⓓ Ⓔ
79. Ⓐ Ⓑ Ⓒ Ⓓ Ⓔ
80. Ⓐ Ⓑ Ⓒ Ⓓ Ⓔ
81. Ⓐ Ⓑ Ⓒ Ⓓ Ⓔ
82. Ⓐ Ⓑ Ⓒ Ⓓ Ⓔ
83. Ⓐ Ⓑ Ⓒ Ⓓ Ⓔ
84. Ⓐ Ⓑ Ⓒ Ⓓ Ⓔ
85. Ⓐ Ⓑ Ⓒ Ⓓ Ⓔ
86. Ⓐ Ⓑ Ⓒ Ⓓ Ⓔ
87. Ⓐ Ⓑ Ⓒ Ⓓ Ⓔ
88. Ⓐ Ⓑ Ⓒ Ⓓ Ⓔ
89. Ⓐ Ⓑ Ⓒ Ⓓ Ⓔ
90. Ⓐ Ⓑ Ⓒ Ⓓ Ⓔ

91. Ⓐ Ⓑ Ⓒ Ⓓ Ⓔ
92. Ⓐ Ⓑ Ⓒ Ⓓ Ⓔ
93. Ⓐ Ⓑ Ⓒ Ⓓ Ⓔ
94. Ⓐ Ⓑ Ⓒ Ⓓ Ⓔ
95. Ⓐ Ⓑ Ⓒ Ⓓ Ⓔ
96. Ⓐ Ⓑ Ⓒ Ⓓ Ⓔ
97. Ⓐ Ⓑ Ⓒ Ⓓ Ⓔ
98. Ⓐ Ⓑ Ⓒ Ⓓ Ⓔ
99. Ⓐ Ⓑ Ⓒ Ⓓ Ⓔ
100. Ⓐ Ⓑ Ⓒ Ⓓ Ⓔ
101. Ⓐ Ⓑ Ⓒ Ⓓ Ⓔ
102. Ⓐ Ⓑ Ⓒ Ⓓ Ⓔ
103. Ⓐ Ⓑ Ⓒ Ⓓ Ⓔ
104. Ⓐ Ⓑ Ⓒ Ⓓ Ⓔ
105. Ⓐ Ⓑ Ⓒ Ⓓ Ⓔ
106. Ⓐ Ⓑ Ⓒ Ⓓ Ⓔ
107. Ⓐ Ⓑ Ⓒ Ⓓ Ⓔ
108. Ⓐ Ⓑ Ⓒ Ⓓ Ⓔ
109. Ⓐ Ⓑ Ⓒ Ⓓ Ⓔ
110. Ⓐ Ⓑ Ⓒ Ⓓ Ⓔ
111. Ⓐ Ⓑ Ⓒ Ⓓ Ⓔ
112. Ⓐ Ⓑ Ⓒ Ⓓ Ⓔ
113. Ⓐ Ⓑ Ⓒ Ⓓ Ⓔ
114. Ⓐ Ⓑ Ⓒ Ⓓ Ⓔ
115. Ⓐ Ⓑ Ⓒ Ⓓ Ⓔ
116. Ⓐ Ⓑ Ⓒ Ⓓ Ⓔ
117. Ⓐ Ⓑ Ⓒ Ⓓ Ⓔ
118. Ⓐ Ⓑ Ⓒ Ⓓ Ⓔ
119. Ⓐ Ⓑ Ⓒ Ⓓ Ⓔ
120. Ⓐ Ⓑ Ⓒ Ⓓ Ⓔ

MODEL EXAMINATION 2

> **Directions:** This test contains 120 questions. Circle the correct answers directly on the page. You have three hours to complete this examination. Each question has a relative weight of 1.0.

1. Which of the following people occupies the position of greatest importance in the maintenance of good employee relations?

   (A) First-line supervisor
   (B) Second-line supervisor
   (C) Department head
   (D) Representative of the personnel agency

2. On being promoted to a supervisory position, an individual should recognize that the position is primarily one of

   (A) security.
   (B) power.
   (C) responsibility.
   (D) authority.

3. Supervision is so essential to effective operation as to justify the rule that every subordinate at the level of execution should be under the _____ supervision of a supervisor. Which of the following best fills the blank in the above sentence?

   (A) constant
   (B) functional
   (C) implied
   (D) direct

4. The main responsibility of anyone who has subordinates working under him is to

   (A) make himself liked and respected by his subordinates.
   (B) create an attitude in his subordinates that will make them receptive toward the policies of the department.
   (C) adopt those procedures that will further the interests of his department.
   (D) get the work done properly.

5. "Sergeants must realize that their capacity and character are accurately reflected by the work of the personnel under them." The foregoing statement is

   (A) valid, because it is found in the rules and regulations.
   (B) invalid, because many capable commanders have some subordinates whose performance is substandard.
   (C) valid, because subordinates perform in accordance with what their superiors require.
   (D) invalid, because a strong commander is conspicuous by the state of his command.

6. A supervisor should realize that the performance of his or her subordinates will tend to meet the standard of work that

   (A) the supervisor is willing to accept.
   (B) the character of the work requires.
   (C) they can achieve with reasonable effort.
   (D) he or she sets as a goal.

7. Command is synonymous with initiative and self-reliance in meeting and accepting responsibility. It follows from this statement that on attaining the rank of sergeant, a person will be expected to consider that she should

    (A) perform her duties without relying on her subordinates at all.
    (B) stand on her own feet and assume full responsibility for her conduct.
    (C) not take advice or suggestions from other members of the department.
    (D) endeavor to revise and improve the administration of the department.

8. A sergeant will most likely secure the respect of the subordinates she supervises if she

    (A) tries to help them solve all their personal problems.
    (B) prods them continually to study the rules and regulations.
    (C) generally overlooks minor infractions of the rules.
    (D) makes it her business to know her job thoroughly.

9. Which of the following subordinates should be promoted to the rank of sergeant?

    (A) Those who have displayed the greatest proficiency in their duties as police officers should be promoted.
    (B) Those who have the greatest length of experience as police officers should be promoted.
    (C) Those who have shown the greatest aptitude for being sergeants should be promoted.
    (D) Those who have the greatest potential qualities of leadership should be promoted.

10. It would be *incorrect* to state that leadership qualities

    (A) are inborn and cannot be developed.
    (B) can be developed if there is sufficient desire on the part of the individual to reinforce or modify the traits he already possesses.
    (C) are the result of environment, experience, and attitudes of the individual.
    (D) enable the person who possesses them to cause others to willingly and voluntarily carry out his desires.

11. To be effective leaders, it is most important that police supervisors

    (A) be born with leadership ability.
    (B) be college graduates.
    (C) have normal intelligence and a willingness to assume responsibility.
    (D) develop an impersonal attitude in human relations.

12. When an employee comes to the supervisor's office to consult him on a personal matter, the supervisor should

    (A) in a friendly fashion, tell him that he does not enter into the private affairs of employees.
    (B) listen attentively, and tell the employee what he would do.
    (C) listen attentively, and through guiding questions induce the employee to think through the problem and arrive at his own solution.
    (D) sympathize with the employee regardless of the problem because that is what the employee wishes to hear.

13. In addition to general administrative ability, one of the desirable qualifications of a supervising officer is the ability to

    (A) publicize himself effectively as an outstanding leader.
    (B) deal with his men in such a manner that disagreements will be eliminated.
    (C) refrain from taking any action that would incite criticism.
    (D) inspire others and to remain open-minded in discriminating between relative values.

14. Of the following, probably the greatest advantage of oral communications as compared to written is the

    (A) informality of the communications atmosphere.
    (B) rapidity with which orders can be carried out.
    (C) opportunity provided for immediate feedback.
    (D) reduced need for structured organization of content.

15. Much has been said in recent years about the advisability of instituting suggestion programs or of inviting subordinates to participate in attempting to find solutions to police problems. In general, the most likely result of instituting either or both of these ideas would be

    (A) an increased motivation of the subordinate officers to do a better job.
    (B) an increased need for disciplinary action against subordinate officers as a result of their feeling more free to introduce new ideas.
    (C) a loss of efficiency resulting from the introduction of new ideas.
    (D) a stifling of initiative among the subordinate officers.

16. During your periodic employee evaluations, based on specific facts related to job performance, you observe that Police Officers Connolly and Mullins work together frequently and do consistently better work than your other subordinates. However, you also observe that Connolly and Mullins do not seem to associate with, nor socialize with, any other members of your unit. They seem to be close friends who do not need or want any association with the other police officers. Under these circumstances you should

    (A) talk to Connolly and Mullins and try to find out what is wrong.
    (B) do nothing; "if it ain't broke, don't fix it."
    (C) let them know that their work is good, but their attitude is not.
    (D) discuss the matter at an open meeting with all your subordinates.

17. Of the following statements concerning subordinates' expressions to a supervisor of their opinions and feelings concerning work situations, the most correct is that

    (A) by listening and responding to such expressions the supervisor encourages the development of complaints.
    (B) the lack of such expressions should indicate to the supervisor that there is a high level of job satisfaction.
    (C) the more the supervisor listens to and responds to such expressions, the more he or she demonstrates lack of supervisory ability.
    (D) by listening and responding to such expressions the supervisor will enable many subordinates to understand and solve their own problems on the job.

18. In making assignments, a superior attempts to fit his subordinates to the jobs. This procedure is

    (A) good, chiefly because it is a definite policy that lends itself to analysis and conclusions.
    (B) poor, chiefly because a job should be fitted to the individual.
    (C) good, chiefly because accomplishment of the mission is the primary goal.
    (D) poor, chiefly because no consideration is paid to human values and relationships.

19. A member will be most inclined to follow a decision enthusiastically if he has

    (A) studied the issues carefully.
    (B) discussed the decision with his peers.
    (C) taken part in shaping the decision.
    (D) been informed of the decision in advance by his immediate supervisor.

20. In a certain jurisdiction, the procedure for patrolling a certain troubled location has been the same for many years and is well known and understood by all police officers. After an intensive study by staff officers, the precinct commander decides to change this patrol procedure substantially. Since he is concerned about the morale of his subordinates, he is eager that the order be understood and accepted. Which one of the following techniques will most likely obtain the greatest acceptance?

    (A) Have the new procedure read at all roll calls and initialed by every subordinate.
    (B) Explain the basis for the decision to make the change in the procedure.
    (C) Issue a carefully written new procedure without any explanation of the basis for the decision to make the change.
    (D) Call a staff meeting of all of his lieutenants and sergeants and read the written procedure to them.

21. The best general rule for a superior officer to follow is to assign work wherever possible on the basis of

    (A) individual abilities.
    (B) expected time to perform the job required.
    (C) previous assignment.
    (D) seniority.

22. The clerical man says to Sergeant Mullins, "Hey sarge, you rated P.O. Connolly as "super- excellent" and the captain wants you to justify this with a special report in writing." Sergeant Mullins responds, "Give me back the form. I'll change it to excellent. He's not that good."

    Sergeant Mullins has just committed the rating error known as
    (A) personal bias.
    (B) central tendency.
    (C) overweighting.
    (D) association error.

23. Of the following, the *best* way for a superior officer to ensure that a subordinate understands an order concerning a job involving significant safety hazards is to

    (A) ask the subordinate if he understands the order.
    (B) give the order in simplified terms the subordinate can understand.
    (C) have the subordinate explain his understanding of the order.
    (D) summarize the order using different terms than those used at first.

24. A captain hears a lieutenant make the following statement to one of his sergeants: "Sergeant, Police Officer Peters has been out sick a lot recently, and I am very much concerned about the staffing problem it has created." With which one of the following kinds of sergeants would this order be most likely to be effective?

    (A) An unreliable sergeant
    (B) An inexperienced sergeant
    (C) An experienced, reliable sergeant
    (D) An antagonistic sergeant

25. Assume that a lieutenant, when giving an order to his subordinates, places responsibility for the order on superior authority. This practice is generally inadvisable, chiefly because the

    (A) lieutenant might appear to be trying to assert more authority than he possesses.
    (B) subordinates might doubt the lieutenant's support of the order.
    (C) superior in whose name the order is given might be unfamiliar with the order.
    (D) lieutenant may have difficulty in determining how well the order is carried out.

26. Shortly before a scheduled inspection of emergency service quarters, Sergeant Smith told Police Officer Jones to obtain the assistance of "a couple of members" and wash the windows of the quarters. Some time later, Sergeant Smith found Police Officer Jones cleaning the windows by himself. When questioned, Jones said that he had asked two members for assistance but they had refused, claiming that they had other work to do. In this situation, the principal blame lies with

    (A) Police Officer Jones for failure to report the situation to Sergeant Smith.
    (B) the two officers for refusing to cooperate.
    (C) both Police Officer Jones for failure to report the situation to Sergeant Smith and the two officers for refusing to cooperate.
    (D) Sergeant Smith for failure to make specific assignments.

27. Sergeant Judy Milowe is preparing her semi-annual evaluation reports of her subordinates. When she comes to Police Officer Mullins' report she says to herself, "You know, I like this guy. He's pleasant and cooperative and he is never late for work, I'm going to give him an above-average rating."

    Sergeant Milowe has committed the error of
    (A) leniency.
    (B) subjectivity.
    (C) overweighting.
    (D) logical error.

28. Since a police superior expects subordinates to carry out commands to the letter, it is most important for the superior to

    (A) check on the execution of all commands immediately.
    (B) issue commands clearly and make sure they are understood.
    (C) issue only commands that seem obviously reasonable to anyone.
    (D) make only one officer responsible for the execution of any command.

29. You observe that an officer under your command is not carrying out a specific assignment in accordance with the instructions you have issued. Of the following, the most important reason why you should have this officer repeat the instructions you gave is that

    (A) instructions can be misunderstood even by excellent officers.
    (B) it will indicate that incorrect instructions were given.
    (C) inefficiency usually has serious consequences.
    (D) oral instructions should be repeated when issued as a safeguard that they are understood.

30. A supervisor observes a definite reluctance on the part of her subordinates to follow her instructions and directions. Of the following, she should *first* investigate to

    (A) determine whether this is apparently a temporary situation.
    (B) discover where she may have failed as a leader.
    (C) learn where she can secure help in the matter.
    (D) remedy failures in the training of the subordinates.

31. A patrol supervisor has issued an order, based on a recently amended department procedure, to a police officer to perform a certain relatively simple routine duty. The police officer does not carry out the order properly in accordance with the amended procedure. Of the following conditions, the one that most indicates that the supervisor also shares the responsibility for this breach of regulations is that the supervisor did not

    (A) attempt to determine if this police officer was best suited for the carrying out of this order.
    (B) explain to the police officer the purpose of the order.
    (C) make any efforts to ascertain the personal preferences of the police officer
    (D) show a copy of the amended procedure to the police officer.

32. A rather complex change is to be made in patrol procedures. As a superior, it is your responsibility to make sure that your subordinates are informed of this change. The one of the following courses of action that is most likely to result in good performance is for you to

    (A) assign one of your best subordinates to explain the order.
    (B) distribute an exact copy of the new order as soon as it becomes available.
    (C) explain the new procedure after your subordinates have had some experience with it.
    (D) explain the new procedure carefully before it is adopted.

33. In giving orders, a superior will give more details at certain times than at other times. The one of the following situations in which the *least* amount of detail should be given is when the order is concerned with a procedure that

    (A) has hazardous features.
    (B) is of a special or infrequent nature.
    (C) has been generally performed in a standardized manner.
    (D) is to be carried out by several subordinates with limited experience.

34. While on patrol, a supervisor is required to issue a fairly important order to a subordinate. Because of the pressure of other duties, the superior issues the order very quickly and briefly while "on the run." An important weakness of the issuance of the orders in this manner is that the

    (A) subordinate is likely to regard the order as less important than it really is.
    (B) superior is giving the subordinate more responsibility than is proper.
    (C) orders require explanation in order to convey the intended meaning.
    (D) the superior is likely to forget this order and to whom it was issued.

35. As a supervisor, you have noticed that after you have issued verbal orders, subordinates seldom ask any questions seeking clarification of such orders. You have also noticed that upon questioning the subordinates while on patrol, few of them have really understood your orders. Of the following courses of action, the one which constitutes the best solution to this problem is for you to

    (A) question the subordinates immediately following the issuance of your orders.
    (B) take disciplinary action against those who are not able to understand your orders.
    (C) issue your orders in written form so that they may be understood more readily.
    (D) request that your commanding officer issue the orders.

36. When previous experience leads a supervisor to believe that instructions given to him for action will produce undesirable results, the *best* procedure to follow generally is for the supervisor to

    (A) indicate to his superior his doubts and reasons for them.
    (B) carry out the instructions as given without question.
    (C) accept the orders but modify them in carrying them out.
    (D) carry out the instructions, calling to his superior's attention any undesirable outcome.

37. You are instructing a group of newly assigned police officers concerning their responsibilities when testifying in court. One of the officers asks, "What should I do when the defense attorney objects to a question asked by the prosecutor?" Your most appropriate response should be

    (A) answer quickly since it is important for your side of the incident to be heard.
    (B) do not answer until the judge has ruled on the objection.
    (C) ask the prosecuting attorney to rephrase the question.
    (D) answer carefully so that your statements do not hurt the people's case.

38. Within the jurisdiction where you are the acting chief, a crime wave has begun in a wealthy residential district. For the past several years, this area has been almost crime free and you have not seen the need for any increased police patrols in that area. In response to complaints from influential residents, your town council has requested that you increase police presence in that area, including foot patrol. You have not been directed to do so, but the request from the town officials has been forceful. You do not have the equipment or personnel to respond to the request because of budget cutbacks. It would be most appropriate for you to

   (A) ask the town board to make the request an order and to put it in writing.
   (B) since you do not have the necessary wherewithal to respond to the request, ignore it.
   (C) reassign personnel from other areas within your jurisdiction to demonstrate to the town board that you are willing to respond to the problem.
   (D) meet with the town board and explain your problem in an effort to secure their assistance if they want you to proceed with the additional police presence in the affected area.

39. You are the ranking officer at the scene of a sexual assault of a 14-year-old girl by a 13-year-old boy, who has been placed under arrest. As the ranking officer you are responsible for responding to the media. You may release the time and place of arrest, the reason for the arrest, the nature of the charges, and

   (A) the name or address of the 14-year-old girl.
   (B) the name or address of the 13-year-old boy.
   (C) the content of any confession, statement, or admission made by the 13-year-old boy.
   (D) the scheduling of the judicial proceedings against the 13-year-old boy.

40. In a downtown area within your jurisdiction, parking has become a serious problem. Merchants have been complaining, residents have been complaining, and generally the area has become the focal point of much community dissatisfaction. You have prevailed upon the local governing body to institute new parking regulations that are designed to alleviate the problem. The new regulations have met with general opposition from persons in the area. Your *first* reaction to this should be to

   (A) determine whether the opposition is truly general or only part of a small vocal group's concern.
   (B) determine whether the people affected thereby understand the reasons behind the new parking restrictions.
   (C) find out whether your officers are at fault because of improper enforcement.
   (D) determine whether the new restrictions are necessary.

Directions: Each of the following questions, 41 to 45, is based upon a group of sentences. The sentences may be scrambled, but when they are correctly arranged, they form a well-organized paragraph. Read the sentences, and then answer the questions by choosing the most appropriate arrangement.

41.
1. The problem of corruption is neither new nor confined to the police.
2. Reports of prior investigations into police corruption make it abundantly clear that police corruption has been a problem for years.
3. On the contrary, in every area where police corruption exists it is paralleled by corruption in other agencies of government.
4. This does not mean that the police have a monopoly on corruption.
(A) 1—2—3—4
(B) 2—1—3—4
(C) 1—2— 4—3
(D) 4—1—2—3

42.
1. To understand these feelings, one must appreciate that an important characteristic of any police department is intense group loyalty.
2. When properly understood, this group loyalty can be used in the fight against corruption.
3. If misunderstood or ignored, then it can undermine anticorruption activities.
4. Feelings of isolation and hostility are experienced by police officers not just in large cities, but everywhere.
(A) 1—2—3—4
(B) 4—1—2—3
(C) 4—2—1—3
(D) 3—2—1—4

43.
1. Everyone agrees that a police officer's life is a dangerous one.
2. It is less generally realized that a police officer works in a sea of hostility.
3. The police officer feels and naturally often returns this hostility.
4. Nobody, whether a burglar or a Sunday motorist, likes to have his activities interfered with.
(A) 1—2—3—4
(B) 1—2—4—3
(C) 4—1—2—3
(D) 2—1—4—3

44.
1. The "rotten-apple" doctrine of corruption has been a basic obstacle to meaningful reform.
2. The doctrine also made difficult, if not impossible, any meaningful attempt at managerial reform.
3. To begin with, it reinforced and gave respectability to the code of silence and made it difficult for someone to publicly disclose the extent of corruption in a department.
4. As a result, departments may fail to take adequate steps to make changes when sincere officers come forward with evidence of corruption.
(A) 1—4—3—2
(B) 4—2—1—3
(C) 2—1—3—4
(D) 1—3—2—4

45.
1. A basic weakness in the present approaches to the problem of corruption is that most agencies rely on police officers to do their investigative work.
2. In the case of district attorneys, there is the additional problem of their close relationship to the police.
3. The district attorneys and the department of investigation, although they have a few nonpolice investigators, depend primarily upon police officers to conduct investigations.
4. These conditions discourage complaints because many citizens just do not trust police officers to investigate each other.
(A) 1—2—3—4
(B) 1—3—2—4
(C) 4—1—3—2
(D) 3—1—4—2

Directions: Answer questions 46 to 50 on the basis of the information provided in the attached line graph. The graph represents "Crimes Against the Person" in your jurisdiction from 1992 to 2000.

Crimes Against the Person from 1992 to 2000

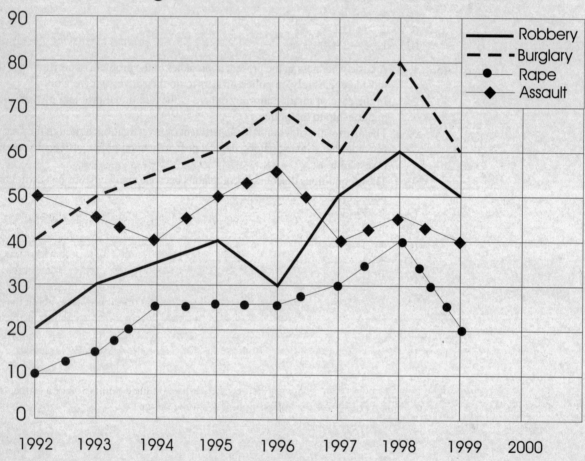

46. In which year was the ratio of robberies to rapes the greatest?

   (A) 1993
   (B) 1997
   (C) 1998
   (D) 1999

47. In which year did the ratio of rapes to robberies *not* change from the preceding year?

   (A) 1993
   (B) 1995
   (C) 1997
   (D) 1998

48. Most nearly, what was the percentage increase in assaults from 1997 to 1998?
    (A) 11
    (B) 13
    (C) 20
    (D) 8

49. Most nearly, what was the percentage decrease in burglaries from 1998 to 1999?
    (A) 15
    (B) 20
    (C) 25
    (D) 50

50. If the number of robberies in 2000 increased by 10 percent over 1999, then, most nearly, how many robberies would there be in 2000?
    (A) 50
    (B) 55
    (C) 60
    (D) 65

Directions: Answer questions 51 to 53 on the basis of the following paragraph.

Automobile tire tracks found at the scene of a crime constitute an important link in the chain of physical evidence. In many cases, they are the only available clues. In some areas, unpaved ground adjoins the highway or paved streets. A suspect will often park his car off the paved portion of the street when committing a crime, sometimes leaving excellent tire tracks. Comparison of the tire track impressions with the tires is possible only when the vehicle has been found. However, the initial problem facing the police is to determine what kind of car probably made the impressions found at the scene of the crime. If the make, model, and year of the car that made the impressions can be determined, then it is obvious that the task of elimination is greatly lessened.

51. When searching for clear signs left by the car used in the commission of a crime, the most likely place for the police to look would be on the
    (A) highway adjoining an unpaved street.
    (B) highway adjacent to a paved street.
    (C) paved street adjacent to the highway.
    (D) unpaved ground adjacent to a highway.

52. Automobile tire tracks found at the scene of a crime are of value as evidence in that they are
    (A) generally sufficient to trap and convict a suspect.
    (B) the most important link in the chain of physical evidence.
    (C) often the only evidence at hand.
    (D) circumstantial rather than direct.

53. The primary reason for the police to try to find out which make, model, and year of car was involved in the commission of a crime is to

(A) compare the tire tracks left at the scene of the crime with the type of tires used on cars of that make.

(B) determine if the mud on the tires of the suspected car matches the mud in the unpaved road near the scene of the crime.

(C) reduce to a large extent the amount of work involved in determining the particular car used in the commission of a crime.

(D) alert the patrol force to question the occupants of all vehicles of this kind.

Directions: Answer questions 54 and 55 on the basis of the following paragraph.

A report of investigation should not be weighed down by a mass of information that is hardly material or only remotely relevant or which fails to prove a point, clarify an issue, or aid the inquiry even by indirection. Some investigative agencies, however, value the report for its own sake, considering it primarily as a justification of the investigative activity contained therein. Every step is listed to show that no logical measure has been overlooked and to demonstrate that the reporting agent is beyond criticism. This system serves to provide reviewing authorities with a ready means of checking subordinates and provides order, method, and routine to investigative activity. In addition, it may offer supervisors and investigators a sense of security; the investigator would know within fairly exact limits what is expected of him and the supervisor may be comforted by the knowledge that his organization may not be reasonably criticized in a particular case on the grounds of obvious omissions or inertia. To the state's attorney and others, however, who must take administrative action on the basis of the report, the irrelevant and immaterial information thwarts the purpose of the investigation by dimming the issues and obscuring the facts that are truly contributory to the proof.

54. From the point of view of the supervising investigator, a drawback of having the investigator prepare the kind of report that the state's attorney would like is that it

(A) gives a biased and one-sided view of what should have been an impartial investigation.

(B) has only limited usefulness as an indication that all proper investigative methods were used by the investigator.

(C) overlooks logical measures, removing the responsibility for taking those measures that the investigator should otherwise have been expected to take.

(D) sets fairly exact limits to what the supervisor can expect of the investigator.

55. District attorneys do not like reports of investigations in which every step is listed because

(A) their administrative action is then based on irrelevant and immaterial information.

(B) it places the investigator beyond criticism, making the responsibility of the district attorney that much greater.

(C) of the difficulty of finding among the mass of information the portion that is meaningful and useful.

(D) the inclusion of indirect or hardly material information is not in accord with the order in which the steps were taken.

Directions: Answer questions 56 and 57 on the basis of the following paragraph.

Pickpockets operate most effectively when there are prospective victims in either heavily congested areas or lonely places. In heavily populated areas, the large number of people about them covers the activities of these thieves. In lonely spots, they have the advantage of working unobserved. The main factor in the pickpocket's success is the selection of the "right" victim. A pickpocket's victim must, at the time of the crime, be inattentive, distracted, or unconscious. If any of these conditions exist, and if the pickpocket is skilled in his operations, the stage is set for a successful larceny. With the coming of winter, the crowds move southward and so do most of the pickpockets. However, some pickpockets will remain in certain areas all year round. They will concentrate on theater districts, bus and railroad terminals, hotels, or large shopping centers. A complete knowledge of the methods of pickpockets and the ability to recognize them come only from long years of experience in performing patient surveillance and trailing of them. This knowledge is essential for the effective control and apprehension of this type of thief.

56. According to this paragraph, the one of the following factors that is *not* necessary for the successful operation of the pickpocket is that

(A) he is proficient in the operations required to pick pockets.
(B) the "right'" potential victims be those who have been the subject of such a theft previously.
(C) his operation be hidden from the view of others.
(D) the potential victim be unaware of the actions of the pickpocket.

57. According to this paragraph, it would be most correct to conclude that police officers who are successful in apprehending pickpockets

(A) are generally those who have had lengthy experience in recognizing all kinds of criminals.
(B) must, by intuition, be able to recognize potential "right" victims.
(C) must follow the pickpockets in their southward movement.
(D) must have acquired specific knowledge and skills in this field.

Directions: Answer questions 58 to 60 on the basis of the following paragraph.

Discontent of some citizens with the practices and policies of local government leads here and there to creation of those American institutions called the local civic associations. These associations are completely outside of government, manned by a few devoted volunteers, understaffed, and with few dues-paying members, they attempt to arouse widespread public opinion on selected issues by presenting facts and ideas. The findings of these civic associations are widely trusted by press and public, and amidst the records of rebuffs received are found more than enough achievements to justify what little their activities cost. Civic associations can, by use of the initiative, get constructive measures placed on the ballot and the influence of these associations is substantial when brought to bear on a referendum question. Civic associations are politically nonpartisan. Hence their vitality is drawn from true political independents, who in most communities are a trifling minority. Except in a few large cities, civic associations are seldom affluent enough to maintain an office or to afford even a small paid staff.

58. It can be inferred from the paragraph that the main reason for the formation of civic associations is to

    (A) provide independent candidates for local public office with an opportunity to be heard.
    (B) bring about changes is the activities of local government.
    (G) allow persons who are politically nonpartisan to express themselves on local public issues.
    (D) permit the small minority of true political independents to supply leadership for nonpartisan causes.

59. According to the paragraph, the statements that civic associations make on issues of general interest are

    (A) accepted by large segments of the public.
    (B) taken at face value only by the few people who are true political independents.
    (C) questioned as to their accuracy by most newspapers.
    (D) expressed as a result of aroused, widespread public opinion.

60. On the basis of the information concerning civic associations contained in the paragraph, it is most accurate to conclude that since

    (A) they deal with many public issues, the cost of their efforts on each issue is small.
    (B) their attempts to attain their objectives often fail and little money is contributed to civic associations.
    (C) they spend little money in their efforts and they are ineffective when they become involved in major issues.
    (D) their achievements outweigh the small cost of their efforts; civic associations are considered worthwhile.

61. "In the clinical approach to disciplinary problems, attention is focused on the basic causes of which the overt actions are merely symptomatic rather than on the specific violations that have brought the employee unfavorable notice." The most accurate implication of this quotation is that the clinical approach

    (A) results in the prompt and more uniform treatment of violators.
    (B) does not evaluate the justice and utility of penalties that may be applied in each case.
    (C) provides for greater insight into the underlying factors that have led to the infractions of discipline.
    (D) avoids the necessity for disciplinary action.

62. Having decided to institute disciplinary action against a subordinate in his command, a sergeant speaks to the subordinate for the purpose of informing him of the action to be taken. At this interview, it would be *least* advisable for the sergeant to explain to the subordinate

    (A) the procedural steps that will follow the institution of disciplinary action.
    (B) the specific reason for the disciplinary action.
    (C) that the purpose of discipline is the punishment of the offender.
    (D) what is expected of the subordinate in the future, especially as related to the behavior that resulted in disciplinary action being taken.

63. The use of positive discipline by a supervisor will enhance the morale of the personnel. Of the following, the *best* example of positive discipline is

    (A) assigning unpleasant duties purely as an educational device.
    (B) reprimanding in public and very soon after the negligent act.
    (C) suggesting methods of work improvement when reviewing work that is poorly done.
    (D) adjusting the severity of the punishment to the severity of the offense.

64. With the proper administration of discipline, actions essentially negative should seldom be necessary. Of the following, the disciplinary attitude that is most consistent with this statement is that

(A) punitive action should be taken primarily to deter more serious infractions of basic rules.

(B) even the most persistent offender can be trained to the point of acceptable performance.

(C) disciplinary actions should usually be accompanied by some form of commendation.

(D) mistakes or poor judgment should be treated essentially as training matters.

65. Which of the following principles is *least* appropriate for effective administration of discipline?

(A) The basic purpose of discipline is the exercise of authority to implement command responsibility.

(B) Every violator should be encouraged to correct his or her faults.

(C) Adequate written records of disciplinary actions should be maintained.

(D) Punishment should be the last resort of the effective disciplinarian.

66. All infractions should be met with equally fair, but firm, treatment, even if the infraction is of a minor nature. For a superior officer to follow this rule generally would be

(A) advisable; alertness on the part of the superior is normal and expected.

(B) inadvisable; the severity of any disciplinary action should not exceed the seriousness of the offense.

(C) advisable; overlooking minor infractions may lead to serious trouble.

(D) inadvisable; the superior officer could occupy his time more profitably by spending it on serious police affairs instead of on trivial matters.

67. Offenses, superficially alike, may be so different fundamentally that uniformity in the corrective measures applied would be, in fact, discriminatory. The most important supervisory implication of this idea for a police supervisor is that this view in practice

(A) contradicts the rule of the certain and firm application of disciplinary measures for all offenses.

(B) requires that punishment for like offenses must be uniformly applied to avoid the rise of discriminatory practices.

(C) seeks to discover the basic reason for the offense as a guide to appropriate corrective measures.

(D) tends to destroy the value of punishment as a corrective device.

68. As a police administrator, you will be called upon to prepare a budget for your agency. Consider the following statements regarding budgeting and determine which one is *not* correct.

(A) As the department administrator, it is your task to inform your jurisdiction's governing body of the economic needy of your agency.

(B) The budget is a function that can facilitate control within the agency.

(C) Budgeting should be viewed as an administration planning function.

(D) A specific time period, close to the end of any budget period, should be set aside for budget preparation.

69. Which budgeting system is utterly simple and will be used mainly by smaller agencies?

(A) Zero-based budgeting

(B) Line-item budgeting

(C) Program budgeting

(D) Performance budgeting

70. As a recently appointed lieutenant, you have decided that disciplinary action is to be taken against a subordinate under your supervision. In this situation, it is most important for you to realize that

   (A) disciplinary action, once decided upon, should be taken quickly.
   (B) disciplinary action should be postponed for reconsideration at a later date when you have acquired more supervisory experience.
   (C) the mildest form of discipline should be tried first.
   (D) you should request your commanding officer to decide whether or not any disciplinary action should be taken.

71. It is a generally accepted principle of supervision that disciplinary action should be taken quickly when it needs to be taken. The statement that best supports taking prompt disciplinary action is that

   (A) the accuracy of official disciplinary records will thereby be insured.
   (B) the offender is more likely to believe that the disciplinary action will be severe.
   (C) the supervisor is more likely to remember the details surrounding the offender's breach of discipline.
   (D) there is an avoidance of the prolonged aggravation caused by later disposition of the case.

72. What is the most proper attitude for you, as a superior officer, to adopt toward complaints from the public?

   (A) Not only accept complaints, but establish a regular procedure by which they may be filed.
   (B) Avoid encouraging correspondence with the public on the subject of complaints.
   (C) Recognize that human nature is such that "grouches" will always be found.
   (D) Remember that your duty is to get the job done well, not to act as a public relations officer.

73. Police public relations has been defined as the combined deliberate effort of all employees of the department to implant in the minds of the people the idea that police officers are friendly, understanding, capable, and willing to be of service to the community. This definition is

   (A) invalid; sometimes information that is critical of police operations must be released to the public.
   (B) valid; if the public image of the department is to be good, then all members must participate.
   (C) invalid; the department must enforce unpopular regulations that offend many individuals.
   (D) valid; every police officer must fully appreciate that the public has a right to know what the department is doing.

74. The most acceptable technique to be used by the police public relations officer is that he or she should

   (A) plan for all members of the department to participate in the departmental public relations program.
   (B) concentrate public relations activities in his or her own office in order to avoid conflicting public statements or activities by subordinates.
   (C) emphasize to the public the information that presents the police in the most favorable light and withhold that which is detrimental to the police position.
   (D) occasionally emphasize to the public the information that is critical of police operations as a public demonstration of the objectivity of the department.

75. Reports need to be as concise as possible. When instructing your subordinates on report writing, which of the following should not be included in a report so that it will be as concise as possible?

    (A) Descriptors
    (B) Police jargon
    (C) Nonessential modifiers
    (D) None of these choices

76. As a practical matter, the criminal investigator should consider his investigation completed when a confession has been properly obtained. This statement is generally

    (A) true; for the investigator to continue the investigation beyond this point would be an inefficient use of his investigative time.
    (B) false; added weight and credibility will probably be given to the confession itself by the jury if the investigator continues with his investigation.
    (C) true; the prosecution of the case may be handicapped if it appears that the investigator is personally interested in obtaining a conviction by continuing his investigation.
    (D) false; attempts should be made to obtain additional evidence that is almost always required to prove guilt beyond a reasonable doubt.

77. What chemical is used to develop latent prints by producing a chemical reaction, generally in a fuming tank or by the use of a fuming wand, and produces a white powder substance on the print?

    (A) Cyanoacrylate
    (B) Silver nitrate
    (C) Iodine
    (D) Ninhydrin

78. It is not possible for anyone, not even the skilled prosecutor, to determine exactly which items of physical evidence found at the scene of a crime will eventually be declared admissible as evidence by the court. For a competent police officer this should mean that

    (A) evidence that has been collected as soon as possible after the commission of the crime is recognized as admissible by skilled prosecutors.
    (B) items of physical evidence should be collected in spite of some doubt as to their admissibility.
    (C) the admissibility of evidence is a technical matter concerning which the police officer has no guides.
    (D) the district attorney or her assistant should be summoned to every crime scene to offer guides as to what may be admissible in evidence.

79. Which of the following guidelines for the collection and care of physical evidence is *incorrect*?

    (A) Each bit of evidence should be collected and preserved as a separate sample whenever necessary to prevent intermingling of known evidence with unknown evidence.
    (B) When evidence is found in the presence of a foreign substance, a sample of this substance should also be obtained.
    (C) Documents should be folded and enclosed in a glassine or other transparent envelope for transportation.
    (D) Identifying marks should be inscribed on large articles of evidence for later identification.

80. Sound police procedures require that the officers assigned examine the scene of an explosion as soon as possible after the explosion, and that photographs and accurately scaled sketches of the scene are made. The chief purpose of such sketches is to

   (A) show the extent of the damage done to persons as compared with the damage done to property.
   (B) provide information about distances and details shown in the photographs.
   (C) enable the officers to testify as to their own observations.
   (D) reduce the time spent on the investigation by pinpointing the seat or center of the explosion.

81. Which of the following chemical tests is *not* used in the identification of bloodstains found at crime scenes?

   (A) Benzidine test
   (B) Phenolphthalein test
   (C) Walker test
   (D) Teichman test

82. Research studies on patterns of informal communication have concluded that most individuals in a group tend to be passive recipients of news, while a few make it their business to spread it around in an organization. With this conclusion in mind, it would be most correct for the sergeant to attempt to identify these few individuals and

   (A) give them the complete facts on important matters in advance of others.
   (B) inform the other subordinates of the identity of these few individuals so that their influence may be minimized.
   (C) keep them informed of the facts on important matters.
   (D) warn them to cease passing along any information to others.

83. Roger has been arrested and is in police custody. When his rights are explained to him, he freely and voluntarily waives those rights and consents to be questioned in the absence of an attorney. While the questioning is going on, Roger says "You know what officer, I think I want my lawyer here to advise me." If you are the interrogating officer, then you should

   (A) explain to Roger that his waiver cannot be rescinded.
   (B) end the interrogation.
   (C) continue the interrogation, but record it on video to show it was not done in a coercive atmosphere.
   (D) tell Roger that he can consult with his attorney when the interrogation is completed.

84. Some of the most persistent and acute problems of administration, especially in large or decentralized organizations such as a large urban police department, stem from deficiencies in horizontal communication. Of the following methods, the one that will tend to diminish this problem the most is the

   (A) emphasis on demonstration and visual aid techniques rather than question-answer methods.
   (B) provision for more face-to-face contacts on policy between subordinate and superior officers.
   (C) greater use of conferences to exchange information between officers of the same rank.
   (D) greater emphasis on the use of clear, concise language in the issue of commands or orders.

85. Which one of the following is the primary purpose of the regular staff meeting in a police agency?

    (A) Initiation of action in order to get the agency's work done
    (B) Staff training and development
    (C) Program and policy determination
    (D) Communication of new policies and procedures

86. The value of the group conference method in supervision lies primarily in the fact that it

    (A) relieves incompetent workers from making decisions and assuming responsibility.
    (B) affords an opportunity for shared thinking and joint participation in solving problems.
    (C) eliminates the necessity for individual conferences with the supervisor.
    (D) assures a uniformity of knowledge and skill of the workers.

87. The twelve-month probationary period of a newly appointed police officer is important to a supervising officer primarily because

    (A) this time is necessary to inculcate in the officer the ideals and objectives for his job and of the department.
    (B) this time is required for the supervising officer and the older members to accept and understand the recruit.
    (C) it serves as a check on the selection process made prior to appointment.
    (D) it is necessary for completion of suitable recruit training and adjustment.

88. It has been stated, that "longevity among the mediocre, rather than leadership, may become in reality the basis of promotion." Applied to selection for promotion to ranks above captain in many departments, this condition may most effectively be prevented by a policy of

    (A) considering the job performance factor in selection for promotion.
    (B) disregarding the experience factor of those being considered for promotion.
    (C) extending of civil service promotion to all ranks.
    (D) lowering the compulsory retirement age.

89. A captain observes that one of his sergeants customarily "does over" a subordinate's work when that subordinate's work is inadequate or unacceptable. The sergeant's reason for this practice is that he sets high standards and requires that all the work of his unit be done well. The captain is evaluating the sergeant. Which one of the following choices most currently states whether the sergeant's practice is good or bad and is also the most important reason for it?

    (A) This practice is good because it results in the work being done well.
    (B) This practice is bad because it corrodes the initiative and morale of the subordinate.
    (C) This practice is bad because it creates in the subordinate a lack of confidence in the sergeant.
    (D) This practice is good because it sets high standards and requires the individual to achieve them.

90. In reviewing a detective's cases in preparation for a periodic evaluation, you note that he has done a uniformly good job with certain kinds of cases, and poor work with other kinds of cases. Of the following, the best approach for you to take in this situation is to

    (A) bring this to the detective's attention, find out why he favors certain clients, and discuss ways in which he can improve his service to all complainants.
    (B) bring this to the detective's attention and suggest that he may need professional counseling, as he seems to be blocked in working with certain cases.
    (C) assign the detective mainly those cases that he handles best and transfer the kinds of cases that he handles poorly to another detective.
    (D) accept the fact that a detective cannot be expected to give uniformly good service to all and take no further action.

91. In which of the following situations would Miranda warnings *not* be required?

    (A) The questioning of a person already placed under arrest
    (B) The questioning of a person suspected of having committed a crime
    (C) The questioning of a person who is in custody, but whose attorney is already present and representing him
    (D) The questioning of an attorney who has been placed under arrest for a serious crime

92. In which of the following situations would Miranda warnings be necessary?

    (A) In the event of volunteered statement
    (B) In the case of a "field investigation" to get the facts as opposed to an "in-custody" interrogation
    (C) In the case of interrogation by a civilian or a private security officer
    (D) In the case of an "in-custody" interrogation of a suspect in the absence of an attorney

93. You are on patrol late at night in a residential area. You observe a man carrying a portable television, several radios, and other objects. You stop him to question him. While you are questioning him he blurts out a confession that he is a burglar. The point in time at which you should give Miranda warnings before asking questions would be

    (A) at the initial stop, since you had probable cause to make an arrest.
    (B) when the suspect gave you evasive answers concerning his activities.
    (C) after the suspect blurts out his confession, since at this point probable cause for the arrest clearly exists.
    (D) at the station house prior to interrogation by detectives.

94. Probable cause is something that must be understood by police officers. Probable cause is best defined as a combination of facts or apparent facts that, viewed through the eyes of an experienced police officer, would lead a person of reasonable caution to believe that a crime is being or has been committed. Which of the following statements is *least* accurate concerning the concept of probable cause?

    (A) Hearsay evidence may form the basis of probable cause.
    (B) The fact of flight from a police officer is universally recognized as a probable cause fact.
    (C) Admissions before an arrest or evasive answers constitute probable cause facts.
    (D) When sufficient probable cause is present, it is not necessary for the police to obtain a search warrant before conducting a search.

95. Which of the following statements is *not* correct concerning the need to have a search warrant?

    (A) Hotel rooms are protected by the Fourth Amendment.
    (B) Houses that are temporarily unoccupied are protected by the Fourth Amendment.
    (C) Landlords and managers of hotels can validly consent to a search of rooms or apartments leased out by them.
    (D) When a person permanently checks out of a hotel room, he or she no longer has a right to privacy in the room and a search of it may be made without a warrant.

96. Certain powers of the police are investigative powers and thus do not require probable cause to put them into action, only some prior factual justification for their use. Which of the following would *not* be considered a police investigative power?

    (A) Stopping suspects
    (B) Frisking suspects
    (C) Attempting to obtain valid consents for search
    (D) Searching for contraband in vehicles

97. No one can dispute the dominant role that hearsay plays in modern police work. This is why the police must know how the courts evaluate hearsay. Which of the following is *least* correct concerning hearsay?

    (A) The hearsay rule does not bar the presentation of hearsay information at probable cause inquiries.
    (B) With respect to hearsay at the probable cause stage, all that is required is that the police officer accepts the information in good faith.
    (C) In determining probable cause that is based on hearsay information, the court will consider the source of the hearsay information.
    (D) At the probable cause stage of an investigation, the usual rules of evidence apply.

98. A health department inspector who is making a routine inspection of a restaurant observes contraband inside the restaurant. She reports it to the police. For the police to go to the restaurant and search it without first obtaining a search warrant would be

    (A) proper, since the source of the information is reliable.
    (B) improper, since a search warrant should be obtained on the basis of the information applied.
    (C) improper, since searches of premises without a warrant are never reasonable.
    (D) proper, since there was probable cause to believe the contraband was there and that it might be moved.

99. Which of the following statements concerning the United States Constitution is *least* accurate?

    (A) The Fourth Amendment insures right to privacy by prohibiting unreasonable searches and seizures.
    (B) The Fifth Amendment protects a citizen from self-incrimination.
    (C) The Sixth Amendment guarantees right to counsel in a proper case.
    (D) The Fourteenth Amendment insures freedom of assembly and petition.

100. A "Penn Register" is most accurately described as

    (A) an electronic device used to identify telephone numbers called.
    (B) an electronic device used in connection with polygraph tests to measure and record certain variations in bodily responses.
    (C) a listing of released convicts maintained by officials at the state penitentiary.
    (D) the required registry record book that must be maintained by all hotels licensed to operate as a hotel.

101. Police Officer Connolly works for you, and he has been late for work five times in the past month. If you consider it advisable to conduct a disciplinary action interview with Officer Connolly, then its primary objective should be to

    (A) convince Officer Connolly to get to work on time.
    (B) make an example of Officer Connolly so that the other officers will not pick up his bad habits.
    (C) convince Officer Connolly that if he is late again, he will be punished.
    (D) make certain that Officer Connolly understands the department's policy concerning lateness.

102. You are in command of a special unit. You have noticed that report processing within your unit is not up to par. You are not sure of the reasons why this unacceptable condition exists, and you decide to interview various members of your unit in an effort to gather facts. Before conducting any of these interviews, it would be best for you to

    (A) ask involved subordinates to prepare a list of recommended changes in procedures.
    (B) let the involved employees know the reasons for the interview.
    (C) compile statistical data regarding the duties of the members involved.
    (D) not divulge any information concerning the interviews so that those involved can approach the interview with an open mind.

103. Occasionally, as a police supervisor, it will be necessary for you to take negative corrective action against a subordinate who has engaged in misconduct. Knowing that this must be done sometimes, which of the following approaches would it be best for you to use?

    (A) Publicize it throughout the department as a preventive measure.
    (B) Carry it out promptly.
    (C) Make certain that similar breaches receive equal punishment.
    (D) Make an apology first so that morale is not adversely affected.

104. Because you have uncovered misconduct on the part of Police Officer Mullins, you have decided to conduct a disciplinary action interview of Officer Mullins. It would be best for you to understand that the purpose of this interview is to

    (A) find out why Officer Mullins misbehaved.
    (B) evaluate the seriousness of Officer Mullins' transgression.
    (C) let Officer Mullins know that his transgression has been discovered.
    (D) change Officer Mullins' attitude and behavior.

105. The ability to communicate clearly has often been said to be the most important single skill that a supervisor should possess. Communications may be oral or they may be written. With respect to written communications, as a knowledgeable police supervisor you should know that, as between you and your subordinates, your written communications will be most effective if

    (A) formal organization channels are used.
    (B) they utilize informality in choice of language.
    (C) they are timely.
    (D) they contain in-depth detail.

106. You are the commander of a unit that has a great deal of contact with the public in your jurisdiction. A good reason for you to meet with and interview these officers periodically is to

    (A) demonstrate your interest in their work.
    (B) use these meetings as a training device.
    (C) gauge public reaction to the policies of your unit.
    (D) convince your subordinates that public sensitivity should be paramount.

107. You have just been appointed to a supervisory rank. You have attended a "command" school where the requisites of good communications skills have been emphasized. Using all of this newly acquired supervisory and administrative know-how, which of the following would be the *best* way for you to give orders and/or directions to subordinates?

    (A) Give a general indication of how the work should be done.
    (B) Describe a general procedure to be followed, but permit your subordinates to work out their own methods.
    (C) Your orders and directions should be exact and no essential points should be left out.
    (D) Point out those areas in which trouble might develop.

108. You are a unit supervisor, and your unit has been experiencing difficult work problems. You have decided to call a conference with the subordinates within your unit concerning these problems. Of the following, the best justification in support of your decision is

    (A) the consultations will serve as a training device for your subordinates.
    (B) by so doing, you can shed some of your responsibility for the results.
    (C) it will permit you to reach the best solution to a given problem more quickly.
    (D) it may increase understanding and develop cooperation.

109. You are a unit supervisor. Police Officer Judy Milowe comes to you with a grievance. You listen attentively to Officer Milowe, which permits her to ventilate and to engage in a mental catharsis. When she has finished with her grievance, it would be best for you to

    (A) convince her that her grievance is not well-founded.
    (B) tell her exactly what you plan to do about it.
    (C) "play" her grievance back to her, in summarized fashion, to be sure that you understand what her grievance is.
    (D) advise her that, when your supervisory duties permit, you will act on her grievance.

110. Which of the following terms best describes the concept of "ventilating" when a subordinate is airing a grievance?

    (A) Fixation
    (B) Catharsis
    (C) Doppler effect
    (D) Brainstorming

111. A supervisor in a unit is faced with a number of tasks to be performed. Of the following tasks, for which would the interview be *least* suitable?

    (A) To obtain information from a suspected employee about alleged criminal activity
    (B) To try to improve the performance of an employee whose work performance has slipped
    (C) To communicate to an employee a new policy of the organization
    (D) To advise an employee with respect to his or her career potential

112. As a supervisor, you conduct periodic staff meetings with your subordinates. At these staff meetings, without fail, you discuss problems being experienced by your unit and by the department. The most likely result of your staff meeting policy is that

    (A) no benefit will result because your subordinates will lose interest in the problems.
    (B) subordinate confidence in the unit and the department will be diminished when they realize there are unsolved problems.
    (C) subordinates, aware of what problems are being faced by the unit and the department, will have a better understanding of the results of their efforts.
    (D) subordinates will become bored with such an approach and will silently say, "No, not again."

113. As a police administrator, you may find it necessary to make and then introduce changes in operations to increase effectiveness and efficiency. Knowing that change sometimes meets with resistance, it would be best for you to

    (A) make certain that your subordinates understand the reasons behind the changed procedures.
    (B) get the support of your subordinate superiors.
    (C) keep the changes simple and then put them into effect promptly.
    (D) compose a written department directive and post it on the bulletin board as an order.

114. Sergeant Connolly has made a street decision regarding a police problem based on the facts at hand. Unfortunately, his decision was erroneous and further action had to be taken to solve the problem. At a critique of the situation later on, Sergeant Connolly readily admitted that he had made an error. Sergeant Connolly, in admitting his error in this way, will probably cause his subordinates to

    (A) lose their respect for him.
    (B) become more confident in his ability.
    (C) be less willing to make decisions on their own.
    (D) more readily admit their own errors if and when they make them.

115. Sergeant Mullins approaches his commanding officer and asks, "Captain, in your opinion, what should I look for to determine whether or not I am succeeding as a supervisor?" Captain Milowe's most appropriate response should be

    (A) "If your subordinates continue to try to advance in rank by studying for promotion, then it means they want to be like you."
    (B) "If your subordinates come to you when they need help and then use your help to get the job done, then consider yourself a success."
    (C) "If no one ever asks for a transfer out of your squad, then you must be doing something right."
    (D) "If they help you to work out and decide how to handle recurring problems, then you are a success."

116. Supervisors, whether interviewing or interrogating, will find questions to be a valuable tool. However, unless caution is exercised, questions may work at cross-purposes to the aims of the interviewer-interrogator. Evaluate the following statements:

    I.   Questions may be used in starting the conversation or delving deeper into a specific area.
    II. Studies have shown that questions framed in negative terms have a tendency to elicit inaccurate responses more frequently than positive questions.
    III. The best questions are those that can be answered with a simple "yes" or "no" reply.
    IV. Leading questions such as, "Don't you like this graveyard shift?" should he avoided.
    (A) All the preceding statements are correct.
    (B) None of the preceding statements is correct.
    (C) Statements I and II are correct, but III and IV are not.
    (D) Statements I, II, and IV are correct, but III is not.

117. The following are three statements that may or may not be valid concerning the interview of two or three victims at the same crime scene.

I. The victims should be interviewed together since the speedy development of information at this point in the investigation is crucial.

II. Taking notes or making tape recordings should be avoided since this tends to upset the victims and may make them reluctant to answer certain questions.

III. The interviewing of all the victims should be done by one investigator rather than by two or more.

Which one of the following best classifies the above statements?

(A) Statement I is generally valid, but II and III are not.

(B) Statement III is generally valid, but I and II are not.

(C) Statements I and II are generally valid, but III is not.

(D) Statements I and III are generally valid, but II is not.

118. You have been directed to prepare an in-service training lecture for the sergeants in your command. The subject matter is discipline. You make each of the following points in your outline. Which would *not* be considered as being necessary for proper discipline within your agency?

(A) Specific internal guides such as rules and regulations should be informal.

(B) All supervisors must make the appropriate use of disciplinary measures.

(C) There must be procedures established for the handling of employee grievances.

(D) Before holding officers accountable for a job, you must delegate sufficient authority to them to carry out that task.

119. The following would be considered primary objectives of a personnel complaint investigation policy, *except* to

(A) protect the integrity and the reputation of the department.

(B) protect the public interest.

(C) protect an employee from an unjust accusation.

(D) insure that all complaints, including anonymous ones, are fully investigated.

120. John Jones calls his neighborhood precinct from his home and volunteers to give the supervisor taking the call information about a double homicide that he witnessed. Of the following, it would be most appropriate for the supervisor to

(A) have the witness interviewed at home as soon as possible.

(B) send a police car to bring the witness in to the police station for an interview.

(C) take down the major items of information over the telephone, but do not interview the witness in person until all other available information has been gathered.

(D) ask the witness to come to the police station immediately for an interview.

MODEL EXAMINATION 2: ANSWERS AND EXPLANATIONS

1. **The correct answer is (A).** Remember, the first-line supervisor exercises the most influence on subordinates and is in the best position to see training needs.

2. **The correct answer is (C).** It has been said that a sergeant's shield should contain the word "responsibility."

3. **The correct answer is (D).** No subordinate should be unsupervised. Even the best officer working for you needs direct supervision.

4. **The correct answer is (D).** Once more, a supervisor's main responsibility is to get the job done.

5. **The correct answer is (C).** As a supervisor, you will receive the kind of performance from your subordinates that you are willing to accept. Set your standards high, but do not make them unreasonable.

6. **The correct answer is (A).** This is the same as in the last question.

7. **The correct answer is (B).** This is the only acceptable response.

8. **The correct answer is (D).** The supervisor who knows her own job thoroughly impresses subordinates with her competence and gains their respect. The supervisor does not have to be able to perform each subordinate's job better than the subordinate.

9. **The correct answer is (D).** Conceptually, this is the ideal. Promotion examinations may limit this ideal.

10. **The correct answer is (A).** Leadership qualities can be developed.

11. **The correct answer is (C).** You do not have to be a genius or a superhero in order to be an effective leader.

12. **The correct answer is (C).** Try to avoid solving the problem for the subordinate. It is better if he or she solves the problem. Remember, you must become involved in personal problems of subordinates when you are asked or when the problem affects job performance.

13. **The correct answer is (D).** The only acceptable response of the choices given.

14. **The correct answer is (C).** The opportunity for immediate feedback is what distinguishes oral from written communication. But remember, written communications should be used for complex operations when many subordinates are involved, or when you want to hold someone strictly accountable.

15. **The correct answer is (A).** This is a form of participative management that tends to be very effective.

16. **The correct answer is (B).** If it becomes a problem, then take steps to correct it.

17. **The correct answer is (D).** This is somewhat related in concept to question 12.

18. **The correct answer is (C).** It is the supervisor's job to get the job done through others.

19. **The correct answer is (C).** Enthusiastic cooperation is an advantage of participatory management.

20. **The correct answer is (B).** Except perhaps in an emergency, it is never wrong to explain. The ideal way to deal with change is to explain the need and then introduce it gradually.

21. **The correct answer is (A).** Doesn't this "get the job done"? But consider that you might want to develop a promising subordinate by assigning tasks to him that are slightly beyond his current ability. Make him stretch.

22. **The correct answer is (B).** Sergeant Mullins is avoiding having to document his "super excellent" rating of P.O. Connolly by downgrading the rating to the more central category of "excellent." If P.O. Connolly really is that good, then he will suffer from this error.

23. **The correct answer is (C).** Have him "play it back" in his own words.

24. **The correct answer is (C).** This is an *implied* order. An implied order must be used sparingly; it cannot be used all the time with everybody. An insensitive sergeant, even if experienced and reliable, might not even recognize an implied order as an order. You must know the officers reporting to you.

25. **The correct answer is (B).** When a supervisor gives an order it must be viewed as his order. He must convey the idea that he is 100 percent behind the order.

26. **The correct answer is (D).** When you delegate you must delegate *authority* as well as *responsibility* (accountability). Remember, delegation never relieves the bass of ultimate responsibility.

27. **The correct answer is (B).** This error is similar to both personal bias and the halo effect.

28. **The correct answer is (B).** You will rarely be wrong if your orders are clear and understandable.

29. **The correct answer is (A).** When in doubt, have him "play it back" in his own words.

30. **The correct answer is (B).** We have seen this concept before. When there is general reluctance to obey, the fault probably lies with the supervisor.

31. **The correct answer is (B).** Explaining the order is always a good option.

32. **The correct answer is (D).** Explain carefully in advance. Remember, if it is a complex matter you should put it in writing.

33. **The correct answer is (C).** When the supervisor establishes objective standards of performance, he can spend more time planning and less time actually supervising details of an operation.

34. **The correct answer is (A).** This is a common sense answer.

35. **The correct answer is (A).** When in doubt, have them "play it back" in their own words.

36. **The correct answer is (A).** You have a duty to make your objections known. Having done so, if your boss tells you to carry out the order, carry it out as long as it is not unlawful.

37. **The correct answer is (B).** In the courtroom, the judge is "the boss." If an attorney has raised an objection to a question, then you must remain silent until the judge rules. Then answer (or do not answer) depending on the ruling.

38. **The correct answer is (D).** The question establishes that you do not have the necessary resources to respond. Explain your problem to the board.

39. **The correct answer is (D).** Age-sensitive material should not be released to the press. Only material of a general nature should be released.

40. **The correct answer is (B).** This is not an easy question. Most competitors tend to choose choice (D), but if the restrictions were not necessary, why were they instituted in the first place? Education might be the key to success. Remember, when reasons for actions are known, resistance can be reduced.

41. **The correct answer is (C).** This is an easy question if you read carefully and think.

42. **The correct answer is (B).** The obvious opening sequence is 4—1.

43. **The correct answer is (B).** A little more thinking is required here. The good reader will realize that 4 must come before 3.

44. **The correct answer is (D).** Sentence 1 is the best opening sentence, and the word "it" in sentence 3 refers to the "rotten-apple" doctrine.

45. **The correct answer is (B).** In sentence 1, there is a reference to "most" agencies. In sentence 3, two of these agencies are dealt with. In sentence 2, one of these two agencies is singled out.

46. **The correct answer is (D).** The ratios of robberies to rapes were as follows:

Year	Robberies	Rapes	Ratio
1993	30	15	2 to 1
1997	50	30	5 to 3
1998	60	40	3 to 2
1999	50	20	5 to 2

The greatest ratio is 5 to 2 = 1999.

47. **The correct answer is (A).** Ratios of rapes to robberies were as follows:

Prior Year		Year in Question		Ratio
1992	10 to 20	1993	15 to 30	Same
1994	25 to 35	1995	25 to 40	Not the same
1996	25 to 30	1997	30 to 50	Not the same
1997	30 to 50	1998	40 to 60	Not the same

The ration of rapes to robberies did not change from 1992 to 1993.

48. **The correct answer is (B).** 1997 Assaults = 40 and 1998 Assaults = 45

$$\frac{5}{40} = \frac{1}{8} = 12.5 \text{ percent} = \text{best answer is 13 percent}$$

49. **The correct answer is (C).** 1998 Burglaries = 80 and 1999 Burglaries = 60

$$\frac{20}{80} = \frac{1}{4} = 25 \text{ percent}$$

50. **The correct answer is (B).** 1999 Robberies = 50

    2000 Robberies = 50 + 10 percent of 50 = 55

51. **The correct answer is (D).** You will find the answer in the third and fourth sentences of the original paragraph.

52. **The correct answer is (C).** The answer is in the second sentence.

53. **The correct answer is (C).** The last sentence answers this question.

54. **The correct answer is (B).** The district attorney does not want a mass of irrelevant material.

55. **The correct answer is (C).** See the last sentence of the paragraph for the answer.

56. **The correct answer is (B).** Previous victims might be on their guard.

57. **The correct answer is (D).** The last two sentences provide the answer.

58. **The correct answer is (B).** The first sentence of the paragraph gives the answer.

59. **The correct answer is (A).** See the third sentence of the original paragraph.

60. **The correct answer is (D).** You will find the answer in the third sentence.

61. **The correct answer is (C).** This is a reading question.

62. **The correct answer is (C).** The purposes of discipline can be remembered as the acronym ASK; change *attitudes*, improve *skills*, and impart *knowledge*.

63. **The correct answer is (C).** Since the purposes of discipline are positive, that is to change attitudes, improve skills, and impart knowledge, positive discipline will improve performance and thereby raise morale. Of course, there are times when positive discipline is inappropriate and fails to work; at such times, negative discipline may be necessary.

64. **The correct answer is (D).** This response is consistent with ASK.

65. **The correct answer is (A).** The basic purpose is to get the job done by using ASK.

66. **The correct answer is (C).** A supervisor should never ignore an observed breach of discipline no matter how minor.

67. **The correct answer is (C).** Corrective measures taken for the *same* breach need not be the same. Suppose that your best worker and your worst worker arrive for work late on the same day at the same time. It is the first time your best worker has been late and this is the earliest your worst worker has ever arrived. Should they be treated *equally*? No, they should be treated *fairly*. Should both latenesses be documented? Yes.

68. **The correct answer is (D).** Budgeting is an ongoing process and preparation should not be limited solely to some fixed period of time.

69. **The correct answer is (B).** This is the simplest budget format. If your agency needs 100 pencils, then there will be a line for pencils such as "100 pencils at $.05 per pencil = $5.00."

70. **The correct answer is (A).** Don't shy away from promptness as a positive way to go when discipline is decided upon.

71. **The correct answer is (D).** This ties in to question 70.

72. **The correct answer is (A).** This is the only acceptable answer.

73. **The correct answer is (B).** Remember, to the citizen in the community, the uniformed officer on patrol *is* the police department.

74. **The correct answer is (A).** Public relations is everybody's job.

75. **The correct answer is (D).** Hopefully, this is an obvious answer. Using unnecessary wording like the "red-colored vehicle," where red denotes color, or meaningless words or phrases, only serves to complicate the report. It is important to encourage subordinates to write in all the essentials of and details of a case in an understandable manner.

76. **The correct answer is (D).** Because of court decisions suppressing confessions, concrete, physical evidence should be sought.

77. **The correct answer is (A).** Cyanoacrylate, also know as the "super-glue" is a method of developing latent prints on small objects that can be placed in a fuming tank or on large objects by using a fuming wand.

78. **The correct answer is (B).** This is the only acceptable response.

79. **The correct answer is (C).** Do not fold documents.

80. **The correct answer is (B).** Photographs provide an accurate record of the scene in general, but may distort relative distances. A photograph also cannot show details of the "other side" of an object. The accurate sketches of a skilled police artist are a vital adjunct to the photographs.

81. **The correct answer is (C).** The Walker or C-Acid Test is used for gunpowder residue.

82. **The correct answer is (C).** They are akin to the informal leaders.

83. **The correct answer is (B).** Once the suspect says he wants a lawyer, his absolute right to counsel is triggered.

84. **The correct answer is (C).** A well-organized conference should be comprised of members of about equal rank when they come from the same organization. In such a conference, there can be much horizontal "give and take" among the like-ranked officers. Another stimulus to horizontal communication in a large, decentralized organization might come from temporarily assigning a patrol supervisor to internal affairs and an internal affairs supervisor to patrol. When such supervisors return to their original assignments, they will bring back an appreciation of the other's position and will thereby enhance horizontal communications. Choices (B) and (D) apply to vertical communications, and choice (A) skirts the question.

85. **The correct answer is (A).** It is imperative to get the job done.

86. **The correct answer is (B).** Shared thinking leading to joint problem-solving is one of the main benefits of a conference. But remember, conferences are costly and time-consuming.

87. **The correct answer is (C).** The probation period is part of the selection process.

88. **The correct answer is (A).** Do not appoint a deputy chief on the basis of seniority, but use performance as the factor.

89. **The correct answer is (B).** Supervisors must not do the work, they must oversee others who do the work. If the supervisor does the job over himself in order to "get it done right," then the subordinate will not learn. Supervisors must resist the temptation to "get their hands dirty" except when demonstrating proper techniques.

90. **The correct answer is (A).** This is the only acceptable response.

91. **The correct answer is (C).** In this case, the attorney informs him of his rights.

92. **The correct answer is (D).** The basic rule is that Miranda warnings are required before *in-custody investigation* can occur.

93. **The correct answer is (C).** Once the suspect blurts out his confession, he is giving probable cause for arrest and is, in effect, placing himself in custody. The suspect who is in custody must be given Miranda warnings before questioning begins.

94. **The correct answer is (D).** When you have "probable cause" you have the basis for obtaining a search warrant. Be careful of choice (A), hearsay is an important factor in establishing probable cause.

95. **The correct answer is (C).** Obviously, this is not true.

96. **The correct answer is (D).** "Searching" requires consent, a search warrant, or probable cause in an emergency.

97. **The correct answer is (D).** Under the usual rules of evidence, hearsay is *incompetent*. But at the probable cause stage, hearsay is important.

98. **The correct answer is (B).** The inspector gave them probable cause and this probable cause should be used to get a warrant.

99. **The correct answer is (D).** The Fourteenth Amendment is the state due process clause. Freedom of assembly and petition are insured by the First Amendment.

100. **The correct answer is (A).** A Penn Register records outgoing phone numbers. A Trap and Trace device records incoming phone numbers. The use of a Penn Register or a Trap and Trace device is usually less controlled than the use of wiretaps, etc.

101. **The correct answer is (A).** Once again, get the job done.

102. **The correct answer is (B).** Note that (B) and (D) are opposite choices.

103. **The correct answer is (B).** Remember, *promptness* of required disciplinary action is not a bad way to go; it is a good way to go.

104. **The correct answer is (D).** Do you remember the acronym ASK? The purpose of discipline is to change *attitudes*, improve *skills*, and impart *knowledge*. Almost always the examiners will be looking for an answer that says," change attitude or behavior."

105. **The correct answer is (C).** What good is the communication if it is not on time?

106. **The correct answer is (C).** Remember, without public support the police objectives cannot be achieved.

107. **The correct answer is (C).** Although choice (B) might have been tempting, choice (C) is correct. What is the opposite of *exact*? It is *inexact*. It is not wrong to be exact. Not leaving out essential points should speak for itself.

108. **The correct answer is (D).** Be careful of choice (C); there is nothing quick about conferences to solve problems.

109. **The correct answer is (C).** Hopefully, this is the obvious answer.

110. **The correct answer is (B).** Everyone should know this concept by now.

111. **The correct answer is (A).** More properly, this would involve an interrogation rather than an interview.

112. **The correct answer is (C).** It is not a negative approach to let subordinates know what problems are being faced within the agency. On the contrary, participation in problem-solving is a motivating activity.

113. **The correct answer is (A).** Understanding the reasons can pave the way to acceptance of changes.

114. **The correct answer is (D).** Decisions must be made and they will not always be good ones. When you make a mistake, *admit* it and keep on trying.

115. **The correct answer is (B).** Your subordinates are getting the job done. Obviously, you are a successful supervisor. Be careful of choice (D). If problems are recurring, then you should not be handling them. You should delegate them and then fall back on the exception principle.

116. **The correct answer is (D).** Questions as in statement III tend to interrupt or stop the train of thought and may bring the interview to an abrupt halt.

117. **The correct answer is (B).** Do not interview together, but do it separately. Taking notes of some sort is probably essential.

118. **The correct answer is (A).** Rules and regulations should be specific and not informal.

119. **The correct answer is (D).** The word "fully" is the eliminator. Anonymous complaints should be investigated insofar as is practical.

120. **The correct answer is (A).** Do not fight this one; this is a proper way to conduct the interview.

MODEL EXAMINATION 3: ANSWER SHEET

1. Ⓐ Ⓑ Ⓒ Ⓓ Ⓔ
2. Ⓐ Ⓑ Ⓒ Ⓓ Ⓔ
3. Ⓐ Ⓑ Ⓒ Ⓓ Ⓔ
4. Ⓐ Ⓑ Ⓒ Ⓓ Ⓔ
5. Ⓐ Ⓑ Ⓒ Ⓓ Ⓔ
6. Ⓐ Ⓑ Ⓒ Ⓓ Ⓔ
7. Ⓐ Ⓑ Ⓒ Ⓓ Ⓔ
8. Ⓐ Ⓑ Ⓒ Ⓓ Ⓔ
9. Ⓐ Ⓑ Ⓒ Ⓓ Ⓔ
10. Ⓐ Ⓑ Ⓒ Ⓓ Ⓔ
11. Ⓐ Ⓑ Ⓒ Ⓓ Ⓔ
12. Ⓐ Ⓑ Ⓒ Ⓓ Ⓔ
13. Ⓐ Ⓑ Ⓒ Ⓓ Ⓔ
14. Ⓐ Ⓑ Ⓒ Ⓓ Ⓔ
15. Ⓐ Ⓑ Ⓒ Ⓓ Ⓔ
16. Ⓐ Ⓑ Ⓒ Ⓓ Ⓔ
17. Ⓐ Ⓑ Ⓒ Ⓓ Ⓔ
18. Ⓐ Ⓑ Ⓒ Ⓓ Ⓔ
19. Ⓐ Ⓑ Ⓒ Ⓓ Ⓔ
20. Ⓐ Ⓑ Ⓒ Ⓓ Ⓔ
21. Ⓐ Ⓑ Ⓒ Ⓓ Ⓔ
22. Ⓐ Ⓑ Ⓒ Ⓓ Ⓔ
23. Ⓐ Ⓑ Ⓒ Ⓓ Ⓔ
24. Ⓐ Ⓑ Ⓒ Ⓓ Ⓔ
25. Ⓐ Ⓑ Ⓒ Ⓓ Ⓔ
26. Ⓐ Ⓑ Ⓒ Ⓓ Ⓔ
27. Ⓐ Ⓑ Ⓒ Ⓓ Ⓔ
28. Ⓐ Ⓑ Ⓒ Ⓓ Ⓔ
29. Ⓐ Ⓑ Ⓒ Ⓓ Ⓔ
30. Ⓐ Ⓑ Ⓒ Ⓓ Ⓔ

31. Ⓐ Ⓑ Ⓒ Ⓓ Ⓔ
32. Ⓐ Ⓑ Ⓒ Ⓓ Ⓔ
33. Ⓐ Ⓑ Ⓒ Ⓓ Ⓔ
34. Ⓐ Ⓑ Ⓒ Ⓓ Ⓔ
35. Ⓐ Ⓑ Ⓒ Ⓓ Ⓔ
36. Ⓐ Ⓑ Ⓒ Ⓓ Ⓔ
37. Ⓐ Ⓑ Ⓒ Ⓓ Ⓔ
38. Ⓐ Ⓑ Ⓒ Ⓓ Ⓔ
39. Ⓐ Ⓑ Ⓒ Ⓓ Ⓔ
40. Ⓐ Ⓑ Ⓒ Ⓓ Ⓔ
41. Ⓐ Ⓑ Ⓒ Ⓓ Ⓔ
42. Ⓐ Ⓑ Ⓒ Ⓓ Ⓔ
43. Ⓐ Ⓑ Ⓒ Ⓓ Ⓔ
44. Ⓐ Ⓑ Ⓒ Ⓓ Ⓔ
45. Ⓐ Ⓑ Ⓒ Ⓓ Ⓔ
46. Ⓐ Ⓑ Ⓒ Ⓓ Ⓔ
47. Ⓐ Ⓑ Ⓒ Ⓓ Ⓔ
48. Ⓐ Ⓑ Ⓒ Ⓓ Ⓔ
49. Ⓐ Ⓑ Ⓒ Ⓓ Ⓔ
50. Ⓐ Ⓑ Ⓒ Ⓓ Ⓔ
51. Ⓐ Ⓑ Ⓒ Ⓓ Ⓔ
52. Ⓐ Ⓑ Ⓒ Ⓓ Ⓔ
53. Ⓐ Ⓑ Ⓒ Ⓓ Ⓔ
54. Ⓐ Ⓑ Ⓒ Ⓓ Ⓔ
55. Ⓐ Ⓑ Ⓒ Ⓓ Ⓔ
56. Ⓐ Ⓑ Ⓒ Ⓓ Ⓔ
57. Ⓐ Ⓑ Ⓒ Ⓓ Ⓔ
58. Ⓐ Ⓑ Ⓒ Ⓓ Ⓔ
59. Ⓐ Ⓑ Ⓒ Ⓓ Ⓔ
60. Ⓐ Ⓑ Ⓒ Ⓓ Ⓔ

61. Ⓐ Ⓑ Ⓒ Ⓓ Ⓔ
62. Ⓐ Ⓑ Ⓒ Ⓓ Ⓔ
63. Ⓐ Ⓑ Ⓒ Ⓓ Ⓔ
64. Ⓐ Ⓑ Ⓒ Ⓓ Ⓔ
65. Ⓐ Ⓑ Ⓒ Ⓓ Ⓔ
66. Ⓐ Ⓑ Ⓒ Ⓓ Ⓔ
67. Ⓐ Ⓑ Ⓒ Ⓓ Ⓔ
68. Ⓐ Ⓑ Ⓒ Ⓓ Ⓔ
69. Ⓐ Ⓑ Ⓒ Ⓓ Ⓔ
70. Ⓐ Ⓑ Ⓒ Ⓓ Ⓔ
71. Ⓐ Ⓑ Ⓒ Ⓓ Ⓔ
72. Ⓐ Ⓑ Ⓒ Ⓓ Ⓔ
73. Ⓐ Ⓑ Ⓒ Ⓓ Ⓔ
74. Ⓐ Ⓑ Ⓒ Ⓓ Ⓔ
75. Ⓐ Ⓑ Ⓒ Ⓓ Ⓔ
76. Ⓐ Ⓑ Ⓒ Ⓓ Ⓔ
77. Ⓐ Ⓑ Ⓒ Ⓓ Ⓔ
78. Ⓐ Ⓑ Ⓒ Ⓓ Ⓔ
79. Ⓐ Ⓑ Ⓒ Ⓓ Ⓔ
80. Ⓐ Ⓑ Ⓒ Ⓓ Ⓔ
81. Ⓐ Ⓑ Ⓒ Ⓓ Ⓔ
82. Ⓐ Ⓑ Ⓒ Ⓓ Ⓔ
83. Ⓐ Ⓑ Ⓒ Ⓓ Ⓔ
84. Ⓐ Ⓑ Ⓒ Ⓓ Ⓔ
85. Ⓐ Ⓑ Ⓒ Ⓓ Ⓔ
86. Ⓐ Ⓑ Ⓒ Ⓓ Ⓔ
87. Ⓐ Ⓑ Ⓒ Ⓓ Ⓔ
88. Ⓐ Ⓑ Ⓒ Ⓓ Ⓔ
89. Ⓐ Ⓑ Ⓒ Ⓓ Ⓔ
90. Ⓐ Ⓑ Ⓒ Ⓓ Ⓔ

91. Ⓐ Ⓑ Ⓒ Ⓓ Ⓔ
92. Ⓐ Ⓑ Ⓒ Ⓓ Ⓔ
93. Ⓐ Ⓑ Ⓒ Ⓓ Ⓔ
94. Ⓐ Ⓑ Ⓒ Ⓓ Ⓔ
95. Ⓐ Ⓑ Ⓒ Ⓓ Ⓔ
96. Ⓐ Ⓑ Ⓒ Ⓓ Ⓔ
97. Ⓐ Ⓑ Ⓒ Ⓓ Ⓔ
98. Ⓐ Ⓑ Ⓒ Ⓓ Ⓔ
99. Ⓐ Ⓑ Ⓒ Ⓓ Ⓔ
100. Ⓐ Ⓑ Ⓒ Ⓓ Ⓔ
101. Ⓐ Ⓑ Ⓒ Ⓓ Ⓔ
102. Ⓐ Ⓑ Ⓒ Ⓓ Ⓔ
103. Ⓐ Ⓑ Ⓒ Ⓓ Ⓔ
104. Ⓐ Ⓑ Ⓒ Ⓓ Ⓔ
105. Ⓐ Ⓑ Ⓒ Ⓓ Ⓔ
106. Ⓐ Ⓑ Ⓒ Ⓓ Ⓔ
107. Ⓐ Ⓑ Ⓒ Ⓓ Ⓔ
108. Ⓐ Ⓑ Ⓒ Ⓓ Ⓔ
109. Ⓐ Ⓑ Ⓒ Ⓓ Ⓔ
110. Ⓐ Ⓑ Ⓒ Ⓓ Ⓔ
111. Ⓐ Ⓑ Ⓒ Ⓓ Ⓔ
112. Ⓐ Ⓑ Ⓒ Ⓓ Ⓔ
113. Ⓐ Ⓑ Ⓒ Ⓓ Ⓔ
114. Ⓐ Ⓑ Ⓒ Ⓓ Ⓔ
115. Ⓐ Ⓑ Ⓒ Ⓓ Ⓔ
116. Ⓐ Ⓑ Ⓒ Ⓓ Ⓔ
117. Ⓐ Ⓑ Ⓒ Ⓓ Ⓔ
118. Ⓐ Ⓑ Ⓒ Ⓓ Ⓔ
119. Ⓐ Ⓑ Ⓒ Ⓓ Ⓔ
120. Ⓐ Ⓑ Ⓒ Ⓓ Ⓔ

MODEL EXAMINATION 3

> **Directions:** This test contains 120 questions. Circle the correct choice directly on the page. You have three hours to complete this examination. Each question has a relative weight of 1.0.

1 A supervisor who is training several inexperienced subordinates on patrol in the best way to handle the various patrol situations likely to arise should respond with them to calls for their services and

(A) avoid correcting any mistakes as they are made, but discuss the overall handling of the situation later.

(B) correct all mistakes as they are made and not discuss the overall handling of the situation later.

(C) correct all mistakes as they are made and then avoid future discussion of these mistakes.

(D) correct serious mistakes as they are made and discuss the overall handling of the situation later.

2. When dealing with newly assigned subordinates, a superior officer has been following the practice of promptly bringing to their attention their first violation of the rules and regulations. This practice is generally

(A) advisable, chiefly because the subordinates must be taught as promptly as possible just who is in charge.

(B) inadvisable, chiefly because the subordinate is relatively new at this point and should be treated with greater leniency.

(C) advisable, chiefly because at this point mild disciplinary measures may be very effective.

(D) inadvisable, chiefly because the subordinate may come to feel that the superior is setting too high a standard of expected performance.

3. Lieutenant Daly is about to prepare P.O. Mullins' evaluation form. On many occasions, Lieutenant Daly and P.O. Mullins have discussed politics. Lieutenant Daly knows that Mullins "subscribes to the same platform" as Daly. As a result, Lieutenant Daly rates Mullins as "superior" in all traits. The rating error committed by Lieutenant Daly is

(A) personal bias.

(B) subjectivity.

(C) halo effect.

(D) central tendency.

4. In order to build a spirit of cooperation among his staff, a supervisor must call attention to correct as well as incorrect behavior in a manner that subordinates will feel is consistent and reasonable. Of the following, the rule for the supervisor to follows is

(A) call attention to incorrect behavior only if it is insignificant, but give praise for any form of correct behavior.

(B) in discussing deficiencies, treat them as problems to be overcome rather than as personal criticisms.

(C) never single out one subordinate for praise in front of the entire staff.

(D) all instances of criticism should be preceded by instances of commendation of equal significance.

5. Assume that as a superior officer you have the task of correcting a subordinate in order to improve the work performance of the group under your supervision. Of the following actions, the one that you should *not* take during a meeting set up for this purpose is to

   (A) criticize the subordinate's performance of his duties.
   (B) compare the subordinate's performance to squad standards.
   (C) end the talk if the subordinate becomes emotional and defensive.
   (D) compare the subordinate's performance to that of others in his group.

6. For a superior who is supervising patrol to make a notation in his memorandum book whenever he strongly reprimands a subordinate verbally is

   (A) inadvisable, chiefly because an undue amount of supervisory time will be devoted to recording such information.
   (B) advisable, chiefly because the superior is developing a fund of information that will be useful in the future handling of the subordinate.
   (C) inadvisable, chiefly because the subordinates may resent such a procedure.
   (D) advisable, chiefly because all subordinates will make greater efforts to improve their job performance since they will not be sure of the nature of the notations.

7. During a disciplinary interview with a subordinate, a supervisor believes that he is unable to maintain an objective attitude because of anger and resentment toward the subordinate. Under these circumstances it would be most appropriate for the supervisor to

   (A) let the subordinate know exactly how he feels and that it will not be easy to "forgive and forget."
   (B) tell the subordinate that he is passing the case on to the precinct commander who will be unbiased in meting out the deserved punishment.
   (C) postpone the interview until a later date before it develops into a subjective discussion.
   (D) try to keep his feelings under control by discussing the behavior that necessitated the interview.

8. As patrol supervisor you are called to the scene of a collision between one of your marked department vehicles and a civilian vehicle. Your investigation discloses that your subordinate was on an emergency radio run and he drove through a controlled intersection with his siren blasting loudly, but without his red and white warning signals activated. A deaf motorist, properly within the intersection, was struck broadside by the police vehicle. Based on this set of facts, it would be most advisable for you

   (A) not take any action other than to direct the preparation of necessary police accident reports.
   (B) direct that a citation be issued to the civilian motorist for failure to yield the right of way.
   (C) direct the issuance of a citation to the police officer involved for violating the provision of law that *requires* sight and sound warnings when the rules of the road are violated.
   (D) bring administrative charges against the police officer involved.

9. You are the patrol supervisor, working a tour of duty from 4 P.M. to 12 midnight. At about 2350 hours you find it necessary to return to headquarters to deal with some required paperwork. You observe several police officers, at various places within 100 feet of headquarters, standing in doorways obviously waiting for midnight when their tour is over. It would be best for you to

   (A) assign them to extra duty as punishment.
   (B) arrange for their transfer to another assignment.
   (C) face them with their misconduct and warn them that if it happens again, then they will be brought up on charges.
   (D) use this as an opportunity to train them about the necessity for remaining on post until properly relieved.

10. It is generally accepted that a superior officer should not reprimand an erring subordinate in front of other subordinates because of the adverse effect of such a procedure upon the subordinate being reprimanded. Such a procedure is also undesirable mainly because it

    (A) demonstrates a lack of knowledge of proper supervisory methods on the part of the superior officer.

    (B) may encourage other superior officers to employ the same procedure with their subordinates.

    (C) will widely reveal the superior officer's techniques of issuing a reprimand and, therefore, lessen its future effectiveness with the other subordinates.

    (D) may evoke undue sympathy for the subordinate being reprimanded and resentment towards the superior.

11. In an attempt to be completely impartial in issuing necessary reprimands to his subordinates, a police supervisor uses the same degree of personal forcefulness for all reprimands. This procedure is

    (A) good; unfairness in imposing discipline can seriously lower the morale of a police agency.

    (B) poor; the more serious error, when committed, should result in a stronger reprimand.

    (C) good; effective discipline is best achieved when the supervisor always maintains a uniform supervisory manner.

    (D) poor; there will be a tendency on the part of the supervisor to generally use less forcefulness than is required.

12. As a patrol supervisor, it has come to your attention that a police officer under your supervision has been accepting free admission, during his off-duty hours, to a theater located in the precinct. You should emphasize to this police officer that the most important reason why such a practice is undesirable is that his acceptance of free admission to the theater

    (A) is a technique used by the theater management to obtain extra police protection.

    (B) may arouse the resentment of the theater patrons who have to pay the regular admission fee.

    (C) may cause him to lose the respect of other businessmen in the precinct.

    (D) may affect his effectiveness in enforcing the law.

13. "Although some assignments will always be favored, a police department should have no 'corner pocket's' or 'Siberia's.'" It logically follows that transfers should never be used as a disciplinary tool. The principal reason for avoiding transfers of such a nature is that

    (A) they do not attempt to discover the causes for unacceptable behavior nor to cure them.

    (B) such transfers are evidence of failure of both the initial selection and promotion processes.

    (C) such transfers serve only to worsen an obviously bad situation.

    (D) the morale of the individual affected is irreparably damaged.

14. Police Officers Mullins and Connolly both arrive late for work on the same day. Mullins has never been late and Connolly has never been on time. For you, as their supervisor, to document both latenesses would be

    (A) proper, since they both did the same thing, they must be treated equally.

    (B) proper, but the action taken against Mullins need not be as severe as that taken against Connolly.

    (C) improper, since Mullins has never been late before a warning should suffice.

    (D) improper, unless they are more than an hour late no documentation need be made.

15. Generally, as a police department becomes more professional, there is the tendency for the crime rate to rise. Which of the following statements best explains this phenomena?

   I. Obviously, more arrests are being made which cause the crime rate to go up.
   II. As citizens feel more confident in the police department, they are more willing to report crimes.
   III. This demonstrates that there is a total misrepresentation of the crime analysis.
   (A) Statements I and II are correct.
   (B) Statements I and III are correct.
   (C) Statement II is the only correct answer.
   (D) None of the statements holds true.

16. The best public relations program for a police department is for it to promote day-by-day, month-by-month, satisfactory public contacts.

   This statement is generally
   (A) false; it does not take into account the influence of present-day public relations techniques.
   (B) true; the police are judged mainly by their regular contacts with the public.
   (C) false; the efficiency of a police agency is being judged to an increasing degree by "cases cleared" indexes.
   (D) true; the efficiency of a department's law enforcement methods determines the public's attitude towards the police.

17. Much of the work of the police officer is by its very nature not particularly conducive to creating good public relations. This is so mainly because

   (A) of a lack of appreciation of the value of an effective public relations policy in many police agencies.
   (B) police efforts have by necessity become increasingly devoted to the control of activity of a noncriminal nature.
   (C) police emphasis has shifted from the apprehension of criminals to the suppression of crime.
   (D) police must hold themselves above the community and view all people as potential suspects.

18. "It is not enough for a police agency's services to be of a high quality. Attention must also be given to the acceptability of these services to the general public." This statement is generally

   (A) false, a superior quality of police service automatically wins public support.
   (B) true, the police can always progress beyond the understanding and support of the public.
   (C) false, the acceptance by the public of police services determines their quality.
   (D) true, the police are generally unable to engage in effective enforcement activity without public support.

19. A specific test for human blood is the

   (A) benzidine test.
   (B) reduced phenolpthalein test.
   (C) precipitin reaction test.
   (D) lurninol test.

20. Postmortem lividity, or "liver mortis," is the dark discoloration (usually dark blue) forming under the skin after death. It is most important to the crime investigator in determining

   (A) whether the body may have been moved after death.
   (B) the exact time of death.
   (C) the amount of heat lost from the body after death.
   (D) whether death was caused by trauma.

21. In a homicide case, if a human body is found with knife wounds that indicate that much blood has been lost, but the amount of blood near the body appears to be less than what one would normally expect to find, then the most logical assumption by a police investigator is that

   (A) the victim lived a considerable time after receiving the fatal wounds.
   (B) the crime was committed in a place other than where the body was found.
   (C) the victim died from some cause other than knife wounds.
   (D) the homicidal attack had been carefully planned by the perpetrator.

22. One of the first clues to something amiss may be the relationship of the dead body to the rest of the scene. One or more factors may give an impression of unreality to the whole picture. In the context of this statement, it would be most correct to state that

   (A) a clean, neatly dressed body lying peacefully on its back with folded hands, in a violently disturbed environment would be conclusive that death had occurred at some other location and the body was moved there after death.
   (B) a violently damaged body found lying in completely peaceful and undisturbed surroundings would arouse strong suspicion that the killer had set the stage prior to the killing and had struck suddenly.
   (C) a body whose parts are defying gravity would indicate that the victim had died in another position, and had been moved to the position in which it was found after rigor mortis had set in.
   (D) a body lying in a peaceful, relaxed position, face down, in completely peaceful surroundings would arouse strong suspicion that some rearrangement had occurred after death.

23. A platoon is faced with a troublesome local problem. The platoon commander calls all his sergeants to a meeting, outlines the problem, and asks them to give spontaneously any ideas that occur to them as possible ways of handling it. Each idea suggested is written down and later is discussed carefully. The chief advantage of the procedure employed by the platoon commander is that

   (A) time is not wasted on needless talk.
   (B) ideas are obtained which otherwise might not be developed.
   (C) there is less tendency for the meeting to stray from the subject under discussion.
   (D) sergeants receive training in analysis of problems and evaluation of solutions.

24. A sergeant made a practice of distributing agendas to all participants the day before a staff meeting was to be held. In general, this practice is

   (A) good; rumors and speculation are held to a minimum.
   (B) bad; participants are less spontaneous and candid in their discussions.
   (C) good; participants can give prior thought to the problems to be discussed.
   (D) bad; the problem of keeping the discussions confidential is made more difficult.

25. As a leader of a conference charged with making decisions on important problems, you may be faced with a situation where most of the group takes one position on a specific problem but one capable member of the group may argue vehemently for a totally different solution. Of the following, the most desirable position for you to take is to

   (A) discourage the dissenter because he is taking up valuable time of the entire group.
   (B) encourage the dissenter, but only if you are more or less in agreement with his position.
   (C) discourage the dissenter because if he is in the minority, then the group will exert enough pressure to break down his arguments anyway.
   (D) encourage they dissenter because the group will be stimulated to reexamine its solutions and consider previously unthought of aspects of the problem.

26. A police officer came to his sergeant with a complaint. The sergeant realized immediately that the complaint was not justified and cut short the conversation with the excuse that he had a report to finish. His method of handling the situation was bad chiefly because the

    (A) absurdity of the police officer's complaint was not made clear to him.
    (B) police officer was not permitted to discuss the matter and get it "off his chest."
    (C) police officer might go over the head of the sergeant.
    (D) sergeant should not have used an excuse for ending the conversation.

27. If an officer comes to a sergeant with a minor grievance that seems of great importance to the officer, then it would be best for the sergeant to

    (A) explain that supervisory personnel should not be involved in petty grievances.
    (B) explain why the grievance is of no importance.
    (C) listen attentively and give the grievance serious consideration.
    (D) redirect the officer's attention to a major department problem.

28. One of your subordinate officers comes to you and complains in an angry manner about your having chosen him for some particular assignment. In your opinion, the subject of the complaint is trivial and unimportant, but it seems to be very important to your subordinate. The best action for you to take in this situation is to

    (A) allow the officer to continue talking until he has calmed down and then explain the reasons for your having chosen him for that particular assignment.
    (B) warn the officer to moderate his tone of voice at once because he is bordering on insubordination.
    (C) tell the officer in an amused tone that he is making a tremendous fuss over an extremely minor matter.
    (D) point out to the officer that you are his immediate superior and that you are running the unit in accordance with official regulations.

29. A subordinate who is one of the most capable and efficient officers in your squad is continually complaining about his assignments, although he is given his fair share of undesirable and desirable tasks. You have noticed that his complaints are undermining the morale of the other subordinates. The best action for you to take is to

    (A) make him your unofficial assistant so that he will get more satisfaction from his work.
    (B) request his transfer to a squad where there will be more opportunity for him to use his capabilities.
    (C) have a confidential talk with him, explain the bad effect of his complaints, and ask him to curb them.
    (D) have a confidential talk with the other officers and ask them not to pay attention to his complaints.

30. When a formal grievance procedure exists, one of the problems involved is that of possibly having to consider overruling an action of a lower level supervisor. Which is the best rule to apply to this problem?

    (A) When the lower level supervisor has made a mistake, it must be corrected.
    (B) Even if the lower level supervisor has made a mistake, he should not be overruled under any circumstances.
    (C) When a lower level supervisor has made a mistake, it must be corrected, but only after third-party arbitration has made a ruling.
    (D) Even if the lower level supervisor has made a mistake, he should not be overruled if an acceptable way can be found to justify his mistake.

31. Assume that the division inspector asks you to conduct a study for him of a particular situation within the department and to recommend necessary changes. After your study, you submit a fairly long report. The section that should come *first* in this report is a

    (A) description of how you went about making the study.
    (B) summary of the conclusions that you reached.
    (C) discussion of possible objections to the recommendations and their refutation.
    (D) plan in which you show how the recommendations can be affected.

32. Using checklists to support fallible memory is common practice. Of the following, probably the greatest disadvantage of the checklist approach is that

    (A) there is a tendency to give equal weight to all factors when, actually, their actual importance might differ greatly.
    (B) time needed to read the items on the list reduces the time available to perform the required functions.
    (C) their detail and length result in the user's tending to ignore or miss those areas covered but frequently encountered.
    (D) the user may perform the investigative or analytical functions intended by the checklist incorrectly.

33. Of the following, which should be considered *first* in deciding whether or not to institute a new reporting system?

    (A) Ease with which the data can be gathered
    (B) Need for the information to be obtained
    (C) Difficulty in obtaining staff to compile the report
    (D) Cost of training staff to compile and use the report

34. It has been stated that daily reports should be based on calendar days from midnight to midnight, rather than 24-hour periods established by shift changes, such as 7 A.M. to 7 A.M. The principal advantage of basing daily reports on calendar days is that

    (A) reports will be comparable with those prepared in cooperation with other agencies.
    (B) the amount of outside assistance required to complete the report is reduced.
    (C) changes in shift reporting times will not destroy the comparative value of the reports.
    (D) the interpretation and prediction of needs for police services are significantly improved.

35. Because a reader reacts to the meaning he associates with a word, we can never be sure what emotional impact a word may carry or how it may effect our readers. The most logical implication of this statement for employees correspond with members of the public is that

    (A) a writer should try to select a neutral word that will not allow room for misinterpretation.
    (B) simple language should be used in writing letters denying requests so that readers are not upset by the denial.
    (C) every writer should adopt a writing style that he or she finds natural and easy.
    (D) whenever there is any doubt as to how a word is defined, the dictionary should be consulted.

36. Of the following, adherence to "democratic" principles in the administration of a large agency means, most nearly,

    (A) encouraging employees to feel that they are participating in planning and policy making.
    (B) giving equal voice to all employees in planning and policy making.
    (C) offering relevant participation of all employees according to their physical competence.
    (D) prompting friendliness, regardless of rank, among all employees at all levels.

37. Perhaps one of the most important rules a new supervisor can learn is that his subordinates will be most cooperative and willing to follow his instructions if he treats them fairly. Of the following, the situation that is the best example of fair treatment is the one in which

    (A) a supervisor assigns all his subordinates exactly the same work.
    (B) working procedures are strictly enforced with no exceptions allowed.
    (C) a supervisor has developed close personal relations with his subordinates and is regarded by them as "one of the boys."
    (D) discipline is exercised consistently, but exceptions may be allowed for legitimate reasons.

38. When a commander practices general supervision, delegates authority, and supervises by results,

    (A) the commander will spend a great deal of time checking for mistakes made by his subordinates.
    (B) his subordinates will not be as well trained as those who are supervised closely.
    (C) the commander will give fewer specific orders and spend more time planning and coordinating than would someone who supervises closely.
    (D) his subordinates will become accustomed to setting their own goals, and standards are likely to fail because they are under less pressure.

39. The supervisor's job brings her closer to such limiting factors in the operation of an agency as faulty administrative structure, shortage of funds and lack of facilities, inadequacies in personnel practices, community pressures, and an excessive workload. For the supervisor to make a practice of communicating to her subordinates her feelings of frustration about such limitations in the work setting would be

    (A) appropriate, because the workers will be more understanding of the supervisor's burdens and frustrations.
    (B) inappropriate, because the climate created will block rather than further the purposes of supervision.
    (C) appropriate, because such communication will create a more democratic climate between the workers and the supervisor.
    (D) inappropriate, because the supervisor must support and condone agency policies and practices in the presence of subordinates.

40. A certain captain has supervised the three sergeants who are described in the following statements.

    I.   Sergeant Monroe is known as a strict disciplinarian who often hands out punishment. Her subordinates do very good work because they fear the certain and serious consequences of disobedience and poor work.
    II. Sergeant Quaid is definitely not a disciplinarian and rarely hands out punishment. His subordinates do very good work, often beyond what is required or what is expected of them.
    III. Sergeant Redford is known as a disciplinarian, but hands out punishment only occasionally. His subordinates do what is required, because they know that their jobs depend on it, but rarely more.

The captain is classifying his sergeants by their supervisory styles. Which one of the following choices most correctly classifies those sergeants who supervise by leadership and those sergeants who supervise by authority?

(A) Statements I, II, and III all supervise by leadership.

(B) Statements I, II, and III all supervise by authority.

(C) Statements I and III supervise by leadership and II supervises by authority.

(D) Statement II supervises by leadership and I and III supervise by authority.

Directions: The following questions, 41 to 45, are based on a group of sentences. The sentences may be scrambled, but when they are correctly arranged they form a well organized paragraph. Read the sentences and then answer the questions about what order to arrange them in.

41.
1. The manager should be particularly cautious when sensitive areas are reached in the course of an interview.
2. They may ask for advice, but actually they want only a chance to talk.
3. Even when giving advice is successful, there is the danger that the employee may become overdependent on his manager and run to him whenever he has a minor problem.
4. In situations like this, what most people want is a sympathetic, understanding listener rather than an adviser.

(A) 2—3—1—4
(B) 1—4—2—3
(C) 3—1—4—2
(D) 1—2—3—4

42.
1. There is also good reason for careful attention to internal communication.
2. Effective communication with those inside the organization makes for fewer misunderstandings and fewer disgruntled employees.
3. Harmony within the business carries over into public relations with outsiders.
4. In the area of office communication, primary attention is usually centered upon relations with outsiders, including customers, suppliers, and others.

(A) 2—3—1—4
(B) 4—1—2—3
(C) 3—2—1—4
(D) 1—3—2—4

43.
1. For one man, everything he does falls under the heading of administration.
2. To a large extent, what the administrative functions of your job are depend on what you say they are.
3. You can talk to a dozen executives without getting two to agree.
4. Another executive will tell you only planning and decision making belong there.

(A) 1—3—2—4
(B) 2—1—3—4
(C) 4—1—2—3
(D) 3—1—4—2

44.
1. Our lawless society is enjoying the greatest of all crime sprees.
2. It is axiomatic that this nation cannot continue with any semblance of an orderly society if the escalating trend in crime and delinquency is allowed to persist.
3. One of the greatest problems facing this nation is the rising tide of serious crime.
4. Included within the word "crime" are, of course, serious acts of delinquency.
(A) 1—2—3—4
(B) 3—1—4—2
(C) 4—3—1—2
(D) 3—4—2—1

45.
1. They are in a strategic position to discover and know youths who are potentially delinquent.
2. The way the police use this knowledge in their contacts with juveniles may help to determine the future attitude of young people toward the law.
3. The police have an important contribution to make to the welfare of youth.
4. Their knowledge of the community's social resources and how to use them may afford or deny some children the opportunity or impetus for wholesome development.
(A) 3—1—2—4
(B) 1—2—3—4
(C) 2—3—1—4
(D) 3—4—1—2

46. Security of tenure in the public service must be viewed in the context of a universal quest for security. If we narrow our application of the term to employment, then the problem of security in the public service is seen to differ from that in private industry only in the need to deal with the peculiar threats to security in governmental organizations principally the danger of making employment contingent upon factors other than the performance of the worker. According to this, the employment status of the public servant

(A) as well as that of the private employee, is affected only by performance.
(B) may be endangered by factors other than poor performance.
(C) changes more rapidly than that of the private employee.
(D) changes less rapidly than that of the private employee.

47. A limitation on the economic analysis of consumers' wants is the subjective nature of consumer satisfaction that may vary considerably among individuals and among cultural groups. From this statement, it is most reasonable to conclude that

(A) objective standards for specific food needs and values even from the physiological point of view are extremely difficult.
(B) direct quantitative measurement of satisfaction derived from goods cannot yield a universal standard.
(C) determination of consumer demand by producers and sellers is not worthwhile.
(D) consumer education to establish nonobjective standards and common satisfaction values, would be of great importance for economic analysis of consumers wants.

48. The most significant improvements in personnel selection procedures can be expected from a program designed to obtain more precise statements of the requirements for a particular position and from the development of procedures that will make it possible to select not just those applicants who are generally best, but those whose abilities and personal characteristics provide the closest fit to the specific job requirements. According to this information, the most desirable applicant for a position is

(A) the one who has all the necessary training, even though he or she lacks the necessary personal characteristics.

(B) the one whose abilities and personal characteristics are of the highest order.

(C) the person who has the greatest interest in obtaining the position.

(D) the one whose qualifications are most nearly the same as the job requirement.

49. If there is to be reasonable consistency of purpose throughout the government, and if there is to be executive responsibility, broad governmental and departmental objectives must be implemented by, and hence related to, the more limited objectives of bureaus and divisions that make up a department. According to this statement, the objectives of a department should be

(A) set up to coordinate the objectives of its subdivisions.

(B) carried out by its subdivisions.

(C) the immediate objectives of its subdivisions.

(D) not related to the objectives of its subdivisions.

50. Every large social organization is characterized by the presence of strong centrifugal forces that tend to generate autonomous operation of segments and counteracting centripetal forces designed to draw the many activities into an integrated unity. The meaning of this statement is *most nearly* that

(A) centrifugal forces are stronger than centripetal forces in a large social organization.

(B) autonomous operation of segments is not consistent with the efficient operation of a large social organization.

(C) a large social organization has tendencies towards decentralization that conflict with other tendencies towards centralization.

(D) unity of organization cannot be achieved unless all centrifugal forces are eliminated or counterbalanced.

51. The *best* method of developing fingerprints on paper is by the use of

(A) copper powder.

(B) ultraviolet rays.

(C) infrared rays.

(D) silver nitrate.

52. In addition to its use in developing secret writing, iodine fumes can be used to

(A) determine if erasures have been made on a document.

(B) develop gunpowder patterns.

(C) distinguish blood from other substances.

(D) develop latent fingerprints.

53. Rifling in the bore of small arms is designed to

(A) increase the speed of the bullet.

(B) decrease the amount of recoil.

(C) prevent the bullet from turning end over end in the air.

(D) mark the bullet for purpose of identification.

54. A test by which an expert can determine from a bullet hole the distance from which a gun was fired is called the

(A) diphenylamine test.

(B) Walker test.

(C) benzidine test.

(D) photomicrograph test.

55. Examinations of a gun wound in the right temple of a victim reveal many powder grains and residue within the wound with a slight burn or scorch on the edge of the wound, but none outside the wound. From these facts, you may most safely deduce that

    (A) smokeless powder was used in the cartridge.
    (B) the victim was shot from a distance greater than 15 inches.
    (C) the muzzle of the gun was pressed against the victim's flesh.
    (D) the muzzle of the gun was at *least* two to four inches from the victim's flesh.

56. Upon examining a piece of glass in connection with a shooting, it is most accurate to state that

    (A) it is difficult to determine the direction from which a shot was fired.
    (B) a craterlike appearance of the hole indicates the exit side of the bullet path.
    (C) the side of the pane with the radial fractures indicates the side of entry of the bullet.
    (D) concentric fractures indicate the side from which the bullet emerged.

57. Report writing is an essential aspect of many functions within police agencies. How do reports assist a department by providing accurate statistical information?

    I.   They don't; this information is supplied by both state and federal agencies.
    II.   They provide information only usable by crime analyst.
    III. They help to allocate resources and budgetary issues.
    (A) Statements I and II are correct.
    (B) Statements II and III are correct.
    (C) Statement III is the only correct answer.
    (D) None of these statements are correct.

58. A simple test for distinguishing a blood stain from other substances is the

    (A) benzidine test.
    (B) alphanapythylamine test.
    (C) diphenylamine test.
    (D) hydrochloric acid test.

59. All of the following are accurate tests for the presence of alcohol in the human body *except* the

    (A) blood test.
    (B) breathalyzer test.
    (C) perspiration test.
    (D) urine test.

60. In the investigation of a rape case, the utilization of ultraviolet light is a useful method

    (A) both to locate stains and to establish that they are semen stains.
    (B) to locate stains, but not to establish whether they are semen stains.
    (C) only to establish whether certain stains are semen stains, after they have been located by some other method.
    (D) neither for finding stains nor for determining their nature.

61. Which of the following statements is *not* accurate?

    (A) A police officer who obtains a handwriting sample does not violate the Fourth Amendment right to privacy but does violate the Fifth Amendment right against self-incrimination.
    (B) A police officer who takes the fingerprints of a suspect does not violate Fifth Amendment rights, but could violate Fourth Amendment rights if the suspect is illegally seized to get his fingerprints.

(C)   If choice (B) had said "voiceprints" instead of "fingerprints," then the answer would be the same.

(D)   If police officers obtain "blood samples" of a suspect under certain controlled conditions, then no Fifth Amendment violation occurs.

62.   Which of the following statements is *least* correct concerning a search "incident to a lawful arrest?"

(A)   The area of search is narrowly limited by the case of *Chimel v. California.*

(B)   Such a search is also limited in time and must be made contemporaneous with the arrest.

(C)   It is an exception to the general rule that warrantless searches are per se unreasonable under the Fourth Amendment.

(D)   Except in the case of vehicle searches, all such searches must be based upon probable cause.

63.   With respect to the burden of proof, consider the following three statements.

I.   At the arrest stage, the burden is to establish a reasonable ground for belief in guilt.

II.   At the arraignment stage, the burden is to make out a prima facie case.

III. At the trial stage, the burden is to prove the defendant guilty beyond a reasonable doubt.

According to law:

(A)   All three statements are correct.

(B)   Only statements II and III are correct.

(C)   Only statements I and III are correct.

(D)   All three statements are incorrect.

64.   Which of the following amendments to the United States Constitution deals with the right to counsel?

(A)   The Fourth Amendment

(B)   The Fifth Amendment

(C)   The Sixth Amendment.

(D)   The Fourteenth Amendment

65.   Assume that several employees require refresher training. Which of the following training methods would be *least* desirable in the circumstances?

(A)   Coaching method with the supervisor teaching a small group of his employees on a nonlecture basis

(B)   Group-think method such as brainstorming that forces employees to participate in the discussion

(C)   Instructional interview where an instructor, not the supervisor, teaches the employee on an individual basis

(D)   Lecture method by instructors enabling employees to take comprehensive notes

66.   The amount learned from a lecture program depends mostly upon the

(A)   motivation of the members of the group.

(B)   intelligence of the members of the group.

(C)   skill of the lecturer in the subject matter of the course.

(D)   extensive use of visual aids.

67. Sergeant Mullins and Lieutenant Milowe are having an informal discussion about discipline in general. Sergeant Mullins says, "I really don't like to bring charges against the cops. The way it turns out in this department, I feel like I'm the one who is in the wrong." Sergeant Mullins' attitude is probably because

    (A) his popularity suffers when he brings charges.
    (B) so much of his time is spent in preparing the charges.
    (C) he knows he will be subjected to cross-examination at the disciplinary hearing.
    (D) public attention is focused on his activities.

68. Sergeant Connolly and Sergeant Mullins are having a discussion about work output and discipline. Sergeant Connolly says, "George, you are too easy on your subordinates. Why don't you demand perfection from them as I do? If I set the standard as high as it can be, then my workers will improve." Sergeant Mullins answers, "Frank, I want to be realistic. I know my troops aren't perfect and I set my standards at what is acceptable to me." The most valid reason in support of Sergeant Mullins' position is

    (A) standards must change when job specifications change.
    (B) allowances must be made for the poorer performers within the agency.
    (C) work schedules should be flexible to allow for planning time.
    (D) standards should be attainable and at the same time surpassable.

69. A training program for officers assigned to traffic law enforcement should include actual practice in simulated situations under simulated conditions. The chief justification for this statement is the education principle that

    (A) the officers will remember what they see better and longer than what they read or hear.
    (B) the officers will learn more effectively by actually performing the act themselves than they would from watching others do it.
    (C) for the officers to perform the simulated act once or twice will enable them to cope with the real situation with little difficulty.
    (D) for the officers to find anything of lasting value in a training program it must employ materials and methods of a practical nature.

70. Which training method is likely to be most effective in developing a specific skill in officers?

    (A) Meticulously planned lectures
    (B) Repeated and supervised practice
    (C) Selected and comprehensive reading
    (D) Well-designed demonstrations using visual aids

71. While on patrol as a sergeant you observe Police Officer Connolly, your most reliable and effective police officer, violating a very old rule that is known by all but observed by very few. When you bring this observed infraction to Connolly's attention he responds, by saying, "Come on sarge, nobody does it that way any more." If Police Officer Connolly is correct, then it would be most appropriate for you to

    (A) insist on Officer Connolly's compliance.
    (B) follow the rule yourself as an example to others.
    (C) ask the other sergeants how they are dealing with it.
    (D) try to determine whether the reason the rule was instituted still exists.

72. Several times during a roll call training lecture, a sergeant restates the major points of his lecture using different words. This teaching technique is most appropriate when

    (A) one of the subordinates in the group is slower than the rest.
    (B) the average subordinate in the group finds the material difficult.
    (C) he himself is somewhat unclear about aspects of the subject matter.
    (D) the amount of material to be covered would not ordinarily fill the available time.

73. Suppose that you are instructing a subordinate in a new procedure. The subordinate appears to be puzzled, but does not ask any questions. The best of the following ways of handling this situation is to

    (A) repeat the instructions.
    (B) rephrase the instructions.
    (C) ask the subordinate to explain the procedure in his own words.
    (D) closely observe the manner in which the instructions are executed.

74. Which method of instructing subordinates in the discharge of their duties would a superior officer find *least* valuable?

    (A) Construct a hypothetical problem that might rarely occur and then discuss the solution with them.
    (B) Have each individual officer, one at a time, step forth so that his mistakes can be explained to the group.
    (C) Observe the errors each officer makes while on duty and then discuss them with each officer individually.
    (D) Refer them to the proper provisions in the rules and procedures when it appears their application might be required.

75. Lieutenant Nunno, just before instructing an officer in the correct method of searching a premises for contraband, explained to the officer why it was important to follow the correct procedure. The lieutenant's action was

    (A) good; a procedure is less likely to be forgotten if its purpose is understood.
    (B) poor; since the importance of searching for contraband is obvious, the explanation is a waste of time.
    (C) good; repetition is an effective aid in learning an operation.
    (D) poor; such an explanation will distract the officer from the main points in the instruction.

76. One of the best indications of interest on the job on the part of subordinates is that they ask questions. Such questions are of value chiefly because they

    (A) provide an excellent guide to the reassignment of subordinates.
    (B) serve to enhance the status of the supervisor when he or she answers them.
    (C) indicate the efficiency of the individuals involved.
    (D) can be utilized as part of the training process.

77. When police officers ask a certain supervisor's advice about handling specific work problems, the supervisor now and then responds to the request by first asking the officer what he thinks should be done. This practice by the supervisor is generally

    (A) bad, since subordinates will not ask questions in the future.
    (B) good, since it motivates subordinates to think about possible solutions.
    (C) bad, since officers will question the motives of the supervisor.
    (D) good, since poorly thought-out action can lead to undesirable results.

78. When delivering a training talk to new officers, a lieutenant who uses technical terms that may not be familiar to the "rookies," acts correctly provided that he

    (A) explains such terms as soon as he uses them.
    (B) invites the rookies to ask questions about anything they do not understand.
    (C) questions the rookies at the end of the lecture to evaluate their grasp of the materials.
    (D) tells the rookies the names of standard police words in which they are to look up the terms.

79. A supervisor is attempting to discuss some important and practical applications of a new law with a group of his subordinates who have little knowledge of this law. He notices that they are impassive and uninterested in the discussion. Of the following, it would be best for the supervisor to

    (A) explain the law and its application carefully and as thoroughly as possible, and ask provocative questions.
    (B) order the group to participate in the discussion since it is for their own good.
    (C) give the factual information on the law and then staff out of the discussion as much as possible.
    (D) postpone further discussion until some future time when the group has shown some interest in the law.

80. A certain Neighborhood Police Team supervisor believes very strongly in participatory supervision. He works hard at permitting subordinates to influence the decision-making process of the team because he believes that participation builds high team motivation and allows the team to exert pressures on its own members for higher-level performance. Which one of the following best states whether or not the supervisor's technique is appropriate and is also the best reason for it?

    (A) The technique is not appropriate, because it will weaken and possibly ruin the supervisor's authority for making the final decision.
    (B) The technique is appropriate, because group pressures, by their very nature, must work to improve the achievement of individual members.
    (C) The technique is not appropriate, because it is possible for group pressures to act to prevent achievement by individual group members.
    (D) The technique is appropriate, because permitting police officers to influence the direction of the team will pay off in increased output and improved job satisfaction.

81. A certain problem has come to the attention of Sergeant Patrick. He informs Santos, one of his subordinates, of the nature of the problem and that it is to be corrected within two weeks. Which one of the following should be Sergeant Patrick's greatest concern at the end of the two- week period?

    (A) How the problem was corrected
    (B) Whether or not the problem has been corrected
    (C) What steps have been taken to correct the problem
    (D) Whether or not there were any difficulties in correcting the problem

82. A police supervisor began a program to accomplish a certain goal. The program created additional work for his officers. After a reasonable period, it was determined that the program did not work out and, therefore, there was no reason for it. Which one of the following choices is the best way to handle a program on which subordinates have spent time and energy, but which has failed?

    (A) Continue using the program until a substitute is found.
    (B) Continue the program until such time as the subordinates themselves recognize the failure.
    (C) Immediately discontinue the program without explaining the reasons far this action to his officers.
    (D) Immediately discontinue the program and explain the reasons for this action to his officers.

83. When delegating work to a subordinate, a supervisor should always tell the subordinate

    (A) each step in the procedure for doing the work.
    (B) how much time to expend.
    (C) what she expects from the officer.
    (D) whether reports are necessary.

84. Superior officers expect to have their instructions obeyed immediately and "to the letter." Regardless of his skill as leader or soundness of judgment, however, every superior officer occasionally will encounter resistance to his orders. Sometimes the unresponsiveness takes the form of a member's respectful questioning of certain instructions under nonemergency conditions. The best way for a superior officer to deal with such a member is to

    (A) suggest that failure to follow orders may be viewed as insubordination.
    (B) repeat the order and request compliance.
    (C) tell him to do the job in any way as long as it gets done.
    (D) ask for his objections to see whether his reasons are valid.

85. Of the following, an order given by a sergeant will most likely be accepted and carried out without resentment if it is

    (A) stated in a simple manner.
    (B) given as a direct command.
    (C) framed as a request.
    (D) given by an immediate superior.

86. A supervisor may make an assignment in the form of a request, a command, or a call for volunteers. It is *least* desirable to make an assignment in the form of a request when

    (A) a subordinate does not like the particular kind of assignment to be given.
    (B) the assignment requires working past the regular closing day.
    (C) an emergency has come up.
    (D) the assignment is not particularly pleasant for anybody.

87. In an emergency situation, when action must be taken immediately, it is best for the supervisor to give orders in the form of

    (A) direct commands that are brief and precise.
    (B) requests, so that his subordinates will not become alarmed.
    (C) suggestions that offer alternative courses of action.
    (D) implied directives, so that his subordinates may use their judgment in carrying them out.

88. The way a supervisor gives an order can affect the way in which it is carried out, since different people require different supervisory methods. Which one of the following is *least* likely to be an example of a good procedure for giving orders?

    (A) Give the order as a request to a reliable officer who has been employed for a long time.
    (B) Give the order as a direct command to a careless, lazy officer.
    (C) Give the order as a direct command to all officers in emergency conditions.
    (D) Give the order as an implied directive to a new, inexperienced officer.

89. Of the following, the *best* way for a sergeant to make sure that an employee understands a verbal order is to

    (A) give the order in a quiet place where there are few distractions.
    (B) have some subordinates explain it to the employee.
    (C) speak loudly, slowly, and distinctly.
    (D) ask the worker to repeat the order in his own words.

90. A police supervisor must order a change in procedures that he is certain will be unpopular. Which one of the following is the *best* way to give the order so as to assure the highest degree of cooperation?

    (A) Give the order in a short, concise but positive manner.
    (B) Post the order in written form just as it was communicated to the supervisor, without comment.
    (C) Give the order and also to give an explanation as to why the order is important.
    (D) Give the order and also to inform the officers that spot checks will be made in the field to make sure that all officers are complying with the order.

91. Personnel experts recommend that supervisors use positive discipline to correct the deficiencies of their subordinates. Which supervisory practice is *not* a recognized form of positive discipline?

    (A) Finding and removing the causes of employee misconduct
    (B) Developing in subordinates good attitudes toward their work
    (C) Assisting subordinates by guiding and counseling them
    (D) Imposing punishment which fits both the violation and the violators

92. Assume that, after a thorough investigation, a sergeant determines that one of his subordinates is guilty of misconduct. The sergeant then tells the subordinate that he wants to speak to him about this matter in a couple of days. The sergeant's action in this situation is basically

    (A) wise, chiefly because it gives the subordinate an opportunity to improve his performance.
    (B) unwise, chiefly because disciplinary action is most effective when taken promptly.
    (C) wise, chiefly because the sergeant has time to consider the form of discipline that will be most effective.
    (D) unwise, chiefly because the sergeant may not recall the reasons for the disciplinary action.

93. For a supervisor to keep records of reprimands to subordinates about infractions of the rules is

    (A) good practice, because these records are valuable to support disciplinary actions recommended or taken.
    (B) poor practice, because such records are evidence of the supervisor's inability to maintain discipline.
    (C) good practice, because such records indicate that the supervisor is doing a good job.
    (D) poor practice, because the best way to correct subordinates is to give them more training.

94. Mullins, a police supervisor who has developed good rapport with his subordinates and is respected for his actions, is interviewing a police officer about a personal problem. The officer says he is bothered in part by continued violations of the law by fellow officers. The officer asks whether Mullins would keep the information strictly confidential if he reveals the nature of the violations committed by the other officers. Which is the best response on the part of Mullins?

    (A) Mullins should agree to hear the information in confidence and then maintain its confidentiality.
    (B) Mullins should agree to hear the information in confidence and then should decide from the nature of the violations whether or not to keep it confidential.

(C) Mullins should refuse to hear the information in confidence and should attempt to convince the officer to reveal the violations so that proper official action can be taken.

(D) Mullins should refuse to hear the information in confidence and should advise the officer that he is going to officially notify higher authority that the officer has information on possible corruption in the department.

95. A police supervisor received an anonymous phone call alleging that one of the officers under his command has committed an act of brutality to a person on his patrol beat. Which one of the following choices best states both the extent to which this anonymous tip should be investigated and also the best reason for it?

(A) It should be ignored because the complainant is trying to stir up trouble.

(B) It should be ignored because there would be no one available to make a direct accusation against the police officer.

(C) It should be investigated to the same extent that an anonymous tip of a crime would be investigated because anonymous personnel complaints should be investigated within practical limits.

(D) It should be investigated to the extent of talking to the officer and finding out what he knows about the complaint because the officer may have some insight into who the anonymous caller might be.

Questions 96 to 100 are to be answered solely on the basis of the information given in the following table.

THEFTS 1995-2000

Year	Total Number of Thefts	Number of Arrests Made	Percentage of Thefts in which Arrests were Made	Number of Convictions Obtained	Percentage of Arrests in which Convictions were Obtained
1995	4,935	1,147	23.2%	?	19.7%
1996	4,828	1,035	21.4%	223	21.5%
1997	5,172	1,077	20.8%	252	23.3%
1998	6,581	1,083	16.4%	226	20.8%
1999	5,277	1,267	24.0%	253	19.9%
2000	5,314	1,432	?	250	17.4%

96. In the column called Percentage of Thefts in which Arrests were Made, the number for the year 2000 is omitted. Which of the following numbers is closest to the number missing from this column?

(A) 27 percent

(B) 26 percent.

(C) 23 percent

(D) 21 percent

97. In the column called Number of Convictions Obtained, the number for the year 1996 is omitted. Which of the following numbers is closest to the number missing from this column?

(A) 220

(B) 225

(C) 240

(D) 250

98. Which is most nearly the sum of the numbers in the column called Total Number of Thefts?

(A) 33,000
(B) 32,500
(C) 32,110
(D) 31,500

99. Which is most nearly the average of the numbers in the column called Number of Arrests Made?

(A) 7,000
(B) 1,125
(C) 1,150
(D) 1,175

100. In which year was the number of thefts in which convictions were obtained most nearly one thirtieth of the total number of thefts?

(A) 1997
(B) 1998
(C) 1999
(D) 2000

101. Sergeant Connolly is in the habit of explaining to police officers the reasons behind many of their activities and how those activities blend into other functions within the department. The best reason for Sergeant Connolly to continue this approach is that

(A) it demonstrates the depth of his knowledge of department functions.
(B) it gives the officers concerned a means of self-improvement.
(C) it impacts positively on a subordinate's desire for promotion.
(D) it may serve as an impetus for each officer to perform his job properly.

102. Sergeant Mullins sometimes delegates tasks to subordinates when they are not fully able to handle them. He knows the subordinates will come up "a little short." The best reason for Sergeant Mullins to continue this supervisory approach is it

(A) demonstrates to subordinates that he is in charge.
(B) may aid in improving the performance of subordinates.
(C) helps him to determine who his least qualified subordinates are.
(D) insures that his best performers will not be given all the tough assignments.

103. Sergeant Milowe is faced with the task of developing a specific skill in one of her subordinates. It would be best for Sergeant Milowe to

(A) develop a series of well-planned lectures.
(B) supervise repeated practice of the skill to be learned.
(C) use a lecture presentation augmented by visual aids.
(D) direct an expert in the field to give demonstrations.

104. Sergeant Connolly is in the habit of giving a broad assignment of work to subordinates rather than a detailed explanation of the task to be performed. If this is considered to be a good practice on Sergeant Connolly's past, then the best reason for considering it proper is

(A) it takes less time to give a broad assignment.
(B) such an approach encourages initiative on the part of the subordinates.
(C) it tends to eliminate duplication of errors.
(D) it requires less training, discipline, and follow up.

105. Police Officer Roger is a promising subordinate who works for Sergeant Mullins. Sergeant Mullins wants to develop Roger's abilities so that Roger is able to take on more challenging assignments. If Sergeant Mullins wants to give Roger a specific assignment that will help Roger to develop, Sergeant Mullins should tell Roger

    (A) that failure will not be tolerated.
    (B) what he expects from him.
    (C) when the task is to be completed.
    (D) the means to be used to accomplish the task.

106. At the scene of a homicide, an investigating detective would act most properly if he or she

    (A) conducted an investigation.
    (B) questioned witnesses.
    (C) searched for evidence.
    (D) surveyed the scene.

107. Look at the four choices given below and choose the one that describes the most important quality that should be possessed by a supervisor.

    (A) Good trainer
    (B) Well-liked and respected
    (C) Motivates well
    (D) Supervises effectively

108. An effective supervisor is a good motivator. Look at the choices given below and determine which factor would be considered the most effective and most long-lasting motivator.

    (A) High salary and benefits
    (B) Free promotion courses for advancement in rank
    (C) Recognition for a job well done
    (D) Job enrichment and decision-making authority

109. Sergeant Milowe has been directed by her chief to introduce a change in a long-established department procedure. The chief is concerned that there will be resistance to the change and he advises Sergeant Milowe to introduce the change in such a way so as to minimize the resistance. With this objective in mind, Sergeant Milowe should

    (A) explain why the changes are necessary and, if possible, introduce the changes gradually.
    (B) post an explanation of the change on the bulletin board and direct subordinates to study it.
    (C) put the change into effect rapidly so that informal leaders do not have a chance to rally the opposition.
    (D) choose the most effective subordinate to demonstrate to all others how much more beneficial the new procedure is.

110. Continuing with the concept in the last question, excessive resistance to change will most likely be caused by the

    (A) effect the change will have on the organization.
    (B) effect the change will have on current methods.
    (C) reasons for the change.
    (D) manner in which the change is introduced by the hierarchy.

111. Which is *least* important in determining the most desirable span of control for the supervisor of a patrol unit in a police agency?

    (A) The kind of work performed by the unit
    (B) The abilities of the supervisor and his subordinates
    (C) The geographic locations where the work will be performed
    (D) The overall size of the agency involved

112. Evaluate the following statements.

    I. As the number of supervisory levels in an organization increases, the span of control decreases.
    II. As the organizational structure is "flattened," the span of control increases.

    (A) Only statement I is valid.
    (B) Only statement II is valid.
    (C) Both statements are valid.
    (D) Neither statement is valid.

113. "To decrease the possibility of communication blockages it is recommended that the span of control in an organization be large." What best explains why a large span of control may improve communications?

    (A) More organizational levels facilitate communications through intervening layers of officers.
    (B) There is a tendency toward group discussions that eliminates the need to communicate through formal channels.
    (C) There are direct lines to key officers although the department may have many organizational levels.
    (D) Fewer organizational levels are necessary and subordinates can communicate more directly with supervisors.

114. Higher level administrators are not able to supervise effectively as many subordinates as a lower level supervisor because

    (A) the administrator's work demands closer supervision.
    (B) the administrator's job is more diverse.
    (C) the supervisory function is increased in work output.
    (D) there is much more detailed work involved at the higher levels.

115. Within your agency, the following superior/subordinate relationships exist: the chief has five captains reporting to him; each captain has two lieutenants reporting to him; each lieutenant has four sergeants reporting to him; each sergeant has six police officers reporting to him. The main criticism of this arrangement should concern the number of

    (A) subordinates reporting to sergeants.
    (B) sergeants reporting to lieutenants.
    (C) lieutenants reporting to captains.
    (D) captains reporting to the chief.

116. The chief said to Sergeant Mullins, "George, want you to handle this matter from start to finish and I want a report from you that I need only approve and sign." The chief is asking for

    (A) the impossible.
    (B) completed staff work.
    (C) a final report.
    (D) a research and planning project.

117. According to respected authorities, most orders should be

    (A) oral.
    (B) written.
    (C) implied.
    (D) requests.

118. Implied orders are usually abstract and deprive the supervisor of

    (A) a follow-up tool.
    (B) authority.
    (C) responsibility.
    (D) command ability.

119. Consider the following circumstances and determine which, if any, will support the use of a written order.

    I.   Complex operations are involved.
    II. Numerous persons are affected.
    III. Strict accountability is desired.
    IV. It is an emergency situation.
    (A) Statements I, II, III, and IV
    (B) Statements I, II, and III, but not IV
    (C) Statements I and II, but not III and IV
    (D) Statements II and III, but not I and IV

120. The decision-making process involves several steps. Rearrange the following steps in the order in which they should occur in the decision-making process after assuming that the first step, an awareness that a real problem exists, has already been taken.

    1. Facts must be obtained.
    2. Data must be evaluated and analyzed.
    3. Alternate approaches should be decided.
    4. The decision must be communicated to subordinates.
    5. A decision must be selected.
    (A) 1—2—3—5—4
    (B) 1—5—4—3—2
    (C) 1—3—5—2—4
    (D) 1—2—5—3—4

MODEL EXAMINATION 3: ANSWERS AND EXPLANATIONS

1. **The correct answer is (D).** In balance, choice (D) is clearly the best answer. Mistakes should not be allowed to continue and they must be corrected at once. Trial and error is *not* a good training technique; discussion of the overall handling of a situation at a later time is an excellent training method.

2. **The correct answer is (C).** The same concept as in question 1; mistakes should be corrected as they occur.

3. **The correct answer is (A).** Subordinates whose views are not compatible with the supervisor's own philosophy are likely to receive a lower rating.

4. **The correct answer is (B).** The act and not the person should be the subject of the criticism.

5. **The correct answer is (D).** Making such comparisons will not bring positive results.

6. **The correct answer is (B).** However, you must always inform the subordinate that you are keeping a record of his derelictions.

7. **The correct answer is (C).** This is one of the very few times when it is proper to postpone taking necessary disciplinary action.

8. **The correct answer is (D).** Be careful of choice (C); the law does not apply to police vehicles, so a citation is not called for. However, the officer did not follow procedures.

9. **The correct answer is (C).** Don't fall for the "Mr. nice guy" approach in choice (D).

10. **The correct answer is (D).** The general rule is to praise in public and to criticize in private. But suppose your subordinate is manhandling a prisoner; will you correct him even if you are in public? Yes!

11. **The correct answer is (B).** This is an easy one based on pure common sense.

12. **The correct answer is (D).** Unfortunately, there is no such thing as a "free lunch."

13. **The correct answer is (A).** Do not *transfer* a problem; solve it. If transfer is the solution (better job match), then the transfer is proper.

14. **The correct answer is (B).** Who knows, perhaps Mullins will never be on time again. The dereliction must be recorded somewhere.

15. **The correct answer is (C).** Interestingly, as police perform more professionally, the crime rate will increase due to citizens having more confidence in the police. Also, the police should find that arrest rates will go up as well. Not only will citizens report more crimes to the police, but they will also be more willing to assist them in solving crimes.

16. **The correct answer is (B).** The most important factor is everyday contacts with public.

17. **The correct answer is (B).** This is the same concept as question 15.

18. **The correct answer is (D).** How true! The public must recognize the need for the services of the police agency, for it is just about impossible to accomplish the police function without the support of the community.

19. **The correct answer is (C).** The precipitin reaction test is a specific lab test for *human* blood. The other tests can identify blood, but cannot specify that it is human blood.

20. **The correct answer is (A).** The lividity is affected by gravity. If the discoloration is at a point on the body not near the ground, then the body was probably moved.

21. **The correct answer is (B).** The same general concept as in question 20. Knife wounds usually cause much bleeding. If there is not much blood around, then the homicide probably occurred elsewhere.

22. **The correct answer is (C).** It is not uncommon for rigor mortis, once it has set in, to defy the ordinary laws of gravity. If a person dies while lying on a flat surface (with both legs outstretched, for instance) and after rigor mortis has set in, the body is removed to another location where there is no support for the legs. The legs will then remain unnaturally outstretched in space; gravity will not overcome the rigidity. The word "conclusive" eliminates choice (A); in choice (B) the body might have been moved from another location; (D) might indicate a death from natural causes.

23. **The correct answer is (B).** This is called "brainstorming" a problem.

24. **The correct answer is (C).** This question is frequently used and the answer is always the same.

25. **The correct answer is (D).** Do not label the dissenter as a troublemaker. He just has a different opinion and perhaps he is right.

26. **The correct answer is (B).** When a subordinate has what is obviously an unjustified grievance, let him vent and try to get him to see it in its proper light. He will know that he has been treated fairly and that his "beef" was aired.

27. **The correct answer is (C).** This is common sense.

28. **The correct answer is (A).** Let him vent and then take time to explain. Suppose you are a lieutenant and a delegation of officers comes to you with a complaint about their sergeant. What should you do? Ask them if they have spoken with the sergeant.

29. **The correct answer is (C).** Take it right to him. These are strong facts.

30. **The correct answer is (A).** Mistakes should not be allowed to stand.

31. **The correct answer is (B).** This can save your boss time.

32. **The correct answer is (A).** That does not mean you should not use checklists. Just be sure you are aware of the problems

33. **The correct answer is (B).** Your first consideration in instituting anything new should be, "is it needed?"

34. **The correct answer is (C).** This is a common sense answer.

35. **The correct answer is (A).** Sensitivity in both speech and writing is absolutely vital to patrol officers, desk officers, and supervisory staff at all levels.

36. **The correct answer is (A).** Democratic supervisors usually foster participatory management.

37. **The correct answer is (D).** A difficult concept, but a proper one. Suppose that the rule is, "No one can have Friday nights off." P.O. Connolly, father of seven children under 10 years of age, is faced with an emergency when his wife is suddenly hospitalized. Should he get Friday night off? Absolutely!

38. **The correct answer is (C).** This commander is doing a terrific job. Subordinates can exercise initiative and resourcefulness in getting the job done, and the supervisor can concentrate on the broader picture.

39. **The correct answer is (B).** As a boss you should not show your frustrations to subordinates. They look to you for leadership.

40. **The correct answer is (D).** This is a long question for an easy answer.

41. **The correct answer is (B).** The obvious opening sentence is 1 and the best second sentence is 4, "Situations like this" in sentence 4 are the "sensitive areas" referred to in sentence 1.

42. **The correct answer is (B).** This is not so easy. Sentence 4 is the opener and refers to outside relations. Sentence 1 is next, hinting at the importance of internal communications.

43. **The correct answer is (D).** This is difficult, but the sequence of 1—4 is crucial.

44. **The correct answer is (D).** Another difficult one, but the sequence of 3—4 is critical. It appears in choices (A) and (D), but the rest of choice (A) is not acceptable.

45. **The correct answer is (A).** At last, an easy one. The critical sequence is 3—1, as in choice (A).

46. **The correct answer is (B).** This is the rationale for having a merit-based civil service. The second sentence speaks of the danger of jeopardizing employment by factors other than performance.

47. **The correct answer is (B).** This is by inference.

48. **The correct answer is (D).** Those whose abilities and personal characteristics provide the closest fit are those whose qualifications are most nearly the same as the job requirements.

49. **The correct answer is (B).** If departmental objectives are implemented by the bureaus and divisions, then they are carried out by its subdivisions.

50. **The correct answer is (C).** Autonomous operation is decentralized and the integrated unity is centralized; counteracting forces conflict.

51. **The correct answer is (D).** This is a popular question.

52. **The correct answer is (D).** Another frequently used question.

53. **The correct answer is (C).** It causes the pellet to spiral.

54. **The correct answer is (B).** This is sometimes called the C-Acid Test.

55. **The correct answer is (C).** Almost common sense.

56. **The correct answer is (B).** The crater is on the exit side.

57. **The correct answer is (C).** Incident reports provide valuable statistical information and when combined with proper planning is one of the most useful tools.

58. **The correct answer is (A).** The positive reaction is a blue-green coloration.

59. **The correct answer is (C).** A frequently used question in some jurisdictions.

60. **The correct answer is (B).** Ultraviolet light will make semen stains glow. Other stains may also appear in ultraviolet light, making it necessary to perform further testing on glowing stains for a positive determination of semen.

61. **The correct answer is (A).** Self-incrimination deals with *testifying* against yourself.

62. **The correct answer is (D).** Search incident to a lawful arrest must be based on probable cause, even in the case of a vehicle emergency.

63. **The correct answer is (A).** Generally accepted standards in law.

64. **The correct answer is (C).** This question was an easy one?perhaps.

65. **The correct answer is (D).** The most ineffective training method is the lecture. Troopers must be well motivated to have it succeed.

66. **The correct answer is (A).** See the answer to question 65.

67. **The correct answer is (C).** This is the only reason advanced that is responsive to the question.

68. **The correct answer is (B).** If perfection is the standard, then there will be many frustrated employees. But be careful, this does not mean that you accept work that is below what your workers are capable of accomplishing. That is a different concept.

69. **The correct answer is (B).** This is a form of role playing and it is effective.

70. **The correct answer is (B).** The question deals with a *specific* skill.

71. **The correct answer is (D).** A tough situation for a first-line supervisor, but that is the acceptable answer.

72. **The correct answer is (B).** Your teaching level should be aimed at the average learner in the group.

73. **The correct answer is (C).** Have him "play it back."

74. **The correct answer is (B).** Why explain mistakes? Besides, this would be embarrassing.

75. **The correct answer is (A).** Remember, it is almost always good to explain.

76. **The correct answer is (D).** Questions can reveal training needs.

77. **The correct answer is (B).** It is the supervisor's job to get them thinking.

78. **The correct answer is (A).** Once more, there is the word "explain."

79. **The correct answer is (A).** You will never miss one again with the word "explain."

80. **The correct answer is (D).** This is another way of saying that participatory management can have positive results.

81. **The correct answer is (B).** Sergeant Patrick assigned Santos to have a problem corrected within two weeks. After two weeks, Sergeant Patrick must follow up to be certain that the problem has been corrected.

82. **The correct answer is (D).** Why continue it, if it does not work? But by all means, explain the reasons for discontinuance to the officers who spent so much time and energy on the new program. This explanation is most important in order to maintain morale.

83. **The correct answer is (C).** If you tell the subordinate what you expect, then you should be covering all the bases.

84. **The correct answer is (D).** Everybody in the department owes a duty to his supervisor to respectfully disagree when he thinks a procedure is wrong. And it is the supervisor's duty to listen and to consider the comments.

85. **The correct answer is (C).** That is what most orders should be.

86. **The correct answer is (C).** This is when a direct command is recommended.

87. **The correct answer is (A).** An emergency demands precise direct commands that will be carried out.

88. **The correct answer is (D).** The implied order is usually reserved for the reliable, experienced subordinate, or when the supervisor is trying to develop a promising employee.

89. **The correct answer is (D).** Have him "play it back."

90. **The correct answer is (C).** Once more, the word "explain."

91. **The correct answer is (D).** Punishment is negative.

92. **The correct answer is (B).** Do not let him wait there wondering what is going to happen.

93. **The correct answer is (A).** But remember, when you intake a record, inform the subordinate.

94. **The correct answer is (C).** When you say you will keep it confidential, you really can put yourself into a terrible spot. Violations by other officers must be acted upon, so you must not promise to keep them confidential. (You may remember a similar question that appeared earlier in this book. The question did not specify the nature of the information that the subordinate offered to provide in exchange for the promise of confidentiality. For some important, useful information, the promise of confidentiality may be justified and appropriate. This is a judgment call.)

95. **The correct answer is (C).** You cannot simply ignore anonymous tips. "Practical limits" is the operative term here. Where there is no witness to question, an investigation cannot be thorough and must not be permitted to displace other important work. But you must never "ignore" allegations of brutality.

96. **The correct answer is (A).** What percent of 5.314 is 1432?

    $5314\overline{)1432.00} = 26.9$ percent

97. **The correct answer is (B).** What is 19.7 percent of 1147?
    $1147 \times .197 = 225.9$

98. **The correct answer is (C).** Just add them.

99. **The correct answer is (D).** Just add them, and divide by 6.

100. **The correct answer is (B).** $1998\text{-}6581 \div 226 = 29.12$
    close to one thirtieth
    1997 $5172 \div 252 = 20.52$
    1999 $5277 \div 254 = 20.86$
    2000 $5314 \div 250 = 21.26$

101. **The correct answer is (D).** The officer who understands how his own work fits into the whole operation is bound to do a better job.

102. **The correct answer is (B).** Mullins is making his subordinates "stretch." If they stretch, then they may grow.

103. **The correct answer is (B).** In choices (A), (C), and (D), the trainer is the active person. In choice (B), the trainee is doing the work. The trainee will learn the skill best by "doing."

104. **The correct answer is (B).** This is a training and development device.

105. **The correct answer is (B).** Some argue that a better answer is (C). But, remember the chapter on techniques for answering civil service questions. Isn't (B) a "broader choice" than (C)? If you told him (B), wouldn't that include (C) within it?

106. **The correct answer is (A).** Use what you learned in the "techniques" chapter. If the detective did choice (A), would that not include choices (B), (C), and (D)? Yes it would. Choice (A), therefore, is the *broadest* choice. Remember, when the chips are down, "technique" can make you a winner.

107. **The correct answer is (D).** This is not quite as obvious, but here again we have the broadest choice. If someone is an effective supervisor, then he or she will be a trainer, communicator, motivator, and will be respected. Do effective supervisors "get the job done?" If they did not, then they would not be effective.

108. **The correct answer is (C).** Be careful of choice (D). Everybody wants recognition. Not everybody wants the responsibility for "calling the shots" and making decisions.

109. **The correct answer is (A).** How often have we said, "explain"? If conditions permit, explain the reasons and introduce changes gradually. However, in an emergency? Duck! They are shooting!?further explanation may not be recommended.

110. **The correct answer is (D).** If the manner of introducing change seems arbitrary and the reasons for change are not explained, excessive resistance may be the consequence.

111. **The correct answer is (D).** The overall size of the agency is irrelevant. What is important is to determine the nature of the work to be performed by the patrol unit and the optimum number of officers to be supervised by the particular supervisor.

112. **The correct answer is (C).** We are, of course, referring to "raw number" span of control.

113. **The correct answer is (D).** Again, we are speaking about the "raw number" span of control.

114. **The correct answer is (B).** The higher level administrator has more to do on her own, thus has less time to supervise many subordinates than does the lower level administrator. Remember the principles of "span of control."

115. **The correct answer is (D).** Too many captains are reporting to the chief. The chief should have the most narrow span of control.

116. **The correct answer is (B).** The definition of "completed staff work" is work that has been completed by the designated staff member and is ready for approval and signature.

117. **The correct answer is (D).** This is not a new concept.

118. **The correct answer is (A).** If orders are subject to more than one interpretation, then they are unenforceable. This is why implied orders should not be used on newly-appointed employees nor on unreliable ones.

119. **The correct answer is (B).** Common sense will tell you that emergency orders should not be written. Some will argue that complex orders should be given orally to allow for immediate feedback to be certain that they are understood, but the preferred rule is to put complex orders into writing so that all the steps are clearly visible.

120. **The correct answer is (A).** This is not a difficult problem.

PART FIVE

Civil Service Career Information Resources

HOW TO FIND A GOVERNMENT JOB

Very often finding a job is a matter of luck. However, we'd like to take some of the luck out of it and make it more directive. Obviously, in police work there are dozens of areas in which you can work and at different levels. We've tried to give you a selection of where to go for jobs, how to apply for them, and this book was written to help you pass your promotion exam and stay within your current area of employment.

FEDERAL JOBS

The Office of Personnel Management (OPM) is the place to start. They have a list of job openings that is updated daily. In addition, they also publish the *Federal Exam Announcement* each quarter during the year. Although they are not responsible for hiring for jobs, they will provide you with access to each hiring agency and there you can get the specific details about each job. You can reach the OPM's telephone line at 912-757-3000. Since it's an automated number, it's available seven days a week, 24 hours a day.

If you are able to use the Internet, then you will find their site easier to use than the telephone line and a lot less expensive. They can be found on the Web at http://www.opm.gov/. You can find here a complete application for federal employment along with instructions on how to fill it out, explanations of federal job categories, and specific job descriptions. You can then search geographically and alphabetically to find out the jobs that have current openings and exactly where the openings are located. In turn, the listings refer you to full vacancy announcements, including qualification requirements and application procedures and deadlines. With adequate equipment you can download the announcement. Or you can then take notes from the information on your screen. Likewise, you can download application forms or even apply electronically using your computer. Or you can follow instructions for getting the proper forms by telephone or mail.

Another excellent source is the *Federal Jobs Digest*, a biweekly newspaper that lists thousands of government jobs, both in the United States and in foreign countries. The Web site features thousands of job listings at any one time. They can be reached at www.jobsfed.com; e-mail: webmaster@jobsfed.com; voice: 1-800-824-5000; or fax: 914-366-0059.

You might also look under the heading "U.S. Government" in the blue pages of your telephone directory for a listing for office of personnel management or federal job information center. A telephone call to this number may give you automated information pertinent to your own area or may direct you to a location at which you can pick up printed materials or conduct a search on a computer touch screen.

There are several other relevant Internet sights for law enforcement jobs listed as follows:
www.lawenforcementjob.com
www.jobs4police.com
www.officer.com
www.govtjobs.com/safe/index.html
As you search the Web, you will probably find dozens of links to other sights.

STATE EMPLOYMENT

Almost every state has its own Web site. In order to access the state systems via the Internet, there's a very simple way to find each state, although it may take some searching once you're online.

To find the state Internet site, enter the following: www.state.__.us. In the blank, enter the two-letter code for that state. For example, for Arizona you would enter www.state.az.us. For Wisconsin, enter www.state.wi.us. Here's a list of the latest URLs for the state sites. Be aware, however, that they may change from time-to-time.

Alabama: www.state.al.us/
Alaska: www.state.ak.us/
Arizona: www.state.az.us/
Arkansas: www.state.ar.us/
California: www.state.ca.us/
Colorado: www.state.co.us/
Connecticut: www.state.ct.us/
Delaware: www.state.de.us/
District of Columbia: www.washingtondc.gov/
Florida: www.state.fl.us/
Georgia: www:state.ga.us/
Hawaii: www.state.hi.us/
Idaho: www.state.id.us/
Illinois: www.state.il.us/
Indiana: www.state.in.us/
Iowa: www.state.ia.us/
Kansas: www.state.ks.us/
Kentucky: www.state:ky.us/
Louisiana: www.state.la.us/
Maine: www.state.me.us/
Maryland: www.state.md.us/
Massachusetts: www.state.ma.us/
Michigan: www. state.mi.us/
Minnesota: www.state.mn.us/
Mississippi: www.state.ms.us/
Missouri: www.state.mo.us/
Montana: www.state.mt.gov/
Nebraska: www.state.ne.us/
Nevada: www.state.nv.us/
New Hampshire: www.state.nh.us/
New Jersey: www.state.nj.us/
New Mexico: www.state.nm.us/
New York: www.state.ny.us/
North Carolina: www.state.nc.us/
North Dakota: www.state.nd.us/
Ohio: www.state.oh.us/
Oklahoma: www.state.ok.us/
Oregon: www.state.or.us/
Pennsylvania: www:state.pa.us/
Rhode Island: www.state.ri.us/
South Carolina: www:state.sc:us/
South Dakota: www.state.sd.us/
Tennessee: www.state.tn.us/
Texas: www.state.tx.us/
Utah: www.state.ut.us/
Vermont: www.state.vt.us/

Virginia: www.state.va.us/
Washington: www.wa.gov/
West Virginia: www.state.wv.us/
Wisconsin: www.state.wi.us/
Wyoming: www.state.wy.us/

If that state also has a Job Bank, you can also find that the same way. This time you would enter www.abj.org/__, and enter the state's two-letter code in the blank space.

LOCAL EMPLOYMENT

To begin with, it's likely you are currently working at your local precinct. When you pass one of the promotion exams, you will either remain there, or be transferred to another location. But obviously, the best way to find a job in your area is to consult the bulletin board, or ask your commanding officer about job availability.

For city and county employment information on the Internet, you may find these through your state's home page. Or, if you're in a large city, it is likely that the city has it's own a Web site. Use some of the popular search vehicles such as Yahoo.com, Ask.com, Altavista.com, and so on to locate other job-related sites. Use search terms such as *jobs*, *employment*, *labor*, *business*, *help wanted*, and so on. Add that to the specific city or state and you'll be surprised at the number of suggested sites you'll get. You might enter into the search box something like *Miami+jobs*. The plus sign (+) indicates that you want both Miami and jobs to be in the same suggested sites.

You should also investigate to see if there is a local (large) city civil service publication that would list upcoming job announcements. For example, in New York City, *The Chief-Leader* is the primary source for upcoming civil service jobs. (You can write to them at 277 Broadway, New York, NY 10007, to order a subscription.) You will also find information about state and federal jobs in the paper.

HOW TO GET A GOVERNMENT JOB

Now that you know where to look for a job, it's important to understand the procedure. The procedure you must follow to get a government job varies little from job to job and from one level of government to another. There are variations in details of course, but certain steps are common to all.

Once you have found a *Notice of Examination* (it may be called an announcement), read it very carefully. If you can get a copy for yourself, then all the better. If not, then take lots of time to take notes. Make sure you have written down all of the details. The Notice of Examination will give a brief job description. It will tell the title of the job and describe some of the job duties and responsibilities. On the basis of the job description, you will decide whether or not you want to try for this job. If the job appeals to you, then you must concentrate on the following:

- **Education and experience requirements**. If you cannot meet these requirements, then do not bother to apply. Government service is very popular and many people apply. The government has more than enough applicants from which to choose. It will not waive requirements for you.

- **Age requirements**. Discrimination on the basis of age is illegal, but a number of jobs demand so much sustained physical effort that they require retirement at an early age. For these positions, there is an entry age limit. If you are already beyond that age, then do not apply. If you are still too young, inquire about the time lag until hiring. It may be that you will reach the minimum age by the time the position is to be filled.

- **Citizenship requirements**. Many jobs are open to all people who are eligible to work in the United States, but all law enforcement jobs and most federal jobs are limited to citizens. If you are well along the way toward citizenship and expect to be naturalized soon, inquire as to your exact status with respect to the job.

■ **Residency requirements**. If there is a residency requirement, then you must live within the prescribed limits or be willing to move. If you are not willing to live in the area, then do not waste time applying.

■ **What forms must be filed**. The Announcement of the position for which you are applying will specify the form of application requested. For most federal jobs, you may submit either the Optional Application for Federal Employment (OF 612) or a resume that fulfills the requirements set forth in the pamphlet, Applying for a Federal Job (OF 510). For other than federal jobs, the Notice of Examination may tell you where you must go or write to get the necessary form or forms. Be sure you secure them all. The application might be a simple form asking nothing more than name, address, citizenship, and social security number or it may be a complex "Experience Paper." An Experience Paper, as its title implies, asks a great deal about education, job training, job experience, and life experience. Typically, the Experience Paper permits no identification by name, sex, or race; the only identifying mark is your social security number. The purpose of this procedure is to avoid permitting bias of any sort to enter into the weighting of responses. The Experience Paper generally follows a short form of application that does include a name. When the rating process is completed, the forms are coordinated by means of the social security number.

■ **Filing dates, place, and fee**. There is great variation in this area. For some positions, you can file your application at any time. Others have a first day and last day for filing. If you file too early or too late, your application will not be considered. Sometimes it is sufficient to have your application postmarked by the last day for filing. More often, your application must be received by the last date. If you are mailing your application, then allow five full business days for it to get there on time. Place of filing will be stated right on the notice. Get the address right! Most applications may be filed by mail, but occasionally in-person filing is specified. Follow directions. Federal and postal positions require no filing fee. Most, but not all, other government jobs do charge a fee for processing your application. The fee is not always the same. Be sure to check this out. If the notice specifies "money order only," plan to purchase a money order. Be sure the money order is made out properly. If you send or present a personal check, your application will be rejected without consideration. Of course, you would never mail cash, but if the announcement specifies "money order only," you cannot submit cash even in person.

■ **How to qualify**. This portion of the Notice will tell you the basis on which the candidate will be chosen. Some examination scores consist of a totaling up of weighted education and experience factors. This type of examination is called "an unassembled exam," because you do not come to one place to take the exam. The exam is based upon your responses on the application and supplementary forms. Obviously these must be very complete for you to get full credit for all that you have learned and accomplished. The Notice may tell you of a qualifying exam, an exam that you must pass in addition to scoring high on an unassembled, written or performance test. Or, the Notice may tell you of a competitive exam written, performance or both. The competitive exam may be described in very general terms or may be described in detail. It is even possible that a few sample questions will be attached. If the date of the exam has been set, that date will appear on the Notice. Write it down.

When you have the application forms in hand, it is important to photocopy them. Fill out the photocopies first. This way you can correct mistakes, change the order of information and add or delete. You can work at fitting what you have to say into the space allowed. Do not exaggerate, but be sure to give yourself credit for responsibilities you took on, for cost-saving ideas you gave your prior employer, for any accomplishments. Be clear and thorough in telling what you have learned and what you can do.

When you are satisfied with your draft, copy over the application onto the form(s). Be sure to include any backup material that is requested. By the same token, do not send more "evidence" than is truly needed to support your claims of qualification. Your application must be complete according to the requirements of the announcement, but must not be overwhelming. You want to command hiring attention by exactly conforming to requirements.

Check over all forms for neatness and completeness. Sign wherever indicated. Attach the fee, if required. Then mail or personally file the application on time.

WARNING! If you are currently employed, do not give your notice now. Stay at your present job. If you are job hunting, continue your search. The time lag between application for a government job and actual employment is always many months; it may even be a year or two. You cannot afford to sit back and wait for the job.

If the Notice of Examination told you that there will be a competitive exam and told you about subjects of the examination, then you can begin to study now. If not, just continue working and await notice of next steps.

When the civil service commission or personnel office to which you submitted your application receives it, the office will date, stamp, log, and open your file. The office may acknowledge receipt with more forms, with sample exam questions, or with a simple receipt slip. Perhaps you may hear nothing at all for months.

Eventually, you will receive a testing date or an interview appointment. Write these on your calendar in red so that you don't let the dates slip by. Write the address to which you are to report in the same place. If you receive an admission ticket for an exam, then be sure to put it in a safe place, but keep it in sight so that you will not forget to take it with you to the exam. With an exam date, you should get information about the exam. Time may be short. Begin to study and prepare right away if you have not already done so.

If the next step is an exam, that exam might be either a paper-and-pencil exam or a performance exam. The exam depends on the nature of the job. The police promotion exams are primarily paper-and-pencil exams, but in order to qualify to take the exams, you must already have experience as a police officer. The written test is most frequently a multiple-choice test, one in which the test-taker chooses the best of four or five answer choices and marks its number on a separate answer sheet. Multiple-choice tests are machine scored. Machine scoring insures accuracy and objectivity. No one can misinterpret your answers. Machine scoring also allows for many applicants to be rated at the same time. It speeds up the process, though if you are waiting to hear about your job, you may doubt this fact.

Occasionally, the written test will consist of an essay portion along with the multiple-choice section or even of essays alone. Essays usually appear at levels above initial entry level where there are fewer applicants and fewer papers to score. On an essay, the examiners are looking for indications that you can organize your thoughts and can express them effectively in writing.

If you are called for an exam, arrive promptly and dress appropriately. Neatness is always appropriate; however, you do not need to dress up for a performance exam or for a written exam. If you will do manual work for your performance exam, then wear clean work clothes. For a written exam, neat, casual clothing is fine.

THE INTERVIEW

If there is no exam and you are called directly to an interview, then what you wear is more important. Take special care to look businesslike and professional. You must not appear to be too casual, and certainly not sloppy. Overdressing is also inappropriate. A neat dress or skirted suit is fine for women; men should wear shirt and tie with suit or slacks and a jacket. And do pay attention to your grooming.

Interviews take up an interviewer's time. If you are called for an interview, then you are under serious consideration. There may still be competition for the job, someone else may be more suited than you, but you are qualified and your skills and background have appealed to someone in the hiring office. The interview may be aimed at getting information about the following:

■ **Your knowledge**. The interviewer wants to know what you know about the area in which you will work. For instance, if you will be doing data entry in a budget office, what do you know about the budget process? Are you at all interested 5n this area of financial planning? You may also be asked questions probing your knowledge of the agency for which you are interviewing. Do you care enough to have educated yourself about the functions and role of the agency, whether it's child welfare, pollution control, or international trade?

■ **Your judgment**. You may be faced with hypothetical situations, job-related or in interpersonal relations, and be asked "What would you do if . . .?" questions. Think carefully before answering. You must be decisive but diplomatic. There are no right answers. The interviewer is aware that you are being put on the spot. How well you can handle this type of question is an indication of your flexibility and maturity.

■ **Your personality**. You will have to be trained and supervised. You will have to work with others. What is your attitude? How will you fit in? The interviewer will be trying to make judgments in these areas on the basis of general conversation with you and from your responses to specific lines of questioning. Be pleasant, polite, and open with your answers, but do not volunteer a great deal of extra information. Stick to the subjects introduced by the interviewer Answer fully, but resist the temptation to ramble.

■ **Your attitude towards work conditions**. These are practical concerns: If the job will require frequent travel for extended periods, how do you feel about it? What is your family's attitude? If you will be very unhappy about the travel, you may leave the job and your training will have been a waste of the taxpayers' money. The interviewer also wants to know how you will react to overtime or irregular shifts.

Remember, working for the government is working for the people. Government revenues come from taxes. The hiring officers have a responsibility to put the right people into the right jobs so as to spend the taxpayers' money most effectively. And, as a government employee, you have a responsibility to give the people (including yourself) their money's worth.

Other steps along the hiring route may be a medical examination, physical performance testing, and psychological interviewing. If there is a written test, these steps do not occur until the written tests are scored and ranked. Steps that require the time of one examiner with one applicant are taken only when there is reasonable expectation of hiring.

MEDICAL EXAMINATION

A medical exam is self-explanatory. If there are eyesight or hearing requirements for the position, then these must be checked against agency standards. Because the occupation of police officer requires standing, lifting, or running, the applicant must be medically able to withstand the rigors. Since all government employers afford some sort of health coverage, there must be assurance of the general health of the employee, or at least full awareness of current or potential problems. Drug testing is often included. Drug testing is legal if applied routinely and equally to all applicants and if notice of it is given beforehand.

PHYSICAL EXAMINATION

Physical performance testing is limited to applicants for physically demanding jobs. As a police officer, you must be able to run, climb, and carry, often under stress of personal danger as well as under the pressures of the immediate situation. Usually the physical performance test is a qualifying test; either you can do it or you can't. Sometimes, especially where speed may be a crucial element, the physical test is competitively scored and enters into the rating the candidate earns for placement on the certification list.

PSYCHOLOGICAL INTERVIEW

Finally, there is the psychological interview. This interview differs from the general information interview or the final hiring and placement interview in that it tries to assess your behavior under stress. Not all applicants for government jobs must be subjected to a psychological interview. It is limited to persons who will carry guns to people who must make very quick decisions at moments of danger and to people who might find themselves under interrogation by hostile forces. In other words, police officers, firefighters, CIA agents, and DEA (Drug Enforcement Agency) agents, to name just a few, must be able to do their jobs without "cracking" under the strain.

Reading all the applications and weeding out the unqualified ones takes time. Weighing education and experience factors takes time. Administering and scoring of exams takes time. Interviews, medical exams, and physical performance tests take time. Verifying references takes time. And, finally, the vacancies must occur and the government agency must have the funds to fill the vacancies.

All of this clarifies why you must not leave a job or a job search at any step along the way. Wait until you are offered your government job before you cut other ties. But when you finally do get that job, you will have a good income, many benefits, and job security.

How to Increase Your Skills in Mathematics

THE LANGUAGE OF MATHEMATICS

Although not every police promotion examination contains questions dealing with math, many jurisdictions do include questions dealing with charts, graphs, and/or manpower distribution, based on statistical information. Note, also, that the job relatedness of these kinds of questions has been upheld by the courts.

Before we look at some actual chart and graph questions, it is necessary that we understand that decimals, fractions, and percentages are related. Once we are comfortable with these relationships, we can proceed to work with the kinds of questions involved in chart and graph interpretation.

In order to solve a mathematical problem, it is essential to know the mathematical meaning of the words used. There are many expressions that have the same meanings in mathematics. These expressions may indicate a relationship between quantities, or an operation (addition, subtraction, multiplication, and division) to be performed. This chapter will help you to recognize some of the mathematical synonyms commonly found in word problems.

DECIMALS

1. A **decimal**, which is a number with a decimal point (.), is actually a fraction, the denominator that is understood to be 10 or some power of 10.

   a. The number of digits, or places, after a decimal point determines which power of 10 the denominator is. If there is one digit, the denominator is understood to be 10; if there are two digits, then the denominator is understood to be 100, etc.

   Examples: $.3 = \frac{3}{10}$, $.57 = \frac{57}{100}$, $.643 = \frac{643}{1000}$

   b. The addition of zeros after a decimal point does not change the value of the decimal. The zeros may be removed without changing the value of the decimal.

   Example: $.7 = .70 = .700$ and vice versa, $.700 = .70 = .7$

   c. Since a decimal point is understood to exist after any whole number, the addition of any number of zeros after such a decimal point does not change the value of the number.

   Example: $2 = 2.0 = 2.00 = 2.000$

ADDITION OF DECIMALS

2. Decimals are added in the same way that whole numbers are added, with the provision that the decimal points must be kept in a vertical line, one under the other. This determines the place of the decimal point in the answer.

Illustration: Add .31, .037, 4, and 5.0017
SOLUTION:
$$
\begin{array}{r}
2.3100 \\
.0370 \\
4.0000 \\
+\ 5.0017 \\
\hline
11.3487
\end{array}
$$

Answer: 11.3487

SUBTRACTION OF DECIMALS

3. Decimals are subtracted in the same way that whole numbers are subtracted, with the provision that, as in addition, the decimal points must be kept in a vertical line, one under the other. This determines the place of the decimal point in the answer.

Illustration: Subtract 4.0037 from 15.3
SOLUTION:
$$
\begin{array}{r}
15.3000 \\
-\ 4.0037 \\
\hline
11.2963
\end{array}
$$

Answer: 11.2963

MULTIPLICATION OF DECIMALS

4. Decimals are multiplied in the same way that whole numbers are multiplied.

   a. The number of decimal places in the product equals the sum of the number of decimal places in the multiplicand and in the multiplier.
   b. If there are fewer places in the product than this sum, then a sufficient number of zeros must be added in front of the product so as to equal the number of places required, and a decimal point is then written in front of the zeros.

Illustration: Multiply 2.372 by .012
SOLUTION:
$$
\begin{array}{r}
2.372 \quad \text{(3 decimal places)} \\
\times\ .012 \quad \text{(3 decimal places)} \\
\hline
4744 \\
2372 \\
\hline
.028464 \quad \text{(6 decimal places)}
\end{array}
$$

Answer: .028464

5. A decimal can be multiplied by a power of 10 by moving the decimal point to the *right* as many places as indicated by the power. If multiplied by 10, the decimal point is moved one place to the right; if multiplied by 100, the decimal point is moved two places to the right; etc.

Examples:
$$
\begin{array}{ll}
.235 \times 10 & = 2.35 \\
2.35 \times 100 & = 235 \\
2.35 \times 1000 & = 2350
\end{array}
$$

DIVISION OF DECIMALS

6. There are four types of division involving decimals:

■ When the dividend only is a decimal

■ When the divisor only is a decimal

■ When both are decimals

■ When neither dividend nor divisor is a decimal

    a. When the dividend only is a decimal, the division is the same as that of whole numbers, except that a decimal point must be placed in the quotient exactly above the decimal point in the dividend.

Illustration: Divide 12.864 by 32

SOLUTION:

$$32\overline{)12.864}^{\,.402}$$

$$\begin{array}{r} 128 \\ \hline 64 \\ 64 \end{array}$$

Answer: .402

    b. When the divisor only is a decimal, the decimal point in the divisor is omitted and as many zeros are placed to the right of the dividend as there were decimal places in the divisor.

Illustration: Divide 211327 by 6.817

SOLUTION:

$$6.817\overline{)211327} = 6817\overline{)211327000}^{\,31000}$$

        (3 decimal places) $\underline{20451}$ (3 zeros added)

                                                   6817

                                                   $\underline{6817}$

Answer: 31000

    c. When both the divisor and dividend are decimals, the decimal point in the divisor is omitted and the decimal point in the dividend must be moved to the right as many decimal places as there were in the divisor. If there are not enough places in the dividend, then zeros must be added to the end of the dividend to make up the difference.

Illustration: Divide 2.62 by .131

SOLUTION: $.131\overline{)2.62} = 131\overline{)2620}^{\,20}$

Answer: 20

d. In instances when neither the divisor nor the dividend is a decimal, a problem may still involve decimals. This occurs in two cases: when the dividend is a smaller number than the divisor; and when it is required to work out a division to a certain number of decimal places. In either case, write in a decimal point after the dividend, add as many zeros as necessary, and place a decimal point in the quotient above that in the dividend.

Illustration: Divide 7 by 50

SOLUTION:

$$
\begin{array}{r}
.14 \\
50\overline{)7.00} \\
\underline{50} \\
200 \\
200
\end{array}
$$

Answer: 14

Illustration: How much is 155 divided by 40, carried out to 3 decimal places?

SOLUTION:

$$
\begin{array}{r}
3.875 \\
40\overline{)155.000} \\
\underline{120} \\
350 \\
\underline{320} \\
300 \\
\underline{280} \\
200
\end{array}
$$

Answer: 3.875

7. A decimal can be divided by a power of 10 by moving the decimal point to the left as many places as indicated by the power. If divided by 10, the decimal point is moved one place to the left; if divided by 100, the decimal point is moved two places to the left; etc. If there are not enough places, then add zeros in front of the number to make up the difference and add a decimal point.

Examples: .4 divided by 10 = .04
                          .4 divided by 100= .004

ROUNDING DECIMALS

8. To round a number to a given decimal place:

a. Locate the given place.
b. If the digit to the right is less than 5, omit all digits following the given place.
c. If the digit to the right is 5 or more, raise the given place by 1 and omit all digits following the given place.

Examples: 4.27   = 4.3 to the nearest tenth
                          .71345 = .713 to the nearest thousandth

9. In problems involving money, answers are usually rounded to the nearest cent.

CONVERSION OF FRACTIONS TO DECIMALS

10. A fraction can be changed to a decimal by dividing the numerator by the denominator and working out the division to as many decimal places as required.

Illustration: Change $\frac{5}{11}$ to a decimal of two places.

SOLUTION:

$$\frac{5}{11} = 11\overline{)5.00}\;{}^{.45\frac{5}{11}}$$

$$\frac{4.44}{60}$$

$$\frac{55}{5}$$

Answer: .45

11. To clear fractions containing a decimal in either the numerator or the denominator, or in both, divide the numerator by denominator.

Illustration: What is the value of $\frac{2.34}{.6}$?

SOLUTION:

$$\frac{2.34}{.6} = .6\overline{)2.34} = 6\overline{)23.4}\;{}^{3.9}$$

$$\frac{18}{54}$$

$$\frac{54}{}$$

Answer: 3.9

CONVERSION OF DECIMALS TO FRACTIONS

12. Since a decimal point indicates a number having a denominator that is a power of 10, a decimal can be expressed as a fraction, the numerator of which is the number itself and the denominator of which is the power indicated by the number of decimal places in the decimal.

Examples: $.3 = \frac{3}{10}$, $.47 = \frac{47}{100}$

13. When the decimal is a mixed number, divide by the power of 10 indicated by its number of decimal places. The fraction does not count as a decimal place.

Illustration: Change $25\frac{1}{3}$ to a fraction.

SOLUTION:
$$25\frac{1}{3} = 25\frac{1}{3} \div 100$$
$$= \frac{76}{3} \times \frac{1}{100}$$
$$= \frac{76}{300} = \frac{19}{75}$$

Answer: $\frac{19}{75}$

14. When to change decimals to fractions:

   a. When dealing with whole numbers, do not change the decimal.

Example: In the problem $12 \times .14$, it is better to keep the decimal:
$$12 \times .14 = 1.68$$

   b. When dealing with fractions, change the decimal to a fraction.

Example: In the problem $\frac{3}{5} \times .17$, it is better to change the decimal to a fraction:

$$\frac{3}{5} \times .17 = \frac{3}{5} \times \frac{17}{100} = \frac{51}{500}$$

15. Because the decimal equivalents of fractions are often used, it is helpful to be familiar with the most common conversions listed as follows:

$\frac{1}{2} = .5$	$\frac{1}{3} = .3333$
$\frac{1}{4} = .25$	$\frac{2}{3} = .6667$
$\frac{3}{4} = .75$	$\frac{1}{6} = .1667$
$\frac{1}{5} = .2$	$\frac{1}{7} = .1429$
$\frac{1}{8} = .125$	$\frac{1}{9} = .1111$
$\frac{1}{16} = .0625$	$\frac{1}{12} = .0833$

FRACTIONS

FRACTIONS AND MIXED NUMBERS

1. A **fraction** is part of a unit.

    a. A fraction has a **numerator** and a **denominator**.

Example: In the fraction $\frac{3}{4}$, 3 is the numerator and 4 is the denominator.

    b. In any fraction, the numerator is being divided by the denominator.

Example: The fraction $\frac{2}{7}$ indicates that 2 is being divided by 7.

    c. In a fraction problem, the whole quantity is 1, which may be expressed by a fraction in which the numerator and denominator are the same number.

Example: If the problem involves $\frac{1}{8}$ of a quantity, then the whole quantity is $\frac{8}{8}$, or 1.

A **mixed number** is an integer together with a fraction, such as $2\frac{3}{5}$, $7\frac{3}{8}$, etc. The integer is the integral part, and the fraction is the fractional part.

3. An **improper fraction** is one in which the numerator is equal to or greater than the denominator, such as $\frac{19}{6}, \frac{25}{4}$ **or** $\frac{10}{10}$.

4. To change a mixed number to an improper fraction:

    a. Multiply the denominator of the fraction by the integer.
    b. Add the numerator to the result.
    c. Place this sum over the denominator of the fraction.

Illustration: Change $3\frac{4}{7}$ to an improper fraction.

SOLUTION:
$$7 \times 3 = 21$$
$$21 + 4 = 25$$
$$3\frac{4}{7} = \frac{25}{7}$$

Answer: $\frac{25}{7}$

5. To change an improper fraction to a mixed number:

    a. Divide the numerator by the denominator. The quotient, disregarding the remainder, is the integral part of the mixed number.
    b. Place the remainder, if any, over the denominator. This is the fractional part of the mixed number.

Illustration: Change $\frac{36}{13}$ to a mixed number.

SOLUTION:

$$13\overline{)36}$$

$$\underline{26}$$

10 remainder

$$\frac{36}{13} = 2\frac{10}{13}$$

Answer: $2\frac{10}{13}$

6. The numerator and denominator of a fraction may be changed by multiplying both by the same number, without affecting the value of the fraction.

Example: The value of the fraction $\frac{2}{5}$ will not be altered if the numerator and the denominator are multiplied by 2, to result in $\frac{4}{10}$.

7. The numerator and denominator of a fraction may be changed by dividing both by the same number without affecting the value of the fraction. This process is called **reducing the fraction**. A fraction that has been reduced as much as possible is said to be in **lowest terms**.

Example: The value of the fraction $\frac{3}{12}$ will not be altered, if the numerator and denominator are divided by 3, to result in $\frac{1}{4}$.

Example: If $\frac{6}{30}$ is reduced to lowest terms (by dividing both numerator and denominator by 6), the result is $\frac{1}{5}$.

8. As a final answer to a problem:

    a. Improper fractions should be changed to mixed numbers.
    b. Fractions should be reduced as far as possible.

PERCENTS

1. The **percent symbol** (%) means "parts of a hundred." Some problems involve expressing a fraction or a decimal as a percent. In other problems, it is necessary to express a percent as a fraction or a decimal in order to perform the calculations.

2. To change a whole number or a decimal to a percent:

    a. Multiply the number by 100.
    b. Affix a percent sign.

    Illustration: Change 3 to a percent.
    SOLUTION: $3 \times 100 = 300$
    $$3 = 300\%$$

    Answer: 300%

    Illustration: Change .67 to a percent.
    SOLUTION: $.67 \times 100 = 67$
    $$= .67 = 67\%$$

    Answer: 67%

    Illustration: Change $4\frac{2}{3}$ to a percent.

    SOLUTION: $4\frac{2}{3} \times 100 = \frac{14}{3} \times 100 = \frac{1400}{3}$
    $$= 466\frac{2}{3}$$
    $$4\frac{2}{3} = 466\frac{2}{3}\%$$

    Answer: $466\frac{2}{3}\%$

4. To remove a percent sign attached to a decimal, divide the decimal by 100. If necessary, the resulting decimal may then be changed to a fraction.

    Illustration: Change .5% to a decimal and to a fraction.
    SOLUTION: $.5\% = .5 \div 100 = .005$
    $$.005 = \frac{5}{1000} = \frac{1}{200}$$

    Answer: $.5\% = .005$
    $$.5\% = \frac{1}{200}$$

5. To remove a percent sign attached to a fraction or mixed number, divide the fraction or mixed number by 100, and reduce, if possible. If necessary, the resulting fraction may then be changed to a decimal.

Illustration: $\frac{3}{4}\%$ to a fraction and to a decimal.

SOLUTION: $\frac{3}{4}\% = \frac{3}{4} \div 100 = \frac{3}{4} \times \frac{1}{100}$

$$= \frac{3}{400}$$

$$\frac{3}{400} = 400 \overline{)3.0000} \,^{.0075}$$

Answer: $\frac{3}{4}\% = \frac{3}{400}$

$$\frac{3}{4}\% = .0075$$

6. To remove a percent sign attached to a decimal that includes a fraction, divide the decimal by 100. If necessary, the resulting number may then be change to a fraction.

Illustration: Change $.5\frac{1}{3}\%$ to a fraction.

SOLUTION: $.5\frac{1}{3}\% = .005\frac{1}{3}$

$$= \frac{5\frac{1}{3}}{1000}$$

$$= 5\frac{1}{3} \div 1000$$

$$= \frac{16}{3} \times \frac{1}{1000}$$

$$= \frac{16}{3000}$$

$$= \frac{2}{375}$$

Answer: $.5\frac{1}{3}\% = \frac{2}{375}$

7. Some fraction percent equivalents are used so frequently that it is helpful to be familiar with them.

$$\frac{1}{25} = 4\%$$

$$\frac{1}{20} = 5\%$$

$$\frac{1}{12} = 8\frac{1}{3}\%$$

$$\frac{1}{10} = 10\%$$

$$\frac{1}{8} = 12\frac{1}{2}\%$$

$$\frac{1}{6} = 16\frac{2}{3}\%$$

$$\frac{1}{5} = 20\%$$

$$\frac{1}{4} = 25\%$$

$$\frac{1}{3} = 33\frac{1}{3}\%$$

$$\frac{1}{2} = 50\%$$

$$\frac{2}{3} = 66\frac{2}{3}\%$$

$$\frac{3}{4} = 75\%$$

RATIO AND PROPORTION

RATIO

1. A **ratio** expresses the relationship between two (or more) quantities in terms of numbers. The mark used to indicate ratio is the colon (:) and is read "to."

Example: The ratio 2:3 is read "2 to 3."

2. A ratio also represents division. Therefore, any ratio of two terms may be written as a fraction, and any fraction may be written as a ratio.

Examples: $3:4 = \dfrac{3}{4}$

$$\frac{5}{6} = 5:6$$

3. To simplify any complicated ratio of two terms containing fractions, decimals, or percents:

    a. Divide the first term by the second.
    b. Write as a fraction in lowest terms.
    c. Write the fraction as a ratio.

Illustration: Simplify the ratio $\dfrac{5}{6} : \dfrac{7}{8}$

$$\frac{5}{6} \div \frac{7}{8} = \frac{5}{6} \times \frac{8}{7} = \frac{40}{42} = \frac{20}{21}$$

$$\frac{20}{21} = 20:21$$

Answer: 20:21

4. To solve problems in which the ratio is given:

    a. Add the terms in the ratio.
    b. Divide the total amount that is to be put into a ratio by this sum.
    c. Multiply each term in the ratio by this quotient.

Illustration: The sum of $360 is divided among three people according to the ratio 3:4:5. How does each one receive?

$3 + 4 + 5 =$	12
$\$360 \div 12 =$	$30
$\$30 \times 3 =$	$90
$\$30 \times 4 =$	$120
$\$30 \times 5 =$	$150

Answer: The money is divided thus: $90, $120, $150.

PROPORTION

5.   a.   A **proportion** indicates the equality of two ratios.

Example: 2:4 = 5:10 is a proportion. This is read "2 is to 4 as 5 is to 10."

     b.   In a proportion, the two outside terms are called the **extremes**, and the two inside terms are called the **means**.

Example: In the proportion 2:4 = 5:10, 2 and 10 are the extremes, and 4 and 5 are the means.

     c.   Proportions are often written in fractional form.

Example: The proportions 2:4 = 5:10 may be written $\dfrac{2}{4} = \dfrac{5}{10}$.

     d.   In any proportion, the product of the means equals the product of the extremes. If the proportion is in fractional form, then the products may be found by cross multiplication.

Example: In $\dfrac{2}{4} = \dfrac{5}{10}$, $4 \times 5 = 2 \times 10$

     e.   The product of the extremes divided by one mean equals the other mean; the products of the means divided by one extreme equals the other extreme.

6.   Many problems in which three terms are given and one term is unknown can be solved by using proportions. To solve such problems:

     a.   Formulate the proportion very carefully according to the facts given. (If any term is misplaced, the solution will be incorrect.) Any symbol may be written in place of the missing term.

     b.   Determine by inspection whether the means or the extremes are known. Multiply the pair that has both terms given.

     c.   Divide this product by the third term given to find the unknown term.

Illustration: The scale on the map shows that 2 cm represents 30 miles of actual length. What is the actual length of a road that is represented by 7 cm on the map?

SOLUTION: The map lengths and the actual lengths are in proportion; that is, they have equal ratios. If *m* stands for the unknown length, the proportion is:

$$\frac{2}{7} = \frac{30}{m}$$

As the proportion is written, m is an extreme and is equal to the product of the means, divided by the other extreme:

$$m = \frac{7 \times 30}{2}$$

$$m = \frac{210}{2}$$

$$m = 105$$

Answer: 7 cm on the map represents 105 miles.

Illustration: If a money bag containing 500 nickels weighs 6 pounds, how much will a money bag containing 1600 nickels weigh?

SOLUTION: The weights of the bags and the number of coins in them are proportional. Suppose that w represents the unknown weight. Then

$$\frac{6}{w} = \frac{500}{1600}$$

The unknown is a mean and is equal to the product of the extremes, divided by the other mean:

$$w = \frac{6 \times 1600}{500}$$
$$w = 19.2$$

Answer: A bag containing 1600 nickels weighs 19.2 pounds.

AVERAGES

Rule: We find an average of several numbers by adding them and dividing the sum by the number of addends (numbers added).

Practice Exercise

Find the average of the following sets of numbers:

1. $42 + 78 + 80 + 36 =$

2. $16 + 42 + 81 + 50 + 26 =$

3. $14 + 46 + 82 + 39 + 62 + 57 =$

4. $38 + 62 + 21 + 18 =$

Answers:

1. Total 236 divided by 4 = 59.

2. Total 215 divided by 5 = 43.

3. Total 300 divided by 6 = 50.

4. Total 139 divided by 4 = 34.75.

Warning: The one basic rule that you must keep in mind is that some things *cannot* be determined by averaging.

Examples:

If I tell you that the total number of crimes in a given 12-month period was 144, and then asked for the monthly average, the answer would be $12\overline{)144} = 12$

This is the monthly average. Does this mean that every month had 12 crimes? No.

Does it mean that any month had to have 12 crimes? No

Could one or more months have had 12 crimes? Yes.

Note: When you get an average, you cannot determine what the individual values are that give you the average.

January	12 crimes	July	0 crimes
February	0 crimes	August	0 crimes
March	12 crimes	September	36 crimes
April	24 crimes	October	0 crimes
May	6 crimes	November	6 crimes
June	18 crimes	December	30 crimes

The yearly total is 144, and the monthly average is 12.

Note: Sometimes the examiner throws in a curve ball by asking for something that cannot be determined by averaging.

Examples:

Q. There are 12 months in the year. If the average monthly incidence of burglary is 2.5, what is the total number of burglaries per year?

A.
$$
\begin{array}{r}
12 \text{ months} \\
\times\ 2.5 \text{ per month} \\
\hline
30
\end{array}
$$

30.0 total burglaries per year.

Q. If the average monthly number of burglaries in 1999 was 2.5, and there was a 25% increase overall in 2000, what was the total number of burglaries in 2000?

A.
$$
\begin{array}{r}
12 \text{ months} \\
\times\ 2.5 \text{ per month} \\
\hline
30
\end{array}
$$

30.0 total burglaries in 1999.

25% increase (of 30) = increase in 2000.

$$
\begin{array}{r}
30 \\
\times .25 \\
\hline
1.50 \\
6.0 \\
\hline
7.50
\end{array}
$$

Therefore, the total number of burglaries in 2000 was 30 plus 7.5 = 37.5 = 38. (You cannot have half of a burglary.)

Q. What was the total number of burglaries for January 1988?

A. It cannot be determined.

Q. What was the total number of burglaries for July 1987?

A. It cannot be determined.

Q. Assume that the average monthly number of larcenies, in 1997 was 5. In 1998, there was a 10% overall increase in larcenies. In 1999, there was a 15% overall increase from 1999. In 2000, there was a 25% overall increase over the 1997 figures. What is the 2000 total for larcenies?

A. 1997 = 5 x 12 = 60

1998 = 10% increase = 66

1999 = 15% increase over 1998 = 76

2000 = 25% increase over 1997 = 75

You should have realized from reading the problem that the *only* percentage computation necessary was the last one.

This projection type problem is additionally an exercise in reading care and ability.

Q. After studying the chart for larcenies committed each year during a five-year period, you list them as follows:

1996 = 200 larcenies

1997 = 220 larcenies

1998 = 300 larcenies

1999 = 175 larcenies

2000 = 225 larcenies

What percentage of the total number of larcenies for this period occurred during 1999?

SOLUTION:

You must first add up all the yearly totals.

200
220
300
175
<u>225</u>
1120 Grand Total

The answer is the percentage arrived at from the following fraction:

$$\frac{175}{1120} = \frac{\text{Total for 1999}}{\text{Grand Total}} = 1120\overline{)175.00} = 15.6\%$$

A. 15.6% of the larcenies occurred in 1999.

SOLVING ACTUAL CHART AND GRAPH PROBLEMS

The following chart and graph problems are offered as typical of the kinds of problems that you should expect on a promotional examination for higher rank.

We urge you to utilize the following guidelines in responding to the following problems:

1. Study the chart or graph carefully *before* you begin to put numbers on a piece of paper.

2. Take careful note of what the chart or graph is *telling* you.

3. Be certain that you know what is examiner is *asking* you.

4. Make sure your computations are neatly written and clearly labeled.

5. Check your answers against the solutions contained in the text. (All of the problems are fully explained.)

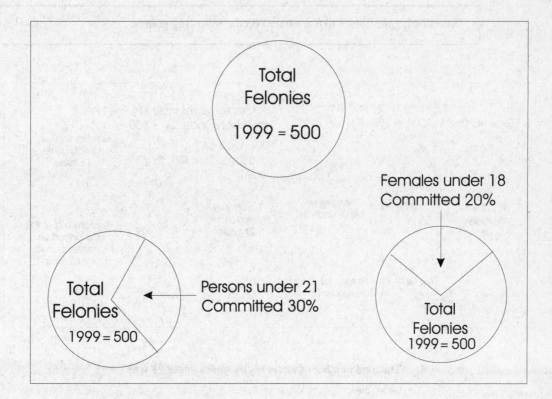

Directions: Questions 1 to 3 are based on the preceding graphs.

1. The number of felonies committed by persons under 21 was
   (A) 140
   (B) 130
   (C) 120
   (D) 150

2. The number of felonies committed by females under 18 was

   (A) 100
   (B) 110
   (C) 120
   (D) 125

3. Assume that the ratio between felonies committed by persons under 21 as compared to the total number of felonies is the same as the ratio of felonies committed by females under 16 to felonies committed by females under 18. The number of felonies by females under 16 would be

   (A) 30
   (B) 35
   (C) 20
   (D) 25

   Remember: The pie graph represents 100 percent of something. If you are given the value of some of the slices, then you can determine the value of the remainder.

   Directions: Questions 4 to 6 are based on the following graphs.

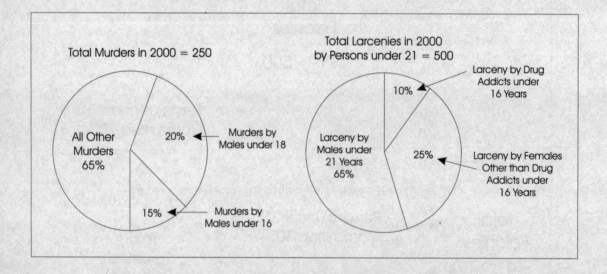

4. The total number of larcenies by males under 21 was

   (A) 300
   (B) 325
   (C) 330
   (D) 350

5. The ratio of larcenies by females to larcenies by males under 21 is most nearly

   (A) 1 to 2
   (B) 1 to 3
   (C) 1 to 4
   (D) 1 to 5

6. If 20% of the larcenies by drug addicts under 16 were committed by female drug addicts under 16, then the number committed by such female drug addicts is most nearly

    (A) 10
    (B) 15
    (C) 20
    (D) 30

Directions: Questions 7 to 10 are based on the following graph.

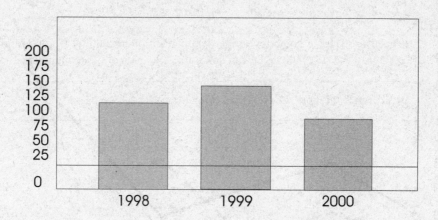

7. What was the percentage change from 1998 to 1999?

    (A) 17% increase
    (B) 18% increase
    (C) 20% increase
    (D) 16% increase

8. The yearly average for the three-year period was

    (A) 162.5
    (B) 160.5
    (C) 160.2
    (D) 125

9. The number of robberies in 1998 was most nearly what percent of the total number of robberies during the three-year period?

    (A) 33
    (B) 30
    (C) 35
    (D) 36

10. The ratio of robberies in 1998 to robberies in 1999 was

    (A) 1 to 1.2
    (B) 1 to 2
    (C) 1 to 2.5
    (D) 1 to 3

Directions: Questions 11 to 17 are based on the following graph.

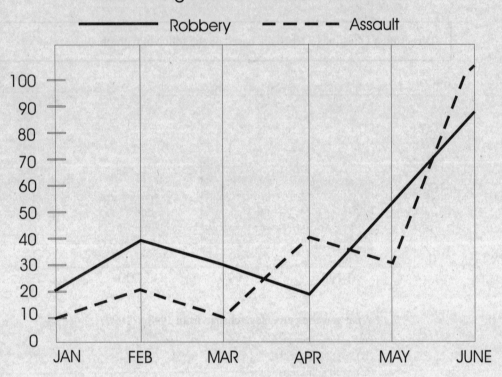

11. The monthly average number of assaults during the six-month period was less than the monthly average of robberies for the same period by what approximate amount?

    (A) 5
    (B) 6
    (C) 7
    (D) 8

12. The ratio of assaults to robberies in the first three months of the period was most nearly

    (A) 1 to 2
    (B) 1 to 4
    (C) 1 to 5
    (D) 1 to 6

13. In which month during the period covered was the ratio of assaults to robberies the greatest?

    (A) April
    (B) June
    (C) March
    (D) January

14. The percentage decrease in robberies from February to March was most nearly

    (A) 12
    (B) 13
    (C) 14
    (D) 15

15. The percentage increase in assaults from May to June was most nearly

    (A) 333
    (B) 33
    (C) 200
    (D) 300

16. What percent of the total robberies during the six-month period occurred during April?

    (A) 8.5
    (B) 10
    (C) 8
    (D) 9

17. Assuming that the number of assaults in July was 10% more than the monthly average of assaults during the six-month period, and assuming that the ratio of assaults to robberies in July is the same as the ratio of assaults to robberies in March, then the number of robberies in July would most nearly be

    (A) 110
    (B) 100
    (C) 105
    (D) 90

Directions: Questions 18 to 21 are based on the following graph.

Motorcycle Registration and Accident Involvement

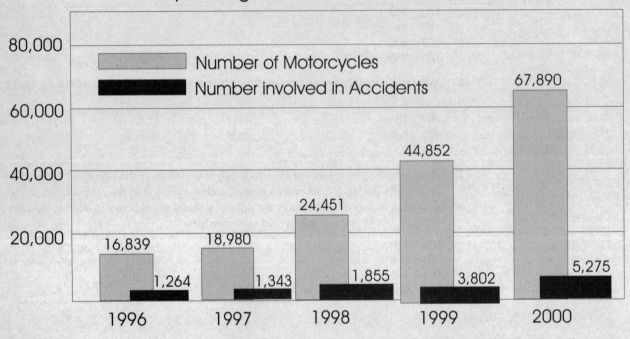

18. The percentage increase in the number of accidents involving motorcycles from 1996 to 1997 was most nearly

    (A) 5
    (B) 6
    (C) 7
    (D) 8

19. The average number of accidents involving motorcycles for the years 1996 through 2000 exceeded the number of accidents involving motorcycles during 1998 by most nearly

    (A) 775
    (B) 800
    (C) 825
    (D) 850

20. In 1999, there were 62,302 accidents involving all types of vehicles. The percentage of these accidents involving motorcycles was most nearly

    (A) 4
    (B) 5
    (C) 6
    (D) 7

21. The ratio of the number of motorcycles to the number of motorcycles involved in accidents was *lowest* in the year of

    (A) 1996
    (B) 1997
    (C) 1998
    (D) 1999

ACCIDENTS

CONTRIBUTING CIRCUMSTANCES	TOTAL	FATAL	INJURY	PROPERTY DAMAGE
No Violation	36571	632	29964	5975
Did Not Have Right of Way	68784	227	39198	29359
Following Too Closely	97259	18	63313	33928
Drive Left of Center	20480	205	9600	10675
Improper Illegal Passing	25031	37	10149	14845
Reckless Driving	74956	415	24098	50443
Speed	38755	835	21899	16021
Passed Stop Sign	15115	74	9001	6040
Ran Traffic Signal	15008	57	10044	4907
Passed Stopped School Bus	77	1	54	22
Failed to Signal	3775	1	1326	2448
Avoiding Object in Road	13891	20	5100	8771
Total Accidents	409702	2522	223746	183434

Directions: Questions 22 to 25 are based on the preceding chart.

---

22. The percentage of fatal accidents in which reckless driving was a contributing circumstance was most nearly

    (A) 15
    (B) 16
    (C) 17
    (D) 18

23. The percentage of injury accidents in which "no violation" was involved is most nearly

    (A) 11
    (B) 12
    (C) 13
    (D) 14

24. The ratio of fatal accidents to injury accidents is most nearly

    (A) 88 to 1
    (B) 48 to 2
    (C) 1 to 88
    (D) 2 to 84

25. If the total number of fatal accidents due to "following too closely" were spread equally throughout the year, the average monthly number of such accidents would be

    (A) 2.5
    (B) 5.1
    (C) 1.2
    (D) 1.5

ANSWERS TO QUESTIONS ON CHART AND GRAPH PROBLEMS

1. **The correct answer is (D).** 30% of 500 = .30 x 500 = 150
2. **The correct answer is (A).** 20% of 500 = .20 x 500 = 100
3. **The correct answer is (A).** The ratio of felonies by persons under 21 to total felonies is the same as the ratio of felonies by females under 16 to felonies by females under 18. Stated numerically, (30% of 500) to 500 is the same as *X* to (20% of 500). So, 150 to

    500 = *X* to 100

    $$\frac{150}{500} = \frac{x}{100}$$

    500*X*   =   15000 .

    X   =   30 felonies by females under 16

4. **The correct answer is (B).** 65% of 500 = .65 x 500 = 325
5. **The correct answer is (B).** Ratio of larcenies by females = 25% to larcenies by males under 21 = 65%. To get the ratio of 25% to 65%, divide each number by 25. 1 to 2:6
6. **The correct answer is (A).** Larcenies by drug addicts under 16 = 10% of 500 = 50 and 20% of 50 (female addicts under 16) = 10.
7. **The correct answer is (C).** 1998 = 125; 1999 = 150. What is the percentage change from 125 to 150?

    1. Draw a line: —

    2. Where you start from goes on bottom $\overline{125}$

    3. The distance traveled (amount of change) goes on top: $\underline{25}$

    $$\frac{25}{125} = \frac{1}{5} = .20 = 20\% \text{ increase}$$

8. **The correct answer is (D).**   1998= 125

    1999 = 150
    2000 = $\underline{100}$.
    375 = three-year total divided by 3 = 125 yearly average

9. **The correct answer is (A).**   1998 = 125   Three-year total = 375

    125 is what percent of 375? $\frac{125}{375} = \frac{1}{3} = .33 = 33\%$

10. **The correct answer is (A).** The ratio of robberies is 1998 (125) to robberies in 1999 (150) is the ratio of 125 to 150. Divide each number by 125. 1 to 1.2

11. **The correct answer is (A).**

Assault		Robbery
10	January	20
20	February	35
10	March	30
40	April	20
30	May	50
100	June	80
210		235

$$6\overline{)210} \quad \genfrac{}{}{0pt}{}{35}{}$$

$$6\overline{)235.0} \quad \genfrac{}{}{0pt}{}{39.2}{}$$

392

−35

42

12. **The correct answer is (A).**

Assault	to	Robbery
January 10	to	20
February 20	to	35
March 10	to	$30\frac{1}{40}$ to $\frac{21}{85}$

1 to 2.1

13. **The correct answer is (A).**

Assault		to	Robbery
April	40	to	20
June	100	to	80
March	10	to	30
January	10	to	20

(A) 40 to 20 = $\frac{40}{20}$ = 2:1

(B) 100 to 80 = $\frac{100}{80}$ = 1.25:1

(C) 10 to 30 = $\frac{10}{30}$ = .33:1

(D) 10 to 20 = $\frac{10}{20}$ = .50:1

14. **The correct answer is (C).**
Robberies
February   35

March   30

$$\frac{5}{35} = 35\overline{)5.000}^{.1428} = .143 = 14.3\%$$

15. **The correct answer is (C).**
Assaults
May   30

June   100

$$\frac{70}{30} = 2.33 = 233\%$$

16. **The correct answer is (A).**

Total Robberies = 235

April Robberies = 20

(20 is what % "of" 235?) $\frac{20}{235} = 235\overline{)20.000}^{.085} = 0.085 = 8.5\%$

17. **The correct answer is (A).** Monthly Average Assaults = 35 (see question 11)

July Assaults = 10% more than 35.

$$\begin{array}{r} 35 \\ \times .10 \\ \hline 3.50 \end{array}$$

July Assaults = (35 + 3.50) = 38.5

July Assaults to Robberies = 38.5 to X

March Assaults to Robberies = 10 to 30

$$\frac{38}{x} \quad \frac{10}{30}$$

$10X = 1155$

$X = 115.5$

18. **The correct answer is (B).**   1996 = 1264

    1997 = 1323

    What is the percentage increase when you start at 1264 and end at 1343?

    $$\frac{79 \text{ (distance traveled)}}{1264 \text{ (where you started)}}$$

    $$\frac{79}{1264} = 0.62 = 6.2\%$$

19. **The correct answer is (D).**

    Accidents Involving Motorcycles
    1996 = 1264
    1997 = 1343
    1998 = 1855
    1999 = 3802
    2000 = <u>5275</u>

    13539 = Total Accidents Involving Motorcycles

    $5\overline{)13539}$ = 2707 average number of accidents involving motorcycles

    Average = 2,707
    1998   = <u>1.855</u>

    852

20. **The correct answer is (C).** 1999 = 62,302 Accidents
    1999 = 3,802 Accidents Involving Motorcycles

    (What % of 62,302 is 3,802?)

    $$\frac{3,802}{62,302} = .061 = 6.1\%$$

21. **The correct answer is (D).**

    Motorcycles to Motorcycles in Accidents
    1996 16839 to 1264 = 13.3 to 1
    1997 18980 to 1343 = 14.1 to 1
    1998 24451 to 1855 = 13.2 to 1
    1999 44852 to 3802 = 11.8 to 1

    Be careful, the question asked for the *lowest* ratio!

22. **The correct answer is (B).** Fatal Accidents = 2,522
    Reckless Driving = 415

    (What % "of" 2522 is 415?)

    $$\frac{415}{2,522} = .164 = 16.4\%$$

23. **The correct answer is (C).** Injury Accidents = 223,746

    No Violations   =   29,964

    (29,964 is what percent "of" 223,746?)

    $$\frac{29,964}{223,746} = .134 = 13.4\%$$

24. **The correct answer is (C).** Fatal Accidents (2,522) to Injury Accidents (223,746) is 2522 to 223,746. Divide each number by 2,522. 1 to 88.

25. **The correct answer is (D).** Fatal due to following too closely = 18 (18 divided by 12 months) = 1.5

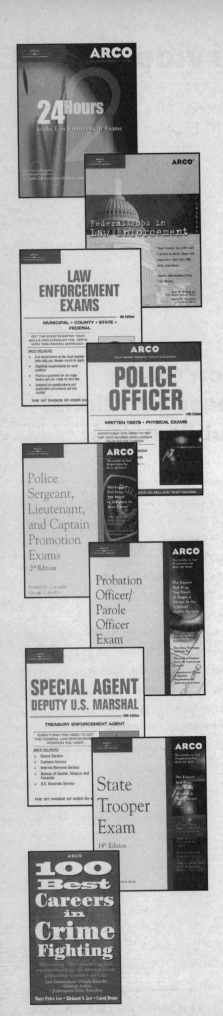